CAMBRIDGE TEXTS IN THE
HISTORY OF POLITICAL THOUGHT

BOLINGBROKE
Political Writings

CAMBRIDGE TEXTS IN THE
HISTORY OF POLITICAL THOUGHT

Series editors

RAYMOND GEUSS

Lecturer in Social and Political Sciences, University of Cambridge

QUENTIN SKINNER

Regius Professor of Modern History in the University of Cambridge

Cambridge Texts in the History of Political Thought is now firmly established as the major student textbook series in political theory. It aims to make available to students all the most important texts in the history of western political thought, from ancient Greece to the early twentieth century. All the familiar classic texts will be included but the series does at the same time seek to enlarge the conventional canon by incorporating an extensive range of less well-known works, many of them never before available in a modern English edition. Wherever possible, texts are published in complete and unabridged form, and translations are specially commissioned for the series. Each volume contains a critical introduction together with chronologies, biographical sketches, a guide to further reading and any necessary glossaries and textual apparatus. When completed, the series will aim to offer an outline of the entire evolution of western political thought.

For a list of titles published in the series, please see end of book.

BOLINGBROKE

Political Writings

EDITED BY

DAVID ARMITAGE

Columbia University

CAMBRIDGE
UNIVERSITY PRESS

PUBLISHED BY THE PRESS SYNDICATE OF THE UNIVERSITY OF CAMBRIDGE
The Pitt Building, Trumpington Street, Cambridge CB2 1RP, United Kingdom

CAMBRIDGE UNIVERSITY PRESS
The Edinburgh Building, Cambridge, CB2 2RU United Kingdom
40 West 20th Street, New York, NY 10011–4211, USA
10 Stamford Road, Oakleigh, Melbourne 3166, Australia

First published 1997

Printed in the United Kingdom at the University Press, Cambridge

Typeset in Ehrhardt 9½/12 pt

A catalogue record for this book is available from the British Library

Library of Congress Cataloguing in Publication data

Bolingbroke, Henry St John, Viscount, 1678–1751.
Political writings/edited by David Armitage.
p.   cm. – (Cambridge texts in the history of political thought)
Includes bibliographical references and indexes.
ISBN 0 521 44393 8 – ISBN 0 521 58697 6 (pbk)
1. Great Britain – Politics and government – 1727–1760.
2. Political sciences – Great Britain.   3. Political parties – Great
Britain.   4. Kings and rulers – Duties.   I. Armitage, David, 1965–.
II. Title.   III. Series.
DA500.B63 1997
320.941′09′033 – dc20   96 35840 CIP

ISBN 0 521 44393 8 hardback
ISBN 0 521 58697 6 paperback

WV

Contents

Acknowledgements

For their help in tracing Bolingbroke's references, I am grateful to Peter Burke, Bob Connor, Constantin Fasolt, Pierre Force, Julian Franklin, Karen Green, Nick Harding and Chad Ludington; Guido Abbattista generously gave me a draft of his edition of *The Idea of a Patriot King* which greatly lightened my task. I owe particular thanks to the members of the Columbia University Seminar on Social and Political Thought, especially Julian Franklin and Melvin Richter, as well as to Joyce Chaplin, Quentin Skinner and Ruth Smith, for their helpful comments on successive versions of the Introduction. Richard Fisher has been a model of editorial patience throughout.

The Columbia University Council on Research and Faculty Development in the Humanities and Social Sciences funded part of the research for this volume, which I completed while a Fellow at the National Humanities Center. My thanks to both institutions for their support.

Introduction

Henry St John, later Viscount Bolingbroke, was born in 1678, the year of the Popish Plot, and died in 1751, nine years before the accession of George III and the subsequent revival of Tory fortunes reshaped the British political landscape. However, Bolingbroke's career as an active politician spanned only the period from the last year of William III's reign, when he first entered Parliament in 1701, to the first of George I, when he was impeached by the overwhelmingly Whig Parliament elected in the aftermath of the Hanoverian succession and the Jacobite rising of 1715. St John's fortunes rose and fell with those of the post-Revolutionary Tory party. His political acumen, charisma and industry had recommended him to Tory leaders, who rapidly promoted him up the ranks of their administration until he held the crowning office of his career, as Secretary of State for the Northern Department during the closing years of the War of the Spanish Succession.

St John was elevated to the Lords as Viscount Bolingbroke in 1712, and in the following year he took credit for negotiating the Treaty of Utrecht which ended the war. Bolingbroke looked set to make a bid for the leadership of his party, until the Whigs won the general elections of 1715 by a landslide, 'after which a new and more melancholy scene for the party, as well as for me, opened itself', as he put it in *A Letter to Sir William Wyndham* (1716). The Tories went into the wilderness of proscription and opposition until 1760, and Bolingbroke fled to his first extended period of exile in France (1714–25). While there he became Secretary of State to the Old Pretender in 1715–16. For many of his associates in the Tory party and the opposition to Walpole, this flirtation with Jacobitism put him beyond the political pale in English politics, despite his association with the Hanoverian heir, Frederick, Prince of Wales, in the late 1730s, and though he protested that he was innocent of the 'treason that claret inspires' (p. 269). Thereafter, he confined his political enterprises to building coalitions and dispensing counsel to the various groups ranged against Sir Robert Walpole. His greatest political writings – the *Dissertation upon Parties*, the letter 'On the Spirit of Patriotism', and *The Idea of a Patriot King* – all sprang from these contexts, and deployed the languages of Whiggism and Toryism, classical republicanism and Stoicism, in defence of the mixed constitution and the common good, in accordance with the order of nature as revealed by reason.

Bolingbroke was a member of the first generation that came to maturity under the Revolution Settlement of 1688. 'Under this constitution the greatest part of the men alive were born', he noted in 1733 (p. 78). This was the constitution under which David Hume, thirty years his junior, and for a time his adversary, grew up; it became the envy of continental contemporaries, such as Voltaire and Montesquieu, both of whom drew upon Bolingbroke as a constitutional authority. The Glorious Revolution had affirmed the Protestantism of the English state, restored the supposedly ancient constitutional balance between monarchy and Parliament, and set the terms for political debate in Britain for the next century. Yet the cost of securing Protestantism was military invasion by the Dutch stadtholder, William of Orange, and entry into the opening stages of a second hundred years war between Britain and France that ended at Waterloo. As Bolingbroke acknowledged in the *Dissertation*, annual parliaments were the offspring of the fiscal necessity of continental warfare. The uneasy political truce negotiated in 1688 soon began to fracture into party strife, as the Whigs benefited from William's patronage, while Tory fortunes only revived with the accession of Queen Anne in 1702. Bolingbroke was the chronicler of these ambivalent consequences, which made and unmade his own political career.

The Glorious Revolution, according to Bolingbroke, had scrambled the traditional markers of party politics. The classic labels of Whig and Tory first appeared in the context of the Exclusion Crisis of 1679–81. The pre-Revolutionary Whigs were those politicians who favoured the exclusion of Charles II's Catholic brother, James, Duke of York, from the succession to the throne; the Tories, those who resisted such tampering with the succession. The national and international dimensions of the Exclusion debate identified Whigs and Tories with distinct positions on the relative powers of Parliament and monarchy, on the Church of England and its toleration of Dissent, and on the menace of international Catholicism. The Exclusionist Whigs demanded the power for Parliament to alter the succession, and hence placed statute above prerogative. They supported toleration for Dissent, yet were fearful of the supposed relationship between popery and arbitrary government, and hence resisted toleration for Catholicism, and proposed vigorous measures against the threatening power of Louis XIV's France. The anti-Exclusionist Tories resisted Parliamentary supremacy in the name of royal power, upheld the exclusivity and sacramental validity of the Church of England, were less wary of international Catholicism, and believed that the danger of altering the succession would be greater than the consequences of a known Catholic taking the English throne. The inept authoritarianism and expedient political and religious somersaults executed by the Duke of York during his reign as James II (1685–88) alienated both Whigs and Tories. Accordingly, the majority of both parties joined forces in 1688 to resist his innovations in Church and state, and ultimately to legitimize the accession of the Dutch invader, William of Orange, to the English throne.

The Glorious Revolution in England was a genuine compromise between Whigs and Tories, achieved under pressure of political necessity, and by means of ideological legerdemain in the Convention Parliament of 1688. No party could be held to have won over the other in 1688, and it seemed for a time that the divisions opened up by the Exclusion Crisis had finally been closed. However, during the course of William's reign, the Whigs emerged as the victors, and they became the natural party of government for most of the eighty years after 1688. Ideological and religious divisions persisted into the first Age of Party, the age of Bolingbroke's political maturity, and the scene for his own early political career.

After 1688, the two parties remained divided over the legacy of the Glorious Revolution and the Church of England's attitude towards Protestant Dissent. Post-Revolutionary Whigs increasingly appealed to the notion of a contract between the crown and the people (or, rather, their representatives as assembled in Parliament), which James II had violated, and to which future monarchs would be held accountable. Tories argued that, since James had abdicated his throne, there had been neither a contract to be broken nor any future right of resistance implied by the Revolution. Instead, subjects should be passively obedient to their monarchs, and could have no justification for resistance. This left Tories open to the charge that they were half-hearted in their support for the Protestant succession, a suspicion that their intolerance of Dissent also raised. The Whigs remained the party of Dissent, the Tories the supporters of Anglicanism at all costs. For High Church Tories, the national church could only be the Church of England or nothing; for Low Church Whigs, it had to be the Church of England with toleration for almost all Protestants. The Whigs' greatest victory was the Toleration Act of 1689, which to Tories smacked of support for heresy and irreligion that put the 'Church in Danger', as their rallying-cry had it. As Bolingbroke noted, the idea of a Whig became inseparably associated with '[t]he power and majesty of the people, an original contract, the authority and independency of Parliament, liberty, resistance, exclusion, abdication, deposition'; that of a Tory with '[d]ivine hereditary, indefeasible right, lineal succession, passive-obedience, prerogative, non-resistance, slavery, nay and sometimes popery too' (p. 5).

The consequences of the post-Revolutionary wars against France sharpened the ideological divisions between the two parties. The Whig war party benefited most obviously from William's patronage, as they were most committed to the anti-Catholicism and anti-Bourbonism of their new monarch, and to the military and fiscal measures needed to finance European warfare. The Tories however baulked at the expense of the continental commitment, and proposed instead a 'blue-water' policy to sap French commercial might by attacking shipping, draining trade-revenues and dispersing their defences by assailing French coastlines and colonies rather than seeking pitched battles on the European continent. The Whigs rode high politically on the benefits of their aggressively interventionist policies, achieving victory in eleven of the twelve general elections held between 1689 and 1715. Nevertheless, it was the Tories – Bolingbroke pre-eminent among them – who gained temporarily from the reaction to the costs of war, as they swept to power in 1713 at the end of the War of the Spanish Succession.

The institutional consequences of making Britain into a fiscal–military state cut across and complicated these party divisions. The financial demands of international warfare accelerated the transformation of England from an overwhelmingly agricultural economy, with a low tax-base, a comparatively unintrusive and informal bureaucracy, and an isolationist stance towards the outside world, into the United Kingdom of Great Britain, home to Europe's greatest financial institutions and most productive system of public credit, an expanding fiscal capacity, a growing and professional bureaucracy, and the financial resources to prosecute continental war, commercial expansion and imperial growth. Whig leadership and investment lay behind the greatest fiscal and institutional innovations after the Revolution, such as the Bank of England and the National Debt, and the benefits of investment in these institutions flowed most of all to Whigs and the so-called 'monied interest'. This alliance between policy and profit, created by royal favour and cemented by the spoils of office, led to the association of a specific 'Court' programme, encompassing high taxation, governmental expansion, financial innovation and international aggression, with the Whigs. The supporters of the competing 'Country' programme protested that half of the tax burden fell on the 'landed interest', feared the growth of the executive, benefited less from the suspicious new institutions, and were sceptical of the benefits to be had from costly continental commitments. Since the bulk of the Whigs were beneficiaries and backers of the Court programme, and the majority of Tories opposed the actions of the Whigs, 'Court' Whigs became counterposed to 'Country' Tories, and the so-called Old Whigs who were committed to the neo-republican constitutional Whiggism of the 1690s joined forces with the Tories in an uneasy oppositional alliance.

The ascendancy of the Whig Robert Walpole to the post of principal, or prime, minister in 1722 sharpened the appeal of a Country interest arrayed against the increasingly powerful Court Whigs. Bolingbroke emerged as the pre-eminent spokesman for this interest, as well as the most talented and mercurial of Walpole's opponents. The chief instrument of his campaign against Walpole was *The Craftsman* (later retitled *The Country Journal*), the journal he founded with the dissident Whig William Pulteney in December 1726 and which carried both the *Remarks on the History of England* (1730–31) and the *Dissertation upon Parties* (1733–34) in the form of weekly editorials. The aim of these publications was to construct a platform for the disparate constituencies which made up the opposition to Walpole, and to convince them that they were bound together not solely by their common enemy but rather by a shared set of political principles.

Bolingbroke's Country platform combined Old Whig and Tory elements in order to put Walpole's regime on the defensive against the charge that it had betrayed the heritage of Whiggism and that its policies endangered the liberty guaranteed by the Revolution Settlement. Bolingbroke reminded Walpole and his ministry of 'the civil faith of the old Whigs' (p. 8), that body of political principles which stretched back through the early years of the eighteenth century, via the works of the Whig apologists for the Revolution and the supporters of Exclusion to the republicanism of the Interregnum. These principles enshrined a classical republican vision of liberty as freedom under the protection of law and of virtue as devotion to the welfare of the community. According to the writers in this tradition, the greatest threats to liberty and virtue were a standing army in time of peace (which could overturn the laws, and deprive citizens of their property by force) and the corruption of the nation's politicians and people by means of bribery, placeholding and a more general lack of moral activity. Bolingbroke's oppositional campaign returned time and again to the charges that the armed forces under Walpole were a threat to 'public liberty', and that the minister's shrewd management of Parliament amounted to packing it with placemen and thereby disabling its function as the assembly of the nation.

To these Whiggish principles Bolingbroke added distinctive planks from earlier Tory platforms, in particular a commitment to maintaining the mixed and balanced constitution. This had its roots in the moderate Toryism of the opening decade of the eighteenth century, which upheld mixed government, the common good, and the moral leadership of the monarchy in response to the Court Whigs' exaltation of the power of Parliament and doctrines of popular sovereignty. For example, in 1701, Sir Humphrey Mackworth's *A Vindication of the Rights of the Commons of England* argued that only internal political divisions could ruin England, that all three parts of the constitution – King, Lords and Commons – must balance one another to safeguard the common good, and that the best guarantee of the national welfare would be a reciprocal relationship between crown and people, for 'no king was ever great and glorious in England, but he, that . . . became the prince of the people'. The twenty-three-year-old Bolingbroke praised Mackworth's work as 'a just draught of our admirable constitution'. The closeness of Mackworth's constitutional vision to that espoused by an Old Whig theorist such as John Toland in *The Art of Governing by Partys* (1701) made it doubly attractive for Bolingbroke's purposes. It could be used to affirm that post-Revolutionary Whigs and Tories had been united in principle, and to argue that their common platform could again provide the impetus for the co-operative enterprise of defending British liberties in the face of Walpolean 'corruption'.

The defeat of Walpole's excise scheme in 1733 and the necessity of general elections in 1734 provided the occasion for the *Dissertation upon Parties*, the greatest monument to Bolingbroke's oppositional activities. Walpole's plan to extend the excise to wine and tobacco encountered a storm of protest from those who feared the imposition of a general excise, and offered the opposition its best opportunity yet to mobilize opinion both inside and outside Parliament. The bill proposed to increase the powers of excise officers, and could therefore be presented as offering a threat to liberty and property, and hence to the very principles of the post-Revolutionary political order. The opposition rallied in Parliament and left Walpole with such slim majorities for his unpopular measure that he was forced to withdraw the bill in June 1733. The onus was now on the opposition to exploit their victory at the elections scheduled for the coming year.

Bolingbroke himself had stayed on the sidelines through most of the Excise Crisis, yet he seized the opportunity offered by Walpole's defeat to produce the decade's most sophisticated statement of Country ideology, in the *Dissertation upon Parties*. Bolingbroke's aim in this series of essays was to keep the opposition together in the face of the impending elections, as well as to undermine the legitimacy of Walpole's shaken government. George II's steadfast support of his chief minister had restored Walpole's standing, and the ministry quickly regained its control over Parliament. This recovery made it all the more necessary for the opposition to maintain a united front, and for its writers to expose the vulnerability of Walpole's ideological position.

Bolingbroke's main strategy in the *Dissertation* was to show that the party divisions of Whig and Tory had been made redundant by the Glorious Revolution. He argued that the only true distinctions were now between Church and Dissent and, most importantly, between Court and Country. All political parties are necessarily ideological coalitions: Bolingbroke exploited this structural fact in the hope of leaving Walpole and his closest supporters isolated from the majority of those who assented to the principles derived from the Revolution. Accordingly, he rewrote the history of seventeenth-century Britain to show Walpole's apostasy from the Old Whig principles which had been forged in the century-long battle against monarchical absolutism.

Bolingbroke's earlier series of essays in *The Craftsman*, the *Remarks on the History of England* (1730–31), had cast British history from the earliest times to the calling of the Long Parliament in 1640 as a perpetual battle between 'prerogative and privilege', the 'spirit of faction' and the 'spirit of liberty'. The first ten letters of the *Dissertation* (published in *The Craftsman* between October 1733 and January 1734) projected this narrative into the later seventeenth century by tracing the 'epidemical taint' (p. 14) of absolutism from the accession of James VI of Scotland to the English throne in 1603, through to the climactic reign of James II. Bolingbroke had promised that the *Dissertation* would trace the origin of parties both civil and ecclesiastical. He therefore argued that the only true divisions in the years after 1660 were those between Churchmen and Dissenters, since the factions of 'roundhead and cavalier' had expired before the Restoration, while Whig and Tory would not arise until the latter years of Charles II's reign. The battle over the exclusion of the Duke of York from the succession allowed the court to use its power to foment faction. The court alone was therefore culpable for having shattered the civil consensus on the common good which had been maintained by the Country party of the 1670s. Bolingbroke hoped to show that the party divisions of 1679–88 had been contingent, temporary, and created only by misguided passions and 'the wily intrigues of the court' (p. 37). The spirit of liberty and the national interest should therefore prevail over manipulation by the court and private interest in the name of the natural and historic 'Country party . . . authorized by the voice of the country' (p. 37).

The ideology of the Country party, as elaborated by Bolingbroke, was recognizably Whig in its conception of the Glorious Revolution. James II had violated the nation's fundamental laws, and had therefore forfeited the throne. There had been no dissolution of government, but the Revolution had restored the ancient constitution and, with it, the 'spirit of liberty, transmitted down from our Saxon ancestors' (p. 82) that had withstood the assaults of faction and prerogative government down the ages. All monarchs since William III had ruled under the 'original contracts' (p. 83) that were the pillars of the Revolution Settlement, the Declaration of Rights (1689) and the Act of Settlement (1701). These guaranteed that the 'rights and privileges of the people' (p. 84) limited the monarchy, and that among those privileges was a limited right of resistance. All were now agreed in their subscription to these original contracts. Extreme exigency alone could justify resistance like that in 1688, Bolingbroke argued, as he took up the argument from necessity originally employed by post-Revolutionary Tories, and later taken up by the anxious Whig managers of the Sacheverell trial in 1710, Walpole among them. There was therefore no foreseeable possibility of justifiable resistance. Nor was it likely that malcontents would attempt to overthrow the government or, at the most extreme, the constitution itself (an admission intended to marginalize the Jacobites, and perhaps to distance Bolingbroke himself from his own earlier associations with the Pretender). The only threat came from those who were attached to the government yet enemies to the constitution, by which Bolingbroke meant Walpole's placemen in Parliament and others who profited from the Whig oligarchy at the cost of abandoning true Whig principles.

Bolingbroke had argued that Whig and Tory had been replaced by Court and Country parties, and that the only true enemies to the principles of the Revolution were Walpole and his supporters. All that remained for him, in his first series of letters, was to provide a criterion for judging political behaviour in the new era of Country consensus. To this end, he proposed a major conceptual distinction between 'government' and 'constitution'. He defined government as the instrumental activity of administration, an evaluatively neutral activity that could be used to describe the conduct of any 'chief magistrate, and inferior magistrates under his direction and influence' (p. 88). Attachment to the principles of the constitution, however, provided the means to judge whether a government was good or bad, and hence whether it fostered the spirit of liberty or the practice of tyranny. 'By constitution', he argued in a classic definition, 'we mean . . . that assemblage of laws, institutions and customs, derived from certain fixed principles of reason, directed to certain fixed objects of public good, that compose the general system, according to which the community hath agreed to be governed' (p. 88). Any government that acted against the common good, or that went against the original contracts which formed the basis of the constitution, could be accused of being 'unconstitutional', a term coined by Bolingbroke himself (p. 124).

In order to convict Walpole's government of unconstitutionality, Bolingbroke turned to two further shibboleths of the Old Whig tradition, standing armies and the corruption of Parliament. Now Walpole was keeping the army on foot, on the pretext of potential Jacobite invasion. Bolingbroke's argument at this point was rather undeveloped, though he was compelled to make it because of the association between tyranny and standing armies which had most recently been affirmed in the 1690s by Old Whig authors such as John Trenchard, John Toland and Andrew Fletcher. His argument that Walpole was corrupting Parliament was more persuasive. If the monarch could sufficiently pack both Houses of Parliament, either through his direct influence or through his chief minister, the balance of powers in the mixed constitution would be destroyed, and with it liberty itself. 'Parliaments are the true guardians of liberty', Bolingbroke asserted, '[b]ut then no slavery can be so effectually brought and fixed upon us as parliamentary slavery' (p. 94). The crucial support of the crown in keeping Walpole in power after the Excise Crisis lent conviction to this argument, and it was on the ground of Parliamentary 'corruption' that the opposition mobilized its attack during the election campaign of 1734.

The diagnosis of corruption provided the link between the *Dissertation*'s first ten letters, 'Letter XI' of the *Dissertation* (first issued as a separate broadside in the spring of 1734), and the work's concluding suite of letters (published in November and December 1734), though Bolingbroke's target shifted from the crown to the

people. The opposition, led by Bolingbroke and his Tory ally Sir
William Wyndham, had put pressure on Walpole by introducing a
bill to repeal the Septennial Act in March 1734. This Act had been
introduced in the wake of the 1715 Jacobite rising as a security
measure on the grounds that elections held at least every three years
(as had been the case since 1694) led to political instability. The bill
of repeal provided the occasion for *The Craftsman Extraordinary
... In Which the Right of the People to Frequent Elections of their
Representatives is Fully Considered*, which Bolingbroke later incorporated as 'Letter XI' of the *Dissertation*. In this pamphlet, Bolingbroke again traced the history of royal management of Parliament
from Richard II to James II to show how the 'essentials of British
liberty', 'freedom of elections, and the frequency, integrity and
independency of parliaments' (p. 101), had been repeatedly threatened, until restored by the Revolution Settlement and forced by the
needs of war. To safeguard that liberty, Bolingbroke argued for
triennial, even annual, parliaments to prevent the entrenchment of
oligarchical government, and hence the unbalancing of the constitution. Later in the century, Rousseau famously remarked that the
English were free only once every seven years, while Paine held that
the existence of the Septennial Act proved that 'there is no constitution in England'. A distinctive feature of later eighteenth-century
British radicalism would be the demand for annual parliaments.
The central place of this argument in the *Dissertation* partly explains
Bolingbroke's reputation among radicals as '[t]he ablest defender of
our liberties and the noblest asserter of the excellence of our constitution as it was established at the Revolution', as the *London Courant*
called him in 1780.

The elections of 1734 returned Walpole and the Whigs to power,
albeit with a reduced majority. Though Bolingbroke spent the
spring of 1734 in Somerset, 'rising early and writing much', he did
not resume publication of the *Dissertation* until the winter of that
year, after the election had been settled. The attempt at coalition-
building had collapsed, the move to repeal the Septennial Act had
failed, and Bolingbroke was now a marginal figure in the counsels
of the opposition. These circumstances may account for the more
leisurely and abstract character of the *Dissertation*'s concluding 'Letters', which returned to the examination of the mixed constitution,
the dangers it faced, and the means to protect it. They may also

account for the greater emphasis Bolingbroke placed on the com-
plicity of the people in their own downfall, as if in reproach to the
electorate for their failure to displace the minister. In 'Letter VII',
he had argued that Charles II had not been able to subvert the
constitution, because only Parliament, and not the people, were corrupted. Now the danger lay in the people lapsing into voluntary
servitude, by their failure to hold their representatives to account
and thereby to safeguard the constitution. 'We may give ourselves
a tyrant in our folly, if we please' (p. 112), he warned, but only if
the people became accomplices in their own enslavement.

In 'Letters XII–XIX' of the *Dissertation*, Bolingbroke turned to history to show the vulnerability of the mixed constitution, and the
necessity of vigilance to protect it. Only a government in which the
three parts – monarchical, aristocratic and democratic – checked
one another's powers, and remained in balance with one another,
could protect true liberty, that is, 'liberty stated and ascertained by
law' (p. 112). The Romans had a monarchical dictator and an aristocratic senate, but lacked a third estate. Their fate was the collapse
of the Republic and imperial tyranny. The aristocracy of fifteenth-
and sixteenth-century Castile had failed to mediate between crown
and people, and had thereby allowed a powerful monarch aided by
a corrupt minister to establish absolutism. Finally, the French
people 'had no real share in the supreme power of government,
either collectively or representatively' (p. 143), so that a powerful
monarchy was able to intimidate the nation's assemblies. These
examples pointed up the excellence of Britain's constitution: it had
not yet collapsed into the tyranny suffered by its fellow Gothic
constitutions in France and Spain, and its spirit of liberty had
survived even the Norman Conquest. Only if the crown were rich,
Parliament corrupt and the people demoralized would ruin come to
Britain. In the end, 'nothing can destroy the constitution of Britain,
but the people of Britain' (p. 167). Bolingbroke argued that the
crown had grown rich from the proceeds of the civil list and the
financial settlement agreed after the Revolution. Parliament was
packed with placemen and office-holders. The task now was to
sustain the incorruptibility of the people themselves. If that were
lost, the balance of the constitution would be upset, and 'then will
the fate of Rome be renewed, in some sort, in Britain' (p. 167).

The *Dissertation* did not end on this chillingly Machiavellian note. Instead, Bolingbroke returned to his crucial distinction between the constitutional and the anti-constitutional parties within British politics. Neither Tories, nor Whigs, nor Dissenters could be expected to protect the constitution alone; instead, the 'constitutionists' must join together in order to resist the forces that would corrupt the constitution: the power of the crown, the profits of speculation, and the connivance of ministers. He also called Walpole to account with a classic republican threat. Walpole's schemes of corruption were ultimately self-defeating, rendering his family's 'riches and honours precarious and insecure, and . . . entailing servitude upon his own race' (p. 188). This was because freedom demanded sacrifice by every citizen for its protection; only if all remained virtuous could the liberty and security of any individual be ensured. Bolingbroke's conception of the subordination of private interest to the common good and his parallel definition of liberty as freedom under law reveal his debt to the classical republican tradition more clearly than either his use of the language of virtue and corruption or his dire warnings of imminent national decline.

The electorate had failed Bolingbroke as much as his allies in the opposition had and he returned to France in 1735, where he adopted the pose of the retired politician-philosopher associated with Cicero and Seneca and, more recently in British political life, with Francis Bacon and the Earl of Clarendon. His first major political work composed in France, the letter 'On the Spirit of Patriotism' (1736), expressed disillusionment with the older generation of opposition politicians in neo-Stoic tones and no longer directed advice to the people but rather counsel to the aristocracy. Bolingbroke addressed his letter to Henry Hyde, Viscount Cornbury, Clarendon's great-grandson, a member of a group of young, largely aristocratic MPs who had been elected to Parliament in 1734. These 'Boy Patriots' were untainted by association with an opposition which had conspicuously failed to cohere in 1733–34, and they could not be accused of the compromises which had dogged Bolingbroke's own career. They promised new hope for the opposition, and Bolingbroke offered counsel designed to call them to their responsibilities and to show that their most important duties were those to the nation itself.

Bolingbroke followed Cicero in arguing that the highest duty was service to one's country, and that the responsibility to serve was calibrated according to one's position in the commonwealth. The greatest responsibility fell on the members of that aristocracy of talent present in every society 'who are born to instruct, to guide, and to preserve' (p. 193). These were the men who were above passion and ambition, and who were born to lead once humans had congregated naturally and submitted to government under the law. Bolingbroke's appeal to natural law in this letter is notable, since he had so signally avoided it in the *Dissertation upon Parties*. In the *Dissertation*, he had mainly relied instead upon history to validate his arguments and, where history was lacking (as in the case of the origins of the British constitution) on immemoriality; in response, Ministerialist writers had monopolized natural jurisprudential argument in their justifications of hierarchy as a counterblast to Bolingbroke's constitutionalism. However, in the letter, he offered an account of the world as a 'moral system' (p. 197), framed by the Creator, whose order was accessible to human reason, and to which all humans should contribute according to their capabilities. Yet this again was consonant with the Stoic conception of duty as conformity to nature. Since men were naturally sociable, and sociability entailed government, service to one's country was therefore 'no chimerical, but a real duty' (p. 201). The satisfactions to be derived from the exercise of one's duty were again calibrated according to the importance of that duty, and the achievement of this highest responsibility would therefore generate the highest of intellectual pleasures.

Bolingbroke returned to the themes of duty and patriotism in his most famous, and later most reviled, political work, *The Idea of a Patriot King* (1738). He had left France for England in the summer of 1738, to sort out his financial affairs, and to stay with his friend Alexander Pope. By this stage, the Patriot opposition to Walpole was rallying around Frederick, Prince of Wales, and was becoming identified with his alternative court at Leicester House. *The Idea of a Patriot King* seems to have arisen from a request by Frederick's Secretary, George Lyttelton, that Pope provide much-needed counsel for the Prince at a time when his popularity was on the rise. Frederick needed to live down a chequered, rakish past, and to prepare himself to be a worthy successor to his father. Bolingbroke, rather than Pope, responded with a mirror for the Prince that completed the intellectual trajectory he had followed in the *Dissertation* and 'On the Spirit of Patriotism'. In the *Dissertation*, he had stated that '[a] popular king of Great Britain will be always not only easy and secure, but in effect absolute. He will be, what the British constitution alone can make any prince, the absolute monarch of a free people' (p. 162). *The Idea of a Patriot King* gave substance to this statement, on the basis of the natural-law principles of the letter 'On the Spirit of Patriotism'.

Bolingbroke had addressed the British people and their representatives in the *Dissertation upon Parties*. In 'On the Spirit of Patriotism', he had turned to the aristocracy. Finally, he directed *The Idea of a Patriot King* to the remaining power in the mixed constitution, the monarchy. Now the duties to be treated were the highest ones, 'the duties of a king to his country' (p. 217). Bolingbroke again derived duties from the principles of divine order and human nature. Though he now argued that government had arisen from human depravity as much as from natural sociability, this inconsistency did not affect his main contention that the aim of government was the happiness of society in accordance with the precepts of the law of nature. To this deistical utilitarianism, Bolingbroke added the republican contention that good government was necessary 'to support legal liberty, and legal liberty to preserve good government' (p. 244). The best constitution to guarantee happiness and liberty would be a monarchy limited by an aristocratic and a democratic element. Should that happiness and liberty be under threat, the best means to restore it would be the accession of such a limited monarch, devoted to the common welfare, protective of the rights of property and liberty, and therefore, in Bolingbroke's terms, truly a 'Patriot King'.

Bolingbroke repudiated extreme party positions on the nature of the monarchy, as he had earlier done in the *Dissertation*. He disavowed the High Tory belief in divine-right kingship, by claiming that any government that promoted the happiness of the people was in accordance with God's laws, and could therefore be called divine, whether it was a monarchy or not. He also rejected the most radical form of Whig contractualism, which would lead to the destruction of the constitution by placing too stringent limitations on the monarchy. However, his failure to define exactly what limitations would be so damaging, and his insistence that the prince ruled solely for the good of his people, made *The Idea of a Patriot King* palatable to Whig oppositionists, just as his insistence upon hereditary right and the necessity of monarchy rendered it acceptable to Tories. Bolingbroke once again provided an ideology for a disparate coalition, this time centred on a prince rather than on a party programme.

The Patriot King would be the enemy of corruption, the father of his people, a moral exemplar and the head of a flourishing commercial empire. He would therefore purge his court of self-interested and ambitious advisers and rely upon the wise counsel of virtuous men. He would exhibit the essential decorum intrinsic to virtue and maintain the unaffected propriety of a gentleman. He would rule above party, favouring one when temporary necessity demanded, yet not permanently enlisting himself with any, for only then could he truly act for the common good. Finally, he would encourage the nation's commerce, foster overseas colonies and avoid continental commitments. He would therefore follow the precepts of the mirror-for-princes tradition, which recommended the avoidance of flattery and the pursuit of good counsel; he would adopt the Country programme of national unity and non-party government promoted by Bolingbroke and his allies throughout the 1730s; he would model himself after the moral advice of Cicero's *De Officiis* (twice paraphrased in the text itself); and he would follow the blue-water foreign and colonial policies espoused by the Tories since the Glorious Revolution.

Bolingbroke chose his sources pointedly in the circumstances of 1738. The tradition of advice to a prince remained alive and well in a culture where the education of the heir to the throne was a major political prize, especially when Frederick's own son George (later George III, for whom his father wrote his own brief advice in 1749) had been born in the summer before Bolingbroke composed *The Idea of a Patriot King*. The Patriot King would be enlisted among the supporters of Cicero (for his stand against corruption, his prosecution of Catiline, and his championing of national unity) against those on the minister's side in the 1730s who accused him of trimming and hypocrisy. More immediately for Bolingbroke's political purposes, the Patriot King's non-partisan leadership (as embodied in Frederick) could offer hope to a Patriot cause which was newly confident of Walpole's weakness in Parliament, especially as commercial grievances against Spain inspired widespread opposition to his policy of peace within and without doors. This last context gave point to the work's closing panegyric of the Patriot King as a latter-day Nerva, combining the traditionally incompatible ideals of *imperium* and *libertas*, or as a new Augustus, at the head of a prosperous and free people, commanding a vast though uncorrupting empire well suited to the maritime capabilities of an island nation. Within a year of Bolingbroke's writing *The Idea of a Patriot King*, Britain had entered the War of Jenkins's Ear, fought to protect the nation's maritime and commercial interests.

Bolingbroke's visions of virtuous princely rule, non-partisan government and a flourishing empire of the seas in *The Idea of a Patriot King* bequeathed enduring legacies to later eighteenth-century British political thought. The work provided a necessary point of reference for all subsequent mirrors for princes after its official publication in 1749, a standard against which radicals held future kings (only one of whom, William IV, seems to have read it), as well as a slur to be cast on the monarchy of George III by Sir Robert Walpole's son, Horace, who accused the young King's tutors of having raised him on prerogative principles derived from Bolingbroke. The work may have had its most enduring influence in the early American republic, where it was read by John Adams and Thomas Jefferson as a blueprint for a presidency above party. This was despite the fact that the benign blue-water patriarchalism promised by Bolingbroke had been subverted by the territorial militarism of the later eighteenth-century British Empire, which the American rebels had attacked with Bolingbrokean accusations of ministerial corruption in the decade before 1776.

Bolingbroke has been largely remembered as the grandfather of English conservatism, though this has done grave historical and intellectual violence to his thought. Such appropriation can be explained by the fact that his political career in office was indeed spent as a Tory; by his promotion of the ideal of patriotism which, since the last round of the British wars against France in the late eighteenth century, has been associated with the xenophobia of the right; and by his appeal for Benjamin Disraeli, who took Bolingbroke as his own model in forming the Young England movement in the 1840s. Yet Bolingbroke's place in the history of political thought was secured by his definition of constitutional government in the *Dissertation upon Parties*, by his revival of a neo-Stoic conception of patriotism in the letter 'On the Spirit of Patriotism' and by his vision of a non-partisan executive in *The Idea of a Patriot King*. All of these ideas still deserve attention from citizens of those nationalistic, commercial, representative republics we call democracies, whether their constitution is presidential or monarchical, congressional or parliamentary, in form.

Principal events in Bolingbroke's life

1678   *September*: born, probably at Lydiard Tregoze, Wiltshire.
        October: mother buried at Lydiard Tregoze; Henry St John baptized at Battersea.
1685   *February*: accession of James II.
1688   *December*: flight of James II; accession of William and Mary.
(?)   Educated at Sheriffhales Dissenting Academy, Shiffnal, Shropshire (?).
1697   'To Mr. Dryden' published in Dryden's translation of *The Works of Virgil*.
1698   Begins two-year grand tour: visits France, Switzerland and Italy.
1701   *February*: elected MP for Wootton Bassett, Wiltshire.
        May: marries Frances Winchcombe.
1702   *March*: death of William III; accession of Anne.
        August: receives honorary degree from Christ Church, Oxford.
1704   *April*: appointed Secretary at War in Godolphin–Marlborough administration.
1708   *February*: resigns from administration.
        April: fails to secure re-election as MP for Wootton Bassett; retires to wife's estate at Bucklebury, Berkshire.
1710   *February–March*: trial of Dr Sacheverell.
        June: appointed Secretary of State for the Northern Department in Harley administration.
        August: *A Letter to the Examiner* (Swift's new journal).

	September: Tory landslide at general election; elected MP for Berkshire.
	November: first meeting with Swift.
1711	*November*: Swift publishes *The Conduct of the Allies*.
1712	*July*: elevated to the Lords as Viscount Bolingbroke and Baron St John.
1713	*April*: Treaty of Utrecht ends War of the Spanish Succession.
1714	*June*: promotes Schism Bill in the Lords.
	July: Harley (Oxford) dismissed by Queen Anne.
	August: death of Anne; accession of George I; Bolingbroke dismissed from Secretaryship.
1715	*February*: Whig landslide at general election.
	March: flees to France.
	June: impeached by Parliament.
	July: accepts earldom from the Pretender and becomes his Secretary of State.
	September: death of Louis XIV.
1716	*March*: dismissed as Pretender's Secretary.
	April: Collapse of Jacobite rising in Scotland; Septennial Act passed by Parliament.
	Writes *Reflections upon Exile* and *A Letter to Sir William Windham* (first published 1752–53).
1718	*October*: death of Frances Winchcombe.
1719	Marries Marie-Claire de Marcilly, Marquise de Villette.
1720	Collapse of the South Sea Company.
	December: leases Château de la Source, near Orléans, where he lives until 1725. During this period, writes *The Substance of Some Letters to M. de Pouilly*, *A Letter Occasioned by One of Archbishop Tillotson's Sermons* and *Reflections Concerning Innate Moral Principles* (first published 1752–54).
1722	Walpole becomes principal minister.
1723	*May*: pardoned under the Great Seal, but not released from 1715 Act of Attainder.
	June–August: back in England.
	Foundation of the Club de l'Entresol in Paris.
1724	*August*: drafts 'Plan for a General History of Europe' in letter to Pope.
1725	Returns to England; settles at Dawley, near Uxbridge.

      May: attainder reversed, but not allowed to return to the Lords.

1726   *October*: Swift publishes *Gulliver's Travels*.

      December: first issue of *The Craftsman* published (5th).

1727   *January*: *The First Vision of Camilick* appears in *The Craftsman*.

      March: *The Occasional Writer, I–III*, appear in *The Craftsman*.

      June: death of George I; accession of George II.

1728   *January*: Gay, *The Beggar's Opera* first performed.

      May: Pope publishes *The Dunciad*.

1729   *August–October*: tours Netherlands and north-west France.

      October: Montesquieu begins visit to England (October 1729–summer 1731)

1730   *The Case of Dunkirk Faithfully Stated and Impartially Considered.*

      September: begins publishing *Remarks on the History of England* in *The Craftsman* under the pseudonym 'Humphrey Oldcastle'.

1731   *May*: publishes concluding letter of *Remarks on the History of England* in *The Craftsman*.

      A Final Answer to the Remarks on the Craftsman's Vindication.

1733   *January–June*: the Excise Crisis.

      February–May: Pope publishes *An Essay on Man*, Epistles I–III (addressed to 'my St John').

      The Freeholder's Political Catechism.

      October: begins publishing the *Dissertation upon Parties* serially in *The Craftsman*.

1734   *The Craftsman Extraordinary . . . In Which the Right of the People to Frequent Elections of their Representatives is Fully Considered.*

      December: concludes publication of the *Dissertation upon Parties* in *The Craftsman*.

1735   Lyttelton publishes *Persian Letters*; James Thomson publishes *The Seasons*.

      February: *The Dissertation upon Parties* appears in book form, dedicated ironically to Walpole.

      May: leaves England for France.

June: settles at Chanteloup, in Touraine.

November: begins writing *Letters on the Study and Use of History*, dedicated to Henry Hyde, Lord Cornbury.

1736   Moves to Argeville, near Fontainebleau.

Writes *A Letter on the Spirit of Patriotism*, addressed `to Lord Cornbury, and (?) *Of the True Use of Retirement and Study*, dedicated to Lord Bathurst.

1738   *March*: Pope, *Epistle to Bolingbroke*.

June: birth of George, son of Frederick, Prince of Wales.

July: returns to England; stays with Pope until April 1739.

Pope prints private edition of *Letters on the Study and Use of History*.

November/December (?): writes *The Idea of a Patriot King*.

1739   *April*: returns to France.

Writes *Of the State of Parties at the Accession of King George the First*.

1740   *June*: death of Sir William Wyndham.

1741   (?) Pope prints edition of The *Idea of a Patriot King*.

1742   *February*: Walpole resigns, and is elevated to the Lords as Earl of Orford.

April: father dies.

Late April/early May–June: in England.

1743   *April–May* and *October*: in England.

1744   *May*: death of Pope.

Returns to England for good, and settles at Battersea.

October: Pope's pirated edition of *The Idea of a Patriot King* mostly destroyed.

1745   *March*: death of Walpole.

October: death of Swift.

Duke of Cumberland crushes Jacobite rebellion.

1746   Publishes [Pope,] *Verses on the Late D—ss of M—. By Mr P—*.

1748   *A Collection of Political Tracts by the Author of the Dissertation on Parties*.

Treaty of Aix-la-Chapelle ends War of the Austrian Succession.

1749   *January–April*: *London Magazine* begins unauthorized reprint of sections from *The Idea of a Patriot King*.

May: *Letters, On the Spirit of Patriotism: On the Idea of a*

Patriot King: And On the State of Parties, At the Accession of King George the First.
July: A Familiar Epistle to the Most Impudent Man Living.
Writes last political tract, *Some Reflections on the Present State of the Nation.*

1750   *March:* wife dies: buried in St Mary's Church, Battersea.

1751   *March:* death of Frederick, Prince of Wales.
December: dies; buried at Battersea.

1752   *March: Letters on the Study and Use of History, Of the True Use of Retirement and Study and Reflections upon Exile.*
Reflections Concerning Innate Moral Principles.

1753   *A Letter to Sir William Wyndham, Some Reflections on the Present State of the Nation and the Letter to Mr Pope.*

1754   *March: The Works of the Late Right Honourable Henry St John, Lord Viscount Bolingbroke* published in five volumes by David Mallet.

Further reading

Biography

H. T. Dickinson, *Bolingbroke* (London, 1970) replaced all earlier accounts, though Walter Sichel, *Bolingbroke and His Times* (2 vols., London, 1901–2) contains material which is still useful. Sheila Biddle, *Bolingbroke and Harley* (London, 1975) and Brean Hammond, *Pope and Bolingbroke: A Study of Friendship and Influence* (Columbia, Missouri, 1984) have since treated two of Bolingbroke's most important relationships in greater detail, Hammond the more revealingly.

Political background

Four major recent syntheses of British history in the 'long' eighteenth century provide a variety of contexts for Bolingbroke's life, works and politics: John Brewer, *The Sinews of Power: War, Money and the English State 1688–1783* (London, 1989); J. C. D. Clark, *English Society 1688–1832: Ideology, Social Structure and Political Practice During the Ancien Regime* (Cambridge, 1985); Linda Colley, *Britons: Forging the Nation 1707–1837* (New Haven, 1992); and Paul Langford, *A Polite and Commercial People? England 1727–1783* (Oxford, 1989). None of these entirely replaces two older synoptic studies of relevance to the study of Bolingbroke and his thought: Betty Kemp, *King and Commons 1660–1832* (London, 1959) and J. H. Plumb, *The Growth of Political Stability in England 1675–1725* (London, 1967).

For a general introduction to the political life of Walpolean Britain see J. H. Plumb, *Sir Robert Walpole* (2 vols., London, 1956, 1960), P. G. M. Dickson, *The Financial Revolution in England: A Study in the Development of Public Credit, 1688–1756* (London, 1967), Paul Langford, *The Excise Crisis: Society and Politics in the Age of Walpole* (Oxford, 1975), H. T. Dickinson, *Walpole and the Whig Supremacy* (London, 1973), Jeremy Black, ed., *Britain in the Age of Walpole* (London, 1984), and Nicholas Rogers, *Whigs and Cities: Popular Politics in the Age of Walpole and Pitt* (Oxford, 1989). The politicization of the press, on which see Jeremy Black, *The English Press in the Eighteenth Century* (London, 1987) and Michael Harris, *London Newspapers in the Age of Walpole: A Study of the Origins of the Modern English Press* (London, 1987), was a major development in Bolingbroke's lifetime; for its impact on political thought see for example Nicholas Phillipson, *Hume* (London, 1989), ch. 2. The best account of the major oppositional organ is Simon Varey, '*The Craftsman 1726–52*' (PhD thesis, Cambridge, 1976), some of whose findings appear in the introduction to *Lord Bolingbroke: Contributions to the Craftsman*, ed. Simon Varey (Oxford, 1982). On the politics of literature during this period, see Maynard Mack, *The Garden and the City: Retirement and Politics in the Later Poetry of Pope, 1731–1743* (Toronto, 1969), Bertrand Goldgar, *Walpole and the Wits: The Relation of Politics to Literature, 1722–1742* (Lincoln, Nebraska, 1976) and, above all, Christine Gerrard, *The Patriot Opposition to Walpole: Politics, Poetry, and National Myth, 1725–1742* (Oxford, 1994). Examples of the literary and visual attacks on Walpole's government can be found in *Political Ballads Illustrating the Administration of Sir Robert Walpole*, ed. Milton Percival (Oxford, 1916) and *Walpole and the Robinocracy*, ed. Paul Langford (Cambridge, 1986). Ruth Smith, *Handel's Oratorios and Eighteenth-Century Thought* (Cambridge, 1995) provides a careful exposition of oppositional thought in a surprising context.

Intellectual background

The most valuable general studies of eighteenth-century British political thought are H. T. Dickinson, *Liberty and Property: Political Ideology in Eighteenth-Century Britain* (London, 1977), J. A. W. Gunn, *Beyond Liberty and Property: The Process of Self-Recognition in Eighteenth-Century Political Thought* (Kingston, Ontario, 1983), and J. G. A. Pocock, *Virtue, Commerce and History: Essays on Political Thought and History, Chiefly in the Eighteenth Century* (Cambridge, 1985), especially Part III, 'The Varieties of Whiggism from Exclusion to Reform: A History of Ideology and Discourse'. The essays in J. G. A. Pocock, ed., *The Varieties of British Political Thought, 1500–1800* (Cambridge, 1994) authoritatively map the broader territory within which Bolingbroke worked and had his greatest influence.

Bolingbroke's specific debts to earlier intellectual traditions have been variously studied. Herbert Butterfield, *The Statecraft of Machiavelli* (London, 1962), ch. 4, is the classic study of his relation to Machiavelli, while Jeffrey Hart, *Viscount Bolingbroke: Tory Humanist* (London, 1965) places Bolingbroke in the context of 'humanism', albeit rather imprecisely defined. Isaac Kramnick, 'An Augustan Reply to Locke: Bolingbroke on Natural Law and the Origin of Government', *Political Science Quarterly* 82 (1967): 571–94, tries to make sense of Bolingbroke's engagement with Hobbes, Locke and the Cambridge Platonists; Knud Haakonssen, *Natural Law and Moral Philosophy: From Grotius to the Scottish Enlightenment* (Cambridge, 1996) has since provided the necessary framework for reconsidering Bolingbroke's natural-law theory. Bernard Cottret, 'Le Roi, les Lords et les Communes: monarchie mixte et états du royaume en Angleterre (XVIᵉ–XVIIIᵉ siècles)', *Annales E.S.C.* 41 (1986): 127–50, places Bolingbroke in the tradition of English reflection on mixed government, while Mark Goldie, 'Tory Political Thought, 1689–1714' (PhD thesis, Cambridge, 1978), reveals the intellectual foundations of aspects of Bolingbroke's programme in post-Revolutionary Tory constitutionalism; on contemporary Whiggism see J. P. Kenyon, *Revolution Principles: The Politics of Party 1689–1720* (Cambridge, 1977).

Bolingbroke's religious thought has not been studied seriously for almost half a century. The classic works remain Leslie Stephen, *History of English Thought in the Eighteenth Century* (2 vols., London, 1876), Norman L. Torrey, *Voltaire and the English Deists* (New Haven, 1930), D. G. James, *The Life of Reason: Hobbes, Locke, Bolingbroke* (London, 1949), and Walter Mackintosh Merrill, *From Statesman to Philosopher: A Study in Bolingbroke's Deism* (London, 1949).

The French context of Bolingbroke's thought would also repay further study. A start might be made with E. R. Briggs, 'The Political Academies of France in the Early Eighteenth Century with Special Reference to the Club de l'Entresol and its Founder, Pierre Joseph Alary' (PhD thesis, Cambridge, 1931), Nannerl O. Keohane, *Philosophy and the State in France: The Renaissance to the Enlightenment* (Princeton, 1980), and Harold E. Ellis, *Boulainvilliers and the French Monarchy: Aristocratic Politics in Eighteenth-Century France* (Ithaca, 1988). In the meantime, see D. J. Fletcher, 'The Intellectual Relations of Bolingbroke with France' (MA thesis, University College of Wales, 1953) and his 'Bolingbroke and the Diffusion of Newtonianism in France', *Studies on Voltaire and the Eighteenth Century* 53 (1967): 29–46. Rex A. Barrell, *Bolingbroke and France* (Lanham, Maryland, 1988) provides a cursory overview.

Bolingbroke's contribution to British historiography has been well studied, especially in Isaac Kramnick, 'Augustan Politics and English Historiography: The Debate on the English Past, 1730–1735', *History and Theory* 6 (1967): 33–56, *Lord Bolingbroke: Historical Writings*, introd. Isaac Kramnick (Chicago, 1972), R. J. Smith, *The Gothic Bequest: Medieval Institutions in British Thought, 1688–1863* (Cambridge, 1987), ch. 2, and the important article by Philip Hicks, 'Bolingbroke, Clarendon and the Role of the Classical Historian', *Eighteenth-Century Studies* 20 (1987): 445–71. Also of interest are D. J. Womersley, 'Lord Bolingbroke and Eighteenth-Century Historiography', *The Eighteenth Century* 28 (1987): 217–34, and Joel Weinsheimer, *Eighteenth-Century Hermeneutics: Philosophy of Interpretation from Locke to Burke* (New Haven, 1993), ch. 3, 'Bolingbroke on History'.

Political thought

Bolingbroke's political thought is most often studied as part of the transformation of early-modern civic humanism into the transatlantic 'Country' ideology of the eighteenth century. J. G. A. Pocock, 'Machiavelli, Harrington and English Political Ideologies in the Eighteenth Century' in his *Politics, Language and Time: Essays on Political Thought and History* (New York, 1971), 104–47, provides the best introduction to this transformation, on which see more broadly Caroline Robbins, *The Eighteenth-Century Common-*

wealthman: Studies in the Transmission, Development and Circumstance of English Liberal Thought from the Restoration of Charles II until the War with the Thirteen Colonies (Cambridge, Mass., 1959) and J. G. A. Pocock, *The Machiavellian Moment: Florentine Political Thought and the Atlantic Republican Tradition* (Princeton, 1975).

The two most influential modern interpretations of Bolingbroke's political thought are Isaac Kramnick, *Bolingbroke and His Circle: The Politics of Nostalgia in the Age of Walpole* (Ithaca, 1968, reissued 1992), the reductionism of which has gone largely unquestioned, and Quentin Skinner, 'The Principles and Practice of Opposition: The Case of Bolingbroke versus Walpole' in Neil McKendrick, ed., *Historical Perspectives: Studies in English Thought and Society in Honour of J. H. Plumb* (London, 1974), 93–128, which makes exemplary use of Bolingbroke to illuminate the wider problem of the relationship between political thought and political action. The only subsequent reassessments have been Simon Varey, *Henry St John, Viscount Bolingbroke* (Boston, 1984) (on Bolingbroke's 'rhetoric', broadly defined) and Shelley Burtt, *Virtue Transformed: Political Argument in England, 1688–1740* (Cambridge, 1992), ch. 5, 'Bolingbroke's Politics of Virtue' (on his deployment of classical notions of public virtue). However, the publication of Guido Abbattista's Italian edition of *L'Idea di un Re Patriota* (Rome, 1995), Bernard Cottret's edition of *Bolingbroke's Political Writings: The Conservative Enlightenment* (London, 1997), and Alexander Pettit's study, *Illusory Consensus: Bolingbroke and the Polemical Response to Walpole, 1730–1737* (Newark, Del., 1997) suggests that one of the periodic revivals of interest in Bolingbroke's political thought is now under way.

Until recently it was assumed that Bolingbroke and the opposition made all the intellectual running during Walpole's ministry. However, Reed Browning, *Political and Constitutional Ideas of the Court Whigs* (Baton Rouge, 1986) and Shelley Burtt, *Virtue Transformed*, ch. 6, 'The Court Whig Conception of Virtue', have made a strong case for the interest and coherence of Ministerialist political thought, stronger than that of Simon Targett, 'Government and Ideology during the Age of Whig Supremacy: The Political Argument of Sir Robert Walpole's Newspaper Propagandists', *The Historical Journal* 37 (1994): 289–317. M. M. Goldsmith, 'Faction Detected: Ideological Consequences of Robert Walpole's Decline and Fall', *History* 64 (1979): 1–19, is a suggestive account of the end of the Walpolean pamphlet wars.

There have been few assessments of Bolingbroke's contribution to political theory. Notable in this respect are the brief studies by J. H. Burns, 'Bolingbroke and the Concept of Constitutional Government', *Political Studies* 10 (1962): 264–76, and J. H. Grainger, 'The Deviations of Lord Bolingbroke', *Australian Journal of Politics and History* 15 (1969): 41–59.

Parties and the *Dissertation upon Parties*

J. A. W. Gunn, *Factions No More: Attitudes to Party in Government and Opposition in Eighteenth-Century England* (London, 1972) provides a good anthology of eighteenth-century theories of party, on which see also Caroline Robbins, '"Discordant Parties": A Study in the Acceptance of Party by Englishmen', *Political Science Quarterly* 73 (1958): 505–29. For complementary narratives see Tim Harris, *Politics under the Later Stuarts: Party Conflict in a Divided Society 1660–1715* (London, 1993), Geoffrey Holmes, *British Politics in the Age of Anne* (London, 1967, revised edition 1987), and Archibald S. Foord, *His Majesty's Opposition 1714–1830* (Oxford, 1964). Linda Colley, *In Defiance of Oligarchy: The Tory Party 1714–1760* (Cambridge, 1982), demythologizes the party context within which Bolingbroke operated. J. C. D. Clark, 'A General Theory of Party, Opposition and Government, 1688–1832', *The Historical Journal* 23 (1980): 295–325, projects a Bolingbrokean analysis of party well into the nineteenth century. Richard Hofstadter, *The Idea of a Party System: The Rise of Legitimate Opposition in the United States, 1780–1840* (Berkeley, 1969), traces the dissolution of Bolingbrokean fears of party in the early American republic.

For treatments of Bolingbroke's own views on party and opposition see especially F. N. Fieldhouse, 'Bolingbroke and the Idea of Non-Party Government', *History* 23 (1938): 41–56, Pat Rogers, 'Swift and Bolingbroke on Faction', *Journal of British Studies* 9 (1970): 71–101, and Kurt Kluxen, *Das Problem der Politischen Opposition* (Freiburg, 1956).

Patriotism and *The Idea of a Patriot King*

H. T. Dickinson, 'Bolingbroke: "The Idea of a Patriot King"', *History Today* 20, 1 (January 1970): 13–19, finds the work overrated;

Simon Varey, 'Hanover, Stuart and the *Patriot King*', *British Journal of Eighteenth-Century Studies* 6 (1983): 163–72, re-opens the question of the Patriot King's identity, albeit unconvincingly. On the relationship between the literature of opposition and the *Patriot King*, M. H. Cable, 'The Idea of a Patriot King in the Propaganda of the Opposition to Walpole', *Philological Quarterly* 18 (1939): 119–30, has been decisively superseded by Christine Gerrard, *The Patriot Opposition to Walpole*, ch. 7, 'Mythologizing the Monarch: Ideas of a Patriot King'.

The changing meaning of patriotism in the course of the eighteenth century can be followed in Hugh Cunningham, 'The Language of Patriotism' and Linda Colley, 'Radical Patriotism in Eighteenth-Century England', in Raphael Samuel, ed., *Patriotism: The Making and Unmaking of British National Identity I: History and Politics* (London, 1989), 57–89, 169–87, and in the more specific studies by Betty Kemp, 'Patriotism, Pledges, and the People' in Martin Gilbert, ed., *A Century of Conflict, 1850–1950: Essays for A. J. P. Taylor* (London, 1966), 37–46; Robert Harris, *A Patriot Press: National Politics and the London Press in the 1740s* (Oxford, 1993); Marie Peters, *Pitt and Popularity: The Patriot Minister and London Opinion during the Seven Years War* (Oxford, 1980); John Brewer, *Party Ideology and Popular Politics at the Accession of George III* (Cambridge, 1976), ch. 6; Linda Colley, 'The Apotheosis of George III: Loyalty, Royalty and the British Nation, 1760–1820', *Past and Present* no. 102 (1984): 94–129; John Sainsbury, *Disaffected Patriots: London Supporters of Revolutionary America, 1769–1782* (Kingston, Ontario, 1982); John Dinwiddy, 'England' in Otto Dann and John Dinwiddy, eds., *Nationalism in the Age of the French Revolution* (London, 1988), 53–70; David Eastwood, 'Patriotism and the English State in the 1790s' in Mark Philp, ed., *The French Revolution and British Popular Politics* (Cambridge, 1991), 146–68; and Eastwood, 'Robert Southey and the Meanings of Patriotism', *Journal of British Studies* 31 (1992): 265–87. David Armitage, 'A Patriot For Whom? The Afterlives of Bolingbroke's Patriot King', forthcoming, *Journal of British Studies* 36 (1997): 397–418, locates Bolingbroke's place in that shift; Maurizio Viroli, *For Love of Country: An Essay on Patriotism and Nationalism* (Oxford, 1995), briefly sets him in the longer history of the rise and fall of republican patriotism.

Legacy

Bolingbroke's relationship to his most important contemporaries is the subject of Robert Shackleton, 'Montesquieu, Bolingbroke and the Separation of Powers', *French Studies* 3 (1949): 25–38, and Duncan Forbes, *Hume's Philosophical Politics* (Cambridge, 1975), ch. 6. The question of Voltaire's debt to Bolingbroke – denied by Norman L. Torrey, 'Bolingbroke and Voltaire – A Fictitious Influence', *Publications of the Modern Languages Association of America* 42 (1927): 788–97 - is briefly reconsidered in J. H. Brumfitt, *Voltaire, Historian* (Oxford, 1958). D. J. Fletcher, 'The Fortunes of Bolingbroke in France in the Eighteenth Century', *Studies on Voltaire and the Eighteenth Century* 47 (1966): 207–32, is more persuasive than his suggestion of a link between Bolingbroke and Rousseau in '*Le Législateur* and *The Patriot King*: A Case of Intellectual Kinship', *Comparative Literature Studies* 6 (1969): 410–18.

Horace Walpole's canard that George III was raised on Bolingbrokean prerogative principles was laid to rest for ever in the introduction to *Letters from George III to Lord Bute, 1756–66*, ed. Romney Sedgwick (London, 1939), and its later career anatomized in Herbert Butterfield, *George III and the Historians* (London, 1957). Bolingbroke's legacy has been more reliably confirmed in relation to the political thought of Burke, the American Revolution and Disraeli. The most extended comparison between Burke and Bolingbroke is Harvey Mansfield, Jr, *Statesmanship and Party Government: A Study of Burke and Bolingbroke* (Chicago, 1965), while J. C. Weston, Jr, 'The Ironic Purpose of Burke's *Vindication* Vindicated', *Journal of the History of Ideas* 19 (1958): 435–41, succinctly reveals Burke's critical evaluation of his predecessor. On Bolingbroke's role as a conduit of 'Country' ideology from Britain to the American colonies, the classic works remain Bernard Bailyn, *The Origins of American Politics* (New York, 1968) and Bailyn, *The Ideological Origins of the American Revolution* (Cambridge, Mass., 1967, revised edition 1992), to which should be added the more specific studies of William D. Liddle, '"A Patriot King or None": Lord Bolingbroke and the American Renunciation of George III', *Journal of American History* 65 (1979): 951–70, Zoltan Haraszti, *John Adams and the Prophets of Progress* (Cambridge, Mass., 1952), ch. 4, 'Bolingbroke, the Ishmael of His Age', and Ralph Ketcham,

Presidents Above Party: The First American Presidency, 1789–1829 (Chapel Hill, 1984). For more sceptical assessments of the influence of the Country tradition in eighteenth-century Britain and America see Jack P. Greene, 'The Concept of Virtue in Late Colonial British America' and Isaac Kramnick, 'Corruption in Eighteenth-Century British and American Political Discourse', in Richard K. Matthews, ed., *Virtue, Corruption, and Self-Interest: Political Values in the Eighteenth Century* (Bethlehem, Pa., 1994), 27–54, 55–75.

Bolingbroke's most conspicuous political imitator was the young Benjamin Disraeli, on whom see Annaliese Dahle, *Disraelis Beziehungen zu Bolingbroke* (Freiburg, 1931) and Richard Faber, *Beaconsfield and Bolingbroke* (London, 1961). His contribution to later English Toryism is examined in Geoffrey Butler, *The Tory Tradition: Bolingbroke, Burke, Disraeli, Salisbury* (London, 1914, reprinted with a preface by R. A. Butler, 1957) and, more briefly, in Sidney W. Jackman, *Man of Mercury: An Appreciation of the Mind of Henry St John, Viscount Bolingbroke* (London, 1965).

The ambiguity of Bolingbroke's contemporary legacy is perhaps indicated by his presence both in *The Faber Book of Conservatism*, ed. Kenneth Baker (London, 1993) and in *Democracy in Britain: A Reader*, ed. Jack Lively and Adam Lively (Oxford, 1994).

Note on texts

In light of the current interest in Bolingbroke's work, the most appropriate response to Burke's famously scathing query, 'Who now reads Bolingbroke? who ever read him through?' might be 'Where should one read Bolingbroke?' There has never been a critical edition of Bolingbroke's works, and none of the three editions of his collected writings (5 vols., London, 1754; 4 vols., Philadelphia, 1841; 4 vols., London, 1844, and later facsimiles) contains either textual apparatus or annotation. Nor are they complete, since none includes Bolingbroke's *A Letter to the Examiner* (London, 1710), *The Case of Dunkirk Faithfully Stated and Impartially Considered* (London, 1730), *The Freeholder's Political Catechism* (London, 1733) or *A Familiar Epistle to the Most Impudent Man Living* (London, 1749), for example. Further essays attributable to Bolingbroke have also been collected in *Lord Bolingbroke: Contributions to the Craftsman*, ed. Simon Varey (Oxford, 1982), and there is now an excellent Italian edition and translation of *L'Idea di un Re Patriota*, ed. Guido Abbattista (Rome, 1995). The best guide to the texts of Bolingbroke's work is Giles G. Barber, 'A Bibliography of Henry Saint John, Viscount Bolingbroke' (B.Litt. thesis, Oxford, 1963).

Alexander Pope noted the prodigious quality of Bolingbroke's memory: 'if he is alone and without books he can sit down by himself (as another man would in his study) and refer to the books, or such a particular subject within them, in his own mind'.[1] However,

---

[1] Joseph Spence, *Observations, Anecdotes, and Characters of Books and Men*, ed. James M. Osborn (2 vols., Oxford, 1966), I, 120.

Bolingbroke's mind frequently played tricks on him and his reconstructions and rememberings are often frustratingly inexact or inaccurate. Although every effort has been made to track the sources of Bolingbroke's quotations and allusions, some remain elusive.

A Dissertation upon Parties

The letters which make up the *Dissertation upon Parties* appeared weekly as editorials in *The Craftsman* between 27 October 1733 and 26 January 1734 (with some breaks) and then again from 9 November to 28 December 1734. In 1735 they were collected with the addition of an ironic dedication to Sir Robert Walpole (here omitted), and of *The Craftsman Extraordinary ... In Which the Right of the People to Frequent Elections of their Representatives is Fully Considered* (1734) as 'Letter XI'. The collection went through five London editions and two Dublin editions during Bolingbroke's lifetime. All later editions followed the 'second', 1735 edition (the first being taken to have been their publication in *The Craftsman*), which incorporated minor substantive revisions to the original periodical texts. Mallet's 1754 edition of Bolingbroke's *Works* reprinted the 1735 text, and this version (checked against the original issues of *The Craftsman* and the 1735 edition) is the basis for the modernized text in this edition. Since this is not a critical edition of Bolingbroke's text, and the variations are slight, I have not reproduced variants from the original editions of *The Craftsman*. However, I have noted the issue and date of publication of the letters, to facilitate comparison. Bolingbroke's footnotes are lettered; editorial notes are numbered.

'On the Spirit of Patriotism'

Bolingbroke wrote 'On the Spirit of Patriotism' in 1736 as a letter to Henry Hyde, Lord Cornbury. It remained in manuscript until May 1749 when it first appeared in Andrew Millar's edition of *Letters, On the Spirit of Patriotism: On the Idea of a Patriot King: And On the State of Parties, At the Accession of King George the First* (London, 1749). This edition presents a modernized version of Millar's text, checked against Mallet's edition of 1754; later variants are indicated by *1754* in the footnotes.

The Idea of a Patriot King

The Idea of a Patriot King is the most bibliographically fraught of Bolingbroke's works. He wrote it in the autumn of 1738 while staying at Twickenham with Alexander Pope. The opposition politician, Lyttelton, had approached Pope in October 1738 to ask him to help the opposition, in particular by providing advice to Frederick, Prince of Wales, which might 'Animate [him] to . . . the Virtue least known to Princes . . . Love of the Publick'.[2] Though friendly with Prince Frederick, Pope was ambivalent about the Patriot cause, and seems not to have complied with Lyttelton's request. However, it is possible that Pope passed the task of counselling Frederick and his advisers to his house-guest, and that *The Idea of a Patriot King* was the resulting mirror for a prince; Lyttelton later wrote that it 'was originally writ in the form of a letter to me. I being then in the Prince's service.'[3]

When Bolingbroke returned to France in April 1739, he entrusted the manuscript of the *Patriot King* to Pope, along with other pieces (probably including the letter 'On the Spirit of Patriotism'), with the instructions that he should produce a small, private edition for the use of the Prince and his closest advisers. Pope had already done something similar in 1738 when he published a private edition of Bolingbroke's *Letters on the Study and Use of History*.[4] Bolingbroke had little reason to believe that his wishes regarding the *Patriot King* had not been followed until after Pope's death in 1744, when he discovered that fifteen hundred copies of the work had been printed under Pope's supervision some years earlier by John Wright under the title *The Idea of a Patriot King: With Respect to the Constitution of Great Britain. By a Person of Quality*.[5] He ordered the destruction of all but a few copies of that edition, and there the matter rested until extracts from *The*

[2] *Correspondence of Alexander Pope. IV: 1736–1744*, ed. George Sherburn (Oxford, 1956), 138–9.
[3] *Memoirs and Correspondence of George, Lord Lyttelton*, ed. R. J. Phillimore (2 vols., London, 1845), II, 428.
[4] George H. Nadel, 'New Light on Bolingbroke's *Letters on History*', *Journal of the History of Ideas* 23 (1962): 550–8.
[5] D. J. McLaverty, *Pope's Printer, John Wright: A Preliminary Study*, Oxford Bibliographical Society Occasional Publication XI (Oxford, 1977), 27 (item 147), suggests 1741 as the date of Pope's edition.

Idea of a Patriot King, preceded by the associated letter 'Of the Private Life of a Prince', appeared in the *London Magazine* in early 1749.[6] Bolingbroke forestalled the work's complete serial republication in May 1749, when Andrew Millar published *Letters, On the Spirit of Patriotism: On the Idea of a Patriot King: And On the State of Parties, At the Accession of George the First*. In the 'Advertisement' to that edition, he accused Pope (though not by name) of breach of trust, and thereby set off one of the literary *causes célèbres* of the eighteenth century, as Pope's supporters rushed to defend his memory and reputation.[7]

Any complete assessment of Bolingbroke's intentions must take account of both texts of the *Patriot King*, and this edition makes their variants available together for the first time in English.[8] The earliest assessment of the state of Bolingbroke's text collated only one surviving copy of Pope's edition against the 1749 text, and reproduced the variants incompletely and inaccurately;[9] subsequent bibliographical discussions have used two or three copies of Pope's edition. For this edition, the copies in the British Library, the Harry Ransom Humanities Center (University of Texas, Austin) and the Beinecke Library (Yale University), as well as a previously unremarked copy in the Robert H. Taylor collection (Firestone Library, Princeton University), have been collated.[10] Though these texts differ in the completeness of their front matter (the British Library copy lacks the title-page and contents pages which are present in the Texas, Yale and Princeton copies), they all contain a complete text of the *Patriot King*, preceded by the 'Author's Preface', paginated 1–8, 1–131, and signed A[1]^r–S[1]^v in fours. In the parts that they share, these four texts are identical in every respect. They are

---

[6] *London Magazine* 18 (January 1749): 3–10; (March 1749): 103–7; (April 1749): 157–60.

[7] The best treatments of this episode, and the textual problems it generated, are Giles Barber, 'Bolingbroke, Pope, and the *Patriot King*', *The Library* 19 (1964): 67–89, and Frank T. Smallwood, 'Bolingbroke vs. Alexander Pope: The Publication of the *Patriot King*', *Papers of the Bibliographical Society of America* 65 (1971): 225–41.

[8] They are also recorded (in Italian) in *L'Idea di un Re Patriota*, ed. Guido Abbattista (Rome, 1995).

[9] Fannie E. Ratchford, 'Pope and the *Patriot King*', *Texas Studies in English* 6 (1926): 157–77; in all textual details this article was superseded by the work of Barber and Smallwood.

[10] *The Idea of a Patriot King: With Respect to the Constitution of Great Britain. By a Person of Quality* (London, n.d.). I am grateful to the keepers of all four collections for making this collation possible.

evidently part of the same run, and therefore in themselves provide no bibliographical evidence to support the suggestion that there may have been 'two states or even editions' before the edition of 1749, one of five or six for Frederick's inner circle, the other, an unauthorized edition of fifteen hundred copies.[11] Though this may indeed have been the case, either no copy of the coterie edition survives, or Pope produced only a single edition, a few copies of which were reserved for immediate, private circulation, while the rest he intended to be saved for a wider audience.

In accordance with the practice of this series, this edition presents a modernized text of *The Idea of a Patriot King*. The 1749 edition of the *Letters* is the copy text, and the footnotes record all substantive variants from the surviving copies of Pope's edition. In the absence of a manuscript of the *Patriot King*,[12] the earlier edition provides the only access to Bolingbroke's original intentions. Even if Bolingbroke exaggerated the scope of the changes made by Pope when he alleged that the poet 'had taken upon him further to divide the subject, and to alter and to omit passages, according to the suggestions of his own fancy',[13] those parts of the original text retained in 1749 can be assumed to be in accord with Bolingbroke's intentions, even if he revised those intentions retrospectively. The earlier edition shows more clearly the *Patriot King*'s origins as a coterie text, directed in particular to Lyttelton (who is addressed in the second person throughout). It also provides evidence of Pope's editorial practices and his reading of the work as an advice-book in the Machiavellian mode, which he subdivided into short chapters on the model of *The Prince*. It is notable that this earlier version contains anti-Jacobite polemic, which one early commentator (followed by later scholars) assumed to be an editorial insertion.[14] Bolingbroke's retention of this passage in 1749 may have been

---

[11] Barber, 'Bolingbroke, Pope, and the *Patriot King*': 80; Barber, 'Some Uncollected Authors XLI: Henry Saint John, Viscount Bolingbroke, 1678–1751', *The Book Collector* 14 (1965): 534–5, suggests 'two versions . . ., one of which the author knew, one slightly amended, of which he did not'.

[12] Though Lyttelton possessed one, 'as it was writ and in my Lord's own hand', in 1748 (*Memoirs*, ed. Phillimore, II, 428).

[13] *Letters, On the Spirit of Patriotism: On the Idea of a Patriot King: And On the State of Parties, At the Accession of King George the First* (London, 1749), vii.

[14] *London Magazine* 18 (May 1749): 199; Simon Varey, 'Hanover, Stuart and the *Patriot King*', *British Journal for Eighteenth-Century Studies* 6 (1983): 167; Christine Gerrard, *The Patriot Opposition to Walpole: Politics, Poetry, and National Myth, 1725–1742* (Oxford, 1994), 205.

dictated by caution, in the aftermath of the '45 and in the attempt to live down his much earlier brush with Jacobitism; however, it is plausible to assume that it reflects Bolingbroke's original intentions in a work intended very precisely for the circle of Frederick, Prince of Wales.

The major difference between Pope's edition and the 1749 text is the inclusion in the latter of advice regarding the prince's private conduct. This material is not included in the earlier edition. It does exist in an earlier printing, the unique copy of which is bound in with the British Library's copy of Pope's edition of *The Idea of a Patriot King*.[15] Though the work is clearly intended to follow directly on from the *Patriot King*,[16] the accompanying internal title-page calls it 'Letter III. Of the Private Life of a Prince'. The section is separately paginated and signed (pp. [2] + 3–28; sigs. A[1]ʳ–D[2]ᵛ), and this – together with the heading, 'Letter III' – suggests that it was intended to join a projected compendium of Boling-broke's political epistles from 1736 to 1738, comprising the letter 'On the Spirit of Patriotism', *The Idea of a Patriot King* and 'Letter III. Of the Private Life of a Prince'. When Bolingbroke published *The Idea of a Patriot King* in 1749, he inserted this material into the main body of the text, and the volume concluded instead with 'Letter III. Of the State of Parties at the Accession of King George'. Subsequent editions have obscured the origins of Bolingbroke's later works, and a full critical edition should probably restore them to the forms in which they were originally composed, whether periodical or epistolary. This edition seeks only for the moment to present his most important political writings and their variants in an accessible modern form.

Bolingbroke evidently made his excisions, revisions and additions on a copy of Pope's edition in order to create the text for the 1749 printing. Material added in the later text is indicated by *1749* in the footnotes; all other textual notes record material either omitted from Pope's text or revised by Bolingbroke.

---

[15] BL shelfmark C.40.g.23. This copy is now also available in the microfilm series *The Eighteenth Century*, reel 4992, item 8.

[16] It begins, 'You observe, that among the several Heads under which I have con-sider'd the Character and Conduct of a Patriot King, I omitted to take notice of One . . .': 'Letter III', 3; compare pp. 280–92 of this edition.

A Dissertation upon Parties

Sir,

To corrupt and to divide are the trite and wicked expedients, by which some ministers in all ages have affected to govern; but especially such as have been least capable of exerting the true arts of government. There is however a difference to be made between these two expedients, to the advantage of the latter, and by consequence between the characters of those who put them in practice.

Every busy, ambitious child of fortune, who hath himself a corrupt heart, and becomes master of a large purse, hath all that is necessary to employ the expedient of corruption with success. A bribe, in the hand of the most blundering coxcomb that ever disgraced honour and wealth and power, will prevail as much as in the hand of a man of sense, and go farther too, if it weigh more. An intriguing chamber-maid may slip a bank-note into a griping paw, as well as the most subtle demon of hell. H—e[2] may govern as triumphantly by this expedient as the great knight his brother, and the great knight as Burghley himself.[3]

But every character cannot attempt the other expedient of dividing, or keeping up divisions, with equal success. There is, indeed, no occasion for any extraordinary genius to divide; and true wisdom despises the infamous task. But there is need of that left-handed wisdom, called cunning,[4] and of those habits in business, called experience. He that is corrupted, co-operates with him that corrupts. He runs into his arms at the first beckon; or, in order sometimes to raise the price, he meets him but half way. On the other hand, to divide, or to maintain and renew the divisions of parties in a state, a system of seduction and fraud is necessary to be carried on. The divided are so far from being accessory to the guilt, that they would not be divided, if they were not first deceived.

---

[1] *Craftsman* 382 (27 October 1733).

[2] H[orac]e: Horatio Walpole (1678–1757), diplomat and long-standing Whig MP (1702–56), younger brother of Sir Robert Walpole.

[3] Sir Robert Walpole was frequently compared to Elizabeth I's chief minister, William Cecil, Lord Burghley (1520–98), though usually in a positive light, as the loyal, upwardly mobile defender of the cause of Protestantism and the crown.

[4] 'We take cunning for a sinister or crooked wisdom': Bacon, *Essays*, 'Of Cunning' in *Francisci Baconis . . . Opera Omnia* (4 vols., London, 1730), III, 332 (compare *Idea of a Patriot King*, p. 255).

From these differences, which I have observed between the two expedients, and the characters and means proper to put them in practice with success, it may be discovered perhaps why, upon former occasions, as I shall hereafter show, the expedient of dividing prospered so much better than that of corrupting; and why, upon some later occasions, the expedient of corrupting succeeds so well in those hands, which are not, and I trust will not be so lucky in maintaining or renewing our party divisions.

Much hath been written by you, Mr D'Anvers,[5] by your correspondents and others, who have drawn their pens in the cause of truth, virtue, and liberty, against the right reverend, as well as undignified, the noble, as well as ignoble assertors of corruption; enough surely to shame those who have not lost all sense of shame, out of so ignominious a crime; and to make those who have not lost every other sense tremble at the consequences of it. We may flatter ourselves that those honest endeavours have had some effect; and have reason to hope that far greater will follow from those illustrious examples of repulses which have been lately given to the grand corrupter, notwithstanding his frequent and insolent declarations that he could seduce whomsoever he had a mind to gain. These hopes are farther confirmed to us by repeated declarations of the sense of Parliament, and will be turned, we doubt not, into certainty, whenever the wisdom of the two Houses shall again think it proper to raise new barriers of law against this encroaching vice.

In the meantime, I think nothing can better answer the design of your papers, nor promote the public good more effectually in the present conjuncture, than to put our countrymen frequently on their guard against the artifice which is clumsily, but industriously employed to maintain, and, if it be possible, to create new divisions amongst them. That day, which our fathers wished to see, and did not see, is now breaking upon us. Shall we suffer this light to be turned again into party-darkness by the incantations of those who would not have passed for conjurers, even in the days of superstition and ignorance? The nation is not only brought into an uniformity of opinion concerning the present administration, by the length and the righteous conduct of it; but we are grown into a unanimity about principles of government, which the most sanguine could

---

[5] Caleb D'Anvers, the pseudonymous editor of *The Craftsman*.

scarce have expected, without extravagance. Certain associations of ideas were made so familiar to us, about half a century ago, and became in the course of time so habitual, that we should not have been able, even a few years ago, to break them, nor have been easily induced to believe, on the faith of any prediction, that experience and the evidence of facts would, in a few years more, break them for us, destroy all our notions of party, and substitute new ones in their room.

The power and majesty of the people, an original contract, the authority and independency of Parliament, liberty, resistance, exclusion, abdication, deposition; these were ideas associated, at that time, to the idea of a Whig, and supposed by every Whig to be incommunicable, and inconsistent with the idea of a Tory.

Divine, hereditary, indefeasible right, lineal succession, passive-obedience, prerogative, non-resistance, slavery, nay and sometimes property too, were associated in many minds to the idea of a Tory, and deemed incommunicable and inconsistent in the same manner, with the idea of a Whig.

But now that which neither side would have believed on the faith of any prediction, is come to pass:

> . . . quod divum promittere nemo
> Auderet, volvenda dies en! attulit ultro.[6]

These associations are broken; these distinct sets of ideas are shuffled out of their order; new combinations force themselves upon us; and it would actually be as absurd to impute to the Tories the principles, which were laid to their charge formerly, as it would be to ascribe to the projector and his faction the name of Whigs, whilst they daily forfeit that character by their actions. The bulk of both parties are really united; united on principles of liberty, in opposition to an obscure remnant of one party, who disown those principles, and a mercenary detachment from the other, who betray them.

How this change for the better comes to have been wrought in an age, when most things have changed for the worse; and since it hath been wrought, why the old distinctions are kept up in some measure, will I think be accounted for in treating this subject far-

---

[6] 'See! The onward roll of time has brought you something which no god would have dared to promise': Virgil, *Aeneid*, IX. 6–7.

ther. At present, what shall we say to these who publicly speak of this national union as impracticable and chimerical, yet privately act against it, with all their might, as a practicable thing, and a real evil to them? If it be as complete and as well cemented, as I imagine it is, and as every honest Briton wishes it may be; nay, if there be nothing more than a strong tendency on all sides towards it, which no man of the least observation and candour will deny; it is surely the duty of every one, who desires the prosperity of his country, to seize the opportunity to cultivate and improve it. If men are to be known by their works, the works of those, who oppose this union, denote them sufficiently. Wicked and unhappy men! who seek their private safety, in opposing public good. Weak and silly men! who vainly imagine that they shall pass for the nation, and the nation for a faction; that they shall be judged in the right, and the whole body of the people in the wrong – On whom would they impose? – How long do they imagine that so unequal a contest can last?

There is no complaint which hath been more constantly in the mouths, no grief hath lain more heavily at the hearts of all good men, than those about our national divisions; about the spirit of party, which inspires animosity and breeds rancour; which hath so often destroyed our inward peace, weakened our national strength, and sullied our glory abroad. It is time therefore that all, who desire to be esteemed good men, and to procure the peace, the strength and the glory of their country by the only means, by which they can be procured effectually, should join their efforts to heal our national divisions, and to change the narrow spirit of party into a diffusive spirit of public benevolence.

That we may be more encouraged to do so, it will be of use perhaps to consider, in some particulars, what advances are already made towards that national union, without which no national good can be expected in such circumstances as ours.

Let us begin with the present temper of the members of the Church of England towards the Dissenters. Those laws, by which the latter were debarred from serving God after their own way, have not been these many years a terror to them.[7] Those which

---

[7] These laws included the Quaker Act (1662); the First and Second Conventicles Acts (1664; 1670); the 'Five Mile' Act (1665); the First and Second Test Acts (1673; 1678); the Occasional Conformity Act (1711; repealed 1719); and the Schism Act (1714; repealed 1719).

were designed to hinder the propagation of their principles, and those which shut the door of all public preferment, even to such amongst them as conformed occasionally, are repealed. Far from desiring to impose any new hardships upon them, even those who have been reputed their enemies, and who have acted as such on several occasions, acknowledge their error. Experience hath removed prejudice. They see that indulgence hath done what severity never could; and from the frankness of these, if I was a Dissenter, I should sooner entertain hopes of future favour, than from the double dealing of those who lean on the Dissenters when they are out of power, and who esteem them a load upon them when they are in it. We are now in the true and only road, which can possibly lead to a perfect reconciliation among Protestants; to the abolition of all their differences; or to terms of difference so little essential, as to deserve none of distinction. These happy ends must be obtained by mutual good will. They never can be obtained by force. It is true, indeed, that force, which is the effect of a majority and superior power, may support a rivalship and erect even counter-establishments. But then, by the same means, our ancient disputes will be revived; the Church will be thought really in danger;[8] and religious feuds, which have been so long and so beneficially kept down, will once more disturb the peace of the state. It is a certain truth, that our religious and civil contests have mutually, and almost alternately, raised and fomented each other. Churchmen and Dissenters have sometimes differed, and sometimes thought, or been made to think, that they differed, at least, as much about civil as religious matters. There can be therefore no way so effectual to compose their differences on the latter, as to improve the growing union between them on the former. 'Idem sentire de republica',[9] to think alike about political affairs, hath been esteemed necessary to constitute and maintain private friendships. It is obviously more essential in public friendships. Bodies of men in the same society can never unite, unless they unite on this principle; and if they once unite on this principle, they will unite on all others, or they will readily and cheerfully make one another easy about them. – Let me

[8] 'The Church in Danger' was the slogan of high-flying Tories in the reign of Queen Anne.
[9] '. . . to feel the same way about the commonwealth': adapted from Cicero, *De Amicitia*, x. 33 ('vel ut de republica non idem sentitur').

speak plainly. It becomes a man to do so, who means honestly. – In our political divisions of Whig and Tory, the Dissenters have adhered to the former, and they want no apology for doing so. They joined themselves to those with whom they agreed, and stood in opposition to those with whom they differed in principles of government. There could be no objection brought against them on this account. They certainly did not follow power. They did not act like a sect, or a faction, who had, and pursued, an interest distinct from the interest of the whole. Their non-conformity hath nothing to do here. They concurred with conformists; and if they had been conformists themselves, as they were Dissenters, they would have acted in the same manner. But if this division of parties, on the same principles, subsists no longer; if there be in truth neither a Tory, nor a Whig, as I have said above, but a Court and a Country party in being; if the political principles, which the Dissenters have formerly avowed, are manifestly pursued on one side; and those which they have opposed, or others equivalent to them in their effects, are pursued on the other; can the Dissenters hesitate about the option they are to make? I am persuaded they cannot. I know that several amongst them do not. What might be, and certainly would be said, if they made their option to stand by the M—,[10] I will not so much as suggest. What must be the consequence of their standing by the nation, in opposition to him, for between these two powers the present contest lies, it is easy to tell, and impossible to deny. They will prove, in this case, to the whole world, that the spirit of liberty animates, and conscience alone determines their conduct. They, who could never brook a regal, will have the merit of saving their country from a ministerial tyranny; and their country will owe them all the acknowledgements, which are due from good and grateful citizens of the same commonwealth.

As to the other great and national division of Whig and Tory; he, who recollects what hath passed in Parliament, and observes what passes out of it, can differ very little in his opinion from what hath been said concerning it. The principal articles of your civil faith, published some time ago, or, to speak more properly, the civil faith of the Old Whigs,[11] are assented and consented to by the

[10] The M[inister]: Sir Robert Walpole.
[11] The Old Whig canon comprised the works of James Harrington, Henry Nevile, James Tyrrell, Robert Molesworth, Andrew Fletcher, John Trenchard, Thomas Gordon, Walter Moyle, Algernon Sidney, Edmund Ludlow and John Toland.

Country party; and I say, upon good authority, that if this creed was made a test of political orthodoxy, there would appear at this time but very few heretics amongst us. How different the case is on the other side, will appear not only from the actions, but from the principles of the Court-party, as we find them avowed in their writings;[12] principles more dangerous to liberty, though not so directly, nor so openly levelled against it, than even any of those, bad as they were, which some of these men value themselves for having formerly opposed.

In short, the Revolution is looked upon by all sides as a new era; but the settlement then made is looked upon by the whole Country party as a new Magna Carta, from whence new interests, new principles of government, new measures of submission, and new obligations arise. From thence we must date both king and people. His majesty derives his title from Acts, made in consequence of it.[13] We likewise derive, not our privileges, for they were always ours, but a more full and explicit declaration, and a more solemn establishment of them from the same period. On this foundation all the reasonable, independent Whigs and Tories unite. They could unite on this alone; for the Whigs have always professed the principles which paved the way for the Revolution; and whatever the Tories may have professed, they acted upon the same principles, or they acted upon none, which would be too absurd to assert, when they brought about that great event, in concert with the rest of the nation, as I shall some time or other prove.

To this Magna Carta, and these principles, let us adhere inviolably, in opposition to the two extremes mentioned by me at the beginning of this letter, viz. to those who disown them, and to those who betray them. – Let neither the polemical skill of Leslie,[14] nor the antique erudition of Bedford,[15] persuade us to put on again those old shackles of false law, false reason, and false gospel, which

---

[12] Prominent ministerialist writers included William Arnall, Ralph Courteville, Benjamin Hoadly, Matthew Concanen, Lord Hervey, James Pitt and Horace Walpole; the main pro-government organs were *The British Journal*, *The Free Briton*, *The London Journal* and *The Daily Gazetteer*.

[13] The Bill of Rights (1689) and the Act of Settlement (1701).

[14] Charles Leslie (1650–1722), Irish-born non-juring religious and political controversialist, editor of *The Rehearsal*, defender of patriarchalism and hereditary succession.

[15] Hilkiah Bedford (1663–1724), non-juring divine and presumed author of *The Hereditary Right of the Crown of England Asserted* (1713) (in fact, by George Harbin), which Bolingbroke attacks in 'Letter VIII' below.

were forged before the Revolution, and broken to pieces by it. – As little let us suffer the arch slyness of G—,[16] the dogmatical dryness of H—[17] or the sousing prostitution of S—[18] to slip new shackles on us, which are inconsistent with the constituent principles of our establishment.[19] – Let us maintain and improve the national union, so happily begun, and bless God for disposing the temper of the nation almost universally to it. – Such a coalition hath been long wanted in this kingdom, and never more than at this important crisis; for on this it will depend whether they, who not only oppose the progress of that growing corruption, which had well nigh over-spread the land, but endeavour to extirpate it by the roots, shall prevail; or they who nourish and propagate it, who eat themselves, and tempt others to eat the baneful fruit it bears. – On this it will depend whether they shall prevail, who constantly insist against the continuance of a standing army in time of peace, agreeably to the principles of our constitution; or they who plead for it, and endeavour to make it a necessary part of that constitution, though incompatible with public liberty. – On this it will depend whether they shall prevail, who endeavour to conceal the frauds which are practised, and to screen the fraudulent, at the risk of ruining credit, and destroying trade, as well as to monopolize in the hands of a few the whole wealth of the nation; or they who do their utmost to bring the former to light, and the latter to punishment, at a time when glaring fraud, or very strong symptoms of fraud, appear in so many parts of public management, from some of the greatest companies down to the turnpike at Hyde Park Corner. – On this it will depend whether they shall prevail, who desire that Great Britain should maintain such a dignity and prudent reserve in the broils of Europe, as become her situation, suit her interest, and alone can enable her to cast the balance; or they who are eager, on every

[16] Edmund 'Codex' Gibson (1669–1748), antiquarian and divine, author of the *Codex Iuris Ecclesiae Anglicanae* (1713), known as 'Walpole's pope' when bishop of London.

[17] Francis Hare (1671–1740), Walpole's tutor at Cambridge, bishop of St Asaph and, latterly, Chichester, author of *Church Authority Vindicated* (1713) and *Scripture Vindicated from the Misrepresentation of the Bishop of Bangor* (1721).

[18] Thomas Sherlock (1678–1761), Walpole's schoolfriend, Gibson's successor as bishop of London, and (like Hare) one of the main antagonists of Benjamin Hoadly in the Bangorian controversy over the authority of the Church.

[19] Compare Pope, *The Dunciad* (1742), III, 204–5: 'Still break the benches, Henley! with thy strain, / While Sherlock, Hare, and Gibson preach in vain.'

occasion, to prostitute her dignity, to pawn her purse, and to sacrifice her commerce, by entangling her not only too much with the other great powers of Europe, from whom she may sometimes want reciprocal engagements, but even with those diminutive powers, from whom it would be ridiculous to expect any.

I am, sir, yours, &c.

LETTER II[1]

Sir,

Whilst I was writing my last letter to you, it came into my thoughts that nothing would illustrate the subject better, nor enforce more strongly the exhortation to an union of parties, in support of that constitution, on the terms of which alone all right to govern us, and all our obligation to obey is now founded, than an enquiry into the rise and progress of our late parties; or a short history of Toryism and Whiggism from their cradle to their grave, with an introductory account of their genealogy and descent.

Your papers have been from the first consecrated to the information of the people of Britain; and I think they may boast very justly a merit singular enough, that of never speaking to the passions, without appealing to the reason of mankind. It is fit they should keep up this character, in the strictest manner, whilst they are employed on the most important subject, and published at the most important crisis. I shall therefore execute my design with sincerity and impartiality. I shall certainly not flatter, and I do not mean to offend. Reasonable men and lovers of truth, in whatever party they have been engaged, will not be offended at writings, which claim no regard but on this account, that they are founded in reason and truth, and speak with boldness what reason and truth conspire to dictate. As for the drummers and trumpeters of faction, who are hired to drown the voice of both in one perpetual din of clamour, and would endeavour to drown, in the same manner, even the dying groans of their country, if she was already brought into that extreme condition; they shall not provoke me to break a most contemptuous silence. The subject is too solemn. They may profane it, by writing on it. Far be it from me to become guilty of the same crime by answering them.

If the enquiry I am going to make into the rise and progress of our late parties should produce in any degree the good which I intend, it will help to confirm and improve the national union, so happily begun, by taking off some remains of shyness, distrust and prejudice, which may still hang about men, who think alike, and who press on from different quarters to the same common point of

---

[1] *Craftsman* 383 (3 November 1733).

view. It will help to unmask more effectually the wicked conduct of those, who labour with all the skill, and, which is much more considerable, with all the authority they possess, to keep up the division of parties; that each of these may continue to be, in its turn, what all of them have been too often and too long, the instruments and the victims of private ambition. It will do something more. A few reflections on the rise and progress of our distemper, and the rise and progress of our cure, will help us of course to make a true judgment on our present state, and will point out to us, better perhaps than any other method, the specific remedies still necessary to preserve our constitution in health and vigour. – Having premised this, I come to the point.

Queen Elizabeth designed, and the nation called, King James to the throne, though the whole Scottish line had been excluded by the will of Henry the Eighth, made indeed under the authority of an Act of Parliament, and yet little regarded either by the Parliament, or the people. As soon as he was on the throne, a flattering Act of Recognition passed;[2] for though all princes are flattered on their first accession, yet those princes are sure to be flattered most, who deserve panegyric least. In this Act the Parliament acknowledged, on the knees of their hearts, such was the cant of the age, the indubitable right, by which they declared that the crown descended to him immediately, on the decease of Queen Elizabeth. Of this Act, and of the use, which some men, very weakly I think, endeavoured to make of it, I shall have occasion to speak hereafter. I would only observe here, that this is the era of hereditary right, and of all those exalted notions, concerning the power and prerogative of kings, and the sacredness of their persons. All together they composed such a system of absurdity as had never been heard of in this country, till that anointed pedant broached them. They have been spoken of pretty much at large in your papers; particularly in some of those published under the name of Oldcastle.[3] To them I refer.

To assert that the extravagant principles of ecclesiastical and civil government, which began to be propagated in this reign, and were carried still higher in the next, gave occasion to those of another

---

[2] Act in 'Recognition of the King's Title to the Crown' (1604), 1 Jac. I. c. 1.
[3] Bolingbroke, *Remarks on the History of England* (1730–31), 'Letters XIX–XX', published in *The Craftsman* under the pseudonym Humphrey Oldcastle.

kind, or of another extreme, which were taught with success, and gained by degrees great vogue in the nation, would be too much. Opinions very different from those which received the sanction of a legal establishment in Church and state, had crept about obscurely, if not silently, even whilst the government of Elizabeth lasted. But this I say; that the principles by which King James and King Charles the First governed, and the excesses of hierarchical and monarchical power, exercised in consequence of them, gave great advantage to the opposite opinions, and entirely occasioned the miseries which followed. Frenzy provoked frenzy, and two species of madness infected the whole mass of the people. It hath cost us a century to lose our wits, and to recover them again.

If our grievances under King Charles the First had been redressed by a sober, regular, parliamentary reformation of the state; or, if the civil war happening, a new government had been established on principles of the constitution, not of faction, of liberty, not of licentiousness, as there was on the abdication of King James the Second; we may conclude, both from reason and experience, that the absurd and slavish doctrines I have mentioned would have been exploded early. They would have been buried in the recent grave of him who first devised them; and the memory of him and of them would have stunk together in the nostrils of mankind. But the contrary fell out. The state was subverted, instead of being reformed; and all the fury of faction and enthusiasm was employed to destroy the constitution to the very foundations. A natural consequence followed. If the principles of King James' and King Charles' reigns had been disgraced by better, they would not have risen again: but they were only kept down for a time by worse; and therefore they rose again at the Restoration, and revived with the monarchy. Thus that epidemical taint, with which King James infected the minds of men, continued upon us: and it is scarce hyperbolical to say, that this prince hath been the original cause of a series of misfortunes to this nation, as deplorable as a lasting infection of our air, of our water, of our earth, would have been. The spirit of his reign was maintained in that of his son (for how could it well be otherwise, when the same ministers were continued in power?), and the events of both produced the civil war. The civil war ended in the death of the King, and the exile of his family. The exile of these princes reconciled them to the religion of Rome, and to the politics of foreign nations, in such degrees as their different characters admitted. Charles sipped a little of the poisonous draught, but enough however to infect his whole conduct. As for James,

> Ille impiger hausit
> Spumantem pateram,[4]

he drank the chalice off to the lowest and foulest dregs.

That principles as absurd as those in their nature, and as terrible in their consequences, such as would shock the common sense of a Samoyede, or an Hottentot, and had just before deluged the nation in blood, should come into vogue again at the Restoration, will not appear strange to those who carry themselves back as it were to that point of time. The wounds of the civil war were bleeding, and the resentments of the cavaliers, who came into power at court and in Parliament, were at their height. No wonder then if few men had, in such a ferment as this, penetration enough to discern, or candour enough to acknowledge, or courage enough to maintain, that the principles we speak of were truly and primarily the cause of all their misfortunes. The events, which proved them so, were recent; but for that very reason, because they were recent, it was natural for men in such a circumstance as this, to make wrong judgments about them. It was natural for the royal party to ascribe all their and their country's misfortunes, without any due distinction, to the principles on which King Charles and even King James had been opposed; and to grow more zealous for those on which the governments of these two princes had been defended, and for which they had suffered. Add to this the national transport, on so great a revolution; the excess of joy which many felt, and many feigned; the adulation employed by many to acquire new merit; and by many to atone for past demerit; and you will find reason to be surprised, not that the same principles of government, as had threatened our liberties once, and must by necessary consequence do so again, were established; but that our liberties were not immediately, and at once given up. That they were saved, we owe not to Parliament, no not to the Convention Parliament,[5] who brought the King home; but to

---

[4] 'He boldly drained the frothing bowl': Virgil, *Aeneid* I. 738–9.
[5] The Convention Parliament, convened in April 1660, laid the groundwork for the Restoration Settlement, until succeeded by the more hard-line Cavalier Parliament (1661–79)

those great and good men, Clarendon and Southampton.[6] Far from taking advantage of the heat and fervour of the times to manage Parliaments into scandalous jobs, and fatal compliances with the crown, to their immortal honour, with gratitude and reverence to their memories be it spoken, they broke the army, stinted the revenue, and threw their master on the affections of his people. – But I return.

Besides these reasons, drawn from the passions of men, others of a more sober kind may be given to account for the making a settlement at the Restoration upon principles too near akin to those which had prevailed before the war, and which had in truth caused it. Certain it is, that although the nonconformists were stunned by the blow they had just received, and though their violence was restrained by the force of the present conjuncture; yet they still existed. Symptoms of this appeared, even whilst the government was settling, and continued to appear long after it was settled. Now, every symptom of this kind renewed the dread of relapsing into those miseries, from which the nation had so lately recovered itself; and this dread had the natural effect of all extreme fears. It hurried men into every principle, as well as measure, which seemed the most opposite to those of the persons feared, and the most likely, though at any other risk, to defeat their design, and to obviate the present danger, real or imaginary. May we not fairly conjecture, for it is but conjecture, something more? In such a temper of mind, and such a situation of circumstances, might not even those, who saw how groundless and dangerous such extravagant notions about the right, power and prerogative of kings were, imagine however that it was a part of prudence to give way to them, and to countenance them in the present conjuncture; to suffer the opinions of the nation to be bent too far on one side, as they had been bent too far on the other; not that they might remain crooked, but that they might become straight?

The same spirit and much the same reasons that determined our settlement, at the Restoration, upon such high principles of monarchy, prevailed relatively to our religious differences, and the settlement of the Church. I shall speak of it with that freedom

---

[6] Thomas Wriothesley, 4th Earl of Southampton (1606–67), close associate of Clarendon, and Lord Treasurer to Charles II (1660–67).

which a man may take, who is conscious that he means nothing but the public good, hath no by-ends, nor is under the influence of serving any particular cause.

I say then very frankly, that the Church and the King having been joined in all the late contests, both by those who attacked them, and those who defended them, ecclesiastical interests, resentments, and animosities came in to the aid of secular, in making the new settlement. Great lenity was shown at the Restoration, in looking backwards; unexampled and unimitated mercy to particular men, which deserved no doubt much applause. This conduct would have gone far towards restoring the nation to its primitive temper and integrity, to its old good manners, its old good humour, and its old good nature (expressions of my Lord Chancellor Clarendon, which I could never read without being moved and softened),[7] if great severity had not been exercised immediately after, in looking forwards, and great rigour used to large bodies of men, which certainly deserves censure, as neither just, nor politic – I say, not just; because there is, after all, a real and a wide difference between moral and party justice. The one is founded in reason; the other takes its colour from the passions of men, and is but another name for injustice. Moral justice carries punishment as far as reparation, and necessary terror require; no farther. Party justice carries it to the full extent of our power, and even to the gorging and sating of our revenge; from whence it follows that injustice and violence once begun, must become perpetual in the successive revolutions of parties, as long as these parties exist. – I say, not politic; because it contradicted the other measures taken for quieting the minds of men. It alarmed all the sects anew; confirmed the implacability, and whetted the rancour of some; disappointed and damped a spirit of reconciliation in others; united them in a common hatred to the Church; and roused in the Church a spirit of intolerance and persecution. This measure was the more imprudent, because the opportunity seemed fair to take advantage of the resentments of the Presbyterians against the other sectaries, and to draw them, without persecuting the others, by the cords of love into the pale of the Church, instead of driving them back by severe usage into their

---

[7] Clarendon's speech as Lord Chancellor at the adjournment of the Convention Parliament, 13 September 1660, in *The Parliamentary and Constitutional History of England* (24 vols., London, 1751–60), XXII, 489.

ancient confederacies.[8] But when resentments of the sort we now mention were let loose, to aggravate those of the other sort, there was no room to be surprised at the violences which followed; and they, who had acted greater, could not complain of these, great as they were, with any very good grace.

If we may believe [a]one, who certainly was not partial against these sects, both Presbyterians and independents had carried the principles of rigour, in the point of conscience, much higher, and acted more implacably upon it, than ever the Church of England hath done, in its angriest fits. The securing themselves therefore against those, who had ruined them and the constitution once already, was a plausible reason for the Church party to give, and I doubt not the true and sole motive of many for exercising, and persisting in the exercise of great severity. General, prudential arguments might, and there is a reason to believe they did, weigh with particular men; but they could have little force, at such a time, on numbers. As little could some other considerations have then, whatever they have now. The promises at Breda, for instance, and the terms of the declaration sent from thence,[9] could not be urged with force to a Parliament, who had no mind, and was strictly under no obligation, to make good such promises as the King had made, beyond his power of promising, if taken absolutely; or from which, if taken conditionally, he was discharged, on the refusal of Parliament to confirm them. – Thus again, the merit pleaded by the Presbyterians, on account of the share they had in the Restoration, which was very real and very considerable, could avail however but little. That they went along with the national torrent, in restoring the constitution of Church and state, could not be denied. But then it was remembered too that these fruits of repentance came late; not till they had been oppressed by another sect, who turned upon them, wrested

---

[a] Dr Burnet, afterwards bishop of Salisbury, in one of his tracts.[10]

---

[8] The Act of Uniformity (1662) enforced subscription to the new Prayer Book and the Thirty-Nine Articles and resulted in the ejection of many leading Presbyterian ministers.

[9] [Gilbert Burnet,] *An Apology for the Church of England* (Amsterdam, 1688?), 2.

[10] Charles II's Declaration of Breda (April 1660) declared 'a liberty to tender consciences', subject to confirmation by an Act of Parliament 'granting that indulgence'.

the power out of their hands, and made them feel, what they had made others feel, the tyranny of a party.

Such reasons and motives, as I have mentioned prevailed; and worse than these would have been sufficient, when the passions of men ran so high, to lay the Dissenters, without any distinction, under extreme hardships. They seemed to be the principal object of the fears and jealousies of Parliament. Addresses were continually made, and the edge of the law continually whetted against them, from 1660 to 1669, when the law for suppressing conventicles, and the last of those penal statutes passed, as I remember.[11] Experience will justify me for saying that this long and extreme rigour was unwise, as well as unjust. It appears, indeed, from the memorials of those times, that they who suffered had given abundant provocation, though not sufficient excuse, to the rigour under which they suffered. Some former hardships which the Dissenters had endured from the Church, made them more violent against it, when they got possession of an usurped power. Just so the violence which they exercised at that time, stimulated the severity they felt in their turn, when the legal constitution of the Church was restored. Notwithstanding all which, I incline, upon very good reasons, to think that this severity was not in the first design of the ministers, nor would have been shown, if another fatal influence had not prevailed. The influence I mean is that of popery. It prevailed from the first moments to the last of the reign of King Charles the Second. The best ministers were frequently driven off their bias by it. The worst had a sure hold on their master, by complying with it. On the occasion now mentioned, this influence and the artifice of the popish faction worked very fatally on the passions of parties, and the private interests of individuals; and the ministers, and the Church, and the Dissenters, were bubbles alike of their common enemy. Barefaced popery could ask no favour, because popery could expect none. Protestant Dissenters were therefore to serve as stalking horses, that papists might creep behind them, and have hopes of being some time or other, admitted with them. The Church party was hallooed on the Dissenters; whilst the Dissenters were encouraged to unite and hold out; whilst they were flattered with an high opinion of their own strength, and the King's favour; and whilst

[11] The Second Conventicles Act did not in fact pass until 1670.

some leading men amongst them, who thought it better to be at the head of a sect than at the tail of an establishment, were perhaps encouraged and confirmed in that thought, by the private applications of the court.

These arts, these wicked arts (for such they were) prevailed; and though the two thousand ministers, who went out of their churches on one day,[12] were far from being all of the same mind, or having one positive consistent scheme; though many of them must have lost their benefices, even if they had complied with the Act of Uniformity, because they were intruders, and in actual possession of benefices legally belonging to others; yet, by uniting in the point of non-conformity, they appeared as one body, and in some sense they were so. Several of them were popular for certain modes of devotion, suited to the humour of the time; and several were men eminent for true learning and unaffected piety. They increased the zeal of their flocks, and created compassion in others. Here the court began to reap the fruits of their management, in the struggle for a toleration. I use the word, though I know it may be simply cavilled at. The first step made was an application to the King, who declared himself ready and willing to dispense, in their favour, with several things in the Act of Uniformity: and thus the Dissenters were made, by the severity of the Parliament and the intrigues of the court, the instruments of introducing a dispensing power.[13] Such attempts were made more than once; but happily failed as often as made, through the vigorous opposition of Parliament; till at last the scene began to open more, and the Dissenters to see that they were made the tools of promoting what they never intended, the advancement of the prerogative above law, and the toleration of popery against it.

To conclude. By such means as I have described, the constitution of parties after the Restoration preserved unhappily too near a resemblance to the constitution of parties before the war. The prerogative was not, indeed, carried so high in some instances, as James

---

[12] Though only 936 ministers were ejected on St Bartholomew's Day 1662, it is estimated that more than 2000 ministers, town lecturers and college Fellows lost their posts in 1660–62.

[13] Charles pressed for the introduction of a dispensing power in the Uniformity Bill in 1662 and proclaimed the use of such a power in his First Declaration of Indulgence in December 1663, though both measures were quashed.

and Charles the First had attempted to carry it. Nay, some supports of it were bought off, and taken away; and others more dangerous, as we have observed, were prevented by the virtue of the men at that time in power. But still the government was established on principles sufficient to invite a king to exercise arbitrary power, and support him by their consequences in the exercise of it afterwards; so that, in this respect, the seeds of future divisions were sowed abundantly. The Dissenters had, indeed, lost much of their credit and all their power. But still they had numbers, and property, and industry, and compassion, for them; so that here was another crop of dissensions planted to nurse up, and to strengthen the other. They did not inflame the contest which followed, into a civil war, as they had helped to do formerly; but I think that without them, and the disunion and hatred among Protestants, consequent upon them, the zeal against popery could not have run into a kind of factious fury, as we shall be obliged to confess it did. I think that fears of falling once more under Presbyterian, or republican power, could not have been wrought up in the manner they were, towards the end of this reign, so as to drown even the fear of popery itself; so as to form a party, in favour of a popish successor; so as to transport both clergy and laity into an avowal of principles, which must have reduced us to be at this time slaves, not freemen, papists, not Protestants; if the very men, who had avowed such principles, had not saved themselves and us, in direct opposition to them. – But I am running into the subject of another letter, when this is grown too prolix already.

I am, sir, yours, &c.

LETTER III[1]

Sir,
The sum of what hath been said, concerning the settlement of Church and state, and the division of parties at the Restoration, amounts to this; that as the attempts of King James and King Charles the First, against the spirit of the constitution, threw the nation into a civil war, and all the miserable consequences, both necessary and contingent, of that calamity; so the fury, enthusiasm and madness of those factions which arose during that unnatural ferment, frightened the nation back, if not into all, yet more generally perhaps than before, into most of the notions that were established to justify the excesses of former reigns. Hereditary, indefeasible right, passive obedience and non-resistance, those corner-stones, which are an improper foundation for any superstructure, but that of tyranny, were made, even by Parliament, the foundation of the monarchy; and all those, who declined an exact and strict conformity to the whole establishment of the Church, even to the most minute parts of it, were deprived of the protection, nay, exposed to the prosecution of the state. Thus one part of the nation stood proscribed by the other; the least, indeed, by the greatest; whereas a little before the greatest stood proscribed by the least. Roundhead and cavalier were, in effect, no more. Whig and Tory were not yet in being. The only two apparent parties were those of Churchmen and Dissenters; and religious differences alone at this time maintained the distinction.

Such was the state of party, upon the meeting of the first parliament called by King Charles the Second, and for some years afterwards, as nearly as I have been able to observe by what I have read in history, and received from tradition. – How the notions then in vogue began to change, and this spirit to decline, some time after the Restoration; how the zeal of Churchmen and Dissenters against one another began to soften, and a Court and Country party to form themselves; how faction mingled itself again in the contest, and renewed the former resentments and jealousies; how Whig and Tory arose, the furious offspring of those inauspicious parents roundhead and cavalier; how the proceedings of one party might

[1] *Craftsman* 384 (10 November 1733).

22

have thrown us back into a civil war, confusion and anarchy; how
the success of the other had like to have entailed tyranny on the
state, and popery in Church; how the Revolution did, and could
alone, deliver us from the grievances we felt, and from the dangers
we feared; how this great event was brought about by a formal
departure of each side from the principles objected to them by the
other; how this renewal of our constitution, on the principles of
liberty, by the most solemn, deliberate, national act, that ever was
made, did not only bind at least every one of those, who concurred
in any degree to bring it about (and that description includes almost
the whole nation); but how absurd it is for any man, who was born
since that era, or who, being born before it, hath been bound by no
particular, legal tie to any other settlement, to be willing to give up
the advantages of the present constitution, any more than he would
give up the privileges of the great charter, which was made and
ratified so many ages ago; all these points are to be now touched in
that summary manner which I have prescribed to myself, and which
will be sufficient, in so plain a case, where men are to be reminded
of what they know already, rather than to be informed, and to be
confirmed, not to be convinced.

I proceed therefore to observe, that the nation began to be indis-
posed to the court, soon after the Restoration. The sale of Dunkirk
helped to ruin a great and good minister, though it be still doubtful
at least, notwithstanding the clamour raised, and the negotiations
with d'Estrades so much insisted upon, whether he was strictly
answerable for this measure.[2] – Who knows how soon the re-
establishment of the same port and harbour may be laid in form to
the charge of those two men, who are strictly and undeniably
answerable for it, and who stagger already under the weight of so
many other just imputations?[3]

The first Dutch war, which was lightly and rashly undertaken,
and which ended ignominiously for the nation, augmented the

[2] Dunkirk (which had been taken by Cromwellian forces in 1658) was sold back to
the French in 1662. Clarendon bore much of the brunt of public fury; d'Estrades
was the French ambassador at the time.
[3] An investigation, initiated by Bolingbroke himself in 1729, revealed that the
French were clandestinely rebuilding the fortifications and harbour of Dunkirk
which the Treaty of Utrecht had agreed would remain unrestored. See [Boling-
broke,] *The Case of Dunkirk Faithfully Stated and Impartially Considered*
(1730).

public indisposition. Nay misfortunes, such as the plague, and the burning of London, as well as mismanagement, had this effect. But we must place at the head of all, a jealousy of popery, which was well founded, and therefore gathered strength daily. This soon heated the minds of men to such a degree, that it seems almost wonderful the plague was not imputed to the papists, as peremptorily as the fire.[4]

The death of my lord Southampton, and the disgrace and banishment of my lord Clarendon, made room for new causes of jealousy and dissatisfaction; and the effects increased in proportion. These two noble lords had stood in the breach against popery and foreign politics; and what one of them said to the other, that is, Southampton of Clarendon, may be applied with justice to both. They were true Protestants, and honest Englishmen.[5] Whilst they were in place, our laws, our religion, and our liberties were in safety. When they were removed, England felt the ill effects of the change; for when they were removed, all those were in danger. How glorious a panegyric is this, in which the unanimous voice of posterity does and must agree? It is preferable surely to all the titles and honours and estates, which those illustrious patriots left behind them: and so I persuade myself it is esteemed by the young noblemen, who are heirs to their virtues as well as their fortunes.[6]

King Charles, and more than him, the duke and the popish faction, were now at liberty to form new schemes; or rather to pursue old ones, with less reserve, against the religion and liberty of England. As soon as the famous cabal had the whole administration of affairs, these designs were pushed without any reserve at all.[7] – I am not writing the history of this reign; nor have I undertaken any thing more than to make a few observations on the several turns of parties in it. I need not therefore descend into particular proofs of the designs which I attribute to the court; nor into a deduction of the measures taken to promote them, and the efforts made to defeat them. That these designs were real, can be doubted of by no man;

---

[4] By the first, Bolingbroke means what is usually called the Second Anglo-Dutch War (1665–67); the great plague hit London in 1665, the Great Fire (which was blamed on Roman Catholics) in 1666.

[5] Source unidentified.

[6] Henry Hyde, Lord Cornbury, was Clarendon's great-grandson, for example.

[7] Clifford, Arlington, Buckingham, Ashley and Lauderdale formed a loose and contentious ministry in 1668–73 known (from their initials) as the Cabal.

since without quoting many printed accounts, which are in the hands of every one, or insisting on other proofs, which have not seen the light, and such there are, the abbot Primi's relation of the secret negotiations between the King and his sister, the duchess of Orléans, published in 1682, as I think, and immediately suppressed,[8] as well as the history of the Jesuit d'Orléans,[9] written on memorials furnished to him by King James the Second, put the whole matter out of dispute, and even beyond the reach of cavil. It is sufficient for my purpose to observe, that the tide of party, which had run so strongly for the court, and had been seldom so much as slackened hitherto, began now to turn, and to run year after year more strongly the other way.

When this Parliament sat down, for it deserves our particular observation that both houses were full of zeal for the present government, and of resentment against the late usurpations, there was but one party in Parliament; and no other party could raise its head in the nation. This might have been the case much longer, probably as long as King Charles had sat on the throne, if the court had been a little honester, or a little wiser. No Parliament ever did more to gain their prince than this. They seemed for several years, to have nothing so much at heart as securing his government, advancing his prerogative, and filling his coffers. The grants they made him were such as passed for instances of profusion in those days; when one million two hundred thousand pounds a year for the civil list, the fleet, the guards and garrisons, and all the ordinary expenses of the government, was thought an exorbitant sum; how little a figure soever it would make in our times, when two thirds of that sum, at least, are appropriated to the use of the civil list singly. But all this was to no purpose: a foreign interest prevailed; a cabal governed; and sometimes the cabal, and sometimes a prime-minister had more credit with the King than the whole body of his people. When the Parliament saw that they could not gain him over to his own, and to their common interest; nor prevail on him by

---

[8] The Abbé Primi [Giovanni Battista Visconti Fassola di Rossa, Conte di San Maiola], *Historia della Guerra d'Olanda* (Paris, 1682); extracts appeared in *An Account of the Reasons which Induced Charles the Second, King of England, to Declare War Against the States-General of the United Provinces in 1672* (London, 1689).

[9] Pierre Joseph d'Orléans, *History of the Revolution in England* (Paris, 1693–4; English trans., London, 1722).

connivance, compliance, and other gentle methods; they turned themselves to such as were rough, but agreeable to law and the custom of Parliament, as well as proportionable to the greatness of the exigency. That they lost their temper, on some particular occasions, must not be denied. They were men, and therefore frail: but their frailties of this kind proceeded from their love of their country. They were transported, when they found that their religion and liberty were constantly in danger from the intrigues of a popish faction; and they would have been so transported, no doubt, if liberty alone had been attacked by a Protestant faction. Then it was, that this High-Church Parliament grew favourable to Protestant Dissenters, and ready to make that just distinction, so long delayed between them and popish recusants, that the whole Protestant interest might unite in the common cause. Then it was, that this prerogative-Parliament defied prerogative, in defence of their own privileges, and of the liberties of their country. Then it was, that this passive-obedience and non-resistance Parliament went the utmost lengths of resistance, in a parliamentary way; and the necessary consequence of the steps they made in this way, must have been resistance in another, if the King had not dropped his ministers, retracted his pretensions, redressed some and given expectation of redressing other grievances. In fine, this pensioner-Parliament, as it hath been styled, with some corruption in the house, and an army sometimes at the door of it, disbanded the army in England, and protested against the militia settled in Scotland by Act of Parliament, and appointed to march for any service, wherein the King's honour, authority, and greatness were concerned, in obedience to the orders of the Privy Council. That I may not multiply particular instances, they not only did their utmost to secure their country against immediate danger, but projected to secure it against remote danger, by an exclusion of the Duke of York from the crown, after they had endeavoured strenuously, but in vain, to prevent his entailing popery more easily upon us, by his marriage with a popish princess; for he had declared himself a papist with as much affectation, as if he expected to grow popular by it; had already begun to approve his zeal, and exercise his talent in conversions, by that of his first wife; and was notoriously the agent of Rome and France, in order to seduce his brother into stronger measures than King Charles was willing to take. King Charles, to use an expression of the lord Halifax[10] of that age, would trot; but his brother would gallop.

When I reflect on the particulars here mentioned, and a great many others, which might be mentioned to the honour of this Parliament, I cannot hear it called the pensioner-Parliament, as it were by way of eminence, without a degree of honest indignation; especially in the age in which we live, and by some of those who affect the most to bestow upon it this ignominious appellation. Pensions indeed, to the amount of seven or eight thousand pounds, as I remember, were discovered to have been given to some members of the House of Commons. But then let it be remembered likewise, that this expedient of corrupting Parliaments began under the administration of that boisterous, over-bearing, dangerous minister, Clifford.[11] As long as there remained any pretence to say that the court was in the interest of the people, the expedient of bribery was neither wanted, nor practised. When the court was evidently in another interest, the necessity and the practice of bribing the representatives of the people commenced. Should a Parliament of Britain act in compliance with a court, against the sense and interest of the nation, mankind would be ready to pronounce very justly that such a Parliament was under the corrupt influence of the court. But, in the case now before us, we have a very comfortable example of a court wicked enough to stand in need of corruption, and to employ it; and of a Parliament virtuous enough to resist the force of this expedient; which Philip of Macedon boasted that he employed to invade the liberties of other countries; and which had been so often employed by men of less genius, as well as rank, to invade the liberties of their own.[12] All that corruption could do in this Parliament, was to maintain the appearance of a Court party, whilst the measures of the court united a Country party, in opposition to them. Neither places nor pensions could hinder courtiers in this Parliament from voting, on many signal occasions, against the court; nor protect either those who drew the King into ill

---

[10] George Savile, Marquess of Halifax (1633–95), 'the Trimmer', statesman and pamphleteer.

[11] Thomas Clifford (1603–73), crypto-Catholic client of James, Duke of York, and member of the Cabal.

[12] Compare Bolingbroke's essay in *The Craftsman* 406 (13 April 1734), citing Cicero, *De Officiis*, II. 15. 53.

measures, nor those who complied with him in them. Nay, this pensioner-Parliament, if it must be still called so, gave one proof of independency, besides that of contriving a test in 1675, to purge their members on oath from all suspicion of corrupt influence, which ought to wipe off this stain from the most corrupt. They drove one of their paymasters out of court, and impeached the other, in the fullness of his power;[13] even at a time, when the King was so weak as to make, or so unhappy as to be forced to make, on account of pensions privately negotiated from France, the cause of the crown and the cause of the minister one, and to blend their interests together.

What I have said to the honour of the long Parliament is just; because in fact the proceedings of that Parliament were agreeable to the representation I have given of them. But now, if some severe censor should appear, and insist that the dame was chaste, only because she was not enough tempted; that more pensions would have made more pensioners; that much money and little prerogative is more dangerous to liberty than much prerogative and little money; and that the worst and weakest minister King Charles ever had, might have been absolute in this very parliament whose charac-ter I defend, if such a minister had been able to enlist, with places, pensions and occasional bribes, not a slender majority, which the defection of a few might at any time defeat, but such a bulky majority, as might impose on itself: if any one, I say, should refine in this manner, and continue to insist that such a minister, with such a purse, would have stood his ground in the Parliament I speak of, with how much contempt and indignation soever he might have been everywhere treated by the people; I shall not presume to assert the contrary. It might have been so. Our safety was owing as much, perhaps, to the poverty of the court, as to the virtue of the Parlia-ment. We might have lost our liberties. But then I would observe before I conclude, that if this be true, the preservation of our religion and liberty, at that time, was owing to these two circum-stances: first, that King Charles was not parsimonious, but squan-dered on his pleasures, what he might have employed to corrupt

---

[13] Ralph Montagu (formerly ambassador to France) was dismissed in July 1678; evidence he revealed led to the impeachment of Lord Treasurer Danby by the Commons in December 1678 for his part in Charles' secret negotiations for French subsidies.

this Parliament; secondly, that the ministers in that reign, fingering no money but the revenue, ordinary and extraordinary, had no opportunity to filch in the pockets of every private man, and to bribe the bubbles very often with their own money; as might be done now, when funding hath been so long in fashion, and the greatest minister hath the means of being the greatest stockjobber, did not the eminent integrity of the minister, and the approved virtue of the age, secure us from any such danger.

We have now brought the deduction of parties very near to the era of Whig and Tory, into which the court found means to divide the nation, and by this division to acquire in the nation a superiority, which had been attempted ineffectually, even by corruption in Parliament. – But this I reserve for another letter, and am,

sir, yours, &c.

Sir,

There is a passage in Tully so extremely applicable to the mischievous, but transitory, prevalence of those principles of government, which King James the First imported into this country, that since it occurs to my memory, I cannot begin this letter better than by quoting it to you, and making a short commentary on it. [a]*Opinionum commenta delet dies, naturae judicia confirmat.*[2] Groundless opinions are destroyed, but rational judgments, or the judgments of nature, are confirmed by time. It is Balbus,[3] who makes this observation very properly, when he is about to prove the existence of a supreme being. The same observation might have been employed as properly, on other occasions, against Balbus himself; and the truth of it might have been exemplified, by comparing the paradoxes and superstitious opinions of his own sect, as well as the tales of an hippocentaur, or a chimera, with the eternal truths of genuine theism, and sound philosophy. In short, the application of it might have been justly made then, and may be so now in numberless instances, taken from the most important subjects, on which the thoughts of men are exercised, or in which their interests, as men and members of society, are concerned.

The authority of a sect, and much more of a state, is able to inspire, and habit to confirm, the most absurd opinions. Passion, or interest, can create zeal. But nothing can give stability and durable uniformity to error. Indolence, or ignorance, may keep it floating, as it were, on the surface of the mind, and sometimes hinder truth from penetrating; or force may maintain it in profession, when the mind assents to it no longer. But such opinions, like human bodies, tend to their dissolution from their birth. They will be soon rejected in theory, where men can think, and in practice, where men can act with freedom. They maintain themselves no longer, than the same means of seduction, which first introduced them, or the same circumstances, which first imposed them, attend and continue to sup-

---

[a] L. 2. *De Nat. Deor.*

[1] *Craftsman* 384 [sc. 385] (17 November 1733).
[2] Cicero, *De Natura Deorum*, II. 2. 5.
[3] The Stoic interlocutor in Cicero's dialogue.

port them. Men are dragged into them, and held down in them, by chains of circumstances. Break but these chains, and the mind returns with a kind of intellectual elasticity to its proper object, truth. This natural motion is so strong, that examples might be cited of men embracing truth in practice, before they were convinced of it in theory. There are cases, where reason, freed from constraint, or roused by necessity, acts in some sort the part of instinct. We are impelled by one, before we have time to form an opinion. We are often determined by the other, against our opinion; that is, before we can be said properly to have changed it. But observe here the perverseness of that rational creature, man. When this happens; when the judgment of nature, for so we may speak after Tully,[4] hath prevailed against the habitual prejudice of opinion; instead of acknowledging the victorious truth, which determined him to act, instead of condemning the erroneous opinion, against which he acted, he is too often apt to endeavour, peevishly and pedantically, to reconcile his actions to his error; nay, to persist in renouncing true, and asserting false maxims, whilst he reaps the benefit, and maintains the consequences of the former.

You see whither we are brought by these general reflections. The absurd opinions (*fictae et vanae*[5] our Roman orator would have called them) about the right, power, and prerogative of kings, were so little able to take a deep root, and to stand the blasts of opposition, that few of those who drew their swords on the side of King Charles the First, were determined to it by them. I assert this fact on contemporary authority; on the authority even of some who were themselves engaged in that cause, from the beginning to the end of our civil wars. A more recent tradition assures us, that when the same opinions revived at the Restoration, they did not sink deep even then into the minds of men; but floated so superficially there, that the Parliament (the very parliament, who had authorized them, and imposed them, as I observed in the last letter) proceeded a great way, and was ready to have proceeded farther, in direct opposition to them. A tradition still more recent will inform us, and that is to be the subject of this letter; that when these opinions revived again, at the latter end of the same reign, with an appearance of greater

---

[4] 'judicium naturae': Cicero, *De Natura Deorum*, II. 2. 5.
[5] 'false and vain': Cicero, *De Natura Deorum*, II. 2. 5 ('opiniones fictas atque vanas').

strength, and of a more national concurrence than ever, they revived but to be exploded more effectually than ever. King Charles made use of them to check the ferment raised against his government; but did not seem to expect that they would subsist long in force. His wiser brother depended much on them; but his dependence was vain. They were, at that time, wearing out apace; and they wore out the faster by the extravagant use which was made of them. They were in the mouths of many, but in the hearts of few; for almost all those who had them in their mouths, acted against them. Thus were these wicked and ridiculous principles of government twice revived, and twice destroyed again, in less than thirty years from the Restoration.

> Ter si resurgat murus aheneus,
> – Ter pereat![6]

The second revival of these principles, for enough hath been said of the first, happened soon after the dissolution of the long Parliament;[7] and there, I think, we must place the birth of Whig and Tory, though these parties did not grow up into full maturity, nor receive their names till about two years afterwards.[8] The dissolution of this Parliament was desired by men of very different complexions; by some, with factious views; by others, on this honest and true maxim, that a standing Parliament, or the same Parliament long continued, changes the very nature of the constitution, in the fundamental article on which the preservation of our whole liberty depends. But whatever motives others might have to desire this dissolution, the motives which prevailed on the King, were probably those. This Parliament not only grew more reserved in their grants of money, and stiff and inflexible in other matters, but seemed to have lost that personal regard which they had hitherto preserved for him. They brought their attacks home to his family; nay, to himself, in the heats which the discovery and prosecution of the Popish Plot occasioned. That on the Queen provoked him. That on

---

[6] 'If the brazen wall should rise three times ... Three times shall it fall!': Horace, *Odes*, III. 3. 65–6.

[7] The Cavalier Parliament was dissolved in January 1679.

[8] 'Whig' and 'Tory' were first used in English political discourse in the spring of 1681, and were popularized in L'Estrange's *Observator* in July of that year: Robert Willman, 'The Origins of "Whig" and "Tory" in English Political Language', *The Historical Journal* 17 (1974): 247–64.

his brother embarrassed him. But that which provoked and embarrassed him both, was the prosecution of the Earl of Danby, in the manner in which it was carried on. I will not descend into the particulars of an affair, at this time so well understood. This minister was turned out, and might have been punished in another manner, and much more severely than I presume any one, who knows the anecdotes of that age, thinks that he deserved to be. But the intention of this attack, according to Rapin, was to show that the King, as well as his brother, was at the head of a conspiracy to destroy the government, and the Protestant religion.[9] This is a very bold assertion, and such a one as I do not pretend to warrant. But thus much is certain; that if the Earl of Danby's impeachment had been tried, he must have justified himself, by showing what every one knew to be true, that the secret negotiations with France, and particularly that for money, were the King's negotiations, not his.

Now, whether the King hoped, by dissolving the Parliament, to stop this prosecution; or to soften that of the Popish Plot; or to defeat the project of excluding the Duke of York; his hopes were all disappointed. The following Parliaments trod in the steps of this. How, indeed, could they do otherwise in those days, when the temper of the people determined the character of the Parliament; when an influence on elections by prerogative, was long since over, and private, indirect means of gaining another more illegal influence were not yet found, or the necessary supports of such means were not yet acquired; when any man, who had desired people, who knew neither his fortune, his character, nor even his person, to choose him their representative in Parliament, that is, to appoint him their trustee, would have been looked upon and treated as a madman; in short, when a Parliament, acting against the declared sense of the nation, would have appeared as surprising a phenomenon in the moral world, as a retrograde motion of the sun, or any other signal deviation of things from their ordinary course in the natural world.

There was indeed one point, which this Parliament had taken extremely to heart, and which was no longer open to the Parliaments that followed; I mean the conduct of the King in foreign affairs, during the war between France, and Holland and her allies,

---

[9] Paul de Rapin-Thoyras, *The History of England*, trans. Nicholas Tindal (15 vols., London, 1726–31), XIV, 171.

which ended by the Treaty of Nijmegen.[10] This war was not made in remote countries. It was made at our door. The motives to it, on the part of the aggressor, were neither injuries received, nor rights invaded; but a spirit of conquest, and barefaced usurpation. The interest we had in it was not such as depended on a long chain of contingencies, and required much subtlety to find out, but plain and immediate. The security, and at one time, the very existence of the Dutch commonwealth depended on the event of it. No wonder then, if the conduct of the King, who joined openly with France at first, and served her privately to better purpose at last, furnished ample matter to the public discontent, and helped to increase the ill humour of succeeding Parliaments on two other points, which were still open, and continued to draw their whole attention, as long as King Charles suffered any to sit, during the rest of his reign.

These two points were the prosecution of persons involved in the Popish Plot, and the exclusion of the Duke of York. The first of these had prepared mankind for the second. The truth is, that if nothing which affected the Duke had been produced, besides Coleman's letters,[11] these proofs of his endeavours to subvert the religion and liberty of the people he pretended to govern, joined to so many others of public notoriety, which showed the whole bent of soul, and the whole scheme of his policy, would have afforded reason more than sufficient for sacrificing the interest, or even the right (if you will call it so) of one man to the preservation of three kingdoms. I know how partial we are in the judgments we make, concerning ourselves, and our own interests. I know that this partiality is the immediate effect of self-love, the strongest spring in the human, nay in the whole animal system; and yet I cannot help being surprised that a man should expect to be trusted with a crown, because he is born a prince, in a country where he could not be trusted by law, and ought not to be trusted in reason, with a constable's staff, if he was born a private person. Let me add, that such an expectation must be deemed more unreasonable in a descendant of Henry the Fourth of France, if possible, than in any

---

[10] The Treaty of Nijmegen (1678) concluded six years of war between France and the Confederates (Holland, Spain and the Empire).

[11] The papers of Edward Coleman, former secretary to the Duke and Duchess of York, furnished evidence in 1678 of a treasonable attempt to subvert Protestantism and Parliament with French help.

other man.[12] The hereditary title of the house of Bourbon, on the extinction of that of Valois, was certainly as clear, and much better established by the laws and usages of France, than the hereditary right of any prince of the house of Stuart to the crown of England; and yet Henry the Fourth, with all the personal qualifications which could recommend a prince to the esteem and love of his subjects, would never have been received into the throne by the French nation, if he had not been of the religion of that nation. On what foundation then could it be expected that a Protestant and a free people should be less animated by religion and liberty both, than their neighbours had been by religion alone; for liberty had nothing to do in that contest? Our fathers were thus animated, at the time I am speaking of. The long Parliament projected the exclusion; and if the design had been carried on, in the spirit of a Country party, it would probably have been carried on with a national concurrence, and would consequently have succeeded in effect, though not perhaps at once, nor in the very form at first proposed.

The violent and sanguinary prosecution of the Popish Plot was intended, no doubt, to make the success of the exclusion more secure, by raising the passions of men so high, that no expedient but an absolute and immediate exclusion, in the terms of the bill, should be thought sufficient. I cannot help saying on this occasion, that I wish this laudable and just design had not been pursued, by wading through the blood of so many men: enemies to our religion and liberty, indeed; but convicted, for the most part on evidence, which could hardly have passed at any other time. I wish we had done nothing which might be interpreted to the disrepute of our own religion, whilst we attempted to proscribe theirs. In fine, I wish, for the honour of my country, that the prosecution on account of this plot, and much more on account of another, which was set up as a kind of retaliation for this, and which caused some of the noblest, as well as some of the meanest blood in the nation to be spilt, could be erased out of the records of history.[13] But there is still a farther reason to wish that greater temper had been joined, at this time, to the same zeal for religion and liberty. Men were made to believe that the King, who had yielded on so many other

---

[12] Charles II and James II's mother, Henrietta Maria, was Henri IV's daughter.
[13] William, Lord Russell, and Algernon Sidney were executed in the wake of the discovery of the Rye House Plot (1679).

occasions, would yield on this; that he, who had given up so many
ministers, would give up his brother at last; and that if the Parliament would accept nothing less than the exclusion in their own
way, it would be extorted from him. Now in this they were fatally
deceived: and I must continue to suspect, till I meet with better
reasons than I have yet found to the contrary, that they were so
deceived by the intrigues of two very opposite cabals; by the Duke
of York's, who were averse to all exclusions, whether absolute, or
limited, but most to the last; and by the Duke of Monmouth's, who
could not find their account in any but an absolute exclusion; nor
in this neither, unless the bill passed without any mention of the
Duke's daughters, as next in succession: to which, as bishop Burnet
tells us, the Prince of Orange was willing to comply, on the faith of
assurances he had received from hence;[14] a fact, which the bishop
might know, and we may therefore take on his word, as extraordinary as it seems. I would only observe that King William, then
Prince of Orange, could have no reason for consenting that his
wife's pretensions to the crown should not be confirmed by an act
which excluded her father, except one; and that was the necessity,
real, or apparent, of uniting different private interests in the public
measure of excluding the Duke of York. Now, if this was his reason,
the same reason proves, what shall be farther confirmed in the next
letter, that a spirit of faction ran through the proceedings of those
who promoted the bill of exclusion: and when faction was opposed
to faction, there is no room to wonder, if that of the court prevailed.
The King, who had not used to show firmness on other occasions,
was firm on this: and the consequence of pushing the exclusion in
this manner, was giving him an opportunity of breaking the
Country party; of dividing the nation into Whig and Tory: of governing himself without Parliaments; and of leaving the throne open
to his brother, not only without our limitations or conditions, but
with a more absolute power established, than any prince of his
family had enjoyed.

As soon as the court had got, by management, a plausible pretence of objecting a spirit of faction to those in the opposition, the
strength of the opposition was broken, because the national union

[14] [Gilbert Burnet,] *Bishop Burnet's History of His Own Times* (3 vols., London, 1724–
34), I, 482.

was dissolved. A Country party must be authorized by the voice of the country. It must be formed on principles of common interest. It cannot be united and maintained on the particular prejudices, any more than it can, or ought to be, directed to the particular interests of any set of men whatsoever. A party, thus constituted, is improperly called party. It is the nation, speaking and acting in the discourse and conduct of particular men. It will prevail in all struggles sooner or later, as long as our constitution subsists; and nothing is more easy to demonstrate than this, that whenever such a party finds it difficult to prevail, our constitution is in danger; and when they find it impossible, our constitution must in fact be altered. On the other hand, whenever the prejudices and interests of particular sets of men prevail, the essence of a Country party is annihilated, and the very appearance of it will soon be lost. Every man will resort in this case to that standard, under which he hath been marshalled in former divisions; to which his inclinations lead him; or which, though he does not entirely approve, yet disapproves the least.

Such a dissolution of a Country party was brought about at the period to which we are now come in our deduction of parties, by the passions, the public pique, and private interest of particular men, and by the wily intrigues of the court. The dissolution of this party, and the new division of the nation into Whig and Tory, brought us into extreme danger. This extreme danger reunited the nation again, and a coalition of parties saved the whole. Such an experience might have showed them, that how opposite soever their professions were, yet they really differed more on negative than on positive principles; that they saw one another in a false light, for the most part, and fought with phantoms, conjured up to maintain their divisions, rather than with real beings. Experience had not this happy effect soon. The swell of the sea continued long after the storm was over; and we have seen these parties kick and cuff like drunken men, when they were both of the same side. – Let us hope that this scene of tragical folly is over, to the disappointment of those who are conscious of past iniquity, or who meditate future mischief. There are no others who wish and endeavour to prolong it.

I am, sir, &c.

Sir,

Nothing is more useful, nothing more necessary, in the conduct of public affairs, than a just discernment of spirits. I mean here not only that natural private sagacity which is conversant about individuals, and enables some men to pry, as it were, into the heads and hearts of others, and to discover within them those latent principles which constitute their true characters, and are often disguised in outward action; but I mean principally that acquired, public, political sagacity, which is of the same kind, though I think not altogether the same thing as the former; which flows from nature too, but requires more to be assisted by experience, and formed by art. This is that superior talent of ministers of state, which is so rarely found in those of other countries, and which abounds so happily at present in those of Great Britain. It is by this, that they discover the most secret dispositions of other courts; and, discovering those dispositions, prevent their designs, or never suffer themselves to be surprised by them. It is by this, that they watch over the public tranquillity at home; foresee what effect every event that happens, and much more every step they make themselves, will have on the sentiments and passions of mankind. This part of human wisdom is therefore everywhere of use; but is of indispensable necessity in free countries, where a greater regard is to be constantly had to the various fluctuations of parties; to the temper, humour, opinion and prejudices of the people. Without such a regard as this, those combinations of peculiar circumstances, which we commonly call conjunctures, can never be improved to the best advantage, by acting in conformity, and in proportion to them; and without improving such conjunctures to the best advantage, it is impossible to achieve any great undertaking, or even to conduct affairs successfully in their ordinary course.

A want of this just discernment of spirits, if I am not extremely mistaken, defeated the designs of those who prosecuted with so much vigour the Popish Plot, and the exclusion of the Duke of York. Several of them were men of very great abilities; and yet we shall have no reason to be suprised that they failed in this point, if

---

[1] *Craftsman* 386 [sc. 387] (1 December 1733).

we reflect how unfit even the greatest genius is to discern the spirit of others, when he hath once overheated his own. All men are fallible: but here lies the difference. Some men, such as I have just mentioned, crossed by difficulties, pressed by exigencies, transported by their own passions, or by the passions of those who fight under their banner, may now and then deviate into error, and into error of long and fatal consequence. But there are some men, such as I shall not mention upon this occasion (because I reserve them for another and a better), who never deviate into the road of good sense; who, crossed by no difficulties, pressed by no exigencies, meeting scarce opposition enough to excite their industry, and guiding a tame well-tutored flock, that follow their bell-wether obstinately, but never tread on his heels: there are men, I say, whose special privilege it is to proceed with all these advantages, deliberately and superciliously, from blunder to blunder, from year to year, in one perpetual maze of confused, incoherent, inconsistent, unmeaning schemes of business.

But having nothing to do with the men of this character at present, I return to those of the former class; to the men who led the Whig party, at its first appearance, in the time of King Charles the Second. The foundation upon which they built all their hopes of success, was this: that they should frighten and force the King into a compliance with them: but they did not enough consider that the methods they took were equally proper to frighten and force a great part of the nation from them, by reason of the particular circumstances of that time. They did not enough consider, that when they began to put their designs in execution, scarce twenty years had passed from the Restoration; and that the highest principles, in favour of the Church and the monarchy, had prevailed almost universally during one half of that time, and very generally during the other half; that they had the accidental passions of the people for them, but the settled habits of thinking against them; that they were going off from a broad to a narrow bottom; from the nation to a part of the nation; and this at a time, when they wanted a more than ordinary concurrence of the whole body. They did not enough consider that they were changing the very nature of their party, and giving an opportunity to the court, which was then become, in the strict sense of the word, a faction, to grow up into a party again, and such a party as would divide, at least, the people with them, upon principles, plausible in those days, and sufficient to raise a spirit capable to disappoint all their endeavours.

The same resentments and prejudices, the same jealousies and fears, which burst out with violence, upon many occasions a few years before, lay still in the hearts of men; latent and quiet, indeed, and wearing out by degrees, but yet easy to be revived, and to be blown up anew. If we compare the conduct of the long Parliament in 1674 and 1675, with the attempts which had been lately made, during the administration of the Cabal; with the secret of the second Dutch war,[2] and many other designs and practices of the court, which were then come lately and very authentically to light; with the state of Scotland, which was then subdued under a real tyranny[3] and with that of Ireland, where, to say no more, the Act of Settlement was but ill observed;[4] if we make this comparison, it will not yet appear that the proceedings of the House of Commons were immoderate, though they were warm; nor factious, though they were vigorous; nor that any danger could be then reasonably apprehended from them, except to the enemies of the constitution in Church and state; and yet even then the old resentments, prejudices, jealousies and fears began to revive; and an apprehension of falling back under the influence of Presbyterians and republican principles began to show itself in the House of Lords, and in the nation. It is true, that this had no immediate consequence; because the Popish Plot broke out soon afterwards like a mighty flame, in which these little fires, that began to burn anew, were lost. This great event made the Church and the Dissenters continue to run into one, as they had begun to do before; and the sole division of parties was that of the Court and the Country, as long as this Parliament lasted. But still it was evident with how delicate an hand every thing that related to our former disputes, required to be touched. It was evident that the least alarm given to the Church, or to those who value themselves on the principles of loyalty then in fashion, would be sufficient to open those wounds which were just skinned over, and to raise two new parties out of the ashes of the old.

[2] By this Bolingbroke means what is usually called the Third Dutch War (1672–74).
[3] The regime of the Duke of Lauderdale in Scotland became increasingly – if ineffectively – authoritarian in Church and state in the mid-1670s.
[4] The Irish Acts of Settlement (1662) and Explanation (1665) attempted to resolve the land disputes between Cromwellian settlers and dispossessed Catholic loyalists.

These parties were not raised, whilst the long Parliament sat; because a general opinion prevailed, and well enough founded on their precedent conduct, that however angry the King might be with the Parliament, or the Parliament with the King, a few popular steps made on one side, and a little money granted on the other, would soften matters between them, and dispose them to forget all former quarrels. As hot therefore as the Parliament grew, and as much as some people might think that they exceeded their bounds; yet still it was difficult to persuade even these people that a Parliament, like this, would push things to the last extremity; destroy the constitution they had settled and supported with so much zeal; or draw the sword against a prince, to whom they had borne so much affection. But in the Parliaments which followed, the case was not the same; and I will state as shortly as I can, upon authorities, which no man likely to contradict me must refuse, what made the difference. These authorities shall be that of Burnet, and that of Rapin; whom I quote, on this occasion, for the same reason that I would quote my lord Clarendon against King Charles the First, or Ludlow for him.[5]

In the year 1676, before we have grounds sufficient to affirm that the design of [a]excluding the Duke of York was formed, but not before we have reason to suspect that it might be in the thoughts of several, those who stood foremost in the opposition to the court, were very industrious to procure a dissolution of the long Parliament; so industrious, that they [b]negotiated the affair with the Duke, who had concurred in a vote for an address to dissolve it; and they undertook [c]that a new parliament should be more inclinable to grant the papists a toleration, than they would ever find this would prove. The papists were in earnest for this measure; since Coleman drew a declaration for justifying it, and since their design in it was to

[a] Burnet's *History of His Own Times*, vol. I, p. 393.[6]
[b] Ibid.
[c] Ibid.

[5] As part of the continuing fight over the legacy of the Civil Wars and Interregnum, the *Memoirs of Edmund Ludlow*, the Puritan, regicide and republican (1617–92), were first published in 1698–99, followed by Clarendon's *History of the Rebellion* in 1702.
[6] Burnet, *History of His Own Times*, I, 393.

divide the [d]King and his people. It is fair to conclude that the
Protestants, who had been in it at the time I mention, upon party
views, were at least as much so, when their views rose higher. This
Parliament had pushed a strict and thorough examination into the
Popish Plot, with great sincerity and zeal. Nay, the project of the
exclusion had been started, though not prosecuted, in the last session. May we not take it for granted however, that they, who were
now resolved to carry the exclusion, in a manner in which they soon
attempted to carry it, and who foresaw by consequence the difficulties that would be opposed to them, and the strong measures
they should be obliged to pursue, in order to overcome these difficulties; I say, might not they think this Parliament much less proper
than any other to engage and persist in such measures? They
thought thus, without doubt; and so far they judged better than the
King, who came into the dissolution; upon very different motives.
But as to the consequence of engaging a new Parliament in such
strong measures, the event showed that the King judged better than
they, in the progress of this affair.

The Dissenters, who had been long persecuted by the parliament,
and bantered and abused by the court, were encouraged by the
conjuncture to lift up their heads. They took advantage of the
horror and indignation, which the discovery of the Popish Plot, and
the use made of this discovery had raised all over the kingdom.
They could not be more zealous in this cause than the members of
the established Church had shown themselves to be; but they cried,
perhaps, louder for it. In short, whatever their management was, or
however they were abetted, certain it is that they were very active,
and very successful too, in the elections of the Parliament which
followed the long Parliament, according to Rapin, who asserts that
many of the members, chosen into this House of Commons, were
Presbyterians.[7] He might have said as much, upon just as good
grounds, of the two Parliaments which followed this; and I shall
speak of them indiscriminately. The leaders, who mustered all their
forces, in order to push the Bill of Exclusion, looked on this turn

[d] Ibid.[8]

[7] Rapin, *History of England*, XIV, 188.
[8] Burnet, *History of His Own Times*, I, 393.

in the elections as an advantage to them: and it might not have been a disadvantage, if they and the Dissenters had improved it with more moderation. But they were far from doing so, as Rapin himself seems to own a little unwillingly, when he says, that complaisance for the Presbyterians were carried, perhaps, too far in the bill for the comprehension of Protestant Dissenters.[9] Bishop Burnet speaks more plainly. He owns that many began to declare openly in favour of the nonconformists; that upon this the nonconformists behaved themselves very indecently; that they fell severely on the body of the clergy; and that they made the bishops and clergy apprehend that a rebellion, and with it the pulling the Church to pieces, was designed.[10] Several other passages of the same strength, and to the same purpose, might be collected from this historian; and he, who reads them, will not be surprised, I think, to find that such proceedings as these, both in Parliament and out of it, gave an alarm to the clergy, and set them to make parallels between the late and the present times; and to infuse the fears and the passions, which agitated them, into the nation. The bishop accuses them, indeed, of doing this with much indecency. But they, who are frightened out of their wits, will be apt to be indecent; and indecency begets indecency.

At the same time that the jealousies of a design to destroy the Church prevailed, others prevailed likewise of a design to alter the government of the state; of a design not only against the successor, but against the possessor of the crown. Many well-meaning men, says bishop Burnet upon one occasion, began to dislike these practices, and to apprehend that a change of government was designed.[11] – The King came to think himself, says the same author upon another occasion, levelled at chiefly, though for decency's sake his brother was only named. Rapin goes farther; for, speaking of the same time, he uses this remarkable expression; that 'Things seemed to be taking the same course as in the year 1640; and there was reason to think that the opposing party had no better intentions towards the king now than the enemies of King Charles the First had towards him.'[12] But whatever some particular men, who knew

[9] Rapin, *History of England*, XIV, 277.
[10] Burnet, *History of His Own Times*, I, 461.
[11] Burnet, *History of His Own Times*, I, 478.
[12] Rapin, *History of England*, XIV, 242 (paraphrased).

themselves irreconcilable with the King, as well as the Duke, or some others, who had still about them a tang of religious enthusiasm and republican whimsies, might intend; I am far from thinking that the party, who promoted the exclusion, meant to destroy, on the contrary it is plain that they meant to preserve, by that very meas-ure, the constitution in Church and state. The reason why I quote these passages, and refer to others of the same kind, is not to show what was really designed, but what was apprehended; for as the distinction of Whig and Tory subsisted long after the real differ-ences were extinguished, so were these parties at first divided, not so much by overt acts committed, as by the apprehensions, which each of them entertained of the intentions of the other. When the resolution was once taken of rejecting all limitations, on the belief artfully, and, I think, knavishly propagated, that the King would yield, if the Parliament persisted; the necessary consequences of the King's adhering inflexibly to his brother were those which followed, those *fulmina parliamentaria*,[13] harsh votes, angry proceedings, addresses, that were in truth remonstrances, projects of associations, pretensions to a power of dispensing with the execution of laws (that very prerogative they had so justly refused to the crown) and many others, which I omit. All these would have been blasts of wind, *bruta fulmina*,[14] no more, if the King had yielded: and that they were pushed in this confidence by the bulk of the party who pushed them, cannot be doubted; since it cannot be doubted that the bulk of the party depended on the King's yielding almost, per-haps, even to the last. Some few might be willing, nay desirous, that he should not yield, and hope to bring things into a state of confusion; which none but madmen, or those, whom their crimes, or their fortunes render desperate, can ever wish to see. But it would be hard, indeed, if parties were to be characterized, not by their common view, or the general tenor of their conduct, but by the private views imputed to some amongst them, or by the particu-lar sallies, into which mistake, surprise, or passion, hath sometimes betrayed the best-intentioned, and even the best-conducted bodies of men. Whig and Tory were now formed into parties; but I think they were not now, nor at any other time, what they believed one

---

[13] 'Parliamentary thunderbolts'.
[14] 'Heavy thunderbolts': Pliny, *Natural History*, II. 113. 8.

another, nor what they have been represented by their enemies, nay by their friends. The Whigs were not roundheads, though the measures they pursued, being stronger than the temper of the nation would then bear, gave occasion to the suspicions I have mentioned. The Tories were not cavaliers, though they took the alarm so sudden and so warm for the Church and the King; and though they carried the principles in favour of the King, at least, whilst the heat of their contests with the opposite party lasted, higher than they had been ever carried before. The Whigs were not Dissenters, nor republicans, though they favoured the former, and though some inconsiderable remains of the latter, might find shelter in their party. The Tories had no disposition to become slaves, or papists, though they abetted the exercise of an exorbitant power by the crown, and though they supported the pretensions of a popish successor to it. – Thus I think about the parties, which arose in the reign of King Charles the Second; and as I deliver my thoughts with frankness, I hope they will be received with candour. Some farther and stronger reasons for receiving them so, may perhaps appear in a subsequent letter.

I am, sir, your, &c.

Sir,

If King Charles the Second could have been prevailed upon to sacrifice the chimerical divine right of his brother to the real interest, and right too, of his people; that happy event would have made him ample amends in future ease and quiet, and the nation in future security, for all precedent disorders, dangers, and fears of danger. But instead of this, he was every day confirmed in the resolution of not giving up, directly and in terms, that right to his brother, which he thought reflected strength on his own. The very measures taken to force him to submit, enabled him to resist. The opposite spirit spent itself in blood and violence. The spirit of him rose visibly in the nation; and he saw very soon the time approach, when he might venture to appeal to his people against his parliament. This time was come, when men were once convinced that a Country party prevailed no longer, but that faction had taken its place. Many appearances, which I have not room to enumerate, served to propagate this opinion; particularly the behaviour and almost avowed pretensions of the Duke of Monmouth; which were carried on even in defiance of the solemn declaration made by the King, that he had never married the Duke's mother.

Some of the worthiest and warmest men, who were engaged for the exclusion, complained themselves, even from the first, of the private interests and factious intrigues which prevailed amongst them. 'I must confess', says a very considerable man, [a]who laid down his life for this cause afterwards, and whose original letter is still extant; 'I must confess, I do not know three men of a mind; and that a spirit of giddiness reigns amongst us, far beyond any I have ever observed in my life.' And yet he had lived and acted in as factious a time as this nation ever saw. He proceeds: 'Some look who is fittest to succeed. – They are for the most part divided between the Prince of Orange, and the Duke of Monmouth. The first hath plainly the most plausible title. – I need not tell you the reasons against Monmouth. The strongest for him are, that whoever

[a] Algernon Sidney.

[1] *Craftsman* 390 (22 December 1733).

46

is opposed to York will have a good party; and all Scotland, which is every day like to be in arms, doth certainly favour him, and may probably be of as much importance in the troubles that are now likely to fall upon us, as they were in the beginning of the last. Others are only upon negatives', &c.[2]

I could easily multiply proofs of this kind; but I think I need not take any pains to show that there was such a faction formed at this time; nor to refute Welwood, who asserts that the Duke of Monmouth was not ambitious to the degree of aspiring to the crown, till after his landing in the west.[3] I will only remark, that the efforts of this faction amongst those who drove on the bill of exclusion, furnished another motive to the division and animosity of parties. The Tories, who had divided from the others, on jealousies of designs to change the constitution in Church and state, began now to apprehend that the opposite party might succeed in another view, and set up a king of their own nomination. A notion then entertained by many, that the worse title a man had, the better King he was likely to make, did not persuade them. They had suffered under the tyranny of a party; many of them had been themselves the abettors of a party-administration; and they feared with reason a party King. Thus personal interests were mingled on both sides with public considerations; and the Duke of York gained a great number of adherents, not by affection to him, but by an aversion to Monmouth; which increased among the Tories, in proportion as the Duke's popularity increased among the Whigs; not by any favourable disposition in the Tories to popery and arbitrary power, but by a dread, as I have observed already, of returning in the least degree under the influence of those principles, and the power of those men, whose yoke had galled the necks of many that were still alive and active on the stage of public affairs. 'Men grew jealous of the design' (says bishop Burnet, speaking of Monmouth's popularity) 'and fancied here was a new civil war to be raised. Upon this, they joined with the Duke's party';[4] meaning the Duke of York's.

[2] Algernon Sidney to Henry Savile, 5/15 May 1679, in *Letters of the Honourable Algernon Sydney, to the Honourable Henry Savile Ambassador to France* (London, 1742), 20–1.
[3] James Welwood, *Memoirs of the Most Material Transactions in England for the Last Hundred Years* (London, 1700), 167.
[4] Burnet, *History of His Own Times*, I, 477.

I say nothing of the apprehensions entertained on one side, and the expectations entertained on the other from Scotland; because though there was, even in the beginning of these struggles, a concert between those who were oppressed by the court there, and those who opposed it here, which grew afterwards into a closer correspondence, and became riper for action; yet the seditious spirit, that gave occasion to these apprehensions and expectations, was roused and exasperated by the inhumanity of the Duke of Lauderdale, who, though a Presbyterian himself, was the butcher of that party; pushed the warmest of them into unjustifiable excesses; revived their silly zeal for the Covenant; and wrought up their enthusiasm even to assassination and rebellion. Let me only observe, that this was plainly the fault of the court, and could not therefore be imputed to the Whigs, whatever use some of that party might propose to make of such a disposition. The violence of the conventiclers was founded high, in order to palliate the severities exercised in the government of that kingdom. But the reasonable men of all parties thought then, as they think now, and always will think, that it is the duty of those who govern, to discern the spirit of the people; to consider even their passions; to have a regard to their weaknesses; and to show indulgence to their prejudices; and that ministers, who punish what they might prevent, are more culpable than those who offend.

As the two parties were formed, so was their division maintained by mutual jealousies and fears; which are often sufficient to nourish themselves, when they have once taken root in the mind; and which were, at this time, watered and cultivated with all the factious industry possible. The most improbable reports, the most idle surmises, carried about in whispers, were sufficient, as I might easily show in various instances, to raise a panic terror in one party, or the other. In both, there were but too many persons on the watch, to improve and to propagate these terrors, and by a frequent repetition of such impressions to raise the alarm and hatred of parties to the highest pitch. He, who went about to allay this extravagant ferment, was called a trimmer; and he, who was in truth a common friend, was sure of being treated like a common enemy. Some, who voted for the bill of exclusion, were very far from being heartily for it; but I have seen good reasons to believe, and such there are even in our public relations, that some of those who voted against it, and

declared for limitations, concurred in the end, though they differed
in the means, with those who promoted the bill. And yet such men
were constantly marked out as favourers of popery and enemies to
their country. Thus in the other party, men, who had no other view
but that of securing their religion and liberty, and who meant
nothing more than to force the court into such compliances as they
judged necessary to establish this security, were stigmatized with
the opprobrious names of fanatic and republican. Thus it happened
in those days; and thus it happens in ours; when any man who
declares against a certain person, against whom the voice of the
nation hath already declared, or complains of things which are so
notorious, that no man in the nation can deny them, is sure to be
followed by the cry of Jacobitism, or republicanism. But there is a
great difference, God be praised, between the two cases. The present cry being void of pretence, is therefore without effect. It is
heard in few places, and believed only in one. – But to return.

When the nation was divided in this manner, the heat of the
parties increased as their contest lasted, according to the usual
course of things. New engagements were daily taken; new provocations and offences were daily given. Public disputes begot private
pique; and private pique supported public disputes with greater
rancour and obstinacy. The opposite principles advanced by the two
parties, were carried higher and higher, as they grew more inflamed;
and the measures they pursued, in order to get the better each of
his adversary, without overmuch regard to any other consequence,
became stronger and stronger, and perhaps equally dangerous. The
meeting of the Parliament at Oxford had a kind of hostile appearance;[5] and as soon as Parliaments were laid aside, which happened
on the sudden and indecent dissolution of this, the appearance grew
worse. No security having been obtained by parliamentary methods,
against the dangers of a popish succession, it is probable that they,
who looked on these dangers as nearest and greatest, began to cast
about how they might secure themselves and their country against
them, by methods of another kind; such as extreme necessity, and
nothing but extreme necessity can authorize. Such methods were
happily pursued and attended with glorious success, a few years
afterwards, when this succession had taken place; and, by taking

---

[5] The Third Exclusion Parliament met at Oxford 21–28 March 1681.

place, had justified all that had been said against it, or foreboded of
it; when the nation was ripe for resistance, and the Prince of Orange
ready and able, from a multitude of fortunate, concurring circumstances, to support so great an enterprise. But the attempts, which
were wise at one time, would have been desperate at the other; and
the measures which produced a revolution in the reign of King
James, would have produced in the reign of King Charles, a civil
war of uncertain event at best: I say of uncertain event at best,
because it seems to me, that whoever revolves in his thoughts the
state of England and Scotland, as well as the situation of our neighbours on the continent, at that time, must be of opinion, that if the
quarrel about the exclusion had broke out into a war, the best cause
would have been the worst supported. The King, more united than
ever with his brother, would have prevailed. What was projected in
1670, and perhaps more than was then intended, would have been
effected; and the religion and liberty of Great Britain would have
been destroyed by consequence.[6] We cannot say, and it would be
presumption to pretend to guess, how far the heads of party had
gone, in Scotland, or in England, into measures for employing force.
Perhaps, little more had passed, in which they who became the
principal sacrifices, were any way concerned, than rash discourse
about dangerous, but rude, indigested schemes, started by men of
wild imaginations, or desperate fortunes, and rather hearkened to
than assented to; nay, possibly despised and neglected by them. But
the court, who wanted a plot to confirm and increase their party,
and to turn the popular tide in their favour, took the first opportunity of having one; which was soon furnished to them by the
imprudent, but honest zeal of some, and by the villainy, as well as
madness of others: and they prosecuted it so severely, with the help
of [b]forward sheriffs, willing juries, bold witnesses and mercenary
judges, that it answered all their ends. The design of assassinating
the King and the Duke, was certainly confined to a few desperate

[b] Burnet.[7]

[6] By the secret clauses of the Treaty of Dover (1670), Louis XIV paid Charles II a
pension in return for Charles' support in the war against the United Provinces,
Spain and the Empire and a pledge to return England to Catholicism at the earliest
opportunity.
[7] Burnet, *History of His Own Times*, I, 538.

villains; but ᶜtoo many had heard it from them, who were both so foolish and so wicked, as not to discover them; and this reflected great prejudice, though I doubt not in many cases very unjustly, against all those who had acted upon better principles, but yet were involved in those prosecutions.

As this event disarmed, dispirited and broke one party, so it strengthened, animated and united the other. The Tories, who looked on the dangers they apprehended from the Whigs to be greater and nearer than those which they had apprehended, as well as the Whigs, before this new division of parties, from a popish succession, were now confirmed in their prejudices. Under this persuasion, they run headlong into all the measures which were taken for enlarging the King's authority, and securing the crown to the Duke of York. The principles of divine hereditary right, of passive obedience, and non-resistance, were revived and propagated with greater zeal than ever. Not only the wild whimsies of enthusiasm, of schoolmen and philosophers, but the plainest dictates of reason were solemnly condemned in favour of them, by learned and reverend bodies of men; who little thought that in five years' time, that is in 1688, they should act conformably to some of the very propositions, which at this time they declared false, seditious and impious.

In short, the Guelphs and Ghibellines were not more animated against each other at any time, than the Tories and Whigs at this;[8] and in such a national temper, considerable steps were made, as they well might be, towards the destruction of our constitution. One of those which Rapin enumerates, and insists upon very gravely, can scarce be mentioned without smiling. 'The King', says he, 'in order to make his people feel the slavery he had newly imposed on them, affected to review his troops; and these troops amounted, by the return of the garrison of Tangier, to four thousand men, effective, and well-armed.'[9] The Whigs, indeed, in those days, were so averse to standing armies, that they thought even those troops, commonly called guards, unlawful; and bishop Burnet argues, in his

---

ᶜ Ibid.[10]

[8] Two powerful rival factions in medieval Italy: the Guelphs supported the Pope against the German emperor, the Ghibellines the emperor against the Pope.
[9] Rapin, *History of England*, XIV, 356 (paraphrased).
[10] Burnet, *History of His Own Times*, I, 538.

reflections on my lord Russell's trial, that a design to seize on them amounted to no more than a design to seize on a part of the King's army.[11] But it is possible that the Tories, who had showed their dislike of standing armies sufficiently in the long Parliament, might think it however no unreasonable thing, when designs of insurrections, and even of assassinations had come so lately to light, that a number of regular troops, sufficient to defend the person of the King, but not sufficient to oppress the liberties of the people, and five times less than we have since seen kept up in the midst of the most secure tranquillity, should be winked at, till these distempers were entirely over.

Another step, which the same author mentions, was indeed of the greatest consequence, and laid the axe to the root of all our liberties at once, by giving the crown such an influence over the elections of members to serve in Parliament, as could not fail to destroy that independency, by which alone the freedom of our government hath been, and can be supported. I mean the proceedings by *quo warranto*, and the other methods taken to force, or persuade, the corporations to surrender their old charters, and accept new ones, under such limitations and conditions as the King thought fit to innovate. These proceedings were violent, the judgments upon them arbitrary, and the other methods employed scandalous. But still it was the end, it was the consequence, that alarmed and terrified all those who had not sold themselves to the court, or who had not lost, in their zeal for party, all regard to their country, much more than the means that were employed upon this occasion. If, instead of garbling corporations by prerogative,[12] the court could have purchased their elections by money, we may reasonably believe that the surer and more silent way would have been taken. But would the alarm have been less among all the friends of liberty? Certainly not. They would have seen that the end was the same, and have disliked those means the more, for being less liable to observation and clamour. A prince, asserting an illegal and dangerous prerogative, and applauded for doing so, and seconded in the

---

[11] Burnet, *History of His Own Times*, I, 555.

[12] Both Charles II and, later, James II used writs of *Quo Warranto* (calling for surrender and scrutiny of charters of rights) against borough charters of incorporation as a means to influence elections and curtail local liberties: Burnet, *History of His Own Times*, I, 527.

attempt by a numerous party in the nation, carried no doubt a very terrible aspect. But still there was room to hope, the violent character of the Duke of York considered (and that hope was actually entertained by many), that the party, who abetted these usurpations of the prerogative, might be soon frightened back again from a Court to a Country interest; in which case, there was room to hope likewise, the milder character and better understanding of the King considered, that the evil might be in some degree redressed, and the consequences of it prevented. It was reasonable for the friends of liberty to expect that men, who were injured, would complain and seek relief, on the first favourable opportunity. But if they had been corrupted, and the practice of selling elections had been once established, I imagine that the friends of liberty would have thought the case more desperate. – It is certainly an easier task, and there is somewhat less provoking, as well as less dangerous in it, to struggle even with a great prince who stands on prerogative, than a weak, but profligate minister, if he hath the means of corruption in his power, and if the luxury and prostitution of the age have enabled him to bring it into fashion. Nothing surely could provoke men, who had the spirit of liberty in their souls, more than to figure to themselves one of these saucy creatures of fortune, whom she raises in the extravagance of her caprice, dispatching his emissaries, ecclesiastical and secular, like so many evil demons, to the north and to the south, to buy the votes of the people with the money of the people, and to choose a representative body, not of the people, but of the enemy of the people, of himself.

This was not the case at the time we are speaking of. It was prerogative, not money, which had like to have destroyed our liberties then. Government was not then carried on by undertakers, to whom so much power was farmed out for returns of so much money, and so much money entrusted for returns of so much power. But though the case was not so desperate, yet was it bad enough in all conscience; and among all the excesses into which the Tories ran, in favour of the crown, and in hopes of fixing dominion in their own party, their zeal to support the methods of garbling corporations was, in my opinion, that which threatened public liberty the most. It hath been reproached to them by many; but if among those who reproached them, there should be some who have shared since that time in the most dangerous practice of corrupting corporations, such men must have fronts of brass, and deserve all the indignation which is due to iniquity, aggravated by impudence. The others abetted, in favour of a prerogative, supposed real by many in those days, and under the pretence at least of law, a power, which gave the crown too much influence in the elections of members of the House of Commons; but these men, if there are any such, have been concerned in a practice, for the sake of their own vile interest, which spreads like a gangrene over the whole body of a nation, and to every branch of government; and which hath never failed, in any one instance, where it hath been suffered, to become the bane of liberty.

We have now carried the two parties through that period of time, when the conduct of both was most liable to the objections made to them by their adversaries. – The Tories acted on the most abject principles of submission to the King; and, on those of hereditary right, were zealous for the succession of a prince, whose bigotry rendered him unfit to rule a Protestant and a free people. – The Whigs maintained the power of Parliament to limit the succession to the crown, and avowed the principle of resistance; in which they had law, example and reason for them. But then the fury of faction was for doing that without Parliament, which could only be legally done by it: and, in order to this, the principles of resistance were extended too far; and the hottest men of the party taking the lead, they acted in an extravagant spirit of licence, rather than a sober spirit of liberty; and the madness of a few, little inferior to that of Cromwell's enthusiasts, dishonoured the whole cause for a time. – My intention was not to have left them here; but to have carried these observations on so far as to justify, notwithstanding these appearances, what is said at the conclusion of my last letter, concerning the true characters of both parties. But either the abundance of matter hath deceived me, or I have wanted skill and time to abridge it; so that I must defer this part of my task, and crave your indulgence, as well as that of your readers, for my prolixity.

I am, sir, &c.

Sir,

I advanced, in the first of these essays, something to this effect; that every clumsy, busy, bungling child of fortune, on whom she bestows the means and the opportunity of corrupting, may govern by this infamous expedient; and, having gratified his ambition and avarice, may have a chance to secure himself from punishment, by destroying the liberties of his country. It was advanced likewise, in the same paper, that every character is not equally fit to govern a people, by dividing them; because some cunning, some experience, nay, some skill to form, and some address to conduct a system of fraud, are necessary in this case. I persuade myself that no man, who read that paper, was at a loss to find an instance to confirm the truth of the first of these propositions; and we have now before us another, which may serve to confirm the truth of the second.

Though I do not think the designs of King Charles the Second either deeply laid, or deeply fixed in his own mind; yet in general they were founded on bad principles, and directed to bad ends. He desired indeed to be easy, and to make his people so; but then he desired both these on such conditions, as were inconsistent with good government, during the whole course of his reign; and with the security of religion and liberty, during the latter part of it. We have seen how the intemperate conduct of many, and the flagitious designs of some among the Whigs, weakened their own party, and gave new strength and new provocations to the other. But we have not yet considered some other advantages, without which these divisions could neither have been fomented, nor supported as they were. Now these advantages arose chiefly from the character and conduct of the King himself. If King Charles had found the nation plunged in corruption; the people choosing their representatives for money, without any other regard; and these representatives of the people, as well as the nobility, reduced by luxury to beg the unhallowed alms of a court; or to receive, like miserable hirelings, the wages of iniquity from a minister: if he had found the nation, I say, in this condition (which extravagant supposition one cannot make without horror) he might have dishonoured her abroad, and

---

[1] *Craftsman* 391 (29 December 1733).

impoverished and oppressed her at home, though he had been the weakest prince on earth, and his ministers the most odious and contemptible men that ever presumed to be ambitious. Our fathers might have fallen into circumstances, which compose the very quintessence of political misery. They might have sold their birth-right for porridge, which was their own. They might have been bubbled by the foolish, bullied by the fearful, and insulted by those whom they despised. They would have deserved to be slaves, and they might have been treated as such. When a free people crouch, like camels, to be loaded, the next at hand, no matter who, mounts them, and they soon feel the whip, and the spur of their tyrant; for a tyrant, whether prince or minister, resembles the devil in many respects, particularly in this. He is often both the tempter and tormentor. He makes the criminal, and he punishes the crime.

But this was not the state of the English nation, at the time we speak of. We were not yet corrupted, nor even quite ripe for corruption. Parties there were; and the contests of these parties gave occasion to the rise and growth of factions; some of which ran into the most seditious practices against the government, and others into the vilest submission to it. But still a spirit of liberty remained in many, uncorrupted and un-extinguished, and such as worked our national deliverance in the days of distress, that soon followed. We were freemen then, in the proper sense and full extent of the words; because not only the laws, which asserted our common rights, were maintained and improved, but private independency, which can alone support public liberty under such a government as ours, was itself supported by some of that ancient economy and simplicity of manners, that were growing, but not grown, out of fashion. Such a people, as we then were, could neither be bought, nor driven; and I think King Charles could not have divided and led them, if he had wanted any of the qualities he possessed, or had held another conduct than he held. Far from being proud, haughty, or brutal, ᵃ"he had not a grain of pride, or vanity, in his whole composition'; but was the most affable, best-bred man alive. He treated his subjects like noblemen, like gentlemen, like freemen, not like vassals,

---

ᵃ Sir William Temple.[2]

[2] (1628–99), diplomat and essayist; source unidentified.

or boors. Whatever notion he had of his hereditary right, he owned his obligation for the crown he wore to his people, as much as he would have been bound to do, in reason, in justice, in honour, and in prudence, if he had stood at the greatest distance from it, in the course of lineal succession, and had been called to it from the low state in which he was before, by the free gift and choice of the nation. His professions were plausible, and his whole behaviour engaging; so that he won upon the hearts, even whilst he lost the good opinion of his subjects, and often balanced their judgment of things, by their personal inclination. These qualities and this part of his conduct went a great way to give him credit with his people, and an hold on their affections. But this was not all. He observed their temper, and he complied with it. He yielded to them in points, from which he had determined, and declared too, that he would never depart. To know when to yield in government, is at least as necessary, as to know when to lose in trade; and he who cannot do the first, is so little likely to govern a kingdom well, that it is more than probable he would govern a shop ill. King Charles gave up to the murmurs of his people, not one or two such ministers as may be found almost behind every desk, those awkward pageants of courts, those wooden images, which princes gild and then worship; but several great and able men, nay, whole cabals of such, who had merit with him, though they had none with the nation. He started often out of the true interest of his people, but the voice of his people almost as often reclaimed him. He made the first Dutch war, but he made the Triple Alliance too.[3] He engaged with France in the war of 1672, but he made a separate peace with Holland. True it is, indeed, that neither the representations of his parliament, nor the desires of his people, could prevail on him to go farther, and to enter in earnest into the war against France. But the confidence between him and his parliament was so broken at that time, that they would not trust him, nor he them. At this I am not surprised, and for that very reason, I confess, I have always been so at the strong and repeated instances made to force him into that war; since it cannot surely be better policy to drive a prince into a war, which he has no inclination to make, than it would be to be drawn by him

[3] The Triple Alliance (1668) brought England, the United Provinces and Sweden together against France.

into a war, if he had no ability to conduct it. In home affairs, besides his frequent concessions, whenever the nation took umbrage at his proceedings, he passed the Test and Habeas Corpus bills,[4] and many others for the public benefit: and I scarce remember any popular act, which stopped at the throne in his time, except that about the militia, which he apprehended to be a dangerous encroachment on his prerogative, and another in favour of the Dissenters, which was contrived, meanly enough, to be stolen off the table in the House of Lords.[5]

What has been touched here, and in former papers, will be sufficient to show, in some measure, how King Charles was enabled to divide a nation so united and so heated as this nation was, on the discovery of the Popish Plot; to oppose so avowedly and so resolutely the exclusion of his brother, the prospect of whose succeeding to the crown was become still more dreadful, even by that small part of Coleman's correspondence, which had come to light: and yet to attach so numerous a party to himself, nay to his brother; to lay aside Parliaments for several years, and not only to stand his ground, but to gain ground in the nation, at the same time. But there is still something more to be added. He had not only prepared for the storm, but he acquired new strength in the midst of it; that is, in the proceedings on the Popish Plot, and the bill of exclusion. He would gladly have kept the former out of Parliament; but when it was once there, he put on the appearances of great zeal for the prosecution of it. These appearances helped him to screen his brother; as the ill success of the Exclusion Bill in the House of Lords, where it was rejected by sixty-three against thirty, helped to screen himself from the violence of the House of Commons. But that which gave him the principal advantage, in the present contests, was another management. As soon as the first preparatory steps were made to the bill of exclusion in 1678, he declared himself, in a speech to his Parliament, ready to pass any bills to make his people safe in the reign of his successor, so they tended not to impeach the right of succession, nor the descent of the crown in

---

[4] The Test Acts passed in 1673 and 1678; the Habeas Corpus Act in 1679.
[5] Charles vetoed the 1678 militia bill because it limited royal control over the militia; on the underhand withdrawal of the bill to repeal the penal laws against nonconformists in the second Exclusion Parliament (1681), see Burnet, *History of His Own Times*, I, 494–5.

the true line. He persisted in his declaration to the last; and if he had done nothing else, I imagine that he would have gained no great popularity. When a free people lie under any grievance, or apprehend any danger, and try to obtain their prince's consent to deliver them from one, or prevent the other, a flat refusal, on his part, reduces them to the melancholy alternative of continuing to submit to one, and to stand exposed to the other, or of freeing themselves from both, without his consent; which can hardly be done by means very consistent with his and their common interest. King Charles was too wise to push the nation to such an extremity. He refused what his Parliament pressed on him, in the manner and on the principle they pressed it; but then his refusal was followed by expedients, which varied the manner, and yet might have been managed so as to produce the effect; and which seemed to save, rather than actually saved, the principle. Numbers concurred, at that time, in avowing the principle; and the tests had made many persons think religion safe; as the King's offers made them think it no fault of his, if it was not made safer. The council had prepared some expedients; and the limitations, and other provisions against a popish successor, proposed directly from the throne by the Chancellor in 1679,[6] went a great way towards binding the hands of such a successor, and lodging the power, taken from him, in the Parliament. But the scheme of expedients, debated in the Oxford Parliament, was a real exclusion from every thing, but the title of a king. The first article banished the Duke of York, during his life, to the distance of five hundred miles from England, Scotland and Ireland; and the tenth, to mention no more, excluded him *ipso facto*, if he came into any of these kingdoms; directed that he should suffer, in this case, as by the former bill; and that the sovereignty should vest forthwith in the regent, that is, in the Princess of Orange. Surely this was not to vote the lion in the lobby into the house. It would have been to vote him out of the house, and lobby both, and only suffer him to be called lion still. I am not ignorant of the refinements urged by Sir William Jones[7] and others against

---

[6] Limitations on a popish successor were proposed to Parliament by Lord Chancellor Finch on 30 April 1679.
[7] Sir William Jones (1631–82), lawyer and Whig MP, who had directed the prosecution of Titus Oates, was credited with a major role in pressing passage of the Exclusion Bill.

this scheme: but I know that men run into errors from both extremes; from that of seeing too much, as well as that of seeing too little; and that the most subtle refiners are apt to miss the true point of political wisdom, which consists in distinguishing justly between what is absolutely best in speculation, and what is the best of things practicable in particular conjunctures. The scheme, no doubt, was built on a manifest absurdity, and was liable to many inconveniencies, difficulties and dangers; but still it was the utmost that could be hoped for at that moment: and the single consideration, one would think, should have been this: whether, united under such an Act of Parliament, they would not have opposed the succession of the Duke of York, with less inconveniency, less difficulty and danger, than disunited, and with the laws against them. The truth is, that as there were men at this time, desirous that the King should be on desperate terms with his Parliament, because they were so themselves; in like manner there were others, who desired, for a reason of the same nature, that the Parliament should be on desperate terms with the King. These were factious interests, and they prevailed against the national interest, which required that the King should be separated at any rate from his brother, instead of being united to him by a fear made common to both. But the die was thrown; and the leaders of the Whig party were resolved. ᵇ'to let all lie in confusion, rather than hearken to any thing, besides the exclusion'. Obstinacy provoked obstinacy. The King grew obstinate, and severe too, against his natural easiness and former clemency of temper. The Tory party grew as obstinate, and as furious on their side, according to a natural tendency in the disposition of all parties: and thus the nation was delivered over, on the death of King Charles, 'à la sottise de son frère'ᶜ; 'to the folly and madness of his brother'.

It was this folly and madness however, that cured the folly and madness of party. As the common danger approached, the impressions of terror which it made, increased. Whig and Tory then felt them alike, and were brought by them, as drunken men

---

ᵇ Burnet's *History*⁸
ᶜ An expression used by King Charles on many occasions.

⁸ Burnet, *History of His Own Times*, I, 486.

sometimes are, to their senses. The events of King James's reign, and the steps by which the Revolution was brought about, are so recent, and so well known, that I shall not descend into any particular mention of them. A few general remarks on the behaviour of his prince, and on the behaviour of parties in his reign, and at the Revolution, will be sufficient to wind up the history of Whig and Tory, and to prove what I have so often asserted, that both sides purged themselves on this great occasion, of the imputations laid to their charge by their adversaries; that the proper and real distinction of the two parties expired at this era, and that although their ghosts have continued to haunt and divide us so many years afterwards, yet there neither is, nor can be any division of parties at this time, reconcilable with common sense, and common honesty, among those who are come on the stage of the world under the present constitution, except those of Churchmen and Dissenters, those of Court and Country.

This behaviour and conduct of King James the Second would be sufficient, if there was no other instance, and there are thousands, to show that as strong prejudices, however got, are the parents, so a weak understanding is the nurse of bigotry, and injustice and violence and cruelty its offspring. This prince was above fifty, when he came to the throne. He had great experience of all kinds; particularly of the temper of this nation, and of the impossibility to attempt introducing popery, without hazarding his crown. But his experience profited him not. His bigotry drew false conclusions from it. He flattered himself that he should be able to play parties against one another, better than his brother had done (which, by the way, was the least of his little talents) and to complete his designs by an authority, which was but too well established. He passed, I think, for a sincere man. Perhaps, he was so; and he spoke always with great emphasis of the word of a king; and yet never was the meanest word so scandalously broken as his. In the debate in 1678, about the Test, when he got a proviso put in for excepting himself, it has been advanced in print, and not denied that I know of, that speaking with [d]"great earnestness, and with tears in his eyes, he solemnly

---

[d] Burnet's *History*.[9]

[9] Burnet, *History of His Own Times*, I, 436.

protested that whatever his religion might be, it should only be a private thing between God and his own soul; and that no effect of it should ever appear in the government'. At his accession to the throne, in council first, and after that in full Parliament, in the face of the nation, he made the strongest declaration in favour of the constitution in Church and state, and took the most solemn engagements to defend and support it. But bigotry burst through all these cobwebs; for such they are to men, transported by a religious delirium, who acquires a strength that those, who are well, have not, and conscientiously break all the obligations of morality. These admirable dispositions in the King were encouraged by the state in which his brother left and he found the nation, and by the complaisance of the Parliament, which he called soon after his accession. They were confirmed, and he was determined to pull off the mask entirely, by the ill success of the Duke of Monmouth and the Earl of Argyll.[10] Bishop Burnet speaks of this Parliament very indecently, and I think very untruly. They were neither men of parts, nor estates, according to him.[11] The truth is, that the circumstances under which we were brought by the factious proceedings of both parties, in the late reign, for and against the court, were such as might perplex the best parts, and puzzle the heads even of the wisest men. A professed, zealous papist, in full and quiet possession of the throne, and, instead of any provision made, or any measures taken against him, the notion and the exercise of the prerogative established at an extravagant height, were such circumstances, as laid the nation almost at the mercy of the King. They therefore, who were the most determined not to part with either their religion, or their liberty, and yet had more to lose in the fray than Dr Burnet, might be willing to look round them, to wait opportunities, and not undertake rashly what can seldom be undertaken twice. It is impossible to believe that their confidence in the King's word was such as they affected. But like drowning men, who saw nothing else to catch at, they caught at a straw. The Duke of Monmouth's expedition into England, and the Earl of Argyll's into Scotland, were so far from

---

[10] Archibald Campbell, 9th Earl of Argyll, led an abortive rising in western Scotland (May–June 1685) in favour of the Duke of Monmouth, who led his own rising in the English west country in June 1685. Both revolts were swiftly crushed, and their leaders executed.

[11] Burnet, *History of His Own Times*, I, 626.

affording the nation any opportunity of mending their condition, that the declaration of the former might draw some of the Dissenters to his standard, as it did; but was calculated to drive the Tory party, most of the Whigs, and in short the bulk of the people from him. The declaration of the latter was founded in the Solemn League and Covenant;[12] and gave so much reason to apprehend that a revival of the same principles, and a renewal of the same tyranny was intended, that we cannot wonder it had no better an effect; though we lament the fate of a worthy and gallant man, whose crime was refusing a test, that should never have been imposed on protestants and freemen, and who had been driven into these extreme resolutions by a series of unjust and tyrannical usage.

Thus were these invasions, in the very beginning of his reign, favourable in some respects to the designs of King James. They fortified, in the minds of men, and jealousies and fears, which had a few years before formed the Tory party, and disposed them by consequence, at least, to keep measures and not break with the King. They gave him the pretence, which he seized very readily, of raising and keeping up a standing army. But, in the event, they forwarded our deliverance from all the dangers to which we were exposed under his government, by precipitating his attempts against our religion and liberty. The same day that the news of the invasion in Scotland was communicated to the Parliament here, the Commons voted that great revenue, which they gave him, and gave him for life. After these invasions were over, they voted a supply, which was intended for the charge of maintaining the additional forces. They offered to pass a law for indemnifying his popish officers from the penalty they had incurred, and to capacitate such others as he should name in a list to be given to the House. In short, they suffered themselves to be drawn to the brink of the precipice: but there they stopped. They would neither give him the whole supply of one million two hundred thousand pounds, which he asked, nor sanctify, by the authority of Parliament, the practice of keeping up a standing army in time of peace; but rejected the words moved for that purpose. They would neither repeal the Test and Penal laws, nor submit to his dispensing, or suspending, which was in effect a

---

[12] Anglo-Scottish agreement of 1643 to establish a Presbyterian church in England in return for Scots aid to the English Parliament against Charles I.

repealing power: that is, they would not cast themselves headlong down the precipice. And because they would not, he quarrelled with them, lost the seven hundred thousand pounds they had voted, rather than suffer them to sit any longer; and never met them more.

Things hastened now to a decision. The King's designs were openly avowed, and desperately pushed. The Church of England opposed them with the utmost vigour. The Dissenters were cajoled by the court; and they, who had been ready to take arms against King Charles, because he was unwilling to exclude his brother, and who had taken arms against this prince, since he was on the throne, became abetters of his usurpations. It were safe to prove this, even by bishop Burnet's account, as much as that is softened; and if the excuses, which have been made for their silence against popery in this critical moment, or for their approving and encouraging the exercise of a dispensing power, are to be received, one may undertake to excuse, on the same principles of reasoning, all those instances of misconduct in the Church party, which I have presumed to censure so freely. But the truth is, these excuses are frivolous. I could quote some that are even burlesque. Let us reverence truth therefore, and condemn the Dissenters as frankly, on this occasion, as we have condemned the members of the Church of England on others.

The Revolution soon followed. Many of the most distinguished Tories, some of those who carried highest the doctrines of passive-obedience and non-resistance, were engaged in it, and the whole nation was ripe for it. The Whigs were zealous in the same cause; but their zeal was not such as, I think, it had been some years before, a zeal without knowledge: I mean, that it was better tempered, and more prudently conducted. Though the King was not the better for his experience, parties were. Both saw their errors. The Tories stopped short in the pursuit of a bad principle. The Whigs reformed the abuse of a good one. Both had sacrificed their country to their party. Both sacrificed, on this occasion, their party to their country. When the Tories and the Whigs were thus coalited, the latter stood no longer in need of any adventitious help. If they did not refuse the assistance of those, who had weakened their cause more by the jealousies and fears to which they gave both occasion and pretence, than they had strengthened it by their number, yet they suffered them to have no influence in their councils, no direction of their conduct. The cause of liberty was no longer made the cause of a party, by being set on such a bottom, and pushed in such a manner, as one party alone approved. The Revolution was plainly designed to restore and secure our government, ecclesiastical and civil, on true foundations; and whatever might happen to the King, there was no room to suspect any change in the constitution. There were some, indeed, concerned in this great and glorious undertaking, who had obstinately preserved or lightly taken up the republican and other whimsies that reigned in the days of usurpation and confusion. If they could have prevailed, and it was no fault of theirs they did not, the coalition of parties had been broken; and, instead of a Revolution, we might have had a civil war, perhaps, not even that sad chance for our religion and liberty. But this leaven was so near worn out, that it could neither corrupt, nor seem any longer to corrupt the mass of the Whig party. The party never had been Presbyterians, nor republicans, any more than they had been Quakers; any more than the Tory party had been papists, when, notwithstanding their aversion to popery, they were undeniably under the accidental influence of popish counsels. But even the appearances were now rectified. The Revolution was a fire, which purged off the dross of both parties; and the dross being purged off, they appeared to be the same metal, and answered the same standard.

I shall deliver my thoughts, on some other occasion, concerning the disputes that arose about the settlements of the crown after the Revolution; and show, if I do not very much deceive myself, that no argument can be drawn from thence against any thing I have advanced.

I am, sir, &c.

Sir,

The slavish principles of passive obedience and non-resistance, which had skulked perhaps in some old homily before King James the First, but were talked, written and preached into vogue in that inglorious reign, and in those of his three successors, were renounced at the Revolution by the last of the several parties who declared for them. Not only the laity, but the clergy embraced and co-operated in the deliverance which the Prince of Orange brought them. Some of our prelates joined to invite him over. Their brethren refused to sign an abhorrence of this invitation. The University of Oxford offered him their plate, and associated for him against their King. In one word, the conduct of the Tories, at this crisis, was such as might have inclined a man to think they had never held resistance unlawful, but had only differed with the Whigs about the degree of oppression, or of danger, which it was necessary to wait, in order to sanctify resistance. Now, it may appear at first a little strange that these principles, which had always gone hand in hand with those of the divine, hereditary, indefeasible right of kings, that were just as well founded in reason, in support of which the example of the primitive Christians might be pompously cited, and to countenance which some texts to the Bible might be piously strained, should not keep their hold, and maintain their influence, as well as the others.

This attachment to hereditary right will appear the more strange, if we consider what regard was shown, at this time, to the difficulties they who had pawned themselves, as it were, for the principles, would be under, when they came to concur in establishing a settlement repugnant to it. That great and solemn resolution, about the abdication of King James, and the vacancy of the throne, might have been expressed in terms much stronger and plainer than it was.[2] I have heard there were persons who had a mind it should be

---

[1] *Craftsman* 393 (12 January 1734).

[2] During debates in the Convention Parliament of 29–31 January 1689, the Commons moved that James II had 'deserted' the throne by fleeing the country, while the Lords amended the resolution to 'abdicated': at stake was the question of whether the throne was thereby vacant and what power – if any – the Convention had to fill it.

so, and who, more attached to the honour, that is, the humour of party, than to the national interest, in this great event, would have turned this resolution, as well as the declaration of the Prince of Orange, to a more express approbation of the Whig and a more express condemnation of the Tory tenets and conduct. But a wiser and honester consideration prevailed. Instead of erecting the new government on the narrow foundations of party systems, the foundations of it were laid as wide, and made as comprehensible as they could be. No man, I believe, at this time thinks that the vote asserted too little; and surely there was no colour of reason, on the side of those who cavilled against it at that time, for asserting too much.

The disputes about the words abdicate, or desert, and about the vacancy of the throne, were indeed fitter for a school than a house of Parliament, and might have been expected in some assembly of pedants, where young students exercised themselves in disputation, but not in such an august assembly as that of the Lords and Commons, met in solemn conference upon the most important occasion. The truth is, that they who formed the opposition, were reduced to maintain strange paradoxes; stranger, in my opinion, than most of those which cast so much ridicule on the Stoics of old.[3] Thus, for instance, they were forced to admit that an oppressed people might seek their remedy in resistance, for they had sought it there themselves; and yet they opposed making use of the only remedy, which could effectually secure them against returns of the same oppression, when resistance had put it in their power, as oppression had given them a right to use this remedy. Surely this must appear a paradox, and a very absurd one too, if we consider that resistance, in all such cases, is the mean, and future security the end; and that the former is impertinent, nay, wicked in the highest degree, if it be not employed to obtain the latter. Thus again, the same men declared themselves willing to secure the nation against the return of King James to that throne which he had abdicated, or, according to them, deserted: nay, some of them were ready, if we may credit the anecdotes of that time, to proceed to such extreme resolutions, as would have been more effectual than justifiable in the eyes of

---

[3] Compare Bolingbroke's dismissive references to Stoic paradoxes in the *Idea of a Patriot King*, p. 240.

mankind; and yet they could not prevail on their scrupulous consciences to declare the throne vacant. They had concurred in the
vote, that it was 'inconsistent with the laws, liberties and religion
of England to have a papist rule over the kingdom'.[4] King James
had followed the pious example of Sigismond,[5] who, not content to
lose the crown of Sweden himself for his religion, had carried his
son away, that he might be bred a papist, and lost it too; and yet
they maintained, though they did not expressly name him, that if
the throne was then, or should be at any time vacant of the father,
it must be reputed instantaneously full of the son, upon the foundation of this silly axiom, that the king never dies. According to
this law, and these politics, King James and his successors, to the
twentieth generation, might have continued abroad, a race of royal
exiles, preserving their indefeasible right to govern, but debarred
from the exercise of it; whilst the nation continued, during all this
time, from century to century, under the dominion of regents, with
regal authority, but without any regal right: an excellent expedient,
sure to keep the monarchy in an hereditary succession! But there
remained none better, on the principles of these men, since the
Prince of Orange had committed the fatal oversight of neglecting to
conquer the nation.[6] His sword would have cut the gordian knot of
hereditary right, and they could have submitted with safe consciences to a conqueror. But to give the crown to a prince, though
they had put the whole administration into his hands; which, by
the way, was high treason, unless the throne was, what they denied
it to be, actually vacant: to give the crown, I say, to a prince who
would not take it, when it was in his power to take it, without their
consent; to settle a new government by agreement and compact,
when the glorious opportunity of establishing it by force and conquest had been unhappily lost: these were propositions to which they
could not consent. King James had violated the fundamental laws,

[4] On 29 January 1689, the Commons resolved (and the Lords concurred) 'that it
hath been found by experience to be inconsistent with the safety and welfare of
this Protestant kingdom to be governed by a Popish Prince'.

[5] The Catholic King of Lutheran Sweden 1592–99, defeated in battle 1598; deposed
1599; also King of Poland 1587–1632.

[6] Some Tories, like Charles Blount (*King William and Queen Mary Conquerors*
(1693)), did go so far as to argue that William's right rested on the grounds of
conquest in a just war; Burke later concurred in the *Reflections on the Revolution
in France*.

which he had promised over and over, and sworn to maintain. He had shown by his first escape, when nothing was more imposed on him than to wait the resolution of a free Parliament, that he would renounce his crown rather than submit to secure effectually the observation of these laws. He had made a second escape, which was voluntary as well as the first, and made on the same principle, against the entreaties of his friends, and the instigations of the same council that had directed his former conduct, and on a letter from the Queen, claiming his promise to do so. Notwithstanding all these reasons, they who maintained the hereditary right of our kings, reduced themselves, and would have reduced their country, to the absurd necessity of altering their constitution, under pretence of preserving it. No king, except a Stuart, was to reign over us: but we might establish a doge, a lord archon,[7] a regent; and thus these warm assertors of monarchy, refusing to be slaves, contended to be republicans. Many more paradoxes of equal extravagance might be cited, which were advanced directly, or which resulted plainly from the arguments employed on one side of the question in those disputes; but the instances I have cited may suffice for our present purpose, and may serve to show, that although difficulties hard to solve in speculation, or to remove in practice, will arise in the pursuit of the most rational principles, yet such absurdities as these can never arise, except from the most irrational, and always must arise from such.

If the persons who maintained this divine, hereditary, indefeasible right of our kings, had thought fit to drop these principles, when they laid aside those of passive obedience and non-resistance, and no tolerable reason can be given why they did not, their conduct would have been consistent and uniform on this great occasion; and this consistency and uniformity would have been productive of great good, by taking away at once even the appearances of all political division in the bulk of the nation. But whilst they laboured to reconcile their present conduct to their ancient system, they were true to neither. They had gone much farther than this would allow, and then they refused to go as far as the other required, in order to be safe, and therefore in order to be justified. They lost every kind of

[7] The Lord Archon is the ruling magistrate in James Harrington's *Commonwealth of Oceana* (1656).

merit: the chimerical merit of adhering to a set of silly principles, the real merit of sacrificing their prejudices to the complete deliverance of their country from the recent danger of popery and arbitrary power. Nay, they did worse, for the mischievous consequences of their conduct were not hurtful to them alone, and at that time alone, but to the public, and even down to these times. They furnished pretence to factions, who kept up a division under the old names, when the differences were really extinguished by the conduct of both parties, because the conduct of both parties was no longer conformable to the principles imputed to them. The Tories had no longer any pretence of fearing the designs of the Whigs, since the Whigs had sufficiently purged themselves from all suspicion of republican views, by their zeal to continue monarchical government, and of latitudinarian schemes in point of religion, by their ready concurrence in preserving our ecclesiastical establishment, and by their insisting on nothing farther, in favour of the Dissenters, than that indulgence which the Church was most willing to grant. The Whigs had as little pretence of fearing the Tories, since the Tories had purged themselves, in the most signal manner, from all suspicion of favouring popery or arbitrary power, by the vigorous resistance they made to both. They had engaged, they had taken the lead in the Revolution, and they were fully determined against the return of King James. The real essences of Whig and Tory were thus destroyed, but the nominal were preserved, and have done since that time a good part of the mischief which the real did before. The opposition made to the settlement of the crown brought this about. An over-curious enquiry into the motives of this opposition would be a task too invidious for me to undertake. Something however may be said upon it. We may say in general, without offence, that private ambition mingled itself early in the great and national concerns of the Revolution; and that it did so more, as the prospect of a new settlement and of the elevation of the Prince of Orange approached. Expectations were raised, disappointments were given or foreseen, and a variety of motives, of the same kind, began to influence very strongly the conduct of the principal actors. Some endeavoured to lay the foundations of their future fortune by demonstrations of a personal attachment to the Prince, which were carried on, I doubt, a little too independently of the regard due to their country, in some cases; particularly, if I mistake not, in that of the

Declaration of Rights,[8] of which we may pronounce, and experience
will justify us, that it was too loose, too imperfect, and nothing
less than proportionable to the importance of the occasion, and the
favourable circumstances of the conjuncture. Others there were,
who imagined that the shortest and surest way for them to take, in
pursuit of the same view, was to make themselves considerable by
opposition, to form a party, and maintain a struggle for personal
power, under the pretence and umbrage of principle. This was,
without doubt, the motive of some particular leading men, and
could not be, at least at first, the motive of numbers. But there was
another motive, which easily became that of numbers, because it
arose out of a fund common to all men, the perversity of human
nature, according to an observation made in one of these letters.[9]
Whilst the event of the Prince of Orange's expedition was unde-
cided, men remained under the full influence of their fears, which
had determined them to act against their prejudices. But when the
Revolution was secure, and these fears were calmed, these prejudices resumed in some degree their former power, and the more for
being revived and encouraged by men of reputation and authority,
who argued for some, and might as reasonably have argued for all
the errors, in contradiction to which most of them had acted, nay,
and were ready to act. With such views, and by such means, were
many brought, at this time, to entangle themselves in a maze of
inextricable absurdities. Had they owned candidly and fairly that
their principles, as well as those of the Whigs, were carried too high
in the former disputes of parties, and that these principles could
not be true, since they found themselves actually in a situation,
wherein it was not possible to act agreeably to them, without manifest absurdity, the distinction, as well as the difference of Whig and
Tory had been at an end. But contrary measures produced a contrary effect. They kept up the appearances, and they could keep up
no more, of a Whig and a Tory party, and with these appearances
a great part of the old animosity. The two names were sounded
about the nation, and men who saw the same ensigns flying, were

---

[8] The Declaration of Rights (13 February 1689) was incorporated as the preamble
to the Bill of Rights (December 1689); it fulsomely asserted in particular the
confidence of the Lords and Commons that William would 'perfect the deliverance so far advanced by him'.

[9] Letter IV, p. 31.

not wise enough to perceive, or not honest enough to own, that the same cause was no longer concerned, but listed themselves on either side, as their prejudices at first, and their inclinations, or other motives, which arose in the progress of their contests, directed them afterwards: Whigs very often under the Tory standard, Tories very often under the Whig standard.

This general representation, which I have made of the state of parties at the Revolution, is, I am verily persuaded, exactly just; and it might be supported by many particular proofs, which I choose rather to suggest than to mention. But if any doubt remains, let us analyse the several parties of that time a little more, reduce them to their first and real principles, and then pronounce whether we find the Whig or the Tory party subsisting among them.

In the first place, there was a party that concurred in making the new settlement; a party that prevailed in Parliament, and was by much the majority of the nation out of it. Were the Whigs this majority? Was this party a Whig party? No man will presume to affirm so notorious an untruth. The Whigs were far from being this majority, and King James must have died on the throne, if the Tories had not concurred to place the Prince of Orange there in his stead. Was this party a Tory party then? Certainly no. The Whigs had been zealous in the same cause, and had contributed to make it successful by their temper, as well as their zeal, by waiting the time of the Tories, or rather the maturity of the conjuncture, and by moderating their principles and their conduct in favour of that coalition, without which the Revolution could have succeeded no more than the exclusion did. We find then here neither a Whig nor a Tory party; for in coalitions of this kind, where two parties are melted as it were into one, neither of them can be said, with truth and propriety, to exist.

There was another party directly opposite to this; a certain number of men, on whom the original taint transmitted down from King James the First, remained still in the full strength of its malignity. These men adhered to those principles, in the natural sense and full extent of them, which the Tories had professed. But yet, the Tories having renounced these principles, or distinguished themselves out of any obligation to observe them, this inconsiderable faction could not be deemed the Tory party, but received the name of Jacobite with more propriety.

Two other parties there were at this time, formed on one common principle, but widely different however, by the different consequences they drew from it. The principle I mean, is that contained in the distinction of a king *de jure*, and a king *de facto*. The famous statute of Henry the Seventh authorized this distinction.[10] The statute was designed principally, no doubt, for the advantage of the subjects, that they might be safe, whichever side prevailed, in an age when the epidemical folly of fighting for different pretenders had spilt oceans of blood on the scaffold, as well as in the field; and yet the statute was designed for the service of kings *de facto* too, and particularly of Henry the Seventh. The author of *Hereditary Right Asserted*[11] would have us believe otherwise; and yet surely nothing can be more evident than this: that if King Henry the Seventh's right had been as unquestionable as he supposes, and I presume to deny that it was, yet he would have been declared a king *de facto* only, if the intrigues of the Duchess of Burgundy, and the faction of York had succeeded; and consequently this provision for the safety of his adherents, in that possible contingency, gave strength to him, as it would have given strength to any other prince, whilst it attached his adherents to him by the apparent security it provided; for this author contends that it did not establish a real security, and advises us to suspend our judgment on the validity of this statute, till we see what the 'opinion of Parliament or the judges may be, whenever a king *de jure* shall dispossess a king *de facto*'.[12] He refers us *ad Calendas Graecas*.[13]

But there are two observations to be made to our present purpose on this statute, which seem to me natural and plain. First, it confounds in effect the very distinction it seems to make; since it secures alike, and, by securing alike, authorizes alike those who adhere to the king *de jure*, and those who adhere to the king *de facto*, provided they adhere to the king in possession. Secondly, it was contrived to hinder people, according to my lord Bacon's sense

[10] The so-called 'De facto' act (1495), 11 Hen. VII. c. 1, which ensured Yorkist allegiance to Henry VII by protecting allegiance to 'the king for the time being' (i.e. any king before Henry himself, but no king other than Henry) from charges of treason.

[11] [George Harbin,] *The Hereditary Right of the Crown of England Asserted* (London, 1713).

[12] Harbin, *Hereditary Right*, 169–71.

[13] 'At the Greek calends' – i.e. never.

of it, 'from busying themselves in prying into the King's title, and that subjects might not trouble themselves with enquiries into the justness of the King's title or quarrel'.[14] Now, upon the foundations of this distinction and this statute, thus understood, they who demurred on the settlement of the crown at the Revolution, might plausibly, though I think very unreasonably, resolve neither to vote, nor act themselves, against those maxims and principles which they had entertained and professed, as maxims of law, and principles of the constitution, and yet resolve to submit sincerely, and adhere faithfully to a new establishment, when it was once made. But the other of the two parties I mentioned drew from the same principle, of distinguishing between a king *de facto* and a king *de jure*, a very different conclusion. They acknowledged one king, and held their allegiance still due to another. They bound themselves by oath to preserve a settlement which they pretended themselves in conscience obliged to subvert. This was to justify perfidy, to sanctify perjury, to remove the sacred boundaries of right and wrong, and, as far as in them lay, to teach mankind to call good evil, and evil good.

Such were the three divisions into which men broke at the Revolution, in opposing the settlement then made, whilst the great body of the nation concurred in it, and Whig and Tory formed in reality but one party. The first of these divisions continued, and became a faction in the state, but made no proselytes, and is worn out by time. The principle of the second was wrong, but it could not be reputed dangerous whilst it lasted, and it seems to have been built on so narrow and slippery a foundation, that it did not continue long in force. I may be more bold in asserting this, since if we look back to the era of the Revolution, and to the times which followed, we shall find among those who voted for a regent, not a king, on the abdication of King James, some illustrious persons who served King William faithfully, who adhered inviolably to our new establishment, and who have been distinguished friends of the succession that hath now taken place. That there have been persons, who deserved to be ranked under the third head, is too notorious to be denied; but I persuade myself that this division hath consisted

[14] Bacon, *History of Henry VII* in *Opera Omnia*, III, 462 (paraphrased); cit. Harbin, *Hereditary Right*, 171.

always of a flux body. On one hand, it is scarce possible to believe that any number of men should be so hardened, as to avow to themselves, and to one another, the acting and persisting to act on a principle so repugnant to every notion and sentiment that harbour in the breasts of social creatures. On the other, we know how the sallies and transports of party, on some occasions, can hurry even reasonable men to act on the most absurd, and honest men to act on the most unjustifiable principles, or both one and the other on no principle at all, according as the object which the prevailing passion presents to them directs. This hath been the case of many since the Revolution, and there are some of all sides, I believe, still alive, sure I am that there were some a few years ago, who know that no side is absolutely unexceptionable in this respect.

I am, sir, &c.

Sir,

But whatever the state of parties was at the Revolution, and for some time afterwards, the settlement made at that time having continued, that state of parties hath changed gradually, though slowly, and hath received at length, according to the necessary course of things, a total alteration. This alteration would have been sooner wrought, if the attempt I have mentioned, to defend principles no longer defensible, had not furnished the occasion and pretence to keep up the appearances of a Tory and a Whig party. Some of those who had been called Tories furnished this pretence. They who had been called Whigs seized and improved it. The advantages to one side, the disadvantages to the other, the mischiefs to the whole, which have ensued, I need not deduce. It shall suffice to observe, that these appearances were the more easy to be kept up, because several men, who had stood conspicuous in opposition to one another before the Revolution, continued an opposition, though not the same, afterwards. Fresh provocations were daily given, and fresh pretences for division daily taken. These contests were present; they recalled those that had passed in the time of King Charles the Second, and both sides forgot that union which their common danger and their common interest had formed at the Revolution. Old reproaches were renewed, new ones invented, against the party called Whigs, when they were as complaisant to a court as ever the Tories had been; against the party called Tories, when they were as jealous of public liberty and as frugal of public money as ever the Whigs had been. Danger to the Church, on one side, and danger to the state, on the other, were apprehended from men who meant no harm to either; for though Dissenters mingled themselves on one side, and Jacobites on the other, and notwithstanding the leanings of parties in favour of those, by whom they were abetted, yet is it a certain truth, that the struggle was in the main for power, not principle; and that there was no formal design laid on one side to destroy the Church, nor on the other the state. The cavils which may be made, and the facts which may be cited, some of older, and some of fresher date, against what hath been here said, do not escape me.

---

[1] *Craftsman* 394 (19 January 1734).

Men of knowledge, and of cool and candid thought, will answer one, and account for the other, without my help; and I cannot resolve, for the sake of the passionate, nor even of the ignorant, to descend upon this subject into a greater detail.

I pass to that which is closer to my present purpose, and of more immediate use; and I say, that as the natural dispositions of men are altered and formed into different moral characters by education, so the spirit of a constitution of government, which is confirmed, improved and strengthened by the course of events, and especially by those of fruitless opposition, in a long tract of time, will have a proportionable influence on the reasoning, the sentiments, and the conduct of those who are subject to it. A different spirit and contrary prejudices may prevail for a time, but the spirit and principles of the constitution will prevail at last. If one be unnatural, and the other absurd, and that is the case in many governments, a vigorous exercise of power, signal rewards, signal punishments, and a variety of other secondary means, which in such constitutions are never wanting, will however maintain, as long as they are employed, both the spirit and the principles. But if the spirit and principles of a constitution be agreeable to nature and the true ends of government, which is the case of the present constitution of the British government, they want no such means to make them prevail. They not only flourish without them, but they would fade and die away with them. As liberty is nourished and supported by such a spirit and such principles, so they are propagated by liberty. Truth and reason are often able to get the better of authority in particular minds; but truth and reason, with authority on their side, will carry numbers, bear down prejudices, and become the very genius of a people. The progress they make is always sure, but sometimes not observable by every eye. Contrary prejudices may seem to maintain themselves in vigour, and these prejudices may be kept up long by passion and by artifice. But when truth and reason continue to act without restraint, a little sooner or a little later, and often when this turn is least expected, the prejudices vanish at once, and truth and reason triumph without any rival.

The constitution of England had been seen in two very different lights for almost a century before the Revolution; so that there is no room to be surprised at the great opposition that appeared, when the Whig and Tory parties arose a very few years before that era, between principles which, as opposite as they were, each side pretended to establish on the nature of one and the same constitution. How this happened hath been often hinted, and I have not here room to explain any farther. Let us be satisfied that it is no longer the case. Our constitution is no longer a mystery; the power of the crown is now exactly limited, the chimera of prerogative removed, and the rights of the subject are no longer problematical, though some things necessary to the more effectual security of them may be still wanting. Under this constitution the greatest part of the men now alive were born. They lie under no pretence of obligation to any other, and to the support of this they are bound by all the ties of society, and all the motives of interest.

Let us prove what we advance; and that we may do so *ad homines*, let us borrow our argument from the great champion of hereditary right. Having mentioned in his introduction what he endeavours pompously, but vainly, to establish in his book in favour of hereditary right, 'a prescription of nine centuries, a continual claim of five hundred and fifty years', he attempts to convince us by a 'novel law, and a modern constitution'.[2] This modern constitution is the Act of Recognition, in the first of King James the First.[3] The declarations there made in favour of hereditary right, are no doubt as strong as words can frame, and the words are such as would tempt one to think, by the fustian they compose, that his majesty himself had penned them. From hence it is concluded, that since 'the vows and acts of fathers bind their posterity, this act, till the society hath revoked it lawfully, lays the same obligation on every member of the society, as if he had personally consented to it'.[4] – If this Act then was lawfully revoked, or repealed, another novel law, contrary to it, might be made equally binding; but neither this Act, nor the Act of the twelfth of Charles the Second, affirming the crown to appertain by just and undoubted right to the King, his heirs and lawful successors,[5] having been expressly repealed, we still lie under the same obligations, and every settlement, contrary to them, and

[2] Harbin, *Hereditary Right*, 13. For a parallel treatment of the flexibility of hereditary right in English history see Bolingbroke, *Remarks on the History of England*, 'Letter xx'.
[3] The 1604 Act mentioned above, p. 13.
[4] Harbin, *Hereditary Right*, 15.
[5] 'An Act for the Confirmation of Judicial Proceedings' (1660), 12 Car. II, c. 12 § 12 ('Recognition of His Majesty's Title').

by consequence the settlement made at the Revolution, is unlawful. Now I ask, was not the will of Henry the Eighth, which excluded the whole Scottish line, made in pursuance, and by the authority of an Act passed in the twenty-fifth year of his reign?[6] Hath not this author justified the validity of this will much to his own satisfaction, and, I believe, to that of his readers? Was this will lawfully revoked? Was this statute expressly repealed? I ask farther, whether hereditary right, and the obligations of subjects to it, could be made immutable and eternal, as this author asserts that they were by the Act of Recognition, without a manifest contradiction to the Act of Queen Elizabeth, which declares the power of Parliament to limit and bind the succession to the crown?[7] Was this Act expressly repealed? That King James the First succeeded lawfully against law, our author is fond to maintain;[8] and the proposition is not unlike that of some popish casuists, who assert that his holiness *jure potest contra jus decernere*,[9] 'can decree rightfully against right'. But if these questions are fairly answered, it will result from such answers, and from the arguments I have quoted, that this novel law, this modern constitution, is a mere illusion; that it never bound any member of the society; and that the parliament had as much right to make the settlement in 1688, notwithstanding the Act of Recognition, as the parliament had to make this Act in 1603, notwithstanding the two Acts I have mentioned, and the will of Henry the Eighth, made by virtue of the first of them. This wayward and forlorn hereditary right must therefore fall to the ground, or be supported by the supposed prescription of nine centuries, and claim of five and a half, which no intelligent man who reads this book, will be persuaded that the author hath proved a jot better, than the uninterrupted succession of popes, from St Peter down to his present holiness, is proved by the learned antiquaries of Italy. If this Act of Recognition be urged, as it sometimes is, to show the declared sense of the three estates of the kingdom, which declaration was obtained, it seems, in an hurry, since the Act was read three times in one House the same day; the declared sense of the three estates, not pronounced in an hurry, but after the most solemn

---

[6] 'An Act Governing the King's Succession' (1534), 25 Hen. VIII, c. 22.
[7] The second Treasons Act (1571), 13 Eliz. c. 1.
[8] Harbin, *Hereditary Right*, 15, 210, 212.
[9] Source unidentified.

debates and conferences, may be urged with much greater weight, in favour of our present settlement. If this Act of Recognition, notwithstanding what hath been objected, be urged as a law which had the assent of a king, in opposition to the proceedings of the Convention, by which King William and Queen Mary were raised to the throne, the answer is obvious and conclusive. The circumstances of the two cases are very different, but when they come to be weighed in a fair balance, those which attended the settlement of the crown on the Revolution, will be found at least as conformable to reason, to law, and to practice, as those which attended the establishment of the Stuart family. Queen Elizabeth designed King James the First to be her successor; the nation concurred to make him so; neither she nor they paid any regard to the law which stood in his way. Their reasons for acting in this manner are easy to be discovered in the history of that time, and on the same authority we may certainly conclude, that they would not have acted in this manner, if King James had been, like his mother, a professed papist. Thus he got into the throne, and when he was there, he got, like other Kings, such a title as he chose to stand upon, agnized, or recognized by his Parliament. The settlement at the Revolution was made by a convention of the lords spiritual and temporal, and a full and free representative of the whole body of the people. When King William and Queen Mary were once settled in the throne, this settlement was continued and confirmed by an assemblage of all the legislative powers. He who will dispute the validity of these proceedings, must show therefore first of all, what hath never yet been shown, no, not by the author I have so often quoted, the invalidity of the proceedings of those Parliaments, which raised Edward the Third and Henry the Fourth to the throne, which were called as irregularly, though by writs in the names of Edward the Second and Richard the Second,[10] as it can be pretended that the Convention was. He must show the invalidity of the proceedings even of that assembly, by which Charles the Second was called home, till their proceedings became valid by a subsequent confirmation. He must show farther, how any of the laws of the princes of the house of Lancaster came

[10] When Edward II was forced to abdicate in 1327 in favour of his son Edward III, Parliament met to ratify the decision and spread the blame; Henry IV claimed the throne after the deposition of Richard II in 1399, and sought quasi-parliamentary approval.

to be constantly received and executed, a little better than the author of *Hereditary Right Asserted* hath done, by assuring us on his word that it was by the 'sufferance of Edward the Fourth and his successors, and the approbation of the people'.[11] He must account for the continuance in force of the laws of Richard the Third, and of Henry the Seventh, a little better than the same author does, by the deficiency of Henry the Seventh's title, which upon another occasion he magnifies, though upon this he affirms it to have been no better than that of Richard the Third, and by the great respect of Henry the Eighth for his father. When this hath been once shown, it will be time to think of a reply. In the meanwhile we will observe, that besides the passion and party-spirit which possess almost all those who write on this subject, there is a distinction which should be constantly made in cases of this nature, and which they never make, or never make exactly enough. They compare the proceedings without comparing the situation. Necessity and self-preservation are the great laws of nature, and may well dispense with the strict observation of the common forms of any particular constitution. Either the Convention must have fallen into the absurdities I have already mentioned, or have called back King James, which would have been still a greater absurdity, or have left their country in absolute anarchy, or have done what they did. What they did, was done as near as possible to the spirit of our constitution, the forms of our laws, and the examples of former times. They had the merit, their posterity hath the benefit, nay, he who would say that they had the guilt, not the merit, must still allow that their posterity hath the benefit, without sharing the guilt; and, upon the whole matter, I will venture to assert, that he who scruples, or pretends to scruple, at this time, the validity of our present constitution, is no wiser, or else no honester, than he would be, who should scruple, or pretend to scruple, the validity of Magna Carta. I have often wished that some profound antiquary of much leisure, would write an elaborate treatise, to assert royal prerogative against the great charter, as well as hereditary right against the Revolution. I am persuaded that he would succeed alike in both. Why, indeed, should a charter, extorted by force, and therefore vicious in its principle, stand on a better foot, or have more regard paid to it,

[11] Harbin, *Hereditary Right*, 154, 157–8, 159.

than a settlement made in opposition to a divine, and therefore indefeasible right? I say, and therefore indefeasible; because if it be not proved to be something more than human, it will hardly be proved indefeasible. But I quit this subject; upon which, perhaps, you may think I have spent my time as ill, as I should have done if I had preached against the Koran at Paul's.[12] It is time to speak of the motives of interest, by which we are bound, as well as by the ties of duty, to support the present constitution.

Upon this head a few words will be sufficient, since I presume that no prejudices can be strong enough to create much diversity of opinion in a case so very clear, and capable of being stated so shortly. Whether the Revolution altered our old constitution for the better, or renewed it, and brought it back to the first principles, and nearer to the primitive institution, shall not be disputed here. I think the latter, and every man must think that one or the other was necessary, who considers, in the first place, how the majesty and authority of the prince began to swell above any pitch, proportionable to the rank of chief magistrate, or supreme head, in a free state; by how many arts the prerogative of the crown had been stretched, and how many precedents, little favourable to liberty, had been set, even before the accession of the Scottish line; and who considers, in the next place, the direct tendency, confirmed by experience, of those principles of government, so frequently mentioned, which composed an avowed system of tyranny and established slavery as a political, a moral, and a religious obligation, which King James the First was too successful in establishing, but neither he nor his descendants were able to pursue. What these considerations made necessary, was done at the Revolution, at least, so far as to put it into our power to do the rest. A spirit of liberty, transmitted down from our Saxon ancestors, and the unknown ages of our government, preserved itself through one almost continual struggle, against the usurpations of our princes, and the vices of our people; and they, whom neither the Plantagenets nor the Tudors could enslave, were incapable of suffering their rights and privileges to be ravished from them by the Stuarts. They bore with the last king of this unhappy race, till it was shameful, as it must have been fatal, to bear any longer; and whilst they asserted their

---

[12] St Paul's Cathedral.

liberties, they refuted and anticipated, by their temper and their patience, all the objections which foreign and domestic abettors of tyranny are apt to make against the conduct of our nation towards their kings. Let us justify this conduct by persisting in it, and continue to ourselves the peculiar honour of maintaining the freedom of our Gothic institution of government, when so many other nations, who enjoyed the same, have lost theirs.[13]

If a divine, indefeasible, hereditary right to govern a community be once acknowledged; a right independent of the community, and which vests in every successive prince immediately on the death of his predecessor, and previously to any engagement taken on his part towards the people; if the people once acknowledge themselves bound to such princes by the ties of passive obedience and non-resistance, by an allegiance unconditional, and not reciprocal to protection; if a kind of oral law, or mysterious cabbala, which pharisees of the black gown and the long robe are always at hand to report and interpret as a prince desires, be once added, like a supplemental code, to the known laws of the land; then, I say, such princes have the power, if not the right, given them, of commencing tyrants, and princes who have the power, are prone to think that they have the right. Such was the state of King and people before the Revolution. By the Revolution, and the settlement since made, this state hath received considerable alterations. A King of Britain is now, strictly and properly, what kings should always be, a member, but the supreme member, or the head of a political body: part of one individual, specific whole, in every respect, distinct from it, or independent of it in none: he can move no longer in another orbit from his people, and, like some superior planet, attract, repel, influence, and direct their motions by his own. He and they are parts of the same system, intimately joined and co-operating together, acting and acted upon, limiting and limited, controlling and controlled by one another; and when he ceases to stand in this relation to them, he ceases to stand in any. The settlements, by virtue of which he governs, are plainly original contracts. His institution is plainly conditional, and he may forfeit his right to allegiance, as undeniably and effectually, as the subject may forfeit his right to protection.

---

[13] The freedom-loving Gothic nations of northern Europe were supposedly the exporters and planters of mixed constitutions. Bolingbroke treats the Saxon origins of Britain's mixed constitution in *Remarks on the History of England*, 'Letter IV'.

There are no longer any hidden reserves of authority, to be let out on occasion, and to overflow the rights and privileges of the people. The laws of the land are known, and they are the sole springs, from whence the prince can derive his pretensions, and the people theirs. It would be to no purpose to illustrate any farther a matter which begins to be so well understood; or to descend into a more particular enumeration of the advantages that result, or may result, from our present settlement. No man, who does not prefer slavery to liberty, or a more precarious security to a better, will declare for such a government, as our national divisions, and a long course, seldom interrupted, of improvident complaisance to the crown, had enabled King James the Second to establish against such a government as was intended by the subsequent settlement: and if there be any such man, I declare that I neither write to him nor for him.

I may assume therefore, without fearing to be accused of begging the question, that the constitution under which we now live, is preferable to that which prevailed at any time before the Revolution. We are arrived, after many struggles, after a deliverance almost miraculous, and such an one as no nation hath reason to expect twice, and after having made some honest improvements on the advantages of our new constitution, very near to that full security, under which men who are free and solicitous to continue so, may sit down, not without watchfulness, for that is never to be suffered to relax under such a government as ours, but without anxiety. The sum therefore of all these discourses, and of all our exhortations to one another, is, and ought to be, that we should not stop short in so important a work. It was begun at the Revolution; but he who thinks it was perfected then, or hath been perfected since, will find himself very much mistaken. The foundations were laid then. We proceeded for some time after that, like the Jews in rebuilding their temple; we carried on the holy work with one hand, and held our swords in the other to defend it.[14] That distraction, that danger is over, and we betray the cause of liberty without any colour of excuse, if we do not complete the glorious building, which will last to ages yet remote, if it be once finished, and

---

[14] Ezra 1–6; compare Hobbes, *Leviathan*, ch. 30: 'They must do . . . as the Jewes did after their return from captivity, in re-edifying the Temple, build with one hand, and hold the Sword in the other . . .'.

will moulder away and fall into ruins, if it remain longer in this imperfect state.

Now that we may see the better how to proceed in the cause of liberty, to complete the freedom, and to secure the duration of our present constitution, it will be of use, I think, to consider what obstacles lie, or may hereafter lie, in our way, and of what nature that opposition is, or may hereafter be, which we may expect to meet. In order to this, let us once more analyse our political divisions; those which may possibly exist now, or hereafter, as we did those which were formed at the Revolution.

One possible division then is that of men angry with the government, and yet resolved to maintain the constitution. This may be the case at any time; under the present wise, virtuous and triumphant administration, and therefore to be sure at any other.

A second possible division is that of men averse to the government, because they are so to the constitution, which I think can never be the case of many; or averse to the constitution, because they are so to the government, which I think may be the case of more. Both of these tend to the same point. One would subvert the government, that they might change the constitution. The other would sacrifice the constitution, that they might subvert the government.

A third possible division, and I seek no more, is that of men attached to the government; or, to speak more properly, to the persons of those who govern; or, to speak more properly still, to the power, profit, or protection they acquire by the favour of these persons, but enemies to the constitution.

Now, as to the first and second of these possible divisions, if there be any such among us, I do not apprehend that we are at present, or can be hereafter in much danger, or that the cause of liberty can meet with much opposition from them; though the second have certainly views more likely to bring slavery upon us, than to promote liberty; and though prudence requires that we should be on our guard against both. The first, indeed, might hope to unite even the bulk of the nation to them, in a weak and oppressive reign. If grievances should grow intolerable under some prince as yet unborn; if redress should become absolutely desperate; if liberty itself should be in imminent peril; the nature of our constitution would justify the resistance, that we ought to believe well enough of posterity to persuade ourselves would be made in such an exigency. But without such an exigency, particular men would flatter themselves extremely, if they hoped to make the nation angry because they were so. Private motives can never influence numbers. When a nation revolts, the injury is national. This case therefore is remote, improbable, nay, impossible, under the lenity, justice and heroical spirit of the present government; and if I mentioned such an imaginary party, it was only done that I might omit none which can be supposed. The projects of the second division, stated in the same hypothetical manner, are surely too extravagant, and their designs too wicked to be dangerous. Disputes may arise hereafter, in some distant time, about ministers, perhaps about Kings; but I persuade myself that this constitution will be, as it ought to be always, distinguished from, and preferred to both, by the British nation. Reasons must arise in process of time, from the very nature of man, to oppose ministers and Kings too; but none can arise, in the nature of things, to oppose such a constitution as ours. Better ministers, better Kings, may be hereafter often wanted, and sometimes found, but a better constituted government never can. Should there be therefore still any such men as we here suppose, among us, they cannot expect, if they are in their senses, a national concurrence, and surely a little reflection will serve to show them, that the same reasons which make them weaker now than they were some years ago, must make them weaker some years hence than they are now.

As to the third division, if any such there be, it is in that our greatest and almost our whole danger centres. The others cannot overthrow, but these may undermine our liberty. Capable of being admitted into power in all courts, and more likely than other men to be so in every court except the present, whose approved penetration and spotless innocence give a certain exclusion to them, they may prevent any further securities from being procured to liberty, till those already established are dissolved or perverted. Since then our principal danger must in all times arise from those who belong to this division, it is necessary to show, before we conclude these discourses, by what means such men may carry on their pernicious designs with effect, and by what means they may be defeated. These considerations will lead us to fix that point, wherein men of all denominations ought to unite, and do unite, and to state the sole distinction of parties, which can be made with truth at this time amongst us.

I am, sir, &c.

LETTER X[1]

Sir,

It may be asked, perhaps, how men who are friends to a government, can be enemies at the same time to the constitution upon which that government is founded. But the answer will be easy, if we consider these two things: first, the true distinction, so often confounded in writing, and almost always in conversation, between constitution and government. By constitution we mean, whenever we speak with propriety and exactness, that assemblage of laws, institutions and customs, derived from certain fixed principles of reason, directed to certain fixed objects of public good, that compose the general system, according to which the community hath agreed to be governed. By government we mean, whenever we speak in the same manner, that particular tenor of conduct which a chief magistrate, and inferior magistrates under his direction and influence, hold in the administration of public affairs. We call this a good government, when the execution of the laws, the observation of the institutions and customs, in short, the whole administration of public affairs, is wisely pursued, and with a strict conformity to the principles and objects of the constitution. We call it a bad government, when it is administered on other principles, and directed to other objects either wickedly or weakly, either by obtaining new laws, which want this conformity, or by perverting old ones which had it; and when this is done without law, or in open violation of the laws, we term it a tyrannical government. In a word, and to bring this home to our own case, constitution is the rule by which our princes ought to govern at all times; government is that by which they actually do govern at any particular time. One may remain immutable; the other may, and as human nature is constituted, must vary. One is the criterion by which we are to try the other; for surely we have a right to do so, since if we are to live in subjection to the government of our Kings, our Kings are to govern in subjection to the constitution; and the conformity or nonconformity of their government to it, prescribes the measure of our submission to them, according to the principles of the Revolution, and of our present settlement; in both of which, though some

[1] *Craftsman* 395 (26 January 1734).

88

remote regard was had to blood, yet the preservation of the constitution manifestly determined the community to the choice then made of the persons who should govern. Another thing to be considered is this: when persons are spoken of as friends to the government, and enemies to the constitution, the term friendship is a little prostituted, in compliance with common usage. Such men are really incapable of friendship; for real friendship can never exist among those who have banished virtue and truth. They have no affection to any but themselves; no regard to any interest except their own. Their sole attachments are such as I mentioned in the last letter, attachments to power and profit, and when they have contracted a load of infamy and guilt in the pursuit of these, an attachment to that protection, which is sufficient to procure them appearances of consideration, and real impunity. They may bear the semblance of affection to their prince, and of zeal for his government; but they who are false to the cause of their country, will not be true to any other; and the very same minister who exalts his master's throne on the ruins of the constitution, that he may govern without control, or retire without danger, would do the reverse of this, if any turn of affairs enabled him to compound, in that manner, the better for himself.

Under a prince therefore tolerably honest, or tolerably wise, such men as these will have no great sway; at least, they will not hold it long. Such a prince will know, that to unite himself to them, is to disunite himself from his people; and that he makes a stupid bargain, if he prefers trick to policy, expedient to system, and a cabal to the nation. Reason and experience will teach him that a prince who does so, must govern weakly, ignominiously and precariously; whilst he, who engages all the hearts, and employs all the heads and hands of his people, governs with strength, with splendour, and with safety, and is sure of rising to a degree of absolute power, by maintaining liberty, which the most successful tyrant could never reach by imposing slavery. But how few men (and princes, by their leaves, are men) have been found in times past, or can be hoped for in times to come, capable of governing by such arts as these? Some cannot propose the ends, nor some employ the means; for some are wicked, and some are weak. This general division runs through the whole race of mankind, of the multitudes designed to obey, and of the few designed to govern. It was this depravity of multitudes, as well as their mutual wants, which obliged men first to enter into societies, to depart from their natural liberty, and to subject themselves to government. It was this depravity of the few (which is often the greater, because born no better than other men, they are educated worse) which obliged men first to subject government to constitution, that they might preserve social, when they gave up natural liberty, and not be oppressed by arbitrary will. Kings may have preceded lawgivers, for aught I know, or have possibly been the first lawgivers, and government by will have been established before government by constitution. Theseus might reign at Athens, and Eurytion at Sparta, long before Solon gave laws to one, and Lycurgus to the other of these cities.[2] Kings had governed Rome, we know, and consuls had succeeded kings, long before the *decemviri*[3] compiled a body of law; and the Saxons had their monarchs before Edgar,[4] though the Saxon laws went under his name. These, and a thousand other instances of the same kind, will never serve to prove what my lord Bacon would prove by them, [a]"that monarchies do not subsist, like other governments, by a precedent law, or compact; that the original submission to them was natural, like the obedience of a child to his parents; and that allegiance to hereditary monarchs is the work of the law of nature'.[5] But that which these examples prove very plainly is, that however men might submit voluntarily in the primitive simplicity of early ages, or be subjected by conquest to a government without a constitution, yet they were never long in discovering that [b]"to live by one man's will became the cause of all men's misery':[6] and therefore they soon rejected the yoke, or made it sit easy on their necks. They instituted

---

[a] Argum., in the case of Postnati.
[b] Hooker's *Eccles. Pol.* L. I. sect. 10.

[2] Theseus and Eurytion were legendary heroic kings of Athens and Sparta respectively; Solon's laws lasted four hundred years in Athens, Lycurgus' seven hundred in Sparta (all are mentioned in Bacon's speech on the case of the post-nati in Bacon, *Opera Omnia*, IV, 193).
[3] The *decemviri* were the ten magistrates who revised the Roman law code in 451 and 450 BCE.
[4] King Edgar (943–75; ruled 959–75) codified the laws and consolidated the administrative and legal achievements of the earlier Anglo-Saxon kings.
[5] Bacon, *Opera Omnia*, IV, 190–1 (paraphrased).
[6] Richard Hooker, *Of the Laws of Ecclesiastical Polity* (London, 1593), I. 10. 5, also cit. Locke, *Second Treatise*, § 94, note and § 111, note.

commonwealths, or they limited monarchies: and here began that struggle between the spirit of liberty and the spirit of dominion, which always hath subsisted, and, that we may not flatter ourselves nor others, must always subsist, except in those instances, of which the most ancient histories furnish so few, the reigns of a Titus, or a Trajan;[7] for it might look like flattery to quote the present most auspicious reign.

To govern a society of freemen by a constitution founded on the eternal rules of right reason, and directed to promote the happiness of the whole, and of every individual, is the noblest prerogative which can belong to humanity; and if man may be said, without profaneness, to imitate God in any case, this is the case: but sure I am he imitates the devil, who is so far from promoting the happiness of others, that he makes his own happiness to consist in the misery of others; who governs by no rule but that of his passions, whatever appearances he is forced sometimes to put on, who endeavours to corrupt the innocent and to enslave the free, whose business is to seduce or betray, whose pleasure is to damn, and whose triumph is to torment. Odious and execrable as this character is, it is the character of every prince who makes use of his power to subvert, or even to weaken that constitution, which ought to be the rule of his government. When such a prince fills a throne with superior parts, liberty is in the utmost peril; nor does the danger diminish in proportion, if he happens to want them. Such men as we are now to speak of (friends to the government and enemies to the constitution) will be always at hand to supply his defects; for as they are the willing instruments of a wicked prince, they are the ready prompters of a weak one. They may sink into the mass of the people, and disappear in a good and a wise reign, or work themselves into power under false colours. *Sed genus immortale manet.*[8] Their race will continue as long as ambition and avarice prevail in the world, and there will be bad citizens as long as there are bad men. The good ought therefore to be always on their guard against them, and whatever disguise they assume, whatever veils they cast over their conduct, they will never be able to deceive those long, who observe constantly the difference between constitution and

---

[7] Titus was Emperor 79–81 CE; Trajan, 98–117 CE: both were renowned for their virtue.

[8] 'But the immortal race remains': Virgil, *Georgics*, IV. 208.

government, and who have virtue enough to preserve the cause of the former, how unprofitable soever it may be at all times, and how unpopular soever at some. – But I ramble too long in generals. It is high time I should come to those particular measures, by which the men I have described are most likely to carry on their designs against our constitution; after which I shall say something of the methods, by which alone their designs may be prevented, or will be defeated, if a national union oppose itself by such methods as these, in time, to them.

Now that I may do this the better, and make what I have to say the more sensibly felt, give me leave to suppose, though I speak of a remote time, and such an one as we ought to hope will never come, that our national circumstances will be just the same as they are now, and our constitution as far distant as it now is from that point of perfection, to which the Revolution ought to have brought it, might have brought it, and hath given the nation a right to expect that it should be brought. The completion of that glorious deliverance is still imperfect, after five and forty years, notwithstanding the hopes then given, the engagements then taken, and the opportunities that have since arisen. How this hath happened, by what arts this justice to the constitution hath been hitherto evaded, sometimes in favour of one government, and sometimes in favour of another, might easily be shown, and proved too, beyond contradiction. But I had rather exhort than reproach, and especially at a time when a strong tendency appears among men of all denominations to such a national union, as will effectually obtain the complete settlement of our constitution, which hath been so long delayed, if it be honestly, prudently and vigorously improved.

It is certain then, that if ever such men as call themselves friends to the government, but are real enemies of the constitution, prevail, they will make it a capital point of their wicked policy to keep up a standing army. False appearances of reason for it will never be wanting, as long as there are pretenders to the crown; though nothing can be more absurd than to employ, in defence of liberty, an instrument so often employed to destroy it; though nothing can be more absurd than to maintain that any government ought to make use of the same expedient to support itself, as another government, on the ruins of which this government stands, was subverted for using; though nothing can be proved more manifestly by experience than these two propositions: that Britain is enabled, by her situation, to support her government, when the bulk of her people are for it, without employing any means inconsistent with her constitution; and that the bulk of the people are not only always for the government, when the government supports the constitution, but are even hard and slow to be detached from it, when the government attacks or undermines the constitution, and when they are by consequence both justified in resisting, and even obliged in conscience to resist the government.

I have heard it argued lately, that pretenders abroad are a security at home, and that a government exposed to their attacks, will never venture to attack the constitution. I have been told too, that these notions were entertained by some who drew many political consequences from them at the Revolution. But if any of those persons are still alive, I persuade myself that they have altered this opinion, since such a situation will furnish at all times pretences or danger; since pretences of danger to a government, whether real of imaginary, will be always urged with plausibility, and generally with success, for obtaining new powers, or for straining old ones; and since whilst those who mean well to the government, are imposed upon by those who mean ill to the constitution, all true concern for the latter is lost in a mistaken zeal for the former, and the most important is ventured to save the least important, when neither one nor the other would have been exposed, if false alarms had not been rashly and too implicitly taken, or if true alarms had not given unnecessary strength to the government, at the expense of weakening the constitution.

Notwithstanding what hath been said, I do not imagine that an army would be employed by these men, directly and at first, against the nation and national liberty. I am far from thinking that any men can arise in future times, capable of attempting, in this manner, what some men in our age, who call themselves friends to the government, have been so weak and so imprudent as to avow in print, and publish to the nation. To destroy British liberty with an army of Britons, is not a measure so sure of success as some people may believe. To corrupt the Parliament is a slower, but might prove a more effectual method; and two or three hundred mercenaries in the two Houses, if they could be listed there, would be more fatal to the constitution, than ten times as many thousands in red and in blue out of them. Parliaments are the true guardians of liberty. For this principally they were instituted; and this is the principal article of that great and noble trust, which the collective body of the people of Britain reposes in the representative. But then no slavery can be so effectually brought and fixed upon us as parliamentary slavery. By the corruption of Parliament, and the absolute influence of a King, or his minister, on the two Houses, we return into that state, to deliver or secure us from which Parliaments were instituted, and are really governed by the arbitrary will of one man. Our whole constitution is at once dissolved. Many securities to liberty are provided, but the integrity which depends on the freedom and the independency of Parliament, is the key-stone that keeps the whole together. If this be shaken, our constitution totters. If it be quite removed, our constitution falls into ruin. That noble fabric, the pride of Britain, the envy of her neighbours, raised by the labour of so many centuries, repaired at the expense of so many millions, and cemented by such a profusion of blood; that noble fabric, I say, which was able to resist the united efforts of so many races of giants, may be demolished by a race of pigmies. The integrity of Parliament is a kind of Palladium, a tutelary goddess, who protects our state. When she is once removed, we may become the prey of any enemies. No Agamemnon, no Achilles will be wanted to take our city. Thersites himself will be sufficient for such a conquest.[9] But I need not dwell any longer on this subject. There is no man, who thinks at all, can fail to see the several fatal consequences, which will necessarily flow from this one source, whenever it shall be opened. If the reason of the thing does not strike him enough, experience must. The single reign of Henry the Eighth will serve to show, that no tyranny can be more severe than that which is exercised by a concert with Parliament;[10] that arbitrary will may be made the sole rule of government, even whilst the names and forms of a free constitution are preserved; that for a prince, or his minister, to become our tyrant, there is no need to abolish Parliaments; there is no need that he who is master of one part of the legislature, should endeavour

---

[9] Agamemnon, King of Mycenae, led the Greeks at the siege of Troy. Achilles was the greatest warrior, Thersites the most ignoble, of the Greeks during the Trojan war.

[10] In *Remarks on the History of England*, 'Letter XI', Bolingbroke argued that Henry VIII 'establish[ed] tyranny by law' through his influence over Parliament.

to abolish the other two, when he can use, upon every occasion, the united strength of the whole; there is no need he should be a tyrant in the gross, when he can be so in detail, nor in name, when he can be so in effect; that for Parliaments to establish tyranny, there is no need therefore to repeal Magna Carta, or any other of the great supports of our liberty. It is enough, if they put themselves corruptly and servilely under the influence of such a prince, or such a minister. – On the whole, I conclude, that in the possible case here supposed, the first and principal object will be to destroy the constitution, under pretence of preserving the government, by corrupting our Parliaments. I am the better founded in concluding that this may happen in some future age, by what we may observe in our own. There is surely but too much reason to suspect that the enemies of our constitution may attempt hereafter to govern by corruption, when we hear and see the friends and advocates of our present most incorrupt minister harangue and scribble in favour of corruption; when it is pleaded for and recommended, as a necessary expedient of government, by some men, of all ranks and orders; not only by professed hirelings, who write that they may eat, but by men who have talked and written themselves already out of their native obscurity and penury, by affecting zeal in the cause of liberty: not only by such as these, but by men whose birth, education and fortune aggravate their crime and their folly; by men, whom honour at least should restrain from favouring so dishonourable a cause; and by men, whose peculiar obligations to preach up morality, should restrain them, at least, from being the preachers of an immorality, above all others, abominable in its nature, and pernicious in its effects.

These men are ready, I know, to tell us, that the influence they plead for is necessary to strengthen the hands of those who govern; that corruption serves to oil the wheels of government, and to render the administration more smooth and easy; and that it can never be of dangerous consequence under the present father of our country.[11] – Absurd and wicked trifters! 'According to them, our excellent constitution' (as one of your correspondents hath observed extremely well) 'is no better than a jumble of incompatible powers,

---

[11] An argument most famously made (in direct response to Bolingbroke) in David Hume, 'Of the Independency of Parliament' (1741).

which would separate and fall to pieces of themselves, unless restrained and upheld by such honourable methods as those of bribery and corruption.' They would prove, 'that the form of our government is defective to a degree of ridiculousness'.[12] But the ridicule, as well as the iniquity, is their own. A good government can want no power, under the present constitution. A bad one may, and it is fit it should. Popularity is the expedient of one, and will effectually support it. Nothing but corruption can support the other. If there was a real deficiency of power in the crown, it ought to be supplied, no doubt. The old whimsies of prerogative should not be revived; but limitations ought to be taken off, or new powers to be given. The friends of liberty acknowledge that a balance of the powers, divided among the three parts of the legislature, is essential to our constitution, and necessary to support it. The friends of liberty therefore would concur, at least to a certain point, with the friends of the ministry; for the former are friends to order, and enemies to licence. For decency's sake, therefore, let the debate be put on this issue. Let it be such a debate as freemen may avow without blushing. To argue from this supposed deficiency of power in the crown, in favour of a scheme of government repugnant to all laws divine and human, is such an instance of abandoned, villainous prostitution, as the most corrupt ages never saw, and as will place the present age, with infamous, pre-eminence, at the head of them, unless the nation do itself justice, and fix the brand on those who ought to bear it. – Thus much for the iniquity of the practice pleaded for. As to the danger of it, let us agree that a prince of such magnanimity and justice as our present monarch, can never be tempted by any sordid motives to forget the recent obligation which he and his family have to the British nation, by whom they were made kings; nor to aim at greater power and wealth than are consistent with the safety of the constitution they are entrusted to preserve, and obliged to secure. Allowing this to be our present case (and concerning our present case, there are not two opinions, I dare say, in the whole nation), yet still the symptoms I have mentioned, show that the poison, with which these pretended friends of the government, and real enemies of the constitution, corrupt the morals of mankind, hath made some progress; and if this progress

[12] *Craftsman* 375 (8 September 1733).

be not immediately checked by proper antidotes, and the power of poisoning taken from these empirics, the disease will grow incurable. The last dismal effect of it may not, or if you please, cannot happen in this reign; but it may, nay it must happen in some other, unless we prevent it effectually and soon: and what season more proper to prevent it in, and to complete the security of our liberties, than the reign of a prince, for whom the nation hath done so much, and from whom, by consequence, the nation hath a right to expect so much? King William delivered us from popery and slavery. There was wisdom in his councils, and fortitude in his conduct. He steered through many real difficulties at home, and he fought our battles abroad; and yet those points of security, which had been neglected, or not sufficiently provided for in the honeymoon of his accession, were continually pressed upon him, during the whole course of his reign. The men who pressed them were called Jacobites, Tories, republicans, and incendiaries too; not from the throne indeed, but by the clamour of those, who showed great indifference at least for the constitution, whilst they affected great zeal for the government. They succeeded however in part, and we enjoy the benefit of their success. If they did not succeed in the whole; if the settlement necessary to secure our liberty, and therefore intended at the Revolution, be not yet complete, let us be persuaded, and let us act on that persuasion, that the honour of completing it was reserved to crown the glories of the present reign. To finish the great work, which King William began, of establishing the liberties of Britain on firm and durable foundations, must be reputed an honour surely; and to whom can this honour belong more justly than to a prince, who emulates, in so remarkable a manner, all the other heroic virtues of his renowned predecessor?

I am, sir, &c.

Sir,

If it was possible for any man, who hath the least knowledge of our constitution, to doubt in good earnest whether the preservation of public freedom depends on the preservation of parliamentary freedom, his doubts might be removed, and his opinions decided, one would imagine, by this single, obvious remark, that all the designs of our princes against liberty, since Parliaments began to be established on the model still subsisting, have been directed constantly to one of these two points, either to obtain such Parliaments as they could govern, or else to stand all the difficulties, and to run all the hazards of governing without Parliaments. The means principally employed to the first of these purposes, have been undue influences on the elections of members of the House of Commons, and on these members when chosen. When such influences could be employed successfully, they have answered all the ends of arbitrary will; and when they could not be so employed, arbitrary will hath been forced to submit to the constitution. This hath been the case, not only since, but before that great change in the balance of property, which began in the reigns of Henry the Seventh, and Henry the Eighth, and carried a great part of that weight into the scale of the commons, which had lain before in the scale of the peers and clergy.[2]

If we look back as far as the close of the fourteenth century, an era pretty near to that when Parliaments received their present form, we shall find both these means employed by one of the worst of our kings, Richard the Second. That he might obtain his will, which was rash, he directed mandates to his sheriffs (officers of the crown, and appointed by the crown; for such they were then, and such they still are) to return certain persons nominated by himself: and thus he acquired an undue influence over the elections. In the next

---

[1] Published separately as *The Craftsman Extraordinary; Or, The Late Dissertation on Parties Continued; In Which the Right of the People to Frequent Elections of their Representatives is Fully Considered* (London, 1734).

[2] Since Harrington's *Oceana*, it had been a commonplace that Henry VII's taming of the barons and the redistribution of property after Henry VIII's dissolution of the monasteries had together effected an irreversible shift in England's balance of power, towards the commons and away from the nobility and clergy; compare 'Letter XVI', p. 155.

place, he obliged the persons thus returned, sometimes by threats and terror, and sometimes by gifts, to consent to those things which were prejudicial to the realm: and thus he acquired an undue influence over the House of Commons.[3] So that, upon the whole, the arbitrary will of a rash, headstrong prince, and the suggestions of his wicked ministers, guided the proceedings of Parliament, and became the law of the land. I might pursue observations of the same kind through several succeeding reigns; but to avoid lengthening these letters, which are grown perhaps too long already, let us descend at once to the reign of King Charles the Second, for in that we shall find examples of all the means which a court that hath common sense, and a prince who will not set his crown on the cast of a die, can take to undermine the foundations of liberty, either by governing Parliaments, or by governing without them.

Now the first attempt of this kind, which King Charles made against the constitution, was this: he improved and managed the spirit of the first Parliament he called, so as to render the two houses obsequious to his will, almost in every case; and having got the triennial bill repealed,[4] he kept the same Parliament in being for many years by prorogations, which crept into custom long before his time, but were still a modern invention with respect to the primitive institution of Parliaments, and wholly repugnant to the ancient practice. Thus he established a standing Parliament, which is, in the nature of it, as dangerous as a standing army, and may become, in some conjunctures, much more fatal to liberty. When the measures of his administration grew too bad, and the tendency of them too apparent to be defended and supported, even in that parliament, and even by a party-spirit, he had recourse to a second attempt, that is, to corruption; and Clifford first lifted a mercenary band of friends to the government against the constitution. – Let us observe on this occasion, and as we pass along, that a national party, such a party as the court adopts, in contradistinction to such a party as it creates, will always retain some national principles, some regard to the constitution. They may be transported, or surprised, during the heat of contest especially, into measures of long

---

[3] See Bolingbroke, *Remarks on the History of England*, 'Letter vi', where Richard II also becomes an antetype of Charles II, ruling tyrannically, manipulating his parliaments, and in thrall to the French.
[4] The 1641 Triennial Act was repealed by the Cavalier Parliament in April 1664.

A Dissertation upon Parties

and fatal consequence. They may be carried on, for a certain time and to a certain point, by the lusts of vengeance and of power, in order to wreak one upon their adversaries, and to secure the other to themselves. But a national party will never be the instruments of completing national ruin. They will become the adversaries of their friends, and the friends of their adversaries, to prevent it; and the minister who persists in so villainous a project, by what name soever he may affect to distinguish himself and his followers, will be found really at the head of a faction, not of a party. But the difference between one and the other is so visible, and the boundaries where party ceases and faction commences, are so strongly marked, that it is sufficient to point at them.

I return therefore, and observe that when the spirit of party failed King Charles, and the corruption he employed proved ineffectual, he resolved to govern for a time without Parliaments, and to employ that time, as soon as he had checked the spirit of one party, by inflaming that of another, in garbling corporations. He had found by experience, that it was impossible to corrupt the stream in any great degree, as long as the fountain continued pure. He applied himself therefore to spread the taint of the court in them, and to poison those springs, from whence the health and vigour of the constitution flow. This was the third, the last, and by much the most dangerous expedient employed by the friends of the government, in the reign of King Charles the Second, to undermine our liberties. The effect of it he did not live to see, but we may easily conjecture what it would have been.

The use I make of what hath been here said is this: the design of the Revolution being not only to save us from the immediate attempts on our religion and liberty, made by King James, but to save us from all other attempts which had been made, or might be made, of the same tendency; to renew and strengthen our constitution; [a]"to establish the peace, honour and happiness of these nations upon lasting foundations, – and to procure a settlement of the religion, and of the liberties and properties of the subjects, upon so sure a foundation, that there might be no danger of the nation's relapsing into the like miseries at any time hereafter'.[5] This being,

[a] See the Prince of Orange's *Declaration*.

[5] [Gilbert Burnet,] *The Declaration of His Highnes William Henry, ... Prince of Orange, &c., Of the Reasons Inducing Him, to Appear in Armes in the Kingdome of England* (The Hague, 1688), 8.

I say, the avowed design of the Revolution, and the nation having engaged in it on a confidence that all this would be effectually performed, the design of the Revolution was not accomplished, the benefit of it was not secured to us, the just expectations of the nation could not be answered, unless the freedom of elections, and the frequency, integrity and independency of Parliaments were sufficiently provided for. These are the essentials of British liberty. Defects in other parts of the constitution can never be fatal, if these are preserved entire. But defects in these will soon destroy the constitution, though every other part of it should be so preserved. However it happened, the truth and notoriety of the fact oblige us to say, that these important conditions, without which liberty can never be secure, were almost wholly neglected at the Revolution. The Claim of Right declares, indeed, that 'elections ought to be free; that freedom of speech and debates ought not to be impeached or questioned out of parliament; and that parliaments ought to be held frequently'.[6] But such declarations, however solemnly made, are nothing better than pompous trifles, if they stand alone; productive of no good; and thus far productive of ill, that they serve to amuse mankind in points of the greatest importance, and wherein it concerns them the most nearly neither to be deceived, nor so much as amused. These were rights, no doubt, to which the nation had an indisputable claim. But then they ought to have been more than claimed, since they had been so often and so lately invaded. That they were not more than claimed, that they were not effectually asserted and secured, at this time, gave very great and immediate dissatisfaction; and they who were called Whigs in those days, distinguished themselves by the loudness of their complaints. Thus for instance, they insisted that there could be no [b]"real settlement; nay, that it was a jest to talk of a settlement, till the manner and time of calling Parliaments, and their fitting when called, were fully determined': and this in order to prevent the practice of

[b] See *Considerations Concerning the State of the Nation*, by Mr Hampden, published in 1692.[7]

[6] The Claim of Right of the Scots Parliament (11 April 1689) was more radical than the English Declaration of Rights, both in its indictment of James and in the demands made of William.
[7] John Hampden, *Some Short Considerations Concerning the State of the Nation* (1692) in *A Collection of State Tracts Publish'd During the Reign of King William III* (3 vols., London, 1705–7), II, 325 (misquoted).

'keeping one and the same Parliament so long on foot, till the majority was corrupted by offices, gifts and pensions'. They insisted that the assurances given at the Revolution had led them to think, that "the ancient, legal course of annually chosen parliaments would have been immediately restored';[8] and the Particular circumstances of King William, who had received the crown by gift of the people, and who had renewed the original contract with the people, which are precisely the circumstances of the present royal family, were urged as particular reasons for the nation to expect his compliance.

The frequent sitting of Parliament was indeed provided for, indirectly and in consequence, by the exigencies of the war, which soon followed the Revolution. This war made annual supplies necessary; and, before it was over, the same necessity of annual sessions of Parliament came to be established, as it continues to this hour, by the great alteration made with relation to the public revenue. The whole public revenue had been the King's formerly. Parliamentary aids were, in those days, extraordinary and occasional; and things came to that pass at last, that Parliaments were more frequently, or more rarely convened, just as courts had more frequent or more rare occasions for such supplies. But King William began to be, and all our princes since him have continued to be, only proprietors for life of that part of the public revenue, which is appropriated to their civil list;[9] although they are entrusted still with the management of the whole, and are even the stewards of the public creditors for that part which is the private property of these creditors. This is the present state, sufficiently known, but necessary to be mentioned particularly on this occasion: and this must continue to be the state, unless some prince should arise hereafter, who, being advised by a desperate minister, abetted by a mercenary faction, supported by a standing army, and instigated, like Richard

---

[c] *An Enquiry, or a Discourse, &c.* published in 1693.

[8] [John Hampden and John Wildman,] *An Enquiry, or a Discourse Between a Yeoman of Kent and a Knight of the Shire, upon the Prorogation of the Parliament to the 2d of May 1693* (1693) in *Collection of State Tracts*, II, 331.
[9] Under the provisions of the Civil List Act (1698), the King received £700,000 p.a. (later increased) for life to pay for the royal household and family, and to cover the costs of civil government.

the Second, by the [d]"rashness of his own temper', may lay rapacious hands on all the funds that have been created, and by applying illegally what he may raise legally, convert the whole to his own use, and so establish arbitrary power, by depriving at one stroke many of his subjects of their property, and all of them of their liberty. Till this happens (and heaven forbid that it should be ever attempted) sessions of Parliament must be annually held, or the government itself be distressed. But neither is this such a direct and full security as the importance of the thing requires; nor does the security of our liberty consist only in frequent sessions of Parliaments, but it consists likewise in frequent new Parliaments. Nay, it consists so much more in this than in the other, that the former may tend without the latter, even more than the discontinuance of Parliaments, to the loss of liberty. This was foreseen by the wisdom of our constitution. According to that, although it became in time, by the course of events, and insensible alterations, no longer necessary to call Parliaments once, or even twice in a year, which had been the more ancient practice, yet still our kings continued under an incapacity of proceeding long in government, with any tolerable ease and safety to themselves, without the concurrence and assistance of these assemblies. According to the same constitution, as Parliaments were to be held, so they were to be chosen frequently; and the opinion, that the 'holding and continuance of Parliaments depended absolutely on the will of the prince',[10] may be justly ranked amongst those attempts, that were made by some men to set the law, whilst others endeavoured to set the gospel, on the side of arbitrary power. This is the plain intent and scheme of our constitution, which provides that the representatives of the people should have frequent opportunities to communicate together about national grievances; to complain of them, and to obtain the redress of them, in an orderly, solemn, legal manner; and that the people should have frequent opportunities of calling their representatives to account, as it were, for the discharge of the trust committed to them, and of approving or disapproving their conduct, by electing or not electing

---

[d] 'Per immoderatam voluntatem'.

[10] Source unidentified. On the prerogative power of calling and dissolving Parliaments see Locke, *Second Treatise*, §§ 156, 167, 215.

them anew. Thus our constitution supposes that princes may abuse their power, and Parliaments betray their trust; and provides, as far as human wisdom can provide, that neither one nor the other may be able to do so long, without a sufficient control. If the crown, indeed, persists in usurping on the liberty of the people, or in any other kind of maladministration; and if the prince who wears it proves deaf, as our princes have sometimes been, to the voice of his Parliament and his people, there remains no remedy in the system of the constitution. The constitution is broken by the obstinacy of the prince, and the ᶜ"people must appeal to heaven in this, as in all other cases, where they have no judge on earth'.[11] Thus if a Parliament should persist in abetting maladministration, or any way give up those liberties which they were entrusted to maintain, no doubt can be made but that the people would be in the same case; since their representatives have no more right to betray them, than their kings have to usurp upon them: and by consequence they would acquire the same right of appealing to heaven, if our constitution had not provided a remedy against this evil, which could not be provided against the other; but our constitution hath provided such a remedy in the frequent succession of new Parliaments, by which there is not time sufficient given, to form a majority of the representatives of the people into a ministerial cabal; or by which, if this should happen, such a cabal must be soon broken. These reflections, and such others as they naturally suggest, are sufficient to convince any thinking man, first, that nothing could make it safe, nor therefore reasonable, to repose in any set of men whatsoever, so great a trust as the collective body delegates to the representative in this kingdom, except the shortness of the term for which this trust is delegated. Secondly, that every prolongation of this term is therefore, in its degree, unsafe for the people; that it weakens their security, and endangers liberty by the very powers given for its preservation. Thirdly, that such prolongations expose the nation, in the possible case of having a corrupt Parliament, to lose the great advantage which our constitution hath provided, of curing the evil, before

ᶜ Locke's *Essay upon Government*, chap. 14.

[11] Locke, *Second Treatise*, § 168: 'The People have no other remedy in this, as in all other cases where they have no Judge on Earth, but to *appeal to Heaven*.'

it grows confirmed and desperate, by the gentle method of choosing
a new representative, and reduce the nation, by consequence, to
have no other alternative than that of submitting or resisting;
though submission will be as grievous, and resistance much more
difficult, when the legislature betrays its trust, than when the king
alone abuses his power. – These reflections, I say, are sufficient to
prove these propositions; and these propositions set before us, in a
very strong light, the necessity of using our utmost efforts that the
true design of our constitution may be pursued as closely as possible, by the reestablishment of annual, or at least of triennial Parliaments.[12] But the importance of the matter, and the particular
seasonableness of the conjuncture, invite me to offer one consideration more upon this head, which I think will not strike the less for
being obvious and plain. It is this. Should a King obtain, for many
years at once, the supplies and powers which used to be granted
annually to him; this would be deemed, I presume, even in the
present age, an unjustifiable measure and an intolerable grievance,
for this plain reason: because it would alter our constitution in the
fundamental article, that requires frequent assemblies of the whole
legislature, in order to assist, and control too, the executive power
which is entrusted with one part of it. Now I ask, is not the article
which requires frequent elections of the representative, by the collective body of the people, in order to secure the latter against the
ill consequences of the possible weakness or corruption of the
former, as fundamental an article, and as essential to the preservation of our liberties as the other? No man dares say that it is not;
at least, no man who deserves our attention. The people of Britain
have as good a right, and a right as necessary to be asserted, to keep
their representatives true to the trust reposed in them, and to the
preservation of the constitution, by the control of frequent elections,
as they have to keep their kings true to the trust reposed in them,
and to the preservation of the constitution, by the control of frequent sittings of Parliament. How comes it then to pass, that we
may observe so great a difference in the sentiments of mankind,
about these two cases? Propose the first, there is no servile friend
of government, who will not affect all that horror at the proposition,

---

[12] By the Septennial Act (1716) the length of Parliaments was extended to seven
years from the three which had obtained since the Triennial Act (1694), subject
to the royal prerogative of prior dissolution.

which every friend of the constitution will really feel. Propose the keeping up septennial, nay, the making decennial Parliaments, the same friends of government will contend strenuously for one, and by consequence for both; since there can be no reason alleged for the first, which is not stronger for the last, and would not be still stronger for a longer term. These reasons, drawn from two or three commonplace topics of pretended conveniency and expediency, or of supposed tranquillity at home, and strength abroad, I need not mention.[13] They have been mentioned by others, and sufficiently refuted. But that which may very justly appear marvellous, is this: that some men, I think not many, who are true friends of the constitution, have been staggered in their opinions, and almost seduced by the false reasonings of these friends of government; though nothing can be more easy than to show, from reason and experience, that convenience, expediency, and domestic tranquillity may be, and in fact have been as well, nay, better secured under triennial, nay, annual Parliaments, than under Parliaments of a longer continuance; and as for strength abroad, that is, national credit and influence, it will depend on the opinion foreign nations have of our national dispositions, and the unanimity of our sentiments. It must be chiefly determined therefore by their knowledge of the real sense of the nation. Now that can appear no way so much as in the natural state of our constitution, by frequent elections; and when it does appear so, it must have another kind of effect than the bare resolutions of a stale, ministerial Parliament, especially if it happens, as it may happen in some future time, that the sense of the nation should appear to be different from the sense of such a Parliament, and that the resolutions of such a Parliament should be avowedly dictated by men, odious and hated, contemptible and contemned both at home and abroad.

But in the supposition that some inconveniencies may arise by frequent elections, which is only allowed for argument's sake, are such inconveniencies, and the trifling consequences of them, to be set in the balance against the danger of weakening any one barrier

[13] The Septennial Act was justified in the wake of the 1715 Jacobite rising on the grounds that, 'a restless and popish faction . . . endeavouring to renew a rebellion within this Kingdom, and an invasion from abroad', triennial Parliaments would 'be destructive to the peace and security of the government' (1 George I, Stat. 2, c. 38).

of our liberty? Every form of government hath advantages and disadvantages peculiar to it. Thus absolute monarchies seem most formed for sudden and vigorous efforts of power, either in attracting or in defending, whilst, in free constitutions, the forms of government must be necessarily more complicated and slow; so that in these, the same secrecy cannot be always kept, nor the same dispatch always made, nor the same steadiness of measures always pursued. Must all these forms, instituted to preserve the checks and controls of the several parts of the constitution on one another, and necessary by consequence to preserve the liberty of the whole, be abandoned therefore, and a free constitution be destroyed, for the sake of some little conveniency or expediency the more in the administration of public affairs? No certainly. We must keep our free constitution, with the small defects belonging to it, or we must change it for an arbitrary government, free perhaps from these defects, but liable to more and to worse. In short, we must make our option; and surely this option is not hard to be made, between the real and permanent blessings of liberty, diffused through a whole nation, and the fantastic and accidental advantages which they who govern, not the body of the people, enjoy under absolute monarchies. I will not multiply instances, though they crowd in upon me. – Two consuls were chosen annually at Rome, and the proconsular power in the government of provinces was limited to a year. Several inconveniencies arose, no doubt, from the strict observation of this institution. Some appear very plain in history: and we may assure ourselves, that many arguments of conveniency, of expediency, of preserving the tranquillity of the city, and of giving strength and weight to the arms and counsels of the commonwealth, were urged to prevail on the people to dispense with these institutions, in favour of Pompey and of Caesar.[14] What was the consequence? The pirates were extirpated, the price of corn was reduced, Spain was held in subjection, Gaul was conquered, the Germans were repulsed, Rome triumphed, her government flourished; but her constitution was destroyed, her liberty was lost. – The law of Habeas Corpus, that noble badge of liberty, which every subject of Britain wears, and by which he is distinguished so eminently, not

---

[14] Pompey made a coalition with Caesar and Crassus to form the first triumvirate in 60 BCE, though rivalry between him and Caesar led to civil war in 49 BCE and (as later republicans often recalled) hastened the collapse of the Roman Republic.

from the slaves alone, but even from the freemen of other countries; the law of Habeas Corpus, I say, may be attended perhaps with some little inconveniencies, in time of sedition and rebellion. – The slow methods of giving money, and the strict appropriations of it, when given, may be attended with some inconveniency likewise, in times of danger, and in great exigencies of the state. – But who will plead for the repeal of the Habeas Corpus Act; or who would not press for the revival of it, if it stood suspended for an indefinite, or even a long term? – Who will say that the practice of giving money without account, or passing votes of credit, by which the purse of the people is taken out of the hands of those whom the people trusted, and put into the hands of those whom they neither did, nor would have trusted; who will say that such a deviation from those rules of Parliament, which ought to be deemed sacred and preserved inviolate, may be established, or should not be opposed by all possible means, if it was established?

If all this be as clear as I imagine it is; if the objections to frequent elections of Parliaments do not lie; or, supposing them to lie, if the danger on one side outweighs vastly the supposed inconveniency on the other; nay, if laws and institutions, not more essential to the preservation of liberty than this ancient and fundamental rule of our constitution, be maintained; and if all men are forced to agree, even they, who wish them perhaps abolished, that they ought to be maintained, for the sake of preserving liberty; let me ask again, how comes it to pass, that we observe so great a difference between the sentiments and reasonings of mankind about frequent sessions of Parliament, and frequent Parliaments; about the case now before us, and all the others that have been mentioned? The only manner, in which I can account for such an inconsistency, is this. The sight of the mind differs very much from the sight of the body, and its operations are frequently the reverse of the other. Objects at a distance appear to the former in their true magnitude, and diminish as they are brought nearer. The event, that created much astonishment, indignation, or terror in prospect, creates less and less as it approaches, and by the time it happens, men have familiarized themselves with it. – If the Romans had been told, in the days of Augustus, that an emperor would succeed, in whose reign an horse should be made consul, they would have been extremely surprised. I believe they were not so much surprised when the thing happened,

when the horse was consul and Caligula emperor.[15] – If it had been
foretold to those patriots at the Revolution, who remembered long
Parliaments, who still felt the smart of them, who struggled hard
for annual, and obtained with much difficulty, at the end of five or
six years, triennial Parliaments, that a time would come, when even
the term of triennial Parliaments would be deemed too short, and a
parliament chosen for three years, would choose itself for four more,
and entail septennial Parliaments on the nation; that this would
happen, and the fruits of their honest labours be lost, in little more
than twenty years; and that it would be brought about, whilst our
government continued on the foundations they had then so newly
laid: if all this had been foretold at the time I mention, it would
have appeared improbable and monstrous to the friends of the Revolution. Yet it hath happened; and in less than twenty years, it is
grown, or is growing, familiar to us. The uniform zeal and complaisance of our Parliaments for the crown, leave little room to
apprehend any attempt to govern without them, or to make them
do in one session the work of seven; though this would be extremely
convenient, no doubt, a great case to future ministers, and a great
saving of expense and time to country gentlemen. But suppose, for
I desire it may be remembered that we reason hypothetically, suppose a Parliament should think fit to give, in the first session, all
the money, all the credit, and all the powers necessary for carrying
on the government, during seven years; and then let those persons,
who will be shocked at this supposition, and yet declare themselves
for septennial parliaments, lay their hands on their hearts, and consider whether such an alteration of the constitution might not grow
familiar to them, and even gain their approbation. I think it would
do so. I am sure it might as reasonably as the other. They would
find the case, in one case, of little attendance, as much as that of
distant elections in the other. The arguments of conveniency,
expediency, public tranquillity, and strength to the government,
would be just as well applied; and if the ministers should, by miracle, make no very exorbitant ill use of such a situation, I doubt
whether he who should plead for annual parliaments then, would
be much better heard by the same persons, than he who pleads for

---

[15] Not all sources agree that Caligula did in fact raise his favourite horse, Incitatus,
to the consulship (though see Suetonius, *Lives of the Caesars*, IV. 55).

frequent elections of Parliaments is now. But let not the lovers of liberty, the friends of our constitution, reason in this manner. Let them remember that danger commences when the breach is made, not when the attack is begun; that he who neglects to stop the leak as soon as it is discovered, in hopes to save his ship by pumping, when the water gushes in with violence, deserves to be drowned; and, to lay aside figures of speech, that our constitution is not, like the schemes of some politicians, a jumble of disjointed, incoherent whimsies, but a noble and wise system, the essential parts of which are so proportioned, and so intimately connected, that a change in one begets a change in the whole; that the frequent elections of Parliament are as much an essential part of this system, as the frequent sittings of Parliament; that the work of the Revolution is imperfect therefore, and our future security precarious, unless our ancient constitution be restored, in this essential part; and that the restoration of it, in this part, is one of those methods, by which alone the pernicious designs of such men as we have mentioned in a former letter,[16] if any such should be ever admitted into power (enemies to the constitution, under the mask of zeal for the government) may be defeated.

I am, sir, &c.

---

[16] 'Letter IX', p. 76.

Sir,

We have observed already, that the constitution of the British government supposes our Kings may abuse their power, and our representatives betray their trust, and provides against both these contingencies, as well as human wisdom can provide. Here let us observe, that the same constitution is very far from supposing the people will ever betray themselves; and yet this case is possible, no doubt. We do not read, I think of more than [a]one nation, who refused liberty when it was offered to them; but we read of many, and have almost seen some, who lost it through their own fault, by the plain and necessary consequences of their own conduct, when they were in full possession of it, and had the means of securing it effectually in their power. A wise and brave people will neither be cozened, nor bullied out of their liberty; but a wise and brave people may cease to be such: they may degenerate; they may sink into sloth and luxury; they may resign themselves to a treacherous conduct; or abet the enemies of the constitution, under a notion of supporting the friends of the government: they may want the sense to discern their danger in time, or the courage to resist, when it stares them in the face. The Tarquins were expelled, and Rome resumed her liberty. Caesar was murdered, and all his race extinct, but Rome remained in bondage. From whence this difference? [b]Machiavel shall account for it. In the days of Tarquin the people of Rome were not yet corrupted. In the days of Caesar they were most corrupt.[2] A free people may be sometimes betrayed; but no people will betray themselves, and sacrifice their liberty, unless they fall into a state of universal corruption: and when they are once fallen into such a

---

[a] The Cappadocians, vid. Strabo, Lib. 12 – 'Libertatem repudiaverunt, ut quam sibi dicerent intolerabilem.'[3]
[b] *Discourses*, Lib. I. c. 17.

---

[1] *Craftsman* 436 (9 November 1734).
[2] Machiavelli, *Discorsi*, I. 17, deals with the difficulty of restoring virtue once a people has regained freedom from the corrupt rule of princes.
[3] '... [the Cappadocians] refused liberty for they said it was unbearable' (when offered it by the Romans, who had ruled Cappadocia through puppet kings until the royal line was extinguished): Strabo, *Geography*, XII. 2. 11 (see also *Remarks on the History of England*, 'Letter II').

state, they will be sure to lose what they deserve no longer to enjoy. To what purpose therefore should our constitution have supposed a case, in which no remedy can avail; a case which can never happen, till the spirit which formed this constitution first, and hath preserved it ever since, shall be totally extinguished; and till it becomes an ideal entity, like the Utopia, existing in the imagination, or memory, nowhere else? As all government began, so all government must end by the people: tyrannical governments by their virtue and courage, and even free governments by their vice and baseness. Our constitution, indeed, makes it impossible to destroy liberty by any sudden blast of popular fury, or by the treachery of a few; for though the many cannot easily hurt, they may easily save themselves. But if the many will concur with the few; if they will advisedly and deliberately suffer their liberty to be taken away by those, to whom they delegate power to preserve it; this no constitution can prevent. God would not support even his own theocracy against the concurrent desire of the children of Israel, but gave them a king in his anger.[4] How then should our human constitution of government support itself against so universal a change, as we here suppose, in the temper and character of our people? It cannot be. We may give ourselves a tyrant in our folly, if we please. But this can never happen till the whole nation falls into a state of political reprobation. Then, and not till then, political damnation will be our lot.

Let us descend into a greater detail, in order to develop these reflections fully, and to push the consequences of them home to ourselves, and to our present state. They deserve our utmost attention, and are so far from being foreign to the subject of these essays upon parties, that they will terminate in the very point at which we began, and wind up the whole in one important lesson.

To proceed then: I say, that if the people of this island should suffer their liberties to be at any time ravished, or stolen from them, they would incur greater blame, and deserve by consequence less pity, than any enslaved and oppressed people ever did. By how much true liberty, that is, liberty stated and ascertained by law, in equal opposition to popular licence and arbitrary will, hath been more boldly asserted, more wisely or more successfully improved,

[4] 1 Samuel 8.

and more firmly established in this than in other countries, by so
much the more heavy would our just condemnation prove in the
case that is here supposed. The virtue of our ancestors, to whom
all these advantages are owing, would aggravate the guilt and the
infamy of their degenerate posterity. There have been ages of gold
and of silver, of brass and of iron, in our little world, as in the great
world, though not in the same order. In which of these ages we are
at present, let others determine. This, at least, is certain, that in all
these ages Britain hath been the temple, as it were, of liberty. Whilst
her sacred fires have been extinguished in so many countries, here
they have been religiously kept alive. Here she hath her saints, her
confessors, and a whole army of martyrs, and the gates of hell have
not hitherto prevailed against her: so that if a fatal reverse is to
happen; if servility and servitude are to overrun the whole world,
like injustice, and liberty is to retire from it, like Astraea, our portion of the abandoned globe will have, at least, the mournful
honour, whenever it happens, of showing her last, her parting
steps.[5]

The ancient Britons are to us the aborigines of our island. We
discover little of them through the gloom of antiquity, and we see
nothing beyond them. This however we know, they were freemen.
Caesar, who visited them in an hostile manner, but did not conquer
them, perhaps was [c]beaten by them; Caesar, I say, bestows very
liberally the title of kings upon their chieftains,[6] and the compilers
of fabulous traditions deduce a series of their monarchs from Samothes,[7] a contemporary of Nimrod. But Caesar affected to swell the
account of his expedition with pompous names; and these writers,
like those whom [d]Strabo mentions, endeavoured to recommend

[c] 'Territa quaesitis ostendit terga Britannis'.[8]
[d] *Geog.* Lib. II.[9]

[5] In the age of iron, before the giants' attack on Olympus, Astraea, the goddess of
justice, was the last of the immortals to leave the earth (Ovid, *Metamorphoses*, I.
150).
[6] Caesar, *De Bello Gallico*, V. 22. I.
[7] Samothes was supposedly the fourth son of Japhet, to whom Noah had allotted
Europe after the Flood: compare Algernon Sidney, *Discourses Concerning Government*, III. 33, on 'the senseless stories of Samothes the son of Japheth and his
magicians'.
[8] 'He showed his frightened back to the Britons whom he had sought out': Lucan,
De Bello Civili, II. 572.
[9] Strabo, *Geography*, XI. 6. 3.

themselves by publishing romances to an ignorant generation, instead of histories. These supposed monarchs were the ᵉheads of little clans, *reguli, vel melioris notae nobiles;*[10] and if our island knew any authority of the kingly sort in those days, it was that of occasional and temporary monarchs, elected in great exigencies, ᶠ*communi consilio, suffragiis multitudinis,*[11] like Cassivellaunus[12] in Britain, or Vercingetorix[13] in Gaul; for, in some cases, examples taken from either of these people will conclude for both. The kings who ruled in Britain after the Romans abandoned the island, in the beginning of the fifth century, held their authority from the people, and governed under the control of national assemblies, as we have great reason to believe, and none to doubt. In short, as far as we can look back, a lawless power, a government by will, never prevailed in Britain.

The Saxons had kings, as well as the Britons. The manner in which they established themselves, and the long wars they waged for and against the Britons, led to and maintained monarchical rule amongst them. But these kings were in their first institution, no doubt, such as Tacitus describes the German kings and princes to have been: ᵍchiefs, who persuaded, rather than commanded;[14] and who were heard in the public assemblies of the nation, according as their age, their nobility, their military fame, or their eloquence gave them authority. How many doughty monarchs, in later and more polite ages, would have slept in cottages, and have worked in stalls, instead of inhabiting palaces, and being cushioned up in thrones, if this rule of government had continued in force? – But the Saxon kings grew into power in time; and among them, as among other

ᵉ Sel. *Anal. Anglo Brit.* Lib. 2. cap. 3. Cam.
ᶠ Caes. *De Bell.* Lib. 5. & 7.
ᵍ De Situ. Mor. & Pop. Germ. Lib. 11.

[10] 'Princelings, or rather better-known nobles': John Selden, *Analecton Anglo-Brittanicum* (Frankfurt, 1615), 17 (I. 3).
[11] '. . . by common consultation and by the votes of the masses': Caesar, *De Bello Gallico*, V. 6. 6 and VII. 63. 6.
[12] British war-leader who headed the resistance to Julius Caesar in 54 BCE: Caesar, *De Bello Gallico*, V.
[13] Chief of the Gallic tribe of the Averni, who was defeated by, triumphed over and executed by Caesar in 46 BCE for rising against Rome in 52 BCE: Caesar, *De Bello Gallico*, VII.
[14] Tacitus, *Germania*, XI.

nations, birth, instead of merit, became, for the sake of order and tranquillity, a title to the throne. However, though these princes might command, and were no longer under the necessity of governing by persuasion, they were still under that of governing to the satisfaction of the people. By what other expedient could they govern men, who were wise enough to preserve and exercise the right of electing their civil magistrates and military officers, and the system of whose government was upheld and carried on by a gradation of popular assemblies, from the inferior courts to the high court of Parliament; for such, or very near such, was the Wittena Gemote,[15] in nature and effect, whenever the word parliament came into use?

The first prince of the Norman race was an absolute conqueror, in the opinion of some men; and I can readily agree that he assumed, in some cases, the power of a tyrant. But supposing all this to be true in the utmost extent, that the friends of absolute monarchy can desire it should be thought so, this, and this alone will result from it: unlimited or absolute monarchy could never be established in Britain; no, not even by conquest. The rights of the people were soon re-asserted; the laws of the Confessor were restored;[16] and the third prince of this race, Henry the First, covenanted in a solemn speech to his people, for their assistance against his brother Robert and the Normans, by promising that sacred charter, which was in other reigns so often and so solemnly confirmed, by engaging to maintain his subjects in [h]their ancient liberties, to follow their advice, and to rule them in peace with prudence and mildness.

---

[h] 'In antiquis vestris libertatibus. Vestris inclinando consiliis. Consultius & mitius, more mansueti principis'. – Vid. Mat. Par.[17]

[15] The ideologists of political Gothicism usually saw the Saxon *witenagemot*, or assembly, as the originary institution of English liberty; Bolingbroke elsewhere identified it as part of a primal mixed government (*Remarks on the History of England*, 'Letter IV').

[16] The restoration of Edward the Confessor's laws after the Norman Conquest was taken to show the continuity of Saxon liberties and the limitation of monarchy by the community's representatives assembled in Parliament: Janelle Greenberg, 'The Confessors' Laws and the Radical Face of the Ancient Constitution', *English Historical Review* 104 (1989): 611–37.

[17] '. . . in their ancient liberties . . . bending to your counsels . . . more advisedly and gently, in the manner of a mild ruler': *Matthaei Paris . . . Historia Major*, ed. William Watts (London, 1684), 52.

I need not descend into more particulars, to show the perpetuity of free government in Britain. Few men, even in this age, are so shamefully unacquainted with the history of their country, as to be ignorant of the principal events and signal revolutions, which have happened since the Norman era. One continued design against liberty hath been carried on by various methods, almost in every reign. In many, the struggles have been violent and bloody. But liberty still hath triumphed over force, over treachery, over corruption, and even under oppression. The altars of tyranny have been demolished as soon as raised; nay, even whilst they were raising, and the priests of that idol have been hewed to pieces: so that I will affirm, without the least apprehension of being disproved, that our constitution is brought nearer than any other constitution ever was, to the most perfect idea of a free system of government. – One observation only I will make, before I leave this head, and it is this. The titles of those kings which were precarious, from circumstances of times, and notions that prevailed, notwithstanding the general acquiescence of the nation to them, afforded so many opportunities to our ancestors of better securing, or improving liberty. They were not such bubbles as to alter, without mending, the government; much less to make revolutions, and suffer by them. They were not such bubbles as to raise princes to the throne, who had no pretence to sit in it but their choice, purely to have the honour of bettering the condition of those princes, without bettering their own in proportion. – If what I have been saying appears a little too digressive from the main scope of this essay, I shall hope for indulgence from this consideration, that the natural effect of such reflections as I have made and suggested, must be to raise in our minds the honest ambition of emulating the virtue and courage of our forefathers, in the cause of liberty; and to inspire a reasonable fear, heightened by shame, of losing what they preserved and delivered down to us, through so many mixtures of different people, of Britons with Saxons, of both with Danes, of all three with Normans, through so many difficulties, so many dangers, so many revolutions, in the course of so many centuries.

There is another reason to be given, why the people of this island would be more inexcusable than any other, if they lost their liberty; and the opening and enforcing of this reason will bring us fully into our subject.

I supposed just now that our liberty might be ravished, or stolen from us; but I think that expression must be retracted, since it will appear, upon due consideration, that our liberty cannot be taken away by the force or fraud alone of those who govern; it cannot be taken away, unless the people are themselves accomplices; and they who are accomplices, cannot be said to suffer by one or the other. Some nations have received the yoke of servitude with little or no struggle; but if ever it is imposed upon us, we must not only hold out our necks to receive it, we must help to put it on. Now, to be passive in such a case is shameful; but to be active, is supreme and unexampled infamy. In order to become slaves, we of this nation must be beforehand what other people have been rendered by a long course of servitude; we must become the most corrupt, most profligate, the most senseless, the most servile nation of wretches, that ever disgraced humanity: for a force sufficient to ravish liberty from us, such as a great standing army is in time of peace, cannot be continued, unless we continue it; nor can the means necessary to steal liberty from us, be long enough employed with effect, unless we give a sanction to their iniquity, and call good evil, and evil good.

It may be said, that even the friends of liberty have sometimes different notions about it, and about the means of maintaining or promoting it; and therefore that even the British nation may possibly, some time or other, approve and concur in measures destructive of their liberty, without any intention to give it up, and much more without changing from the character which they have hitherto borne among the societies of mankind, to that infamous character I have just now supposed. If this were true, it would only furnish more reasons to be always on our guard, to be jealous of every extraordinary demand, and to reject constantly every proposition, though never so specious, that had a tendency to weaken the barriers of liberty, or to raise a strength superior to theirs. But I confess I do not think we can be led blindfold so far as the brink of the precipice. I know that all words, which are signs of complex ideas, furnish matter of mistake and cavil. We dispute about justice, for instance, and fancy that we have different opinions about the same thing; whilst, by some little difference in the composition of our ideas, it happens that we have only different opinions about different things, and should be of the same opinion about the same thing.

But this, I presume, cannot happen in the case before us. All disputes about liberty in this country, and at this time, must be disputes for and against the self-same fixed and invariable set of ideas, whatever the disputants on one side of the question may pretend, in order to conceal what it is not yet very safe to avow. No disputes can possibly arise from different conceptions of anything so clearly stated, and so precisely determined, as the fundamental principles are, on which our whole liberty rests.

If liberty be that delicious and wholesome fruit, on which the British nation hath fed for so many ages, and to which we owe our riches, our strength, and all the advantages we boast of, the British constitution is the tree that bears this fruit, and will continue to bear it, as long as we are careful to fence it in, and trench it round, against the beasts of the field, and the insects of the earth. To speak without a figure, our constitution is a system of government suited to the genius of our nation, and even to our situation. The experience of many hundred years hath shown, that by preserving this constitution inviolate, or by drawing it back to the principles on which it was originally founded, whenever it shall be made to swerve from them, we may secure to ourselves, and to our latest posterity, the possession of that liberty which we have long enjoyed.[18] What would we more? What other liberty than this do we seek? And if we seek no other, is not this marked out in such characters as he that runs may read? As our constitution therefore ought to be, what it seldom is, the rule of government, so let us make the conformity, or repugnancy of things to this constitution, the rule by which we accept them as favourable, or reject them as dangerous to liberty. They who talk of liberty in Britain on any other principles than those of the British constitution, talk impertinently at best, and much charity is requisite to believe no worse of them. But they who distinguish between practicable and impracticable liberty, in order to insinuate what they mean, or they mean nothing, that the liberty established by the true scheme of our constitution is of the impracticable kind; and they who endeavour, both in speculation and practice, to elude and pervert the forms, and to ridicule and explode the spirit of this constitution: these men are

---

[18] On the necessity of a frequent return to first principles to safeguard the liberty of the republic see Machiavelli, *Discorsi*, III.1.

enemies, open and avowed enemies to it, and by consequence to British liberty, which cannot be supported on any other bottom. – Some men there are, the pests of society I think them, who pretend a great regard to religion in general, but who take every opportunity of declaiming publicly against that system of religion, or at least against that church establishment, which is received in Britain. Just so the men of whom I have been speaking affect a great regard to liberty in general, but they dislike so much the system of liberty established in Britain, that they are incessant in their endeavours to puzzle the plainest thing in the world, and to refine and distinguish away the life and strength of our constitution, in favour of the little, present, momentary turns, which they are retained to serve. What now would be the consequence, if all these endeavours should succeed? I am persuaded that the great philosophers, divines, lawyers, and politicians, who exert them, have not yet prepared and agreed upon the plans of a new religion, and of new constitutions in Church and state. We should find ourselves therefore without any form of religion or civil government. The first set of these missionaries would take off all the restraints of religion from the governed, and the latter set would remove, or render ineffectual, all the limitations and controls, which liberty hath prescribed to those that govern, and disjoint the whole frame of our constitution. Entire dissolution of manners, confusion, anarchy, or perhaps absolute monarchy, would follow; for it is possible, nay probable, that in such a state as this, and amidst such a rout of lawless savages, men would choose this government, absurd as it is, rather than have no government at all.

But here again it may be said, that as liberty is a word of uncertain signification, so is constitution; that men have taught the most opposite doctrines, and pretended at least to build them on the principles of the constitution; that the rule therefore of determining our notions of liberty by the principles of our constitution, is no rule, and we are by consequence just where we were before. But the answer is ready. It is true that there were formerly men who persisted long in the attempt to talk and write that chimera called prerogative into vogue; to contend that it was something real, a right inherent in the crown, founded in the constitution of our government; and equally necessary to support the just authority of the prince, and to protect the subject. How we had like to have lost our liberty by the prevalence of such doctrines, by the consequences drawn from them, and the practices built upon them, hath been touched in the deduction of the state of parties. But happily this kind of progression from a free to a slavish constitution of government, was stopped at the Revolution, and the notions themselves are so exploded in the course of six and forty years, that they are entertained at this hour by no set of men, whose numbers or importance give them any pretence to be reckoned among our national parties. – It is as true, that there are now men who pursue the very same design by different methods. The former attacked, these undermine our liberty. The former were the beasts of the field hinted at above; these are the insects of the earth; and like other insects, though sprung from dirt, and the vilest of the animal kind, they can nibble, and gnaw, and poison; and, if they are suffered to multiply and work on, they can lay the most fruitful country waste. Corruption and dependency are their favourite topics. They plead for the first as a laudable expedient of government; and for the last, I mean corrupt, private dependency, as an essential part of our constitution. When they have perplexed, as much as they are able, our ideas of dependency and independency, they reason, if I may give their sophisms so good a name, as if the independency of each part of the legislature, of the king particularly, arose from the dependency of the other parts on that part. Now this is both false and absurd. – It is false, because the constitutional independency of each part of the legislature arises from hence, that distinct rights, powers and privileges are assigned to it by the constitution. But then this independency of one part can be so little said to arise from the dependency of another, that it consists properly and truly in the free, unbiassed, uninfluenced and independent exercise of these rights, powers and privileges, by each part, in as ample an extent as the constitution allows, or, in other words, as far as that point, where the constitution stops this free exercise, and submits the proceedings of one part, not to the private influence, but to the public control of the other parts. Before this point, the independency of each part is meant by the constitution to be absolute. From this point, the constitutional dependency of each part on the others commences. To talk to natural independency belonging to the kingly office, to an house of peers, or an house of commons, the institutions of art, not of nature, is impertinent. – It is absurd, because it absolutely destroys the very thing it is advanced to establish; for if A's independency arises from the dependency of B, and B's independency from the dependency of A, then are A and B both dependent, and there is no such thing as constitutional independency at all. The crown is the source of honours, and hath the disposal of public employments. This no man disputes; nor would any man, I believe, go about to alter. But will it follow that the 'constitutional independency of the king would be lost, because the House of Commons give the supplies, if he had not the power of giving part of this money, in places and pensions, back again to the members of that house? It would be easy for me to turn this whole profound reasoning into many, even ridiculous lights; but the subject creates other sentiments than those of mirth, though the logic employed about it deserves a ludicrous, not a serious treatment. – I ask pardon for having said so much upon so slight an occasion, and I proceed.

Notwithstanding all these endeavours to puzzle our constitution, formerly in favour of that prerogative, by the weight of which it must have been crushed, and actually at this time in favour of that corruption and corrupt dependency by which it would be soon demolished; the main principles of the British constitution are simple and obvious, and fixed, as well as any truths can be fixed, in the minds of men, by the most determinate ideas. The state of our constitution then affords an easy and unerring rule, by which to judge of the state of our liberty. The improvement or decay of one, denotes the improvement or decay of the other; and the strength or weakness of one, the safety or danger of the other. We cannot lose our liberty, unless we lose our constitution; nor lose our constitution, unless we are accomplices to the violations of it; for this constitution is better fitted than any, ancient or modern, ever was, not only to preserve liberty, but to provide for its own duration, and to become immortal, if any thing human could be so.

I am, sir, &c.

---

[i] Vide *London Jour.* Sept. 28, 1734.[19]

[19] *London Journal* 744 (29 September 1734).

Sir,

Much hath been said occasionally, in the course of these letters, concerning the beauty and excellency of the British constitution. I shall make, however, no excuse for returning to the same subject, upon an occasion which introduces it so naturally, and indeed so necessarily. Nothing can be more apposite to the professed design of these writings; nothing of more real, and more present use. Let me speak plainly. We have been all of us, those of every side, and of every denomination, accustomed too long to value ourselves, foolishly or knavishly, on our zeal for this or that party, or for this or that government; and to make a merit of straining the constitution different ways, in order to serve the different purposes of each. It is high time we should all learn, if that be still possible, to value ourselves in the first place on our zeal for the constitution; to make all governments, and much more all parties, bow to that, and to suffer that to bow to none. But how shall this constitution be known, unless we make it the subject of careful enquiry, and of frequent and sober reflection? Or unknown, how shall it become, what it ought to be, the object of our admiration, our love and our zeal? Many of those who reap the greatest advantages from it, pass it by unregarded, with equal folly and ingratitude. Many take a transient, inattentive view of it. Many again consider it in part only, or behold it in a narrow, pedantic light. Instead of this, we should view it often. We should pierce through the form to the soul of it. We should contemplate the noble object in all its parts, and in the whole, and render it as familiar to our intellectual fight, as the most common sensible objects are to our corporeal sight. [a]*Quam illa ardentes amores excitaret sui, si videretur?*[2] Well may it be allowed me to apply to so glorious an effort of human wisdom, what Tully says after Plato, in the *Phaedrus*, if I mistake not, of wisdom herself.

[a] Cic. *De Finib*. L. 2.

[1] *Craftsman* 437 (16 November 1734).
[2] 'If we could see [wisdom], what burning passions would she inspire?': Cicero, *De Finibus* II. 16. 52 (citing Plato, *Phaedrus*, 250D); compare *Idea of a Patriot King*, p. 292.

'All public regiment', says Mr Hooker, 'hath arisen from deliberate advice, consultation and composition between men.'[3] The proposition is undoubtedly and universally true. It is as true in the kingdom of Morocco, as it is in the kingdom of Britain; and the undeniable consequences which flow from it are obvious. We are not to wonder, however, if men do not look up to this original of government, nor trace these consequences from it in most countries. In the institution of governments, too great powers have been usually given, and too great confidence reposed, either at first, or in process of time. These powers have subsisted, have been confirmed by more time, and increased by the very nature of power, which is the properest instrument of its own propagation. But the original composition, for want of being expressed, or sufficiently implied, or frequently recurred to by the forms of the government, hath been forgot, or hath grown so obsolete, that they whose interest required that no such thing should be believed, have thought themselves at liberty boldly to deny it; and not only so, but to suppose some other original of government. Strange systems of policy, and stranger of religion, have been devised to support and sanctify these usurpations. Education hath been set on the same side; and saucy authority hath prevailed against the clearest light of nature, and the plainest dictates of common sense. No man who hath read and looked abroad into the world, and made a reasonable use of either, will think this too strange to be true; since there is no demonstrated truth (such truths I mean as are here spoken of) which may not be rendered, at least, very problematical, by long, uniform, positive contradiction; nor any demonstrated lie, which may not be rendered probable to many, and certain to some, by a long, uniform, positive affirmation; according to a just observation made by father Paul somewhere or other, on occasion of Constantine's supposed grant, and other cheats of the court of Rome.[4] But we of this country have been more happy. Our original contract hath been recurred to often, and as many cavils as have been made, as many jests as have been broke about this expression, we might safely defy the assertors of absolute monarchy and arbitrary will, if there were any worth our regard, to produce any one point of time, since which we know any

---

[3] Hooker, *Ecclesiastical Polity*, I. 10. 4.
[4] Presumably Paolo Sarpi (1552–1623), Venetian controversialist, sceptic and historian, though Bolingbroke's recollection is mistaken.

thing of our constitution, wherein the whole scheme of it would not have been one monstrous absurdity, unless an original contract had been supposed. They must have been blinded therefore by ignorance, or passion, or prejudice, who did not always see that there is such a thing necessarily, and in the very nature of our constitution; and that they might as well doubt whether the foundations of an ancient, solid building were suited and proportioned to the elevation and form of it, as whether our constitution was established by composition and contract. Sure I am that they must be worse than blind, if any such there are, who do not confess at this time, and under the present settlement, that our constitution is in the strictest sense a bargain, a conditional contract between the prince and the people, as it always hath been, and still is, between the representative and collective bodies of the nation.

That this bargain may not be broken, on the part of the prince with the people (though the executive power be trusted to the prince, to be exercised according to such rules, and by the ministry of such officers as are prescribed by the laws and customs of this kingdom), the legislative, or supreme power, is vested by our constitution in three estates, whereof the king is one. Whilst the members of the other two preserve their private independency, and those estates are consequently under no dependency, except that which is in the scheme of our constitution, this control on the first will always be sufficient; and a bad king, let him be as bold as he may please to be thought, must stand in awe of an honest parliament.

That this bargain may not be broken, on the part of the representative body, with the collective body of the nation, it is not only a principal, declared right of the people of Britain, that the election of members to sit in Parliament shall be free, but it hath been a principal part of the care and attention of Parliaments, for more than three hundred years, to watch over this freedom, and to secure it, by removing all influence of the crown, and all other corrupt influence, from these elections. This care and this attention have gone still farther. They have provided, as far as they have been suffered to provide hitherto, by the constitutional dependency of one House on the other, and of both on the crown, that all such influence should be removed from the members after they are chosen. Even here the providence of our constitution hath not stopped. Lest all other provisions should be ineffectual to keep the members of the House of Commons out of this unconstitutional dependency, which some men presume, with a silly dogmatical air of triumph, to suppose necessary to support the constitutional independency of the crown, the wisdom of our constitution hath thought fit that the representatives of the people should not have time to forget that they are such; that they are empowered to act for the people, not against them. In a word, our constitution means, that the members of this body should be kept, as it were, to their good behaviour, by the frequent returns of new elections. It does all that a constitution can do, all that can be done by legal provisions, to secure the interests of the people, by maintaining the integrity of their trustees: and lest all this should fail, it gives frequent opportunities to the people to secure their interests themselves, by mending their choice of their trustees; so that as a bad King must stand in awe of an honest Parliament, a corrupt House of Commons must stand in awe of an honest people.

Between these two estates, or branches of the legislative power, there stands a third, the house of peers; which may seem in theory, perhaps, too much under the influence of the crown, to be a proper control upon it, because the sole right of creating peers resides in the crown; whereas the crown hath no right to intermeddle in the electing commoners. This would be the case, and an intolerable one indeed, if the crown should exercise this right often, as it had been exercised sometimes with universal and most just disapprobation. It is possible too that this may come to be the case, in some future age, by the method of electing peers to sit in Parliament, for one part of the same kingdom, by the frequent translations of bishops, and by other means, if the wisdom and virtue of the present age, and the favourable opportunity of the present auspicious and indulgent reign do not prevent it. But in all other respects, the persons who are once created peers, and their posterity, according to the scheme of the constitution, having a right to sit and debate, and vote in the house of peers, which cannot be taken from them, except by forfeiture; all influence of the kind I have mentioned seems to be again removed, and their share in the government depending neither on the King nor the people, they constitute a middle order, and are properly mediators between the other two, in the eye of our constitution.

It is by this mixture of monarchical, aristocratical and democratical power, blended together in one system, and by these three estates balancing one another, that our free constitution of government hath been preserved so long inviolate, or hath been brought back, after having suffered violations, to its original principles, and been renewed, and improved too, by frequent and salutary revolutions. It is by this that weak and wicked princes have been opposed, restrained, reformed, punished by Parliaments; that the real, and perhaps the doubtful, exorbitancies of Parliaments have been reduced by the crown, and that the heat of one House hath been moderated, or the spirit raised, by the proceedings of the other. Parliaments have had a good effect on the people, by keeping them quiet; and the people on parliaments, by keeping them within bounds, which they were tempted to transgress. A just confidence in the safe, regular, Parliamentary methods of redressing grievances hath often made the freest, and not the most patient people on earth, bear the greatest grievances much longer than people held under stronger restraints, and more used to oppression, who had not the same confidence, nor the same expectation, have borne even less. The cries of the people, and the terror of approaching elections, have defeated the most dangerous projects for beggaring and enslaving the nation; and the majority without doors hath obliged the majority within doors to truckle to the minority. In a word, two things may be said with truth of our constitution, which I think neither can, nor ever could be said of any other. It secures society against the miseries which are inseparable from simple forms of government, and is liable as little as possible to the inconveniencies that arise in mixed forms. It cannot become uneasy to the prince, or people, unless the former be egregiously weak or wicked; nor be destroyed, unless the latter be excessively and universally corrupt. – But these general assertions require to be a little better explained.

By simple forms of government, I mean such as lodge the whole supreme power, absolutely and without control, either in a single person, or in the principal persons of the community, or in the whole body of the people. Such governments are governments of arbitrary will, and therefore of all imaginable absurdities the most absurd. They stand in direct opposition to the sole motive of submission to any government whatsoever; for if men quit the state, and renounce the rights of nature (one of which is, to be sure, that of being governed by their own will), they do this, that they may not remain exposed to the arbitrary will of other men, the weakest to that of the strongest, the few to that of the many. Now, in submitting to any simple form of government whatever, they establish what they mean to avoid, and for fear of being exposed to arbitrary will sometimes, they choose to be governed by it always. These governments do not only degenerate into tyranny, they are tyranny in their very institution; and they who submit to them are slaves, not subjects, however the supreme power may be exercised: for tyranny and slavery do not so properly consist in the stripes that are given and received, as in the power of giving them at pleasure, and the necessity of receiving them, whenever and for whatever they are inflicted. Absolute democracy may appear to some, in abstracted speculation, a less deviation from nature than monarchy, and more agreeable to reason, because here it is the will of the whole community, that governs the whole community, and because reason does certainly instruct every man, even from a consciousness of his own frailty, the *impotentia animi* [5] of the Latin writers, to trust as little power as possible to any other man. But still it must be confessed, that if it be unsafe for a people to trust too much power to a prince, it is unsafe for them likewise to keep too much power to themselves. Absolute monarchy is tyranny; but absolute democracy is tyranny and anarchy both. If aristocracy be placed between these two extremes, it is placed on a slippery ridge, and must fall into one or the other, according to the natural course of human affairs; if the few who govern are united, into tyranny, perhaps, more severe than any other; if they are disunited, into factions and disorders as great as those of the most tumultuous democracy.

From such observations, and many of the same kind and tendency, it hath been concluded very reasonably, that the best form of government must be one compounded of these three, and in which they are all so tempered, that each may produce the good effects, and be restrained by the counterworkings of the other two, from producing the bad effects that are natural to it. Thus much is evident. But then how to fix that just proportion of each, how to hit that happy temperament of them all in one system, is a difficulty that hath perplexed the wisest politicians, and the most famous legislators. Let me quote one of the greatest writers of antiquity.

[5] '. . . poverty of spirit'.

[b]Tacitus acknowledges, in the fourth book of his *Annals*, what is here advanced; but he thinks such a constitution of government rather a subject of fine speculation than of practice. He thinks it much more likely that such a system should continue to be admired and praised in idea, than established in fact; and if it happens ever to be established, he does not imagine it can be supported long. Not only the real difficulties which his sagacity presented to his mind, but his reflections on the constitution and fate of the Roman commonwealth might lead Tacitus into this despondency. But what the refinements of Roman policy could not do, hath been done in this island, upon foundations laid by the rough simplicity of our northern ancestors.

It would be a curious and entertaining amusement, to reduce the constitutions of the Roman government, and of those which were formed on the ruins of that empire, particularly of our own, to their first principles; to observe in which they agree, and in which they differ, and the uniform or various tendencies of each; to mark the latent, as well as apparent causes of their rise and fall; how well or how ill they were contrived for triumphs abroad, or peace at home; for vain grandeur, or real prosperity; for resisting corruption, or being ruined by it. Such an analysis and enquiry would be, I imagine, not only amusing but useful. At least, it would be more so than any rhapsody of general reflections, huddled together with little order or designs; for these leave no systematical impressions on the mind; nothing but a confusion of ideas, often bright and glittering, seldom instructive. But a work of this kind would be too voluminous and too aspiring for these little essays, and the humble author of them. He will therefore keep to his point, and content himself to make some of those observations alone, which seem proper to illustrate and prove what he hath advanced, that the British constitution is a plain and sufficient rule of judgment and conduct to us in everything that regards our liberty; for preserving of

---

[b] 'Cunctas nationes & urbes populus, aut primores, aut singuli regunt. Delecta ex his & constituta reipublicae forma, laudari facilius quam evenire; vel, si evenit, haud diuturna esse potest.'[6]

[6] 'All nations and cities are ruled by the people, the leading inhabitants, or a single person. The form of a republic chosen and made up from these elements is easier to praise than to produce while, if it does arise, it will not last long': Tacitus, *Annals*, IV. 33. 1.

which, as well as for securing its own duration, it is better fitted than any other.

There was so great a mixture of monarchical power in the Roman commonwealth, that ᶜLivy dates the original of liberty from the expulsion of the Tarquins, rather because the consular dignity was made annual, than because the regal power had suffered any diminution in that change. The dictatorial power, the most absolute that can be imagined, was introduced in eight, or at farthest in eleven years afterwards, and may therefore be reckoned coeval with the commonwealth;[7] and whatever diminution either this or the consular power might suffer, the axes and the rods were terrible to the last, especially when they were carried before a dictator, for whom the tribunes of the people were not a match, as they were for the consuls. But though there were three sorts of power exercised, there were but two orders, or estates established in this commonwealth, the patricians and the plebeians, and the supreme power was divided accordingly between the senate and the collective, nor a representative, body of the people. These two orders or estates had frequent contests, and well they might, since they had very opposite interests. ᵈAgrarian laws, for instance, began to be promulgated within three and twenty years, and continued to the end of the commonwealth to produce the same disorders. How inconsistent, indeed, was that plan of government, which required so much hard service of the people; and which, leaving them so much power in the distribution of power, left them so little property in the distribution of property? Such an inequality of property, and of the means of acquiring it, cannot subsist in an equal commonwealth;

ᶜ Libertatis originem inde magis, quia annuum imperium consulare factum est, quam quod diminutum quicquam sit ex regia potestate numeres. Omnia jura, omnia insignia primi consules tenuere. Lib. cap. 1.[8]

ᵈ Tum primum lex agraria promulgata est; nunquam deinde usque ad hanc memoriam sine maximis motibus rerum agitata. Liv. 1. 2. c. 41.[9]

---

[7] The office of dictator was first proposed in 501 BCE (Livy, *Histories*, II. 18. 4).

[8] 'One can reckon the beginning of liberty as proceeding from the fact that the consuls' authority was limited to a year rather than to any diminution of their power compared to that of the kings. The first consuls held all the same rights and insignia': Livy, *Histories*, II. 1. 7–8 (507 BCE).

[9] 'This was the first time that an agrarian law was proposed, and from that day to within living memory it has never been brought up without creating the greatest disturbances': Livy, *Histories*, II. 41. 3 (484 BCE)

and I much apprehend that any near approaches to a monopoly of property, would not be long endured even in a monarchy. – But I return to my first observation.

Though the Romans made frequent experience of the cruel mischiefs, and even extreme danger to liberty, which attended almost every variance of the two estates, yet did they never fall upon any safe or effectual method of preventing these disputes, or of reconciling them without violence. The old expedients alone subsisted; and surely they were not only violent, but extra-constitutional. When the senate was inflexible, the people had immediate recourse to sedition. When the people was refractory, the senate had recourse to a dictator. The latter had an approbation which could not be given to the former, and was a legal institution; notwithstanding which I make no scruple of saying that it was at least as inconsistent with a free constitution of government as the former. Sedition was temporary anarchy. A dictator was a tyrant for six months, unless he thought fit to abdicate sooner. The constitution was suspended, and endangered by both. It might have been destroyed by the excesses of one. It was destroyed by the bare duration of the other. If the Romans had annually elected out of their tribes a certain number of men to represent the people instead of depending on their tribunes; (a sort of bullying magistracy, and often a very corrupt one) and if this representative body had been one estate, and had acted as such, the consuls might very well have supplied the place of a third estate, and have been safely trusted, even more independently of the senate than they were, with the executive power. But the want of a third estate in the Roman system of government, and of a representative body, to act for the collective body, maintained one perpetual ferment, which often increased into a storm, but never subsided into a calm. The state of Rome, and of the greatest men in that commonwealth, would have deserved pity rather than envy, even in the best times, if their defective constitution had not made such a state of ᵉtrouble and tumult the price

---

ᵉ 'Conciones magistratuum paene pernoctantium in rostris. – Accusationes potentium reorum, & assignatae etiam domibus inimicitiae. – Procerum factiones, & assidua senatus adversum plebem certamina'. *Dial. de Orat.* Quinctil. Tacito inscrip.[10]

[10] '. . . the harangues of magistrates who spent almost the whole night on the hustings . . . the impeachments of powerful criminals, and hereditary feuds between whole families . . . factions of the aristocracy, and long-drawn-out struggles by the Senate against the people': Tacitus, *Dialogus de Oratore,* XXXVI. 3.

they paid for the maintenance of their liberty. But this was not the whole price. Whilst Rome advanced triumphantly in conquering the world, as her orators, poets and historians have expressed themselves; that is, a few nations round the Mediterranean sea, and little more; her citizens turned against one another those weapons, which were put into their hands against the enemies of Rome. Mutual proscriptions and bloody massacres followed; each party triumphed in its turn; they were more animated and better disciplined by their contests; both grew stronger; the commonwealth alone grew weaker; and Pompey and Caesar finished the last tragical scene, which Marius and Sulla began.[11] In fine, the Roman commonwealth would have been dissolved much sooner than it was, by the defects I have mentioned, which many circumstances concurred to aggravate, if such a spirit of wisdom, as well as courage, and such an enthusiasm for the grandeur, the majesty, and the duration of their empire had not possessed this people, as never possessed any other. When this spirit decayed, when this enthusiasm cooled, the constitution could not help, nay, worked against itself. That dictatorial power, on which the senate had always depended for preserving it, completed the ruin of it, in the hands of Caesar; and that tribunitial power, to which the people had always trusted the defence of their liberty, confirmed their slavery in the hands of Augustus.

I am, sir, &c.

---

[11] Cornelius Sulla defeated his rival Caius Marius in 82 BCE and became Dictator. One strand of early-modern republicanism (including Machiavelli and Harrington) dated the decline of Rome from the beginnings of Sulla's dictatorship and saw its nadir under Julius and Augustus.

Sir,

The defects, which I have presumed to censure in the Roman constitution of government, were avoided in some of those that were established on the breaking of that empire, by the northern nations and the Goths; for I suspect that the Goths were not properly and strictly a northern nation, any more than the Huns and the Alans, though they have been often confounded, and I believe by myself.[2] – Let us cast our eyes on Spain and France.

We cannot arrive, as far as my scanty knowledge informs me, at any particular and authentic account of the scheme of that government which the western Goths established, when, driven out of Gaul by the Franks, they drove the Vandals and the Alans out of Spain; nor distinguish very accurately between such institutions as were parts of the original Gothic plan, and such as were introduced into the several kingdoms that formed themselves on the reconquest of the country by the Spaniards from the Arabs and Moors. The original of the Cortes particularly is quite in the dark, as we are assured by a very [a]industrious enquirer and judicious writer. Thus much, however, we may assert, that the Gothic kings were at first elective, and always limited, even after they became hereditary; and that the Cortes, whenever it was established, was an assembly, that may be more truly compared to a British Parliament than the assembly of the states of France could ever pretend to be. Churchmen had wriggled themselves into a share of temporal power among the Goths, as they did in every country where they were admitted to preach the gospel, though without any authority from the gospel; so that the Cortes consisted of prelates, as well as dukes, masters of orders, earls and ricoshomes,[3] who composed the whole body of the nobility; and of the procurators of the commons; that is, of the citizens and burgesses, chosen by the cities and boroughs

---

[a] Dr Geddes in his *Miscell. Tracts.*[4]

[1] *Craftsman* 438 (23 November 1734).
[2] *Remarks on the History of England*, 'Letter IV'.
[3] Michael Geddes, *Miscellaneous Tracts* (3 vols., London, 1702), I, 321–2.
[4] '[T]he common Title of the Barons of *Spain*': Geddes, *Miscellaneous Tracts*, I, 328.

to represent and act for the whole body of the commons. To preserve the independency of this assembly, these procurators were to
be paid by the corporations for which they served; the king was to
give no office of salary to any of them; nay, a [b]'resumption of
rewards, granted to members of the Cortes',[5] was once at least
debated, if not enacted. In short, he was not to name their president,
nor even to send letters unopened to any of them. No money could
be raised on the subjects, without the consent of this assembly; and
it was a standing maxim, or order, that redress of grievances should
precede the grants of supplies. Such a frame of government as this
seems built to duration; and, in fact, if it had not been undermined,
it could not have been demolished. The manner in which it was
both undermined and demolished totally at last, deserves the attention of every man in Britain. It was undermined by the influence of
the court, too much connived at and too long tolerated, on the
members of the Cortes. Prostitute wretches were found in those
days, I doubt not, as well as in ours, to maintain that the necessary
independency of the prince could not be supported, without
allowing a corrupt dependency of the Cortes on him; and they had
in those days such success in Castile, as we ought to hope they will
never obtain in Britain. When corrupt majorities were thus secured,
pretences were not wanting, nor will they ever be so, for making
concessions to the crown, repugnant to the spirit of the constitution,
and even inconsistent with the forms of it. Such pretences, however
plausible, would not have been admitted by men zealous to preserve
their liberty; because any real danger, remote as well as immediate,
to a free constitution, would in their balance outweigh all considerations of real expediency, and much more all the frivolous pretences
of that kind. But the [c]members of the Cortes were no longer such
men, when Castile lost her liberties under Charles the Fifth.[6] The
custom of bribing the representatives of the commons, by gifts and
promises, and so securing a majority to the court, had long pre-

[b] Dr Geddes in his *Miscell. Tracts.*
[c] Dr Geddes in his *Miscell. Tracts.*[7]

[5] Geddes, *Miscellaneous Tracts*, I, 240 (paraphrased).
[6] Charles V was Holy Roman Emperor 1519–58; as Charles I, he was King of Spain 1516–56.
[7] Geddes, *Miscellaneous Tracts*, I, 230.

vailed, as we have just now said; and after that, it is not to be wondered at if excises, given for eight years only, became perpetual; if money was granted before grievances were redressed; and if the precedent set in the time of Henry the Second, was followed in all succeeding reigns. The Cortes gave this prince a supply, for making war on the Moors; but the [d]sum being represented by the court to be insufficient for the service, it was carried that, in case of a deficiency, the king might raise, without calling a Cortes, the money necessary to make good that deficiency. This vote of credit gave an incurable fatal wound to that constitution. I call it a vote of credit, though the powers it gave seem to be less than those which are given by some modern votes of credit; for surely there is a difference, and not a small one, between a power to raise money directly on the people, for a service known, and already approved, and provided for in part, by their representatives, and a power to borrow money, on the national credit, for services unknown, and to lay the nation under an obligation of paying for that which it is possible their representatives may disapprove.

This precedent having been made in favour of one king, and in one particular conjuncture, it became a prevailing argument in favour of every other king, and in every other conjuncture: for though it may be, nay must be, in the vast variety of characters, and of conjunctures, prudent and just to grant in favour of some princes, and upon some occasions, what it would be neither prudent nor just to grant in favour of other princes, and upon other occasions, yet such is the merit of every prince who fills a throne, or rather such is the servile adulation paid to power, in what hands soever it be lodged, that general and almost universal experience shows this rule, which no man of sense would break in the management of his private interests, absolutely reversed in the management of the most important, national interests. The inference to be drawn from hence is plainly this, that the inconveniency or danger of refusing to every prince, and in every conjuncture, such things as are inconsistent with the constitution of a free government, must be always less than the inconveniency or danger of granting them to any prince, and in any conjuncture.

[d] Ibid.[8]

[8] Geddes, *Miscellaneous Tracts*, I, 331; Henry II, King of Castile 1369–79.

Let me add this farther observation, which presents itself so naturally after the former. Though it be proper in all limited monarchies to watch and guard against all concessions, or usurpations, that may destroy the balance of power, on which the preservation of liberty depends; yet is it certain that concessions to the crown from the other constituent parts of the legislature are almost alone to be feared. There is no danger that the crown should make them to the others; and on this head the people may very safely trust to those who wear it, and those who serve it. The nobility will not make them to the commons, without great struggles, which give time for interpositions, nor the commons to the nobility. But both may be easily induced to make them to the crown. The reasons of this difference are obvious enough; for, first, a king is really nothing more than a supreme magistrate, instituted for the service of the community, which requires that the executive power should be vested in a single person. He hath, indeed, a crown on his head, a sceptre in his hand, and velvet robes on his back, and he sits elevated in a throne, whilst others stand on the ground about him; and all this to denote that he is a king, and to draw the attention and reverence of the vulgar. Just so another man wears a mitre on his head, a crosier in his hand, and lawn sleeves, and sits in a purple elbow-chair, to denote that he is a bishop, and to excite the devotion of the multitude, who receive his benediction very thankfully on their knees. But still the king, as well as the bishop, holds an office, and owes a service. *Officium est imperare, non regnum.*[9] The King, when he commands, discharges a trust, and performs a duty, as well as the subject, when he obeys. Notwithstanding which, kings are apt to see themselves in another light, and experience shows us that even they who made them what they are, are apt to take them for what they are not. From hence it happened in Spain, and may happen possibly in other countries, that the kings, instead of being satisfied with and thankful for the dignity, honour, power and wealth, which they possessed in so eminent a degree above all other magistrates and members of the commonwealth, repined at their being possessed of no more. What they had was given them by the constitution; and what they had not was reserved by the same authority to the nobility and to the commons. But they proceeded, and

[9] 'To rule is a duty, not a realm [alone]'; source unidentified.

135

their sycophants reasoned, as if the sole power of the government, and the whole wealth of the nation, belonged of right to them, and the limitations of the monarchy were so many usurpations on the monarch. – In the second place, besides this constant desire of encroaching, there is another reason why concessions to the crown are more to be guarded against than others, in limited monarchies. The regal power resides in one person. The other shares of the supreme power are assigned to bodies of men. From hence it follows that the interest of the king, and the interest of the crown, cannot well be divided in the mind of a prince; whereas the interest of each individual may be distinguished from the interest of the nobility or of the commons, and still more from that of the nation, in the minds of those who compose an house of peers, or who are representatives of the people. A king cannot be tempted to give up the interest of the crown, because he cannot give up this public interest, without giving up his private interest; whereas the members of such assemblies may promote their private interest, by sacrificing to it that of the public. Several other reasons might be insisted upon, to establish the truth of the observation we have made, and to show how unfairly they argue, who all along suppose that the independency of the crown may as easily be lost, and the balance of power be destroyed on that side, by concessions from the prince, and usurpations on him, as the independency of the lords or commons may be lost, and the balance of power be destroyed on that side, by concessions to the prince, and by his usurpations. Such reasons, for instance, might be drawn from the difference of that influence which the crown hath on the other estates, and which the other estates have on the crown; as well as from the difference of the pretences, which may be urged on behalf of the crown, or of the nobility, or commons, to obtain such concessions; for supposing them all co-equal, as parts of the legislature, yet if it be considered that the executive power is solely in the crown; that the disposition of public money, as well as public employments, is a part of this power; that this power is in continual exercise, and may immediately affect, more or less, at one time or at another, every particular man, peer as well as commoner; whereas the other powers are exercised occasionally, are continued or suspended, in great measure, at the will of the prince, and are employed chiefly in matters of general, not particular concern; in fine, if it be considered farther, that the powers exercised by assemblies of peers and commoners, whether these assemblies be regarded as parts of the legislature, as the great councils of the nation, or as the judges and prosecutors of enormous offenders, are few and simple, directed to notorious purposes, conducted by rules always known, always the same, and always sufficient to these purposes: whereas the branches of executive power are numerous and complicated, the rules various, and the purposes often unknown, often contingent; so that it may become difficult to judge either of the utility of the purposes, or of the sufficiency of the powers: if all these things be considered, I say, we shall not be at a loss to determine on which side the danger to liberty, in a limited monarchy, lies; and whether concessions to the crown, in prejudice of the constitution, are not more likely to be made, than concessions from it.

Happy had it been for the people of Castile, if they had seen this danger in time, and had remedied, whilst the remedies were in their power, those defects in their constitution, whatever they were, which gave their kings by degrees such an influence over the Cortes, as overturned at last the whole constitution, and gained to the German race, that began to reign in Charles the Fifth (for his father Philip is scarce to be reckoned), such an absolute power as the Gothic kings had never been able to obtain. Though Charles the Fifth was a very able prince, yet the honour, for such it will be esteemed by some men, or more truly the infamy of enslaving Castile, must not be ascribed to his superior capacity, nor to that of his ministers. Had he been the merest tool, a thing of straw, but something less than a scarecrow, and unable to protect the property of his subjects, he might still have taken their liberties from them in that conjuncture, as he did most effectually. Corruption was established; a majority of the Cortes was bribed; the nobility was detached from the common interest by titles, places, pensions, and grants; and the clergy in general, for exceptions there were, took no farther share in it than their particular piques, or some indirect and fleeting considerations inspired them to take. The nation saw itself betrayed, and the commons protested loudly against the proceedings of their representatives. But this was the very point for which the enemies of the Castilian constitution waited; and as soon as a pretence for employing force was given them, they muffled themselves up in that threadbare cloak of zeal for the government, and

stabbed their country to the heart. An ordinance of the Cortes had
been made about an hundred years before, against increasing the
standing forces of the kingdom to more than four thousand soldiers
in garrisons, and fifteen hundred ginets.[10] This ordinance had not
been very well observed. The long wars with the Moors made
armies often necessary, when there was no actual war. The danger
of being invaded by the Moors, for every Moorish king was deemed
a pretender to the throne, might serve to make them so represented;
and when this reason failed entirely, as it did by the conquest of
Granada,[11] the last possession of these people in Spain, pretences
for keeping armies on foot were still to be found. There were still
Moorish factions; the new Christians were Moors in their hearts;
amongst the old Christians there were several who favoured them;
the people were not to be trusted with their own preservation.
Chiévres, the rapacious minister of Charles the Fifth, and his journeymen, for so were those Spaniards called, according to Dr
Geddes, who did not care how much their country was plundered
by foreigners, provided they shared the spoils;[12] Chiévres, I say, and
his journeymen, a real faction, and perhaps not a great one, were
the last friends of the government. The rest of the nation were open
or secret enemies. According to this excellent logic, the former were
to be protected in blundering, for they were guilty of that too, as
well as in plundering; and the latter were to be oppressed for com-
plaining. The nation was sacrificed to a faction, and an excellent
constitution destroyed, in favour of a profligate government. This
destruction however would not have been so easily accomplished,
nor would Castilians alone have enslaved Castile to a foreign race,
after asserting their liberty so often, and so boldly, against princes
of their own country, if two other circumstances had not concurred.
Ferdinand had conquered Navarre,[13] and a regular, disciplined army
defended that conquest against the French. This army, which was
at hand, marched into Castile, defeated the commons, and extinguished liberty in a country where it had been long declining. The

[10] In 1390: Geddes, *Miscellaneous Tracts*, I, 334; 'ginets', or jennets, were Spanish
light cavalry.
[11] Granada was reconquered by the Castilian crown in January 1492.
[12] Geddes, *Miscellaneous Tracts*, I, 231. Guillaume de Croy, Sieur de Chiévres (1458–
1521), was Grand Chamberlain to Charles V.
[13] Ferdinand of Aragon's army conquered Navarre in July 1512.

nobility was detached from the commons by grants of land, amongst other considerations, as I said above; and the commons renewed their contest on this head, perhaps unjustly, to be sure very unseasonably. The commons however were justified for taking arms, in the opinion of the nobility, and even in that of Adrian,[14] who governed during the absence of Charles, whose preceptor he had been; for this honest man, too honest to be long endured on the papal throne, where he was afterwards placed, affirmed that all the troubles of Castile were caused by the King, and by his covetous and tyrannical ministers. The conduct of the commons upon this great occasion, was in many instances rash and violent, as well as ill advised and weak. But they were tumultuous assemblies driven into despair; and the nobility, who might have had great sway amongst them, and might have helped to regulate their fire, and to keep them sober, helped on the contrary to make them mad, either by neglecting them, or by taking part against them, till it was too late; and then complained of their being mad, with as ill a grace as the principal men of Rome, who helped to corrupt that people, complained of their corruption, and assigned it as a reason for depriving them of their liberty.

There cannot be a greater solecism in politics than that of a nobility, under monarchical government, who suffer the liberty of the commons to be taken away. In aristocracies, the nobility get whatever the commons lose; but in monarchies, the crown alone is the gainer, and the certain consequence of their helping to enslave the commons, must be that of being enslaved themselves at last. How, indeed, should it be otherwise, since the liberty of the commons cannot be taken away, unless the constitution be first broken; and since neither the peers, nor any one else, can hold their privileges or their properties, by a better tenure than that of arbitrary will, when the constitution is once broken? Was it possible to doubt of this truth, we might find the proof of it, without going out of the country where we are; I mean Spain. Amongst all the surprising phenomena which have appeared in the world of late years, there are none that have struck mankind with more astonishment, than those instances of persons raised to the highest posts of power, authority and com-

---

[14] Adrian of Utrecht (1459–1523), Pope Adrian VI, was regent of Castile 1520–22.

mand, nay to empire, who had not, either from their obscure birth, or their low talents, or their still lower habits, the least occasion even to dream of such elevation. Among other countries Spain hath had her share of them; and the grandees, as they are pompously styled, the successors of those men, who thought to rise on the ruin of the commons of Castile; they, who have the vain honour of cocking their hats in the presence of their prince, have been seen to stand at awful distance, or approach with respectful cringe, in the presence of a parasite and buffoon.

I know full well that in such governments as we speak of here, it is both the duty and interest of the nobility to oppose the excesses of the commons; but I know too that they have another duty, which they are not to leave undone; another point of interest, which they are not to neglect: and therefore I have spoken of this second estate in our government as of a middle order, that are properly mediators between the other two, in the eye of our constitution. Whilst the peers maintain this character, they will be able to discharge this duty; but they would cease to be so, if it was possible they should ever become the tools of faction, or the vassals of a minister. In mediations of this kind, different from those that are more commonly called such, mediators mingle in the contest, are parties concerned, and can by that alone expect to mediate with effect, whether they be considered as bodies of men, or individuals. When the commons are assisted by the peers in their reasonable endeavours to promote or restore frugality, to secure liberty, and to correct all sorts of maladministration; the peers will have, both collectively and separately, a credit with the people, as well as with the representatives of the people; by which they may contribute to check the latter, whenever an House of Commons shall grow unreasonable, factious, or seditious. But if the peers of the realm neglect, or oppose the commons in their just attempts, and forfeit by consequence the character of impartiality, and even the air of independency, the peers will then add little strength to the crown, whenever the evil day comes, and have as little power to prevent it from coming. There was a time, our fathers saw it, when an House of Commons destroyed, instead of supporting, the constitution, and introduced tyranny, under pretence of excluding slavery. I think it might be shown, from the anecdotes of that age, that this could not have happened, if the court had not been so long and so partially abetted by the greatest part of the nobility and clergy, both in the House of Lords and out of it. An universal and timely concurrence with the spirit of the Commons, which was pious in the true sense of the word at first, would have had, I presume, the full effect that every honest man proposed in a parliamentary reformation of the state; and those fatal opportunities, that were afterwards given to the republican, Presbyterian and independent factions, would have been avoided. But they who could have trimmed (for there is a wise and honest, as well as a silly and corrupt trimming) or have mediated with success, lost the power of doing either; some by abetting the crown so long, for fear of the Commons, and others by concurring with the Commons so far, for fear of the crown, that the people in general had no confidence in the former, and that the latter were afraid to trust their prince after all they had done against him. If any men had trusted to the plausible professions of the court at that time, and the court had subdued the opposite party, we may judge, without any breach of charity, that these men would have found themselves deceived. Just so, if any men who meant the reformation, not the destruction of the state, believed in the canting reformers of that age, such men were no doubt egregiously deceived. But I confess myself of opinion, and surely upon no improbable grounds, that there were few, or no such men. The good intentions of the court were distrusted even by those who took arms for the King; and the ill intentions of many of the leaders on the other side were suspected, no doubt by many who took arms for the Parliament. But two of the three estates being ripe for the rashest enterprises, and the third being in no condition to mediate, the extremes clashed, without any power sufficient to interpose; and when the sword was drawn, the sword could alone decide. I conclude therefore, from these two examples, that as there cannot be a greater error in politics than that of a nobility, who assist a prince to take away the liberties and privileges of the commons, which was the case in Castile, so the surest way of preventing that terrible dilemma, wherein men are obliged to choose either submission to tyrannical government, or concurrence with an enraged and no longer governable people, which hath been the case in Castile and Britain both, is for the nobility, and the principal men amongst the commons, to engage so early in the cause of liberty, that the former may be always in condition to mediate with effect, and the latter have always power to allay the intemperate heat of their own body.

I am, sir, &c.

Sir,

But to resume the comparison of other constitutions of government with our own, I say, that if the Gothic constitution in Spain, either by original defects, or by deviating from, and not being reduced again in time to its first principles, was destroyed through the corruption of parliaments, and by the force of an army, one of which betrayed, and the other conquered the commons of Castile; the commons of France seem either not to have had, or to have lost, in the dark beginnings of that monarchy, all share in the supreme, legislative power. The great, original defect of having but two estates to share the supreme power, is an objection common to the Roman, and to the French constitution, with this difference: of the three simple forms of government, the monarchical, the aristocratical, and the democratical, Rome wanted the first, and France hath always wanted the last. Rome had a nobility and a commonalty, but no magistracy fitted by its institution to answer the purposes of that supreme magistrate, who is called king even in limited monarchies. France hath always had a king and a nobility, and hath felt in their turns all the evils of monarchical and aristocratical tyranny. But the people have not had, I presume, since the government of the Franks was fully established on this side of the Rhine, and the form of their monarchy settled, any share in the supreme power, either collectively or representatively, how much soever a contrary notion may have been countenanced by some writers, and have been generally entertained, at least in other countries.

There is no nation in the world, says Mézeray, more illustrious, nor any whose original is more obscure than that of the French.[2] They who would dispute the first, could hardly dispute the last; and it is no business of mine to controvert either. As dark as their original is, we may discover enough to establish what hath been said, and to carry on the comparison we are making.

The Franks were a nation of Germany, seated at one time between the Elbe, Rhine and Neckar, and at another, that is, in

---

[1] *Craftsman* 439 (30 November 1734).
[2] François Eudes de Mézeray, *Histoire de France, Depuis Faramond Jusqu'au Regne de Louis le Juste* (3 vols., Paris, 1685), I, 90.

the reign of Theodosius the younger,[3] extending themselves on the
German side of the Rhine, from Cologne down to Nijmegen, and
still lower. What is known therefore of the government of the
ancient Germans, either from Tacitus, or any other good authority,
may be properly applied to their government, whilst they continued
in Germany, and even after they settled in Gaul, till such times as
we find, by relations more modern, that a different form of government prevailed amongst them. Now it seems to me extremely plain,
that a different form of government did prevail amongst them even
from the time of Clovis, the conqueror of Gaul.[4] Thus, for instance,
that passage in Tacitus, where he says [a]"that the ancient Germans
took their kings on account of nobility, and their generals on
account of valour; that the power of their kings was not absolute
and unlimited; and that their generals commanded by the authority
which their example, rather than their power gave them'; that passage, I say, is properly enough applied to the Franks before, and
perhaps during the conquest of Gaul; but very improperly afterwards, when [b]Clovis, both king and general of that people, had
founded the monarchy which he transmitted to his posterity. That
the nation of the Franks was divided into several tribes, or clans,
and that these were governed by several little princes, cannot be
doubted. – *Habebat quot pagos, tot paene duces.*[5] That a general was
chosen to command the whole with sovereign authority, but according to certain rules made by common consent, whenever any great
enterprise was undertaken, and that Clovis himself, though he succeeded his father Childeric in commanding over a part of the
Franks, was chosen in this manner, and for this purpose, is certain.
In his first expedition, he led an army of free-booters, and was
obliged by compact to divide the spoil by lots amongst them. The

[a] 'Reges ex nobilitate, duces ex virtute sumunt; nec regibus infinita, nec libera
potestas; & duces exemplo potius quam imperio praesunt'. *De Mor. Germ.*[6]
[b] Boulainv. *Mem. Hist.*[7]

[3] Theodosius II, emperor of the eastern Empire 408–50.
[4] Clovis, King of the Franks 481–511.
[5] 'They had almost as many rulers as villages.'
[6] Tacitus, *Germania*, VII. I.
[7] Henri de Boulainvilliers, 'Mémoires Historiques' in *Etat de la France . . . Avec des
Mémoires Historiques sur l'Ancien Gouvernement de Cette Monarchie jusqu'à Hugues
Capet*, ed. Philippe Mercier (3 vols., London, 1727–28), I, 10.

story, which so many authors have told, after Gregory of Tours, of a private soldier, who refused to leave to his disposition a vessel of gold, that had been taken out of a church at Rheims, and broke it before his face,[8] is a proof that he was nothing more at first than I have represented him, the head of a troop of adventurers, who chose him to lead them, but made their conditions with him. The Franks therefore might be at this time, in some sense, "all free, perfectly equal, and independent'; but will it follow from hence that they continued to be so, in any sense, after Clovis had founded their monarchy; had destroyed all their little kings; united in one body, and under his own domination, all their little states, and changed the form of their government, by appointing dukes, earls, vicars, and other magistrates, to govern under him, according to the model of government in the latter Roman empire? Certainly not. However this change was brought about, and to whatever it was owing, the monarchy of the Franks in Gaul was built on the ruins of their former government. This Boulainvilliers himself confesses, when he says (though not very accurately nor consistently, as I imagine, in calling their former government a kind of aristocracy) that 'the principle of union, which founded the monarchy on the ruins of a kind of aristocracy, was the mistaken ambition of particular men'.[9] In short, proofs enough may be collected out of this very author, to show that the government of the Franks, even under the first race of their kings, was not only different from the German government, but in some respects founded on quite opposite principles. One of these respects, which is immediately to my purpose, I shall mention.

The general assemblies that were held at first in the month of March, and afterwards in the month of May, were national assemblies, indeed, but not such as the ancient Germans held; among whom the [d]principal men consulted and decided about the least, and the whole body of the people about the greatest affairs. In these

[c] Boulainv. *Mem. Hist.*[10]
[d] 'De minoribus principes, de majoribus omnes'. Tacit.[11]

[8] Gregory of Tours, *History of the Franks*, II, 27.
[9] Boulainvilliers, 'Mémoires Historiques' in *Etat de la France*, I, 34.
[10] Boulainvilliers, 'Mémoires Historiques' in *Etat de la France*, I, 16.
[11] 'On minor matters the leaders [debate], on major matters everyone does': Tacitus, *Germania*, XI. 1.

assemblies of the French the people had nothing to do, unless we reckon for something the function of ᶜhollowing, which the author I have just now quoted assigns them, and which he says that custom had rendered necessary. In one word, the people had not any share in the supreme power, either collectively or representatively, in the original plan of the French government. Whether they acquired any share in this power afterwards, let us enquire next. ᶠMézeray pretends, and indeed the whole history of France vouches for him, ᵍ"that no nation ever honoured their nobility so much as the French; amongst whom the nobility was not only exempt from all sorts of impositions and charges, but commanded absolutely all inferior ranks, who were almost in a state of servitude'. How could it be otherwise, when the nobility, and chief magistrates, and the clergy, composed alone the national councils, or parliaments, and even exercised distributive justice all over the kingdom? Their power increased, as that of the kings of the first race diminished. Charles Martel,[12] indeed, who trusted to that battle-axe which gave him his name, and to foreign troops, laid aside the national assemblies, neglected the nobility, and misused even the clergy, who damned him for it. But Pepin[13] found it necessary to regain both, and attach them to his interest, in order to mount the throne. By attaching them, he attached the whole nation to him. Childeric was deposed, and he chosen king in a general assembly held at Soissons, which Mézeray calls most improperly, since the expression communicates a false idea to his reader, the states, 'les états'.[14] These assemblies,

---

ᶜ 'Ills (that is the French) laisserent passer aux hauts magistrats, les ducs, les comtes, & les vicaires, le droit de la nation entiere; de sortque le commun n'eut plus d'autres fonctions dans les assemblées réelles, que d'y paroitre pours les acclamations, que l'usage rendoit necessaires'. Boulainv. *Mem. Hist.*[15]

ᶠ L. 2.

ᵍ'Jamais nation n'honora tant la noblesse que celle la; car non seulement elle etoit exempte de toute sorte d'impots, et corvées, mais commandoit à baguette à ses inferieurs, sur lesquels elle avoit presque droit de servitude'.[16]

[12] Charles Martel (c. 688–741), grandfather of Charlemagne, defeated the Moors at Poitiers in 732.
[13] Pepin the Short, King of the Franks 751–68, son of Charles Martel, and father of Charlemagne, founder of the Carolingian dynasty.
[14] Mézeray, *Histoire de France*, I, 351.
[15] Boulainvilliers, 'Mémoires Historiques' in *Etat de la France*, I, 47.
[16] Mézeray, *Histoire de France*, untraced.

in his time, in that of his son Charles the Great, and so on, consisted of the nobility and clergy alone; and once more it is beyond all dispute certain, that the people had no more share in these national councils, under the second, than under the first race of the kings of France.

When the third race of these kings began in Hugues Capet,[17] the lords were so powerful in their estates, and so independent in their governments, that he was forced to come to a Kind of composition with them. They became sovereigns, each in his territory, but held of the crown, and acknowledged the King for the supreme lord. There was scarce a town which had not a little sovereign, scarce a castle without some little tyrant. The parliaments, in these ages, took several turns; 'Ills prirent divers plis', as [g]Pasquier expressed himself, but still they consisted of princes, great lords, bishops and abbots, who decided in them their disputes with one another, and with the King, and maintained by these means a sort of national confederacy, or federal union of many states, politically united under one head. Such assemblies as these, under the second and third race, were the original institutions, from whence the [h]parliaments of France have proceeded, as many alterations as they have received, and as much as they are now changed: so that we may safely affirm the parliaments of France never gave the people any share in the government of that kingdom; and whoever entertains a notion that the assemblies of the states did, or that [i]these assemblies are of great antiquity, or that they are the foundation of the liberty of the people of that country, will find himself, on due examination, grossly deceived.

These assemblies of the three estates, the nobility, clergy and commons, were invented first by [j]Philip le Bel.[18] They were entirely

[g] *Recherches de la France.*[19]
[h] Primitive origine & institution des parlements. Ibid.[20]
[i] Ibid.[21]
[j] 'L'assemblée des états. – fut une idée toute nouvelle de Philippe le Bel, & jusqu' alors entierement inusitée'. Boulanv. *Let. sur les Anciens Parl. de France.*[22]

[17] Hugues Capet, King of France 987–96, founder of the Capetian dynasty.
[18] Philip le Bel, King of France 1286–1314.
[19] Etienne Pasquier, *Les Recherches de la France* (Paris, 1596), fol. 30C.
[20] Pasquier, *Recherches*, fol. 30C.
[21] Pasquier, *Recherches*, fol. 30C.
[22] Boulainvilliers, 'Lettres sur les Anciens Parlements de France' in *Etat de la France*, III, 70.

unknown before the year 1301. The people had no right to any
such assemblies; and when they were instituted, they were plainly
designed for nothing less than the good of the people. Long after
the establishment of the Capetian race, when taxes grew heavy, and
were laid on and levied very arbitrarily, [k]seditions and rebellions of
an oppressed people, who had no other recourse, followed. To prevent these, not only writs, or orders, were sent to the nobility and
clergy, in the several sheriffwicks and bailiwicks, but to the commons, to assemble and take into consideration how to redress grievances, and support the public expenses; and after such consideration
had amongst themselves, to depute some persons of each order, or
estate, to confer together in the place appointed for holding such
general assemblies. [l]'The commons were added to these assemblies,'
says Pasquier, 'against the ancient order or practice of France, for
no other reason than this, that the principal burden, or charge, was
to fall upon them.' This was the true reason. Redress of grievances
had no part in the schemes of that rapacious and profuse prince,
who was the author of this institution; and he that considers the
manner in which these assemblies were convened, the powers they
were suffered to exercise, the subordination in which the commons
particularly were kept, and the habitual, unavoidable influence
under which they lay, will be easily convinced that such assemblies
were fitted to do the jobs and sanctify the iniquity of the court, and
nothing more. If at any time they make any good ordinances for the
reformation of the state, [m]'these ordinances are', says honest Pasquier, 'like fine pieces of tapestry, hung up to make a show to posterity'. They have no other effect. 'But the imposition granted to
the king hath its full effect.' I conclude therefore, and upon sufficient grounds, that even since the establishment of these assemblies of the estates, in the beginning of the fourteenth century, the

[k] Pasqu. *Rech.*[23]
[l] 'Le roturier fut expres ajouté, contre l'ancien ordre de la France, à cette assemblée', &c.[24]
[m] '– Ces sont belles tapisseries, qui servent seulement de parade à une posterité.
Cependant l'impost que l'on accorde au roy est fort bien mis à effct.'[25]

[23] Pasquier, *Recherches*, fol. 55 B–D.
[24] Pasquier, *Recherches*, fol. 54G.
[25] Pasquier, *Recherches*, fol. 54G.

people of France have had no real share in the supreme power of the government, either collectively or representatively.

I might illustrate and prove what is here advanced, by the example of every assembly of the states of France, of which we have any good accounts, from the first in 1301 to the last that was held, as I remember, in 1614. But such a deduction would carry us too far. I shall content myself therefore with making two observations.

First, that these farces, for such these assemblies were, and such they were designed to be, owe their institution not only to one of the worst kings, but to one of the worst ministers that France ever saw, Enguerand de Marigny,[26] who was called the coadjutor and the governor of the kingdom; the most insolent, the most avaricious, and the most prodigal man of his age. The great ability of this minister, on which his whole merit with a greedy master was raised, consisted in making his administration a system of violence and fraud, in order to plunder and enslave the people. When he durst not employ one, he turned himself to the other; and how grossly and impudently he managed even fraud, it may not be improper to take notice, in one instance, because we shall see the better, by this instance, what the nature and effect of these assemblies were, of which we speak, and what use the court made of them from their first institution. Enguerand de Marigny then meeting with great opposition to ⁿsome taxes he had devised, proposed the calling an assembly of the states, and hoped probably that he might gain the commons to favour the intention he had of extending these taxes to the nobility and clergy. A great scaffold was erected. The King, the lords and the clergy took their places on it. The commons attended at the foot of it. The minister made a most vehement declamation, to stir the passions of the audience, and made no scruple of insinuating in it, what neither he nor his master intended to perform a promise of reimbursing, after the expedition proposed, what the people should give to the King. The King rose from his throne, and advanced to the extremity of the scaffold, that he might second by his looks the harangue of his treasurer, and see who those were

---

ⁿ Boulainv. *Let. sur les Anciens Parl. de France.*[27]

[26] Enguerand de Marigny (*c*. 1275–1315), principal counsellor and treasurer of Philip le Bel.
[27] Boulainvilliers, 'Lettres' in *Etat de la France*, III, 74.

that refused, or consented to the aid he demanded. The deputies of Paris promised to give a sufficient supply, or to follow the King in their persons to the war. The other deputies concurred in this great engagement, and the assembly broke up, without any farther deliberation, or any ordinance of the estates. But an ordinance of the King soon followed; a °general excise was imposed by his authority, as if it had been the grant of the estates to him; and his minister had a number of harpies ready, whom he let loose to desolate the kingdom, by levying this infamous tax, for the consideration of some little advance made to the King. If you ask what were the consequences of these proceedings, it will be sufficient to mention two. The tax of a fifth on the revenues of the subject, which is the proportion of our land-tax of four shillings in the pound, was continued, though the general excise had been imposed; and ᵖEnguerand de Marigny was hanged in the succeeding reign for this amongst other crimes, though not by an assembly of the estates; for the estates had neither the opportunity nor the power of resenting the greatest insult that could be offered them, and the greatest injury that could be done to the nation.

The next observation I have to make is very short, but I think very pertinent, and very important. – This example shows us clearly how true it is, that no instruments of tyranny can be found so sure and effectual as an assembly of the estates of a realm, when such an assembly is so constituted as to want the power, which was from the first the case of the three estates in France, and the same must happen when they are so managed as to want the will, which became at last the case of the Cortes in Spain, to secure the liberty and defend the property of the people, against such kings as Philip le Bel, and such coadjutors as Marigny. This prince and his minister has strained prerogative to the utmost, and had governed by it very tyrannically. Whilst this expedient would do, they tried no other;

° '– Six deniers par livre de toutes les merchandises, victuailles, boissons, & denrées, – Vendues dans le royaume'. Boulainv. *Let. sur les Anciens Parl. de France.*[28]

ᵖ Mézeray, Daniel, &c. sous Louis Hutin.[29]

---

[28] Boulainvilliers, 'Lettres' in *Etat de la France*, III, 75.

[29] Enguerand de Marigny was executed in April 1315: Mézeray, *Histoire de France*, II, 354.

but when they apprehended it might fail them, they added a deputation of the commons to the assembly of the estates; that, seeming to create a new control on the crown, they might in reality give greater scope and freer exercise to arbitrary will. The friends of liberty therefore, who live under limited monarchies, cannot be too careful to preserve their constitution in vigour, nor too fearful lest their representatives should be so influenced as to neglect their privileges, misapply their powers, and depart from their integrity; since these friends of liberty see that the greatest masters of tyranny have judged the form, without the spirit, of a free government more favourable to their schemes of oppression, than all the authority that absolute monarchy can give; and that they made an innovation in the form of their government on this very motive, and for this very purpose.

I am, sir, &c.

Sir,
I have dwelt long, perhaps too long, on the last head. I was induced
to it, not only because the account I have given, according to the
truth of history, is contrary to the national prejudices of many
people on this subject, as I hinted before; but principally because
the great point of strength and security, on which the freedom of
our constitution rests, will appear in a fuller light, by being thus
contrasted with the constitution of the French government. Both
their ancestors and ours came out of Germany, and had probably
much the same manners, the same customs, and the same forms of
government. But as they proceeded differently in the conquests they
made, so did they in the establishments that followed. The conquest
of Britain was a work of time, and the Saxon monarchy was long in
forming. The conquest of Gaul was carried on with greater rapidity,
and the French monarchy was sooner found. From hence some
reasons might be drawn to account, amongst others, for that great
difference between the constitutions of the two monarchies, which
these two German nations founded, at no great distance of time, in
Britain and in Gaul. But I shall not indulge myself in guessing at
the reasons, or accidents, that determined the Franks to the division
they made of their people, and to the form of government they
established. Whatever reasons or accidents determined them, this is
certain, that the distinction of lord and vassal became the general
distinction of the whole nation; that the [a]commons amongst them
were little better than slaves, whatever they had been in Germany;
and that they were so inured to servitude under their kings, prelates
and lords, that they looked on themselves at last, not justly, but
unjustly, as men who had no right, no, not even a right by nature,
to any share in the government of that community whereof they
made so vastly the principal part.

---

[a] 'Le people, d'un autre coté, se fait justice, reconnoissant combien la condition
naturelle le doit eloigner du concours du government, & dans se sentiment ne se
fait entendre que par requête'. Boulainv. *Let. sur les An. Parl.*[2]

[1] *Craftsman* 440 (7 December 1734).
[2] Boulainvilliers, 'Lettres' in *Etat de la France*, III, 72.

In Britain another constitution was formed, and another spirit prevailed. The Saxons had a [b]nobility too, arising from personal valour, or wisdom, continued by blood, and sometimes conferred by the prince, however legally at first it matters not to enquire, on such as held great offices about his person.[3] All these were the adelings, or nobles, an handful in comparison of the *frilingi*, or freeborn, who made the body of the Saxon people. The freedom of this people was erected on two columns, that have proved more durable than brass. They were parties to the making, and to the executing all the general laws of the kingdom.[4] They shared the legislative power; were joined to the lords in the administration of justice; and no magistrate, or officer, could exercise jurisdiction, nor authority over them, no not ecclesiastical, without their consent and election. The *comites ex plebe*, who were chosen for this last function, the administration of justice, made one rank amongst the Saxon commonalty. The *custodes pagani*, such as had an helmet, a coat of mail, and a gilt sword, for their ordinary arms, whether they fought on foot, or on horseback, made another rank; and the plain *pagani*, or ceorles, made the lowest.[5] But even these were totally distinct from, and far superior to the *lazzi*, or slaves, nay to the free *lazzi*, such as had been slaves, and were become free. The ceorles were freemen to all intents and purposes, and in all the essentials of liberty, as much as the Saxons of any superior rank, and were capable of rising to any superior rank by merit, or by favour.

These are the sources, from which all the distinction of rank and degree, that exist at this day amongst us, have flowed. These are the general principles of all our liberties. That this Saxon constitution hath varied in many particulars, and at several periods of time, I am far from denying. That it did so, for instance, on the entry of the Normans, though certainly not near so much as many have been willing to believe, and to make others believe, is allowed. Nay, let it be allowed for argument's sake, and not otherwise, that during the first confusion, and the subsequent disorders which

---

[b] Nat. Bacon. *Hist. & Pol. Dis.*

[3] Nathaniel Bacon, *An Historical and Political Discourse of the Laws & Government of England* (2 vols., London, 1682; reissued 1689), I, 33.
[4] Bacon, *Historical and Political Discourse*, I, 34–5.
[5] Bacon, *Historical and Political Discourse*, I, 35.

necessarily accompany and follow so great and so violent a revolution, the scheme of the Saxon constitution was broken, and the liberties of the people invaded, as well as the crown usurped. Let us even agree that laws were made, without the consent of the people; that officers and magistrates, civil, military and ecclesiastical, were imposed without their election: in one word, that these Norman kings, and the lords, had mounted each other too high to be lords over freemen, and that the government was entirely monarchical and aristocratical, without any exercise of democratical power. Let all this be granted, and the utmost that can be made of it will amount to this, that confusion and violence at the entry, and for some time after, under the government of a foreign race, introduced many illegal practices, and some foreign principles of policy, contrary to the spirit, and letter too, of the ancient constitution; and that these kings and the lords 'abused their power over the freemen, by extortion and oppression, as lords over tenants'.[6] But it will remain true, that neither kings nor lords, nor both together, "'could prevail over them, or gain their consent to give their right, or the law, up to the king's beck. But still the law remained arbiter both of king and people, and the parliament supreme expounder and judge both of it and them.'[7] Though the branches were lopped, and the tree lost its beauty for a time, yet the root remained untouched, was set in a good soil, and had taken strong hold in it: so that care and culture, and time were indeed required, and our ancestors were forced to water it, if I may use such an expression, with their blood; but with this care, and culture, and time, and blood, it shot up again with greater strength than ever, that we might sit quiet and happy under the shade of it; for if the same form was not exactly restored in every part, a tree of the same king, and as beautiful, and as luxuriant as the former, grew up from the same root.

To bring our discourse to that point which is here immediately concerned, Parliaments were never interrupted, nor the right of any estate taken away, however the exercise of it might be disturbed. Nay, they soon took the forms they still preserve, were constituted

c Nat. Bacon summary conclus. of the first part of *Hist. and Pol. Disc.*

6 Bacon, *Historical and Political Discourse*, I, 199.
7 Bacon, *Historical and Political Discourse*, I, 199.

almost as they now are, and were entirely built on the same general principles, as well as directed to the same purposes.

When I say that they were constituted almost as they now are, I do not mean to enter into any of those minute questions, about which a man may employ much time and study, and have as little true and useful knowledge of our constitution as the most ignorant man alive. But I propose to make a short reflection or two on the property and power of the three estates that compose our Parliament, as they stood formerly, and as they now stand; because although our Parliaments were composed of king, lords and commons in those days, as well as these, yet the difference of the weight which each of these estates hath cast into the scale of government, at different periods, does in effect make some difference in the constitution of Parliaments: and by considering this difference, our thoughts will be led the better to judge of the true poise of our constitution, on maintaining which our all depends; since the nearer we keep to it, the safer our liberty is, and since every variation from it is dangerous to our liberty, in a degree proportionable to such variation. Property then, and power by consequence, have changed hands, or rather have shifted much in the same hands since the Norman era. Kings, lords and the Church were in those days, and long afterwards, the great proprietors; and by the nature of tenures, as well as by the bulk of their estates, they held the commons in no small subjection, and seem to have governed without much regard to them, or to their concurrence, in many cases. But the regard that was not paid them at first, the kings, the lords and the Church found it necessary to pay them in a short time; and that authority, that weight in the balance of power, which property did not give them, they soon acquired, or rather resumed by their numbers, and by the circumstances that followed. By the circumstances that followed, I mean the great disorders in the state, and the civil wars, which the ambition of princes, of the nobility, and of the Church too, created. In all these conflicts, some of the commons [d]"holding for the king, who promised liberty from the lords, and others siding with the lords, who promised them liberty from the king',[8] they

[d] Nat. Bacon *Hist. and Pol. Disc.* conclus. of the 2d part.

[8] Bacon, *Historical and Political Discourse*, II, 177.

came off better in the end than their principals, and an example
rarely to be paralleled was set; for general liberty was nursed by
these means, under the wings of particular ambition. In later days,
when the nation, harassed and spent by the long wars of York and
Lancaster, seemed glad to settle under the stable government; and
in this temper gave many advantages to the cunning of Henry the
Seventh, which the violence of his son improved; it is certain that
the commons suffered extremely from the avarice of one, the profusion of the other, and the highstrained prerogative of both. But
then their sufferings were temporary, and may be said to have ended
with these reigns; whereas the sufferings of the nobility and the
Church were permanent and irretrievable. 'The king and his council', says the author I quoted last, 'under colour of liveries and
retainders, brought the whole kingdom to be of their livery.'[9] It was
so. But still the commons lost nothing, and gained much. They
were more under subjection to the crown; but they were less under
subjection to the lords and the Church. Not only the dependencies
on these were broken, but the lords and the Church were made
more dependent on the crown than the commons had been on them.
The lords were obliged to attend the court at their own expense,
and might alienate their estates to defray this expense. A great part
of the lands of the Church were confiscated and parcelled out to
those who could buy, at very cheap rates; and the increase of trade,
which begun about this time to be very considerable, put the commons into a condition of being the buyers. Thus were the old foundations of property and power sapped on one side, and new foundations laid on the other. Some of the weight of the Church
continued in the scale of the lords, and some of it hath gone since
into that of the commons. The parliamentary control of the crown
did not become less, but it became more equally and more usefully
placed. Democracy was so well poised with aristocracy, after this
great change, that if they divided, they could not invade one
another; and if they united, they could not be invaded by the monarchy. Far different was the case in other countries, where the
crown got the better of the lords, and baffled, at least in some
degree, the monstrous attempts of ecclesiastical usurpation. In
France, for instance, when the encroachments of the papal power

[9] Bacon, *Historical and Political Discourse*, II, 143.

were checked, the Church compounded with the crown, and an alliance succeeded, of the monarchy with the hierarchy. But if the Church was able to compound, the nobility was forced to submit in that kingdom; so that the authority and wealth of the Church being fixed on the side of the crown, the whole strength and influence of the nobility being taken from them, and incorporated with the power of the crown, and the commons having nothing to do in that government but to pay taxes, and carry arms, the kings of France are become absolute monarchs; and whatever liberty, or appearance of liberty, there was in that constitution, it is totally destroyed.

When I say that Parliaments were entirely built on the same general principles, as well as directed to the same purposes, as they still are, I shall be justified by the whole tenor of our history, and of our law. Let us consider this in a case the plainest imaginable, though it suffers so much debate through the effrontery of some men. Let us consider it relatively to that great principle, that Parliaments ought to be independent of the crown, in all respects, except such as are settled by the law and custom of Parliament, and concerning which there is no dispute. Now, this general principle hath not only been always the same, but it hath been always so declared, in the most authentic and solemn manner; and Parliaments have not been more intent on any national concern whatever, than on maintaining this principle, and securing the effects of it. I say, Parliaments have been constantly thus intent, and especially in the best times, during more than three centuries at least; for I would not go back too far, nor grope unnecessarily in the dark. What else did those laws mean, that were made in the time of the Lancaster kings, to regulate the elections, and to prevent the influence which Richard the Second had illegally and arbitrarily employed,[10] and which there was room to fear that other princes might employ? What else do all those resolutions, all those declarations, all those remonstrances, all those Acts of Parliament mean, that have been made so often, and enforced so strongly, from time to time, and from those days to these, against the influence of the crown, either on the elections, or on the members of Parliament? I should be ashamed to ask any more questions of this kind, or to descend into any detail, in order to prove what every clerk of a justice of peace, nay, almost every

[10] Compare Bolingbroke, *Remarks on the History of England*, 'Letter vii'.

day-labourer, knows. But there is another question, which I must
ask. If this be so, what do those men mean, who are employed, or
rather, what does he mean who employs them, to plead in all places,
and on all occasions, even the most solemn, in favour of this very
influence, nay, of the very worst sort of it, of that influence which
is created immediately by corruption; for to that their arguments
reach by undeniable consequences? Reason is against him and them;
since it is a plain absurdity to suppose a control on the crown (and
they have not yet ventured to suppose the contrary, that I know of)
and to establish, at the same time, a power, and even a right, in the
crown, to render this control useless. Experience is against them;
since the examples of other countries, and at some times (former
times I mean) of our own, have proved, that a prince may govern
according to his arbitrary will, or that of his more arbitrary minister,
as absolutely, and much more securely with, than without the concurrence of a Parliament. Authority, even the uniform authority of
our whole legislature, is against them. The voice of our law gives
them the lie. How then shall we account for this proceeding; this
open and desperate attack upon our constitution, and therefore
upon our liberty? Have these great men made any nice discovery,
that escaped the blunt sagacity of our ancestors formerly, and is
above the narrow conceptions of all other men, except themselves,
at this time? Is it less fit than the wisdom of this nation hath judged
it to be, for so many ages, that kings should govern under the constitutional control of two other estates? Or is it less fit that they
should govern so, for the time to come, than it was for the time
past? We shall hear, for aught I know, even in this age, that kings
are God's vicegerents; that they are, next to him and his son Christ
Jesus, supreme moderators and governors. We shall hear again, perhaps, of their hereditary, their divine, their indefeasible right, and
the rest of that silly cant, which was invented to make the usurpations of prerogative go down the better. But will even this alter
the case? Will this make it unworthy of them to submit to the
full control of such a constitution as God himself approved, in the
institution of the Jewish senate? Moses was undoubtedly God's
vicegerent. He was, if ever man was so, next and immediately under
God, a supreme moderator and governor. He was ͤinspired, and

ͤ Exod. xviii.[11]

[11] Exodus 18: 17–27.

assisted in a supernatural manner; and yet he took the advice of his father-in-law Jethro, the priest of Midian. He associated to himself in the government of the commonwealth, or he bade the people take, as he says in [f]another place, or choose, 'wise men and understanding, and known among the tribes', that they might be associated to him. He found himself unequal to the talk of governing alone, and he expostulated with God upon it. [g]'I am not able to bear all this people alone. Have I conceived all this people? Have I begotten them? If thou deal thus with me, kill me, I pray thee, out of hand.' Whether they, who deduce from hence the institution of sanhedrins, are in the right, or they who assign them a more modern date, against the opinion of the Jewish doctors themselves, whose authority our doctors receive implicitly enough in some cases, and reject as arbitrarily in others, it matters not to enquire. Let us leave the dispute to the partisans of Joseph Scaliger and Petavius, of father Simon and Le Clerc.[12] Thus much is certain. A great sanhedrin subsisted at Jerusalem, even at the coming of the Messiah, as well as inferior sanhedrins in several parts of Palestine; which form of government bore some resemblance to our old Saxon constitution; and he who takes the trouble of looking into [h]Mr Selden, will find that the great sanhedrin had as much authority, and exercised as much power, as ever Parliaments did, or witanegemots could claim. That God approved a kind of parliamentary establishment, and a division of the supreme power between his vicegerent Moses and the seventy elders, to whom he gave some of the spirit that was on Moses, the quotations I refer to from holy writ do sufficiently prove. After this, it cannot be said, I think, to derogate from the majesty of any prince, let us entertain as high notions of

---

[f] Deut. i.[13]

[g] Numb. xi.[14]

[h] Seld. *De Syned. & Praef. Iurid. Vet. Ebraeorum.*[15]

---

[12] Joseph Scaliger (1540–1609), noted French classicist and chronologer; Dionysius Petavius (Denis Petau) (1583–1652), French chronologer, universal historian and controverter of Scaliger; Richard Simon (1638–1712), French Oratorian, biblical scholar and chronologer, whose *Critical History of the Old Testament* (Eng. trans., London, 1682) provided one of the foundations of English deism; Jean Le Clerc (1657–1736), encyclopaedist and biblical scholar.

[13] Deuteronomy 1: 13.

[14] Numbers 11: 12–15.

[15] John Selden, *De Synedriis et Praefecturis Iuridicis Veterum Ebraeorum* (3 vols., London, 1650–55).

this majesty as we please, that he is relieved from the burden of governing alone; that he is obliged to share the supreme power with the nobility and commonalty of the realm; and that he is hindered from destroying, either directly or indirectly, that independency of those other estates, which can alone preserve, this division of the supreme power, really, as well as apparently. But perhaps these great and honest men have discovered a necessity of putting the members, or a majority of the members of Parliament, under the influence of the crown, in order to preserve this very constitution. Let us see therefore what dangers this expedient is fitted to prevent. – Are we afraid that an House of Commons, unless restrained by places and pensions, should give up the constitution to the lords, and establish an aristocracy? This fear would be ridiculous surely; and he who should argue against such a supposition, would make himself so. – Are we afraid that an House of Commons, unless restrained in this manner, should usurp more power than belongs to them, and establish a kind of democratical tyranny? But they would have, in opposition to them, a power sufficient to defeat their designs: the united power of the crown, and of the House of Lords. Formerly, indeed, they succeeded in an attempt of this kind; and the King and the lords may, at any time, throw too much power into their scale, and set the sense and spirit of the people on their side, as was done at that time. But this neither hath been, nor can be done, unless both King and lords conduct themselves so ill, that the mischiefs to be apprehended from their prevalency appear as great, or greater, than those which are to be apprehended from the prevalency of the commons. Let it be remembered too, that as the King and lords may give too much power and popularity to the commons, so the lords and commons may give too much power to the crown. The difference will lie only here; that the King and lords will never do the first designedly; whereas there is a possibility that the lords and commons may be induced, in some age less virtuous than the present, by places, pensions and other gratifications, bestowed on a majority of those assemblies, to do the last designedly. What now remains to be urged, in favour of this expedient? From what danger are we to be protected by it? Shall we be told that Parliaments will not pursue the national interest, unless their members are bought into it by the crown? Something like this hath been advanced, I have heard; and nothing more impudent, nor more silly could be advanced. A court that is truly in the interest of the nation, will have, nay, must have a concurrence of Parliament, as it would be easy, if it was needful, to show. Time and trouble, indeed, may be sometimes required to lead independent men, who judge for themselves, and comply because they are convinced; whereas neither one nor the other are wanting, to determine such as hold to a court by a corrupt dependency on it: for they are soon disciplined, and ready to perform the whole exercise of parliamentary mercenaries at the beat of a drum. Some inconveniencies may likewise arise, for that which I have just mentioned does not deserve the name, from the independency of Parliaments. Ministers, for instance, may be called to account by the passion, by the prejudice, if you will, of such assemblies, oftener, perhaps, than they deserve to be; or their errors may be censured, or their faults be punished, in a greater degree, and with more rigour, not only than true political justice requires, which should always be tempered with mercy, but even than strict justice exacts. But as one of these is a fault, if it be a fault, on the best side, and as the other will certainly happen very seldom, it does not seem reasonable, that a door should be opened to corruption and dependency, in order to prevent them. Nay, farther, this vigilance, and this severity of Parliaments, which we here suppose, will not fail to have some very good effects, that are more than sufficient to balance the supposed ill effects. Among the rest, they may render the rash, who are in power, more cautious, and the bold more modest. They may render fools less fond of power, and awe even knaves into honesty. It were better, surely, that able and good men should now and then suffer, nay, the good man who suffered would be himself of this opinion, than that the adulation and servility of Parliaments, which are the necessary consequences of corruption and dependency, should ever contribute to make the court become, in any future age, a sanctuary for pickpockets, and an hospital for changelings.

I am, sir, &c.

Sir,

The great alteration we have spoken of, in property and power, brought our constitution, by slow degrees, and through many struggles and dangers, so near the most perfect idea of a free system of government, that nothing would be now wanting to complete it, if effectual means were found of securing the independency of Parliament against corruption, as well as it is secured against prerogative. Our Kings have lost little of the gaudy plumage of the crown. Some of their superfluous power, indeed, hath been bought, and more hath been wrested from them. Notwithstanding which, it is a very demonstrable truth, that the crown must sit lighter and more secure on the head of a wise prince (and no constitution provides for, though every constitution should provide against, a weak prince), since the great change of property and power in favour of the commons, than ever it did before. Our Kings are no longer exposed, as some of the greatest of them have been, to the insults of turbulent, ambitious lords, or haughty prelates. It is no longer in the power of a few factious noblemen to draw armies into the field, and oblige their prince to fight for his crown, to fight to gain it, and to fight to keep it; as Edward the Fourth did, I think, in nine pitched battles.[2] To make the prince uneasy, or insecure, as we are now constituted, the whole body of the people must be uneasy under his government. A popular King of Great Britain will be always not only easy and secure, but in effect absolute. He will be, what the British constitution alone can make any prince, the absolute monarch of a free people; and this popularity is so easily acquired, a King gains the public confidence and affection at so cheap a rate, that he must be poor indeed in all the kingly virtues, who does not purchase them, and establish true popularity upon them.

If the condition of our Kings is mended in many respects, and made worse in none, that of the nation is mended in every respect, by the great improvements of our constitution; which are due prin-

---

[1] *Craftsman* 441 (14 December 1734).
[2] The most famous battles in the Wars of the Roses fought by Edward IV (1442–83) King of England 1461–70, 1471–83) in defence of his crown against Henry VI were Barnet and Tewkesbury (both fought in 1471).

cipally to the change I have mentioned, as the advances we have made in trade, and in national wealth and power, are due principally to these improvements. It is by these, that the subjects of Great Britain enjoy hitherto such a freedom of their persons, and such a security of their property, as no other people can boast. Hence that great encouragement of industry; hence that broad and solid foundation of credit, which must always continue, unless the weight of taxes, and the oppression of tax-gatherers make it worth no man's while to be industrious any longer, and unless national credit be reduced, by length of time, and private management, to rest no longer on its natural and original foundation, but on the feeble props of yearly expedients, and daily tricks; by which a system, that ought to be the plainest and fairest imaginable, will become of course a dark, intricate, and wicked mystery of stockjobbing.

But the great advantage we are to insist upon here, which hath arisen to the whole nation from the alteration in the state of property and power, is this: that we have been brought by it to the true poise of a mixed government, constituted like ours in the three simple forms. The democratical power is no longer kept under the same dependencies; and if an House of Commons should now fail to assert that independent share in the supreme legislative power, which the constitution assigns to this assembly, it could not proceed, as it might and sometimes did formerly, from the nature of tenures, and many other unavoidable restraints; it could proceed alone from the corruption of particular men, who threw themselves into a voluntary dependency. The democratical power of our constitution is not sufficient to overtop the monarchical and aristocratical; but it is sufficient to counterwork and balance any other power by its own strength, and without the fatal necessity of favouring the ambition of the crown against the lords, or that of the lords against the crown. Nay more, as our government is now constituted, the three estates have not only one common interest, which they always had; but they have, considered as estates, no separate, contradictory interest. Our constitution gives so much grandeur, so much authority and power to the crown, and our Parliaments give so immense a revenue, that no prince hath any real interest to desire more, who looks on himself as the supreme magistrate of a free people; for if we suppose inordinate ambition, or avarice, to make part of his character, these passions are insatiable: but then for this very reason, because they are so, there ought to be no account held of them; and though a prince may measure his demands, a people, who are in their senses, will never measure their concessions by them.

The property of the commons is not only become far superior to that of the lords upon the whole, but in the detail there are few, very few, instances to be produced of greater shares of private property amongst the latter, than amongst the former; and as the property of the commons is greater, so it is equally free. There are no badges of servitude on one side; no pretence of any superiority, except those of title and rank, on the other. The peers are, in some points, I speak it with all the respect due to them, commoners with coronets on their coats of arms; and affecting to act as such, it is plain they desire very wisely to be taken for such, on many occasions. The interests on these two estates then, with regard to property, are the same; and their particular rights and privileges are now so well ascertained, and so distinguished, that as the proximity of their interests of one sort should always unite them, so the distance of those of another sort cannot easily make them clash. In short, these two orders, according to the present constitution (and how different is it from that of Rome, or, in the last respect, even from that of Spain, not to mention that of France?) have no temptation, and scarce the means, of invading each other: so that they may the better, and the more effectually, employ their vigilance, and unite their efforts, whenever it shall be necessary, against the encroachments of the crown, from whose shackles they have both emancipated themselves, whether the attempts to impose these shackles again are carried on by prerogative, or by the more formidable enemy of liberty, corruption.

It hath been observed already, that although the crown hath the sole power of creating peers, yet the independency of the peerage on the crown is secured by this: that their rights and privileges cannot be taken from them, at the will of the crown. Could the crown unmake, as well as make peers, it would be a jest to talk of three estates, since there would be virtually, and in effect, but two; and therefore our constitution hath provided against it. But the commons of Great Britain can make, and at proper seasons, and in a proper manner, unmake their representatives; by which means, many inconveniencies and mischiefs are avoided, and many wise and just ends obtained. The peers of the realm can, the commons cannot, assemble in their collective body, without exceeding those numbers, amongst whom the quiet, order, decency and solemnity of a senate may be preserved. The peers therefore sit in Parliament in their collective, the commons in their representative body. The peers have an inherent, the commons a delegated right. The peers are therefore accountable for their conduct, as all other men are, to God, to their own consciences, to the tribunal of public fame, and to no other. But the commons are accountable to another tribunal, as well as to these, to that of their constituents; before which they must frequently appear, according to the true intent of our constitution, to have a censure, or approbation, passed on their conduct, by the refusal, or grant of new powers to the particular members. Thus the collective body of the people of Great Britain delegate, but do not give up, trust, but do not alienate their right and their power, and cannot be undone by having beggary or slavery brought upon them, unless they co-operate to their own undoing, and in one word betray themselves.

We cannot therefore subscribe to those two sayings of my Lord Bacon, which are quoted to this effect; 'That England can never be undone, unless by Parliaments;[3] and that there is nothing, which a Parliament cannot do.'[4] – Great Britain, according to our present constitution cannot be undone by Parliaments; for there is something which a Parliament cannot do. A Parliament cannot annul the constitution; and whilst that is preserved, though our condition may be bad, it cannot be irretrievably so. The legislative is a supreme, and may be called, in one sense, an absolute, but in none an arbitrary power. [a]"It is limited to the public good of the society. It is a power, that hath no other end but preservation, and therefore can never have a right to destroy, enslave, or designedly to impoverish the subjects; for the obligations of the law of nature cease not in

[a] Locke's *Essay on Civil Government*, c. 11. of the extent of the legislative power.[5]

---

[3] A commonplace, though not always attributed to Bacon, e.g. [John Toland,] *The Art of Governing by Partys* (London, 1701), 56; *Craftsman* 427 (7 September 1734); William Blackstone, *Commentaries on the Laws of England* (4 vols., London, 1765–9), I, 156–7.

[4] The classic doctrine of the omnipotence of parliamentary sovereignty, attributed to the 2nd Earl of Pembroke (1534–1601) with the qualification 'but make a man a woman, and a woman a man'.

[5] Locke, *Second Treatise*, § 135.

society, &c.' – If you therefore put so extravagant a case, as to suppose the two houses of Parliament concurring to make at once a formal cession of their own rights and privileges, and of those of the whole nation to the crown, and ask who hath the right, and the means, to resist the supreme legislative power? I answer, the whole nation hath the right; and a people who deserve to enjoy liberty, will find the means. An attempt of this kind would break the bargain between the king and the nation, between the representative and collective body of the people, and would dissolve the constitution. From hence it follows, that the nation which hath a right to preserve this constitution, hath a right to resist an attempt, that leaves no other means of preserving it but those of resistance. From hence it follows, that if the constitution was actually dissolved, as it would be by such an attempt of the three estates, the people would return to their original, their natural right, the right of restoring the same constitution, or of making a new one. No power on earth could claim any right of imposing a constitution upon them; and less than any that King, those lords, and those commons, who, having been entrusted to preserve, had destroyed the former. – But to suppose a case more within the bounds of possibility, though one would be tempted to think it as little within those of probability, let us suppose our Parliaments, in some future generation, to grow so corrupt, and the crown so rich, that a pecuniary influence constantly prevailing over the majority, they should assemble for little else than to establish grievances, instead of redressing them; to approve the measures of the court, without information; to engage their country in alliances, in treaties, in wars, without examination; and to give money without account, and almost without stint. The case would be deplorable. Our constitution itself would become our grievance, whilst this corruption prevailed; and if it prevailed long, our constitution could not last long; because this slow progress would lead to the destruction of it as surely as the more concise method of giving it up at once. But, in this case, the constitution would help itself, and effectually too, unless the whole mass of the people was tainted, and the electors were become no honester than the elected. Much time would be required to beggar and enslave the nation, in this manner. It could scarce be the work of one Parliament, though Parliaments should continue to be septennial. It could not be the work of a triennial Parliament most certainly: and the people of

Great Britain would have none to blame but themselves; because, as the constitution is a sure rule of action to those whom they choose to act for them, so it is likewise a sure rule of judgment to them, in the choice of their trustees, and particularly of such as have represented them already. In short, nothing can destroy the constitution of Britain, but the people of Britain: and whenever the people of Britain become so degenerate and base, as to be induced by corruption, for they are no longer in danger of being awed by prerogative, to choose persons to represent them in Parliament, whom they have found by experience to be under an influence, arising from private interest, dependants on a court, and the creatures of a minister; or others, who are unknown to the people, that elect them, and bring no recommendations but that which they carry in their purses; then may the enemies of our constitution boast that they have got the better of it, and that it is no longer able to preserve itself, nor to defend liberty. Then will that trite, proverbial speech be verified in our case, 'that the corruptions of the best things are the worst';[6] for then will that very change in the state of property and power, which improved our constitution so much, contribute to the destruction of it; and we may even wish for those little tyrants, the great lords and the great prelates again, to oppose the encroachments of the crown. How preferable will subjection to those powerful landlords (whom the commonalty were accustomed to serve; and by whom, if they suffered on one hand, they had considerable advantages on the other), how preferable, indeed, will this subjection appear to them, when they shall see the whole nation oppressed by a few upstarts in power; often by the meanest, always by the worst of their fellow-subjects; by men, who owe their elevation and riches neither to merit nor birth, but to the favour of weak princes, and to the spoils of their country, beggared by their rapine. Then will the fate of Rome be renewed, in some sort, in Britain. The grandeur of Rome was the work of many centuries, the effect of much wisdom, and the price of much blood. She maintained her grandeur, whilst she preserved her virtue; but when luxury grew up to favour corruption, and corruption to nourish luxury, then Rome grew venal; the election of her magistrates, the

---

[6] Compare David Hume, 'Of Superstition and Enthusiasm' (1741), '. . . *the corruption of the best things produces the worst*, is grown into a maxim, and is commonly proved'.

sentences of her judges, the decrees of her senate, all was sold: for her liberty was sold when these were sold; and her riches, her power, her glory could not long survive her liberty. She, who had been the envy, as well as the mistress of nations, fell to be an object of their scorn, or their pity. They had seen and felt that she governed other people by will, and her own by law. They beheld her governed herself by will; by the arbitrary will of the worst of her own citizens, of the worst of both sexes, of the worst of human kind; by Caligula, by Claudius, by Nero, by Messalina, by Agrippina, by Poppaea, by Narcissus, by Callistus, by Pallas;[7] by princes that were stupid or mad; by women that were abandoned to ambition and to lust; by ministers that were emancipated slaves, parasites and panders, insolent and rapacious. In this miserable state, the few that retained some sparks of the old Roman spirit, had double cause to mourn in private; for it was not safe even to mourn in public. They mourned the loss of the liberty and grandeur of Rome; and they mourned that both should be sacrificed to wretches whose crimes would have been punished, and whose talents would scarce have recommended them to the meanest offices, in the virtuous and prosperous ages of the commonwealth. Into such a state, the difference of times and of other circumstances considered, at least, into a state as miserable as this, will the people of Britain both fall, and deserve to fall, if they suffer, under any pretence, or by any hands, that constitution to be destroyed, which cannot be destroyed, unless they suffer it; unless they co-operate with the enemies of it, by renewing an exploded distinction of parties; by electing those to represent them, who are hired to betray them; or by submitting tamely, when the mask is taken off, or falls off, and the attempt to bring beggary and slavery is avowed, or can be no longer concealed. If ever this happens, the friends of liberty, should any such remain, will have one option still left; and they will rather choose, no doubt, to die the last of British freemen, than bear to live the first of British slaves.

I am, sir, &c.

---

[7] Caligula (emperor 37–41), Claudius (emperor 41–54), Nero (emperor 54–68), Messalina (wife of Claudius), Agrippina (mother of Nero) and Poppaea (wife of Nero) were all bywords for cruelty and sensuality. Narcissus was Claudius' secretary; Callistus, Caligula's freedman; and Pallas, Claudius' freedman, who helped Nero to the throne.

Sir,

If we had proposed nothing more to ourselves, in writing this dissertation on parties, than the entertainment, such as it is, of your readers, and our own amusement; we should not have dwelt, perhaps, so much on the nature of the British constitution, nor have recurred so often to assert the necessary independency of Parliaments on the crown. But we had another motive, which we are neither afraid, nor ashamed to avow. This necessary independency of Parliaments, in which the essence of our constitution, and by consequence of our liberty consists, seems to be in great, not to say, in imminent danger of being lost. They who are alarmed at every thing that is said in favour of our constitution, and of British liberty, and who are prejudiced against every man who writes or speaks in defence of them, may take, or affect to take, and try to give offence at this expression. But we desire to be understood, as we have explained our meaning upon some former occasion. We understand our constitution to be in danger, not only when it is attacked, but as soon as a breach is made, by which it may be attacked; and we understand this danger to be greater, or less, in proportion to the breach that is made, and without any regard to the probability or improbability of an attack. This explanation of our meaning is the better founded, because the nation hath an undoubted right to preserve the constitution not only inviolate, but secure from violations. Should corruption prevail among the members, which we trust will never happen, as notoriously as it does in the elections of Parliament, we all know how much the magnanimity of our present King would scorn to take so mean an advantage over the nation; how much, on the contrary, his heroical spirit would prompt him to maintain the liberty even of a degenerate people, who might deserve no longer the enjoyment of so invaluable a blessing, but who could never deserve to have it taken from them by a prince of that family, which was raised by them to the throne, for no other reason but to preserve it. All this we know; and the nation may have, no doubt, the same confidence in every future King of the same illustrious and royal house. But this will not alter the case; nor make that,

[1] *Craftsman* 442 (21 December 1734).

which I call danger, cease to be such. Should angels and arch-angels come down from heaven to govern us, the same danger would exist, until the springs, from whence it arises, were cut off; not because some angels and arch-angels have fallen, and from being the guardians, have become the tempters and tormentors of mankind, and others therefore may fall; but because, as private liberty cannot be deemed secure under a government, wherein law, the proper and sole security of it, is dependent on will; so public liberty must be in danger, whenever a free constitution, the proper and sole security of it, is dependent on will; and a free constitution, like ours, is dependent on will, whenever the will of one estate can direct the conduct of all three.

Having thus explained what I mean by danger, and taken away all colour for cavil, it remains that I prove this danger to be real, and not the phantom of a crazy imagination, or a prejudiced mind. This shall be done therefore as shortly as I am able, and by an undeniable deduction of facts.

He who undertakes to govern a free people by corruption, and to lead them by a false interest, against their true interest, cannot boast the honour of the invention. The expedient is as old as the world, and he can pretend to no other honour than that of being an humble imitator of the devil. To corrupt our Parliaments hath been often attempted, as well as to divide our people, in favour of prerogative, and in order to let the arbitrary will of our princes loose from the restraints of law. We observed this in speaking of the reign of Charles the Second: but the efforts then made were ineffectual. The frugal habits of the former age were not entirely lost in that; which, I presume, may be reckoned as one cause of the noble stands that were then made by our Parliaments in opposition to the court. But not to ascribe more honour than is due, perhaps, to our fathers, the revenue of the crown was, at that time, so small (I speak comparatively; for, in every other respect, it was very ample) and the profusion of that prince on his pleasures was so great, that no minister of King Charles the Second could find sums sufficient to buy a Parliament. He stood therefore on his prerogative, strained it as far as he durst, and made all the use of it he could. The revenue of the crown was greatly increased in the reign of King James the Second, and was given most unwisely for life. I say, most unwisely; for as a prince who hath an heart and head to govern well, cannot stand in need of such a grant; so a prince who hath neither, does not deserve it: and therefore, whatever the generosity of our countrymen to their princes may carry them to do at any time, they might leave this undone at all times, without any reflection on their prudence, or even their generosity. The reign of King James was short; and during this short reign he rested on that prerogative, which he knew was a cheaper expedient than corruption, and which he vainly flattered himself was enough confirmed to support the measures he took, for subverting the religion, the laws, and the liberty of Britain. Thus were men brought, by the conduct of these two princes, to fix their eyes on prerogative, as the sole instrument of tyranny, and to forget that corruption had been employed, though unsuccessfully, by King Charles, and might have been employed with greater force, and perhaps more success, by King James. The cry of the nation was for a free Parliament, and no man seemed to doubt, in that ferment, but that a Parliament must be free, when the influence which the crown had usurped in the precedent reigns over the elections, was removed, as it was by the Revolution. But this general inadvertency, as well as the particular neglect of those who took the lead in national affairs at that time, is the more surprising, because corruption having been so lately employed, among other means, to render Parliaments dependent on the crown, the danger of corruption was, by consequence, one of those dangers against which the nation had a right to be secured, as well as a promise of being so, according to the terms of the Prince of Orange's declaration. Those persons especially, who had exclaimed so loudly against place-men and pensioners, in the reign of King Charles, and who complained, at this instant, so bitterly of the undue influence that had been employed, in small boroughs chiefly, to promote the elections of the Parliament which sat in the reign of King James, ought to have been attentive, one would think, to take the glorious opportunity that was furnished them by a new settlement of the crown, and of the constitution, to secure the independency of Parliaments effectually for the future. Machiavel observes, and makes it the title of one of his discourses, that 'a free government, in order to maintain itself free, hath need, every day, of some new provisions in favour of liberty'.[2] The truth of this observation, and the reasons that support

[2] Machiavelli, *Discorsi*, III. 49.

it, are obvious. But as every day may not furnish opportunities of making some of those new and necessary provisions, no day that does furnish the opportunity ought to be neglected. The Romans had been so liberal in bestowing the right of citizens on strangers, that the power of their elections began to fall into such hands as the constitution had not intended to trust with them. Quintus Fabius saw the growing evil; and being censor, he took the opportunity; confined all these new elections into four tribes; put it out of their power to turn the elections, as they had done, whilst their numbers were divided among all the tribes; freed his country from this danger; restored the constitution, according to the true intent and meaning of it; and obtained, by universal suffrage, the title of Maximus.[3] If a spirit like this had prevailed among us, at the time we speak of, something like this would have been done: and surely something like it ought to have been done; for the Revolution was, in many instances, and it ought to have been so in all, one of those renewals of our constitution that we have often mentioned. If it had been such, with respect to the elections of members to serve in Parliament, these elections might have been drawn back to the ancient principle on which they had been established; and the rule of property, which was followed anciently, and was perverted by innumerable changes that length of time produced, might have been restored; by which the communities to whom the right of electing was trusted, as well as the qualifications of the electors and the elected, might have been settled in proportion to the present state of things. Such a remedy might have wrought a radical cure of the evil that threatens our constitution; whereas it is much to be apprehended, even from experience, that all others are merely palliative; and yet the palliative must be employed, no doubt, till the specific can be procured.

But nothing of this kind was done at the Revolution. Pleased that the open attacks on our constitution were defeated and prevented, men entertained no thought of the secret attacks that might be carried on against the independency of Parliaments; as if our dangers could be but of one kind, and could arise but from one family. Soon after the Revolution, indeed, men of all sides, and of all denomi-

---

[3] Quintus Fabius Maximus (?–203 BCE), noted Roman statesman, gained military eminence in the Punic Wars to add to his domestic honours. Bolingbroke here paraphrases Machiavelli, *Discorsi*, III. 49.

nations (for it was not a party-cause, though it was endeavoured to be made such) began to perceive not only that nothing effectual had been done to hinder the undue influence of the crown in elections, and an over-balance of the creatures of the court in Parliament, but that the means of exercising such an influence, at the will of the crown, were unawares and insensibly increased, and every day increasing. In a word, they began to see that the foundations were laid of giving as great power to the crown indirectly, as the prerogative, which they had formerly dreaded so much, could give directly, and of establishing universal corruption. The first hath happened, and we pray that the last never may.

The net revenue of the crown, at the abdication of King James, amounted to somewhat more than two millions, without any tax on land, or malt, and without a multitude of grievous impositions and excises, that have been since heaped on the nation. It is plain, and it was so then, that this revenue might have been so increased, as to answer annually the great annual expenses, in which we engaged soon afterwards. In this case, the people would not have had a greater, nay nor so great a burden to bear, as they had in the course of the two wars that followed; and, at the end of these wars,[4] they would have found themselves with little or no load upon them, instead of crouching under a debt of fifty millions. That this method was not taken, furnishes matter of very melancholy reflection to the present, and will do so to future generations. But these reflections are no part of my subject. How it came to pass that a method so practicable, and so eligible, was not taken (whether this was owing to private interest, to party-cunning of different and opposite kinds, or to an unhappy refinement in politics, that contracting national debts, under a new establishment, was an effectual expedient to attach men to this establishment), I shall not presume to say. All three might have their share, perhaps, in determining for another measure. At least it is a point, on which the men of that time have spoken with much prejudice, and little candour. But however that might be, certain it is that we began to borrow at high interest, to anticipate and mortgage, immediately after the Revolution: and having once begun, there was no remedy; we were forced to proceed

---

[4] The Nine Years War (1688–97) and the War of the Spanish Succession (1702–13).

in the same manner, through the course of two mighty wars. Formerly, the whole expense of the state was borne by the crown; and when this expense grew, upon extraordinary occasions, too great for the revenue of the crown to bear, the people aided the crown, if they approved the occasions of the expense. These grants were properly aids, no more: for the revenue of the crown was engaged in the first place, and therefore it might seem reasonable that the crown should have the levying and management of the whole; of these aids, as well as of the standing revenue. But it happened in this case, as it does in many; the reason of the thing ceased, and the thing continued. A separate, private revenue, or a civil list, as we commonly call it, was assigned to the crown. From that time, the former order hath been reversed. Our Kings, instead of contributing most, have contributed nothing to the public charge; and the people of Britain, instead of giving occasionally aids to the crown, have taken upon themselves the whole load of ordinary and extraordinary expenses, for which they annually provide. Notwithstanding this vast alteration in the state of the revenue, and the interest of the King and the people in the management of it, the same forms of granting aids to the crown, and of levying taxes, and of managing the public treasure, have been continued; so that the people stand obliged (for the crown, that is trusted with the whole, is bound for nothing) to make good all deficiencies, though they have no share in the management of the revenue. Our Kings, since the establishment of the civil list, have not only a private and separate estate, but receive a kind of rent-charge out of the public estate, to maintain their honour and dignity, nothing else: and whether the public estate thrive, or not, this rent-charge must be made good to them; at least, as it hath been settled on our present most gracious monarch, if the funds appropriated produce the double of that immense revenue of eight hundred thousand pounds a year, which hath been so liberally given him for life, the whole is his, without account; but if they fail in any degree to produce it, the entire national fund is engaged to make up the difference. But although our Kings have thus no longer any immediate interest in the public estate, they are trusted with the entire management of it. They are not only stewards for the public, but they condescend to be such for all those private persons, who are the creditors of the public, and have the additional trouble of managing about three millions a year, on this head.

Now this new settlement, which appears absurd in speculation, how wise soever it may have been thought contrived for practice, hath had this evident and inevitable consequence. As we have annually increased our funds, and our taxes, we have annually increased the power of the crown; and these funds and taxes being established and laid for perpetuity, or for terms equivalent to perpetuity, in the sense here intended, this increase of power must not only continue, but still increase, as long as the system of economy subsists. How this increase of power arises from the increase of funds and taxes, and the influence of the crown grows, in proportion to the burden on the people, heavier, hath been explained so much in the debates on a late detestable occasion, that much less needs to be said on the subject here.[5] If we consider, in the increase of taxes, nothing more than the increase of officers first, by which a vast number of new dependants on the crown are created in every part of the kingdom (dependants as numerous, and certainly more prevalent than all the tenants and wards of the crown were anciently); and secondly, the powers given to the treasury, and other inferior officers, on account of these taxes, which are at least as great and as grievous, in this free government of ours, as any that are exercised in the most arbitrary government, on the same occasions; if we consider this alone, we shall find reason sufficient to conclude, that although the power of prerogative was more open, and more noisy in its operations, yet the power thus acquired is more real and may prove more dangerous for this very reason, because it is more covered, and more silent. That men began to see, very soon after the Revolution, the danger arising from hence to our constitution, as I said above, is most certain. No less than seven Acts were made, in King William's reign, to prevent undue influences on elections;[6] and one of the Acts, as I remember, for I have it not before me, is grounded on this fact, [a]"that the officers of the excise had frequently, by threats and promises,

---

[a] Tertio Gul. & Mar.

[5] The Excise Crisis of 1733.
[6] All revenue officials, as governmental place-holders, were debarred from the House of Commons by a series of Acts passed between 1694 and 1701.

prevailed on electors, and absolutely debarred them of the freedom of voting'. What hath been done, or attempted to be done, since that time, in the same view, and what hath been done, or attempted to be done, both in the reign of King William and since, to prevent an undue influence on the elected, as well as on the electors, I need not recapitulate. They are matters of fresh date, and enough known. Upon the whole, this change in the state and property of the public revenue hath made a change in our constitution, not yet perhaps attended to sufficiently, but such an one however as deserves our utmost attention, since it gives a power, unknown in former times, to one of the three estates; and since public liberty is not guarded against the dangers that may arise from this power, as it was, and as it is now more than ever, against the dangers that used to arise from the powers formerly possessed or claimed by the crown. Formerly, prerogative was kept in sight, and provisions were made against the effects and encroachments of it, as often as occasion required, and opportunity offered. They who called themselves friends to the government, in those days, opposed these provisions. They who were friends to the constitution, promoted them. That the same thing should happen again, in a similar case, we must expect. But as the friends of the constitution, in times past, were not deterred, tempted, nor wearied, whilst they defended it against dangers of one kind, and by their honest perseverance delivered it down, not only safe, but more improved, to posterity; let us flatter ourselves with this agreeable hope, that the friends of the constitution, at this time, and in all times to come, will be neither deterred, tempted, not wearied in the same generous cause, in watching and guarding it against dangers of another kind; and that they will deliver it down, in like manner, to future generations. Sure I am there are reasons, and those of no small moment, why they should be more watchful, more upon their guard, more bold, and more incessant in their endeavours, if possible, even than the assertors of British liberty were formerly; and the enumeration of some of these reasons is an article not to be omitted on this occasion.

I am, sir, &c.

Sir,

As the means then of influencing by prerogative, and of governing by force, were considered to be increased formerly, upon every increase of power to the crown, so are the means of influencing by money, and of governing by corruption, to be considered as increased now, upon that increase of power which hath accrued to the crown by the new constitution of the revenue since the Revolution. Nay farther. Not only the means of corrupting are increased, on the part of the crown, but the facility of employing these means with success is increased, on the part of the people, on the part of the electors, and of the elected. Nay, farther still. These means and this facility are not only increased, but the power of the crown to corrupt, as I have hinted already, and the proneness of the people to be corrupted, must continue to increase on the same principles, unless a stop be put to the growing wealth and power of one, and the growing depravity of the other. We are, to be sure, in no danger from any advantage his majesty will take of this situation; but if advantage be not taken in favour of our constitution, of the present most happy reign, of the mild and beneficent temper of our heroical monarch, of the generous principle, instilled by nature, and improved by philosophy, of his royal consort, it may be supposed, for we speak hypothetically all along, as the reader will please to remember, even where the precaution is not used; it may be supposed, I say, that pretended friends to the government, and real enemies to this constitution, no matter whether they are such by principle, or become such by the crimes, will get into superior power, in some future time, and under some weak or wicked prince: and whenever this happens, the subversion of our constitution, and of our liberty by consequence, will be the most easy enterprise imaginable; because nothing can be more easy than the creation of an anti-constitutional dependency of the two houses of Parliament on the crown will be in that case; and because such a dependency of the two houses is as real a subversion of our constitution as an absolute abolishment of Parliaments would be.

[1] *Craftsman* 443 (28 December 1734).

The first of those means of corruption, that have grown up, or been increased, since the Revolution, which I shall mention, is the establishment of the civil list; not so much on account of the manner in which it was originally given, as on account of that in which it hath been since given, and of the vast augmentations that have been made to it;[2] augmentations, that may be doubled or trebled, in times to come, upon the same motives, under the same and other pretences; in short, just as speciously as they have been made. The revenue of King James the Second, as it stood at his abdication, hath been mentioned; and it would not be hard to show, by indisputable computations, that they who apprehended he might be able to govern without Parliaments, or to buy Parliaments, if he wanted their assistance, had good reason for such apprehensions, notwithstanding the expense he was at, over and above all the ordinary charges of the government, in maintaining against law a great standing army of sixteen or eighteen thousand men. – But to go back to the reign of King Charles the Second, whose revenue was much less. The patriots of that age, even when this revenue was computed at no more than one million two hundred thousand pounds a year, took great alarm at the pecuniary influence it might create, and looked upon it, and spoke of it, as a fund for corruption. Now, if this revenue could afford a fund for corruption, when, besides maintaining the honour and dignity of the crown, it was to defray all the other expenses of the state, and among the rest, those of a small army, and a great fleet; what would the same patriots think of a revenue of eight hundred thousand pounds, or a million a year, applicable to the particular expenses of the crown alone, and not one farthing of which sacred treasure was ever diverted to any national use? They would have the same just confidence, no doubt, as we have in his present majesty; but they would say as we do, that so immense a private, or separate revenue, may become hereafter an inexhaustible fund of corruption: and therefore that the independency of Parliaments is, and must be in real danger, till some remedies, as effectual against the pecuniary influence, as have been found against the prerogative of the crown, are provided. They would show that a small sum, in aid of places and pensions, of fears

---

[2] Under the provisions of the settlement at George II's accession in 1727, the crown became entitled to the surplus revenues from the civil list, over and above the £800,000 guaranteed by Parliament.

and expectations, might serve for the ordinary charge of annual corruption; and that a small saving reserved every year might produce, at the end of seven, a fund sufficient for the extraordinary charge of septennial and national corruption.

But again. If we suppose the civil list to become an insufficient fund for these purposes, by the profusion of some future King (and nothing less than the most extravagant profusion can make it so), or if we suppose that some future King may join to so many ill qualities, as leave him no means of governing but by corruption, a sordid avarice, that renders him unable to open his coffers, even for this use; yet will a very little iniquitous cunning suffice to create funds for corruption, that may come in aid of the civil list. It is natural for men to be less frugal, when others are to pay for their want of frugality. Our Kings therefore may become more apt to take, and our ministers to advise such engagements as plunge the nation, at every turn, into vast expense, since the load which fell, in part at least, on the crown formerly, falls entire on the people now. But besides this general reason to promote a want of frugality, there may arise particular reasons, of more positive and more pernicious effect. A weak administration, for instance, may pretend public necessity, when private inability alone hath formed the conjuncture; and frequent and extravagant supplies may be asked and obtained, to do, or to undo, by the weight of money, what might have been attained, or prevented, by a little foresight, and by a prudent conduct. A wicked administration may propose to impoverish the people; to render them as submissive and as abject as the subjects, the boors, or the slaves, in some foreign countries, and to beggar them out of their sturdiness. But there is another view, that may be common to a weak and a wicked administration both. In such an age as we suppose, public money will be easily granted, and public accounts rarely, or incuriously inspected. The ministers therefore, though never so weak, may be impudent enough to ask, and able enough to get frequent supplies, on national pretences, for private purposes. The consequences of this are manifold; for, in general, the more money passes through their hands, the more opportunities they have of gain; and, in particular, they may share, if they please, in every bad bargain they make for the public; and the worse their bargain, the better their share will be. Thus an immense subsidy given to some little prince, who deals in soldiers, or an immense arrear stated in favour of these little merchants of human flesh, may be so ordered as to steal enough from the public to replenish the royal coffers, to glut the ministers, to feed some of their hungry creatures, and to bribe a Parliament besides. Several of these occasional jobs may be, and, no doubt, will be contrived, in such an age, and by such means as we here suppose, and may be justly reckoned as so many auxiliary funds, belonging to the great aggregate fund of corruption. Let us, however, break off from discoursing of these, which may be more easily and more frequently contrived under the present, but might have been contrived under the former constitutions of the revenue; and let us turn our discourse, to speak of that great source of corruption, which was opened soon after the Revolution; which was unknown before it; and which hath spread, since it was opened, like the box of Pandora, innumerable evils over this unhappy country.

The increase and continuance of taxes acquire to the crown, by multiplying officers of the revenue, and by arming them with formidable powers against the rest of their fellow-subjects, a degree of power, the weight of which the inferior ranks of our people have long felt, and they most, who are most useful to the commonwealth, and which even the superior ranks may feel one time or other; for I presume it would not be difficult to show how a full exercise of the powers that are in being, with, or even without some little additions to them, for the improvement of the revenue, that stale pretence for oppression, might oblige the greatest lord in the land to bow as low to a commissioner of the customs, or excise, or to some subaltern harpy, as any nobleman or gentleman in France can be obliged to bow to the intendant of his province. But the establishment of public funds, on the credit of these taxes, hath been productive of more and greater mischiefs than the taxes themselves, not only by increasing the means of corruption, and the power of the crown, but by the effect it hath had on the spirit of the nation, on our manners, and our morals. It is impossible to look back, without grief, on the necessary and unavoidable consequences of this establishment; or without indignation on that mystery of iniquity,[3] to which this establishment gave occasion, which hath been raised upon it, and carried on, for almost half a century, by

---

[3] II Thessalonians 2: 7.

means of it. It is impossible to look forward, without horror, on the consequences that may still follow. The ordinary expenses of our government are defrayed, in great measure, by anticipation and mortgages. In time of peace, in days of prosperity, as we boast them to be, we contract new debts, and we create new funds. What must we do in war, and in national distress? What will happen, when we have mortgaged and funded all we have to mortgage and to fund; when we have mortgaged to new creditors that sinking fund which was mortgaged to other creditors not yet paid off; when we have mortgaged all the product of our land, and even our land itself? Who can answer, that when we come to such extremities, or have them more nearly in prospect, ten millions of people will bear any longer to be hewers of wood, and drawers of water,[4] to maintain the two hundredth part of that number at ease, and in plenty? Who can answer, that the whole body of the people will suffer themselves to be treated, in favour of an handful of men (for they who monopolize the whole power, and may in time monopolize the whole property of the funds, are indeed but an handful), who can answer, that the whole body of the people will suffer themselves to be treated, in favour of such an handful, as the poor Indians are, in favour of the Spaniards; to be parcelled out in lots, as it were; and to be assigned, like these Indians to the Spanish planters, to toil and starve for the proprietors of the several funds?[5] Who can answer, that a scheme, which oppresses the farmer, ruins the manufacturer, breaks the merchant, discourages industry, and reduces fraud into system; which beggars so often the fair adventurer and innocent proprietor; which drains continually a portion of our national wealth away to foreigners, and draws most perniciously the rest of that immense property that was diffused among thousands, into the pockets of a few; who can answer that such a scheme will be always endured? – But I have run, before I was aware, from my subject, which requires no more than that I should take notice of the establishment of the public funds, as it furnishes new means of corruption on the part of the crown, and new facilities to these means, on the part of the people.

---

[4] Joshua 9: 21, 23.
[5] The *encomienda* system in Spanish America (abolished in 1720) granted a land-owner the labour of a specified number of Indians, in return for his protection and tutelage.

Now this, I suppose, hath need of no proof, and of little explanation; for, first, the whole art of stockjobbing, the whole mystery of iniquity mentioned above, arises from this establishment, and is employed about the funds; and, secondly, the main springs that turn, or may turn, the artificial wheel of credit, and make the paper estates that are fastened to it, rise or fall, lurk behind the veil of the treasury. From hence it follows, that if this office should be ever unrighteously administered; if there should ever be at the head of it, one of those veteran sharpers, who hath learned by experience how to improve the folly, and aggravate the misfortunes of his fellow-subjects, of the innocent, of the poor, of the widow, and of the orphan, to his own, or any other private advantage; it follows, I say, that he must have it in his power, and there can be no doubt of his will, to employ two methods of corruption, without any encumbrance to the civil list. Such a ministerial jobber may employ the opportunities of gaining on the funds, that he can frequently create by a thousand various artifices (notwithstanding the excellent provisions that have been lately made against the infamous practice of stockjobbing, by the wisdom of the legislature, and which we promise ourselves will be still improved),[6] and he may apply the gains that are thus made, to corruption, in aid of the civil list. He may corrupt men with their own spoils, and bribe even those whom he reduced by his clandestine practices to that penury which could alone make them capable of being bribed; or, when he hath to do with men of another character (for no rank alone will be sufficient to raise them, in such an age, above the most direct and prostitute corruption), he may bribe them by a whisper, initiate them into his mystery to gain them, and then secure them by a participation of the same fraud and the same profit.

Though this reasoning be hypothetical, yet the suppositions are not strained, nor unnatural; for as the meanest grubs on earth have raised themselves by stockjobbing to the rank and port of noblemen and gentlemen; so may noblemen and gentlemen debase themselves to their meanness, and acquire the same spirit, by following the same trade. That luxury which began to spread after the Restoration of King Charles the Second, hath increased ever since; hath

[6] The 1733 Act 'to prevent the infamous Practice of Stock-Jobbing' (7 George II. c. 8) sought to end speculative dealing in stock options, though it was never effectively applied.

descended from the highest to the lowest ranks of our people, and is become national. Now nothing can be more certain than this, that national luxury and national poverty may, in time, establish national prostitution. Besides this, it is to be considered, that the immense wealth of particular men is a circumstance which always atttends national poverty, and is in a great measure the cause of it. We may apply already to our country thus much at least of that which Sallust makes Cato say of the state of Rome; and I wish we could apply no more, – *Habemus luxuriam, atque avaritiam; publice egestatem, privatim opulentiam;*[7] 'luxury and avarice, public want and private wealth abound'. Now, as public want, or general poverty, for in that sense I take it here, will lay numbers of men open to the attacks of corruption; so private wealth will have the same effect, especially where luxury prevails, on some of those who do not feel the public want; for there is imaginary as well as real poverty. He who thought himself rich before, may begin to think himself poor, when he compares his wealth, and the expense he is able to make, with those men whom he hath been used to esteem, and perhaps justly, far inferior to himself in all respects. He who would have been ashamed to participate in fraud, or to yield to corruption, may begin to think the fault venial, when he sees men who were far below him, rise above him by fraud and by corruption; when he sees them maintain themselves by these means in an elevation which they could not have acquired by the contrary virtues, if they had had them. Thus may contraries unite in their effect, and poverty and wealth combine to facilitate the means and the progress of corruption. Thus may the great thieves of the nation do more, and less reparable mischief, by the practices they introduce and the examples they set, than by the actual robberies they commit. *Plusque exemplo quam peccato nocent,*[8] to use an expression of Tully, in one of his books of laws.

Much more might be said, concerning the increase of power which the crown hath acquired, and must continue to acquire, according to the present constitution and management of the revenue. Much more might be said to show that the power of money, as the world is now constituted, is real power, and that all power, without this, is imaginary; that the prince who gets prerogative

---

[7] Sallust, *Bellum Catilinae*, LII. 22. 2.
[8] '. . . they do more harm by their example than by their offence': Cicero, *De Legibus*, III. 14. 32.

alone, gets a phantom; but that he who gets money, even without prerogative, gets something real, and will be as much stronger than his neighbours, and his people too, as he hath a greater command of money. In fine, a great deal more might be said to show how much corruption is a more deadly weapon than the highest prerogative, in the hands of men who are enemies to such a constitution of government as ours is. – But I hasten to a conclusion.

If then a spirit of rapine and venality, of fraud and corruption, continue to diffuse themselves, not only luxury and avarice, but every kind of immorality will follow; and the whole may be improved by such ways as have been sketched out, and by others, whenever the nation falls under a bad government, till the prince on the throne shall not be able to say, speaking of his whole people, even that which Philip the Second said, speaking of the corruption of his own court; 'They all take money, except myself and Sapena.'[9] Britain will then be in that very condition in which, and in which alone, her constitution, and her liberty by consequence, may be destroyed; because the people may, in a state of universal corruption, and will in no other, either suffer others to betray them, or betray themselves. How near a progress we have made towards this state, I determine not. This I say; it is time for every man, who is desirous to preserve the British constitution, and to preserve it secure, to contribute all he can to prevent the ill effects of that new influence and power which have gained strength in every reign since the Revolution; of those means of corruption that may be employed, one time or other on the part of the crown, and of that proneness to corruption on the part of the people, that hath been long growing, and still grows. It may otherwise happen, that these causes remaining in force, their effects will become too strong to be checked, and will ensure the ruin of the best constitution upon earth, whenever the men in power shall think their grandeur or their safety concerned in the ruin of it. We are not exposed at present, most certainly, to any such contingency; but the bare possibility of being so is a reason sufficient to awaken and alarm every honest man. Hath not every such man, indeed, reason to be alarmed, when he hears the cause of corruption publicly pleaded, and when men are suffered, nay paid by somebody or other, to plead this unrighteous

[9] Source unidentified.

cause, as if it was that of our most righteous government. Had we lived when the Star Chamber tyrannized,[10] and many other extravagant powers were exercised, under the authority of the crown, we should have found fault as much as we dared, no doubt, and yet have waited patiently, perhaps, for some favourable opportunity of redressing the grievances. But when we heard these acts of power justified as legal and constitutional, and the prerogative, by virtue of which they were done, claimed as a right in the crown, we should have taken the alarm, I presume, as hot as our predecessors did. Thus, in the case now before us, corruption may have been practised in some degree, perhaps, at all times. But then it hath been always kept under by the shame and danger, that attended both the corrupter and the corrupted. It hath been always complained of, never defended, and endeavours have been used, from time to time, with general applause, to prevent it. But according to the principles now avowed, these endeavours were unjust; they ought to be repented of; and the Acts made in consequence of them ought to be repealed: for the constitutional independency of the crown cannot be supported, unless the crown have the right and the means of taking their independency from the other parts of the legislature, by keeping the members of those assemblies under a pecuniary influence. Let no man think that the absurdity and profligacy of these doctrines secure us against the effect of them. They may soon grow into vogue, and be reputed as sacred truths as any of those falsehoods, that are established by the systems of policy and religion, in many other countries. What can be too absurd, or too profligate, for an absurd and profligate, or for a superstitious people?

But if we should apprehend the effects of these doctrines as little as we esteem the doctors who preach them, yet still the alarm is given by them, and it would be stupidity, or somewhat much worse than stupidity, not to take it. We despise the drummers and trumpeters of an enemy's army (for I resume the allusion that I applied in the first of these discourses)[11] but when we hear the noise of their drums and trumpets, we take the alarm, and conclude the enemy is near. The friends of our constitution therefore are in the right to join issue upon this point with the enemies of it, and to fix upon this

[10] The King's Council sat as a court of law in the Star Chamber of Westminster Palace; its reputation for torture and tyranny has been greatly exaggerated.
[11] Above, 'Letter II', p. 12.

principal and real distinction and difference, the present division of parties; since parties we must have; and since those which subsisted formerly are quite extinguished, notwithstanding all the wicked endeavours of some men, who can have no merit but party-merit, nor safety but in faction, to revive them. If there was merit, and surely there was great merit, in opposing the assertors of prerogative formerly, when it rose so high as to endanger our liberty; there is great merit in opposing the assertors of corruption now, and in exposing the means by which this expedient may be improved to the ruin of our constitution, and therefore of our liberty. Nay, the merit is greater in some respects, if corruption be in itself, in its own nature, and in the present circumstances of the nation, and dispositions of the people, more dangerous than prerogative ever was; and if the means of establishing a government of arbitrary will, by corruption, be more likely to prove effectual than those of doing it by prerogative ever were. That it should ever become harder to save our country from the effects of corruption, than it was to defeat the efforts of prerogative, God forbid. – On the whole matter, a dissertation upon parties could not wind itself up more properly, we think, than by showing that the British constitution of government deserves, above all others, the constant attention, and care to maintain it, of the people who are so happy as to live under it; that it may be weakened for want of attention, which is a degree of danger; but that it cannot be destroyed, unless the peers and the commons, that is, the whole body of the people, unite to destroy it, which is a degree of madness, and such a monstrous iniquity, as nothing but confirmed and universal corruption can produce; that since the time, when all our dangers from prerogative ceased, new dangers to this constitution, more silent and less observed, are arisen; and, finally, that as nothing can be more ridiculous than to preserve the nominal division of Whig and Tory parties, which subsisted before the Revolution, when the difference of principles, that could alone make the distinction real, exists no longer; so nothing can be more reasonable than to admit the nominal division of constitutionists and anti-constitutionists, or of a Court and a Country party, at this time, when an avowed difference of principles makes this distinction real. That this distinction is real cannot be denied, as long as there are men amongst us, who argue for, and who promote even a corrupt dependency of the members of the two houses of Parliament on the crown; and others who maintain that such a dependency of the members takes away the constitutional independency of the two houses, and that this independency lost, our constitution is a dead letter, and we shall be only in a worse condition by preserving the forms of it.

To reduce therefore our present parties to this single division, our present disputes to this single contest, and to fix our principal attention on this object of danger, too long and too much neglected, hath been and is the sole design of these discourses. The design may have been insufficiently executed, but it is honest; but it is of the last importance; and whatever the enemies of our constitution, who call themselves the friends of the government, may say, to amuse and impose on the weak, ignorant, and trifling part of mankind, the importance of it will be felt every day, and every hour, more and more, till it be felt by every man in Britain. Let us hope, and endeavour by all possible means, that it may not be felt too late; and to encourage the constitutionists, or Country party, in this attempt, let us consider from whom an opposition to it is to be expected. – Shall it be expected then from those, who have passed under the denomination of Tories? Certainly not. They feel as much as any men in Britain, the preference that ought to be given to that system of government which was established by the Revolution, and in which they took so great a share, and show themselves as ready to render that great work, which was left and still continues imperfect, complete. – Shall this opposition be expected from the Dissenters? It cannot be. Shall they, who pretend to greater purity than others, become the advocates of corruption? Shall they contribute their endeavours to undermine the best constitution of government they can hope to enjoy, unless they hope to rise on the ruins of it, and to form another on their own model? As religious sects, they deserve indulgence, and they have it; but they are too wise not to see that, as a faction in the state, they would deserve none. – In fine, shall this opposition be expected from those who have been called Whigs? That too is impossible. Their predecessors asserted the independency of Parliaments, and struggled hard against corruption, in former reigns. When the rest of mankind embrace the same principles, and pursue the same ends, shall they renounce one, and run counter to the other? Shall they own themselves against one method of destroying our constitution, but for another? Against making kings independent on Parliaments by prerogative, but for making Parliaments dependent on kings by corruption? Shall they give the enemies of the Revolution a plausible pretence to say that nothing more was meant by them at least, than a change of government, in which they hoped to find their particular and party account? This would be to cast black and odious colours on the Revolution, indeed; more black, and more odious than any than it was in the power of a ᵃvain, forward, turbulent preacher to cast, by his frothy declamations. But the Whigs are so far from opposing the endeavours to preserve our constitution, that they co-operate to promote the success of them; and that, however personal prejudices, personal partialities, and old habits, that are daily wearing off, may be still entertained by some amongst them, all the independent men, who pass under that name, unite in the common cause of liberty and their country. – It remains therefore that no national party can be formed in opposition to those, who endeavour to secure the independency of Parliaments against the new influence of the crown, and against corruption; nor any strength be exerted, except that of a faction, composed of the refuse of all parties, gleaned up by one who hath none for him. – I would willingly carry this farther; and, in doing so, I shall not advance a paradox, unless it be supposed, which I think would be a greater paradox, that a man may have abilities to destroy the constitution, and yet not sense enough to see his remote, as well as immediate, his family, as well as personal interest. I say then, that if a design of raising the power of the crown above any pitch of prerogative, and of reducing Parliaments to an absolute dependency, as well as a faction to support this design, be formed; the very man who forms such a design, and such a faction, must be infatuated, if he can with very sincerely his own success. His first design, we are sure, will be that of raising a great family, and heaping upon it riches and honours. Shall his second design be that of rendering these riches and honours precarious and insecure, and of entailing servitude on his own race; for it will be impossible to exempt them from the common calamity? Nothing

---

ᵃ Doctor Sacheverell.[12]

[12] In 1709 the High Churchman, Dr Henry Sacheverell, preached in St Paul's Cathedral against the Glorious Revolution and the practice of toleration, for which he was impeached by the Whigs for 'high crimes and misdemeanours'.

but despair, that is fear void of hope, arising from a consciousness of guilt, can drive any man into such a design. But, in this case, there will be fear opposed to fear, and one of these fears may be allayed by hope. The fear of being called to a severe account may be mitigated by the hope of escaping. Where is the insolent, rapacious, odious minister, that may not entertain some hope, as well as fear, when he sets before his eyes the examples of those who have gone before him? Pallas was the favourite of Agrippina. He governed like the master of the empire, and supported her pride and ambition by his counsels and services, as he had been raised to power and was maintained in it by her credit, whilst her credit lasted. [b]Nero dismissed him; and seeing him go from court with a crowd at his heels, said pleasantly enough, as if it had been spoken of a dictator, that he went to abdicate. But Pallas carried off the spoils of the empire with him; all scores were quitted between him and the public; and, according to the bargain he had made, he was called to no account. Many such examples might be cited to comfort with hope the most guilty minister, who is wise, if not honest enough, to stop in the career of iniquity, before the measure of it be entirely filled, pressed down, and running over. But if one of those bubbles of fortune, who thinks he always shall escape, because he always hath escaped, not content to wound a free constitution of government, should resolve to make it expire under his administration; the condition of such an one, however he may flatter himself, or be flattered by others, must be ten times more wretched and forlorn than the worst of those to which his cruelty hath reduced multitudes – For what? – If he succeeds in his sacrilegious designs (they are of as deep a die, at least), he may hope for impunity,

[b] 'Nero insensius iis, quibus superbia muliebris innitebatur, demovet Pallantem cura rerum, quis a Claudio impositus, velut arbitrum regni agebat; ferebaturque, digrediente eo, magna prosequentium multitudine, non absurde dixisse, ire Pallantem ut ejuraret. Sane pepigerat Pallas, ne cujus facti in praeteritum interrogaretur, paresque rationes cum republica haberet'. Tacit. *An.* L. 13.[13]

[13] 'Furious with those who abetted such arrogance in a woman, Nero removed Pallas from looking after the business with which she had been entrusted by Claudius, and in which he acted as kingmaker. It was said that as Nero was leaving with a host of attendants, he wittily remarked that Pallas was going to swear him out of office. Pallas had in fact stipulated that he should not be questioned for anything he had done before, and that he should have a clean slate with the state': Tacitus, *Annals*, XIII. 14. I.

perhaps, to his grey hairs, and be suffered to languish through the infirmities of old age, with an inward remorse more pungent than any of them; but he is sure to entail servitude on his whole race, and indelible infamy on his memory. If he fails, he misses of that impunity, to which he sacrificed his country; he draws triple vengeance on his own head; and exposes his innocent family to a thousand misfortunes, of which it will not be the least, whether he succeeds or fails, that they descended from him. – But whatever ministers may govern, whatever factions may arise, let the friends of liberty lay aside the groundless distinctions, which are employed to amuse and betray them; let them continue to coalite; let them hold fast their integrity, and support with spirit and perseverance the cause of their country, and they will confirm the good, reclaim the bad, vanquish the incorrigible, and make the British constitution triumph, even over corruption.

I have now gone through the task I imposed on myself, and shall only add these few words. There was an engagement taken, in the beginning of these discourses, not to flatter. I have kept this engagement, and have spoken with great freedom; but I hope with the justice and moderation, and decency that I intended, of persons and of things. This freedom entitles me to expect that no parallels, no innuendoes should be supposed to carry my sense farther than I have expressed it. The reasonable part of mankind will not disappoint so reasonable an expectation. But there are a set of creatures, who have no mercy on paper, to use an expression of ᶜJuvenal, and who are ready to answer, even when they are absolute strangers to the subject. Unable to follow a thread of fact and argument, they play with words, and turn and wrest particular passages. They have done mine that honour, as I am told, and have once or twice seen. They may do the same again, whenever they please, secure from any reply, unless they have sense enough, or their patron for them, to take for a reply the story I am going to tell you, and which you may find related a little differently in one of the *Spectators*.[14] The story is this.

ᶜ '– stulta est clementia –
– periturae parcere chartae'.[15]

[14] *The Spectator* 568 (16 July 1714) (adapted).
[15] 'It is foolish mercy . . . to spare paper that will go to waste': Juvenal, *Satires*, I. 17–18.

A certain pragmatical fellow, in a certain village, took it into his head to write the names of the squire, of all his family, of the principal parish officers, and of some of the notable members of the vestry, in the margins of the *Whole Duty of Man*,[16] over against every sin, which he found mentioned in that most excellent treatise. The clamour was great, and all the neighbourhood was in an uproar. At last, the minister was called in, upon this great emergency; a pious and prudent divine, and the same, for ought I know, who was a member of the Spectator's club. He heard them with patience; with so much, that he brought them to talk one after the other. When he had heard them, he pronounced that they were all in the wrong; that the book was written against sins of all kinds, whoever should be guilty of them; but that the innocent would give occasion to unjust suspicions by all this clamour, and that the guilty would convict themselves. They took his advice. The *Whole Duty of Man* hath been read ever since, with much edification, by all the parishioners. The innocent hath been most certainly confirmed in virtue, and we hope the guilty have been reformed from vice.

I am, sir, &c.

---

[16] [Richard Allestree,] *The Practice of Christian Graces, or The Whole Duty of Man* (1658), the most widely read Anglican devotional treatise of the seventeenth and eighteenth centuries.

On the Spirit of Patriotism

My Lord,   1736.

You have engaged me on a subject which interrupts the series of those letters I was writing to you;[1] but it is one, which, I confess, I have very much at heart. I shall therefore explain myself fully, nor blush to reason on principles that are out of fashion among men, who intend nothing by serving the public, but to feed their avarice, their vanity, and their luxury, without the sense of any duty they owe to God or man.

It seems to me, that in order to maintain the moral system of the world at a certain point, far below that of ideal perfection (for we are made capable of conceiving what we are incapable of attaining), but however sufficient upon the whole to constitute a state easy and happy, or at the worst tolerable: I say, it seems to me, that the author of nature has thought fit to mingle from time to time, among the societies of men, a few, and but a few of those, on whom he is graciously pleased to bestow a larger proportion of the ethereal spirit than is given in the ordinary course of his providence to the sons of men. These are they who engross almost the whole reason of the species, who are born to instruct, to guide, and to preserve; who are designed to be the tutors and the guardians of human kind. When they prove such, they exhibit to us examples of the highest virtue, and the truest piety: and they deserve to have their festivals kept, instead of that pack of anchorites and enthusiasts, with whose

---

[1] The *Letters on the Study and Use of History*, dedicated to Henry Hyde, Viscount Cornbury, 6 November 1735.

names the calendar is crowded and disgraced. When these men apply their talents to other purposes, when they strive to be great and despise being good, they commit a most sacrilegious breach of trust; they pervert the means, they defeat as far as lies in them the designs of providence, and disturb in some sort the system of infinite wisdom. To misapply these talents is the most diffused, and therefore the greatest of crimes in its nature and consequence; but to keep them unexerted, and unemployed, is a crime too. Look about you, my Lord, from the palace to the cottage; you will find that the bulk of mankind is made to breathe the air of this atmosphere, to roam about this globe, and to consume, like the courtiers of Alcinous, the fruits of the earth. *Nos numerus sumus et fruges consumere nati.*[2] When they have trod this insipid round a certain number of years, and begot others to do the same after them, they have lived; and if they have performed, in some tolerable degree, the ordinary moral duties of life, they have done all they were born to do. Look about you again, my Lord, nay look into your own breast, and you will find that there are superior spirits, men who show even from their infancy, though it be not always perceived by others, perhaps not always felt by themselves, that they were born for something more, and better. These are the men to whom the part I mentioned is assigned. Their talents denote their general designation; and the opportunities of conforming themselves to it, that arise in the course of things, or that are presented to them by any circumstances of rank and situation in the society to which they belong, denote the particular vocation which it is not lawful for them to resist, nor even to neglect. The duration of the lives of such men as these is to be determined, I think, by the length and importance of the parts they act, not by the number of years that pass between their coming into the world, and their going out of it. Whether the piece be of three, or of five acts, the part may be long: and he who sustains it through the whole may be said to die in the fulness of years; whilst he, who declines it sooner, may be said not to live out half his days.

---

[2] 'We [Penelope's good-for-nothing suitors, and the young courtiers of Alcinous] are mere cyphers, and consume the fruits of the earth': Horace, *Epistles*, I. 2. 27. Odysseus visits the luxurious court of Alcinous, King of the Phaeacians, in Homer, *Odyssey*, VII.

I have sometimes represented to myself the vulgar, who are acci-
dentally distinguished by the titles of king and subject, of lord and
vassal, of noblemen and peasant; and the few who are distinguished
by nature so essentially from the herd of mankind, that (figure
apart) they seem to be of another species, in this manner. The
former come into the world and continue in it like Dutch* travellers
in a foreign country. Everything they meet has the grace of·novelty:
and they are fond alike of everything that is new. They wander
about from one object to another, of vain curiosity, or inelegant
pleasure. If they are industrious, they show their industry in copy-
ing signs, and collecting mottoes and epitaphs. They loiter, or they
trifle away their whole time: and their presence or their absence
would be equally unperceived, if caprice or accident did not raise
them often to stations, wherein their stupidity, their vices, or their
follies, make them a public misfortune. The latter come into the
world, or at least continue in it after the effects of surprise and
inexperience are over, like men who are sent on more important
errands. They observe with distinction, they admire with knowledge. They may indulge themselves in pleasure; but as their industry is not employed about trifles, so their amusements are not made
the business of their lives. Such men cannot pass unperceived
through a country. If they retire from the world, their splendour
accompanies them, and enlightens even the obscurity of their
retreat. If they take a part in public life, the effect is never indifferent. They either appear like ministers of divine vengeance, and their
course through the world is marked by desolation and oppression,
by poverty and servitude: or they are the guardian angels of the
country they inhabit, busy to avert even the most distant evil, and
to maintain or to procure peace, plenty, and the greatest of human
blessings, liberty.

From the observation, that superiority of parts is often employed
to do superior mischief, no consequence can be drawn against the
truth I endeavour to establish. Reason collects the will of God from
the constitution of things, in this as in other cases; but in no case
does the divine power impel us necessarily to conform ourselves to
this will: and therefore from the misapplication of superior parts to

* Dutch] German *1754*

195

the hurt, no argument can be drawn against this position, that they were given for the good of mankind. Reason deceive us not: we deceive ourselves, and suffer our wills to be determined by other motives. Montaigne or Charron would say, 'l'homme se pipe',[3] 'man is at once his own sharper, and his own bubble'.[4] Human nature is her own bawd, says Tully, *blanda conciliatrix et quasi lena sui.*[5] He who considers the universal wants, imperfections, and vices of his kind, must agree that men were intended not only for society, but to unite in commonwealths, and to submit to laws. *Legum idcirco omnes servi sumus, ut liberi esse possimus.*[6] And yet this very man will be seduced by his own passions, or the passions and examples of others, to think, or to act as if he thought, the very contrary. So he who is conscious of superior endowments, such as render him more capable than the generality of men to secure and improve the advantages of social life, by preserving the commonwealth in strength and splendour, even he may be seduced to think, or to act as if he thought, that these endowments were given him for the gratification of his ambition, and his other passions; and that there is no difference between vice and virtue, between a knave and an honest man, but one which a prince, who died not many years ago, asserted, 'that men of great sense were therefore knaves, and men of little sense were therefore honest'.[7] But in neither of these cases will the truth and reason of things be altered, by such examples of human frailty. It will be still true, and reason will still demonstrate, that all men are directed, by the general constitution of human nature, to submit to government; and that some men are in a particular manner designed to take care of that government on which the common happiness depends. The use that reason will make of such examples will be only this, that since men are so apt, in every form of life and every degree of understanding, to act against their

---

[3] Compare Montaigne, *Essais*, I. 4: '. . . l'âme en ses passions se pipe plustost elle mesme' ('the soul in its passions deceives itself above all'). The phrase does not appear in Pierre Charron, *De la Sagesse*.

[4] Source unidentified.

[5] '. . . a tempting matchmaker, and as it were her own bawd': Cicero, *De Natura Deorum*, I. 77.

[6] '. . . for that reason we are all slaves of the law, so that we can be free': Cicero, *Pro Cluentio*, LIII. 146; compare [Bolingbroke,] *The Freeholder's Political Catechism* (1733), 4: 'I am free not from the Law, but by the Law.'

[7] Source unidentified.

interest and their duty too, without benevolence to mankind, or regard to the divine will, it is the more incumbent on those who have this benevolence and this regard at heart, to employ all the means that the nature of the government allows, and that rank, circumstances of situation, or superiority of talents, give them, to oppose evil, and promote good government; and contribute thus to preserve the moral system of the world, at that point of imperfection at least, which seems to have been prescribed to it by the great creator of every system of beings.

Give me leave now, my Lord, to cast my eyes for a moment homeward, and to apply what I have been saying to the present state of Britain. That there is no profusion of the ethereal spirit to be observed among us, and that we do not abound with men of superior genius, I am ready to confess; but I think there is no ground for the complaints I have heard made, as if nature had not done her part in our age, as well as in former ages, by producing men capable of serving the commonwealth. The manners of our fore-fathers were, I believe, in many respects better: they had more probity perhaps, they had certainly more show of honour, and greater industry. But still nature sows alike, though we do not reap alike. There are, and as there always have been, there always will be such creatures in government as I have described above. Fortune maintains a kind of rivalship with wisdom, and piques herself often in favour of fools as well as knaves. Socrates used to say, that although no man undertakes a trade he has not learned, even the meanest; yet every one thinks himself sufficiently qualified for the hardest of all trades, that of government.[8] He said this upon the experience he had in Greece. He would not change his opinion if he lived now in Britain. But however, such characters as these would do little hurt, generally speaking, or would not do it long, if they stood alone. To do great hurt, some genius, some knowledge, some talents in short, natural or acquired, are necessary: less indeed, far less than are required to do good, but always some. Yet I imagine, not the worst minister could do all the mischief he does by the misapplication of his talents alone, if it were not for the misapplication of much better talents than his by some who join with him, and the non-application, or the faint and unsteady

[8] Plato, *Protagoras*, 319B-D.

exercise of their talents by some who oppose him; as well as the general remissness of mankind in acquiring knowledge, and in improving the parts which God has given them for the service of the public. These are the great springs of national misfortunes. There have been monsters in other ages, and other countries, as well as ours; but they have never continued their devastations long, when there were heroes to oppose them. We will suppose a man imprudent, rash, presumptuous, ungracious, insolent and profligate, in speculation as well as practice. He can bribe, but he cannot seduce; he can buy, but he cannot gain; he can lie, but he cannot deceive. From whence then has such a man his strength? From the general corruption of the people, nursed up to a full maturity under his administration; from the venality of all orders and all ranks of men, some of whom are so prostitute, that they set themselves to sale, and even prevent application? This would be the answer, and it would be a true one as far as it goes; but it does not account for the whole. Corruption could not spread with so much success, though reduced into system; and though some ministers, with equal impudence and folly, avowed it by themselves and their advocates, to be the principal expedient by which they governed, if a long and almost unobserved progression of causes and effects, did not prepare the conjuncture. Let me explain it and apply it, as I conceive it. One party had given their whole attention, during several years, to the project of enriching themselves, and impoverishing the rest of the nation; and, by these and other means, of establishing their dominion under the government and with the favour of a family, who were foreigners, and therefore might believe, that they were established on the throne by the good will and strength of this party alone.[9] This party in general were so intent on these views, and many of them, I fear, are so still, that they did not advert in time to the necessary consequences of the measures they abetted; nor did they consider, that the power they raised, and by which they hoped to govern their country, would govern them with the very rod of iron they forged, and would be the power of a prince or minister, not that of a party long. Another party continued sour, sullen, and inactive, with judgments so weak, and passions so strong, that even experience, and a severe one surely, was lost upon them.[10] They

---

[9] The Court Whigs, who enthusiastically embraced the Hanoverian succession in 1714.
[10] The Jacobites, who stood by the Stuart line.

waited, like the Jews, for a Messiah, that may never come; and under whom, if he did come, they would be strangely disappointed in their expectations of glory and triumph, and universal dominion. Whilst they waited, they were marked out like the Jews, a distinct race, hewers of wood and drawers of water,[11] scarce members of the community, though born in the country. All indifferent men stood as it were at a gaze: and the few, who were jealous of the court, were still more jealous of one another; so that a strength sufficient to oppose bad ministers was not easy to be formed. When this strength was formed, and the insufficiency or iniquity of the administration was daily exposed to public view, many adhered at first to the minister, and others were since gained to his cause, because they knew nothing of the constitution of their own, nor of the history of other countries; but imagined wildly, that things always went as they saw them go, and that liberty has been, and therefore may be preserved under the influence of the same corruption. Others perhaps were weak enough to be frightened at first, as some are hypocritical enough to pretend to be still, with the appellations of Tory and Jacobite, which are always ridiculously given to every man who does not bow to the brazen image that the King has set up. Others again might be persuaded, that no fatal use at least would be made of the power acquired by corruption; and men of superior parts might and may still flatter themselves, that if this power should be so employed, they shall have time and means to stop the effects of it. The first of these are seduced by their ignorance and futility; the second, if they are not hypocrites, by their prejudices; the third, by their partiality and blind confidence; the last, by their presumptions; and all of them by the mammon of unrighteousness, their private interest, which they endeavour to palliate and to reconcile as well as they can to that of the public: *et caeca cupiditate corrupti, non intelligunt se, dum vendant, et venire.*[12]

According to this representation, which I take to be true, your Lordship will agree that our unfortunate country affords an example in proof of what is asserted above. The Dutch* travellers I spoke of, men of the ordinary, or below the ordinary size of understand-

* Dutch] German *1754*

[11] Joshua 9: 21, 23; compare *Dissertation upon Parties*, 'Letter XIX', above, p. 181.
[12] '. . . and corrupted by blind greed, they did not realize that, while they were selling, they were being sold': Seneca, *De Constantia*, II. 2.

ing, though they are called by caprice, or lifted any other way into power, cannot do great and long mischief, in a country of liberty; unless men of genius, knowledge, and experience, misapply these talents, and become their leaders. A ministerial faction would have as little ability to do hurt, as they have inclination to do good, if they were not formed and conducted by one of better parts than they: nor would such a minister be able to support, at the head of this trusty phalanx, the ignominious tyranny imposed on his country, if other men, of better parts and much more consequence than himself, were not drawn in to misapply these parts to the vilest drudgery imaginable; the daily drudgery of explaining nonsense, covering ignorance, disguising folly, concealing and even justifying fraud and corruption; instead of employing their knowledge, their elocution, their skill, experience and authority, to correct the administration and to guard the constitution. But this is not all: the example shows a great deal more. Your Lordship's experience as well as mine will justify what I am going to say. It shows further, that such a conjuncture could not be rendered effectual to preserve power in some of the weakest and some of the worst hands in the kingdom, if there was not a non-application, or a faint and unsteady exercise of parts on one side, as well as an iniquitous misapplication of them on the other: and I cannot help saying, let it fall where it will, what I have said perhaps already, that the former is a crime but one degree inferior to the latter. The more genius, industry, and spirit are employed to destroy, the harder the task of saving our country becomes; but the duty increases with the difficulty, if the principles on which I reason are true. In such exigencies it is not enough that genius be opposed to genius, spirit must be matched by spirit. They, who go about to destroy, are animated from the first by ambition and avarice, the love of power and of money: fear makes them often desperate at last. They must be opposed therefore, or they will be opposed in vain, by a spirit able to cope with ambition, avarice, and despair itself: by a spirit able to cope with these passions, when they are favoured and fortified by the weakness of a nation, and the strength of a government. In such exigencies there is little difference, as to the merit or the effect, between opposing faintly and unsteadily, and not opposing at all: nay the former may be of worse consequence in certain circumstances than the latter. And this is a truth I wish with all my heart you may not see verified

in our country, where many, I fear, undertake opposition not as a
duty, but as an adventure: and looking on themselves like volun-
teers, not like men listed in the service, they deem themselves at
liberty to take as much or as little of this trouble, and to continue
in it as long, or end it as soon as they please. It is but a few years
ago, that not the merchants alone, but the whole nation, took fire
at the project of new excises.[13] The project was opposed, not on
mercantile considerations and interests alone, but on the true principles of liberty. In Parliament, the opposition was strenuously
enough supported for a time; but there was so little disposition to
guide and improve the spirit, that the chief concern of those who
took the lead seemed applied to keep it down; and yet your Lordship remembers how high it continued against the projector; till it
was calmed just before the elections of the present Parliament, by
the remarkable indolence and inactivity of the last session of the
last.[14] But these friends of ours, my Lord, are as much mistaken in
their ethics, as the event will show they have been in their politics.

The service of our country is no chimerical, but a real duty. He
who admits the proofs of any other moral duty, drawn from the
constitution of human nature, or from the moral fitness and
unfitness of things, must admit them in favour of this duty, or be
reduced to the most absurd inconsistency. When he has once admitted the duty on these proofs, it will be no difficult matter to demonstrate to him, that his obligation to the performance of it is in proportion to the means and the opportunities he has of performing it;
and that nothing can discharge him from this obligation as long as
he has these means and these opportunities in his power, and as
long as his country continues in the same want of his services.
These obligations then to the public service may become obligations
for life on certain persons. No doubt they may: and shall this consideration become a reason for denying or evading them? On the
contrary, sure it should become a reason for acknowledging and
fulfilling them, with the greatest gratitude to the Supreme Being,

---

[13] Walpole's attempt to reduce the land tax to a shilling in the pound and to increase
the excise accordingly resulted in the press and petitioning campaign of 1733 (the
'Excise Crisis') which led to the withdrawal of his proposals and almost to the
collapse of his ministry.
[14] Elections were held in the aftermath of the Excise Crisis in April–May 1734; the
new Parliament began sitting in January 1735.

who has made us capable of acting so excellent a part, and of the utmost benevolence to mankind. Superior talents, and superior rank amongst our fellow creatures, whether acquired by birth, or by the course of accidents, and the success of our own industry, are noble prerogatives. Shall he who possesses them repine at the obligation they lay him under, of passing his whole life in the noblest occupation of which human nature is capable? To what higher station, to what greater glory can any mortal aspire, than to be, during the whole course of his life, the support of good, the control of bad government, and the guardian of public liberty? To be driven from hence by successful tyranny, by loss of health or of parts, or by the force of accidents, is to be degraded in such a manner as to deserve pity, and not to incur blame: but to degrade ourselves, to descend voluntarily, and by choice, from the highest to a lower, perhaps to the lowest rank among the sons of Adam; to abandon the government of men for that of hounds and horses, the care of a kingdom for that of a parish, and a scene of great and generous efforts in public life, for one of trifling amusements and low cares, of sloth and of idleness, what is it, my Lord? I had rather your Lordship should name it than I. Will it be said that it is hard to exact from some men, in favour of others, that they should renounce all the pleasures of life, and drudge all their days in business, that others may indulge themselves in ease? It will be said without grounds. A life dedicated to the service of our country admits the full use, and no life should admit the abuse, of pleasures: the least are consistent with a constant discharge of our public duty, the greatest arise from it. The common, the sensual pleasures to which nature prompts us, and which reason therefore does not forbid, though she should always direct, are so far from being excluded out of a life of business, that they are sometimes necessary in it, and are always heightened by it: those of the table, for instance, may be ordered so as to promote that which the elder Cato calls *vitae conjunctionem*.[15] In the midst of public duties, private studies, and an extreme old age, he found time to frequent the *sodalitates*, or clubs of friends at Rome, and to sit up all night with his neighbours in the country of the Sabines. Cato's virtue often glowed with wine: and the love of women did not hinder Caesar from forming and executing the

[15] '. . . the bond of life': Cicero, *De Senectute*, XIII. 45.

greatest projects that ambition ever suggested. But if Caesar, whilst
he laboured to destroy the liberties of his country, enjoyed these
inferior pleasures of life, which a man who labours to save those
liberties may enjoy as well as he; there are superior pleasures in a
busy life that Caesar never knew, those, I mean, that arise from a
faithful discharge of our duty to the commonwealth. Neither Montaigne in writing his essays, nor Descartes[16] in building new worlds,
nor Burnet[17] in framing an antediluvian earth, no nor Newton in
discovering and establishing the true laws of nature on experiment
and a sublimer geometry, felt more intellectual joys, than he feels
who is a real patriot, who bends all the force of his understanding,
and directs all his thoughts and actions, to the good of his country.
When such a man forms a political scheme, and adjusts various and
seemingly independent parts in it to one great and good design, he
is transported by imagination, or absorbed in meditation, as much
and as agreeably as they: and the satisfaction that arises from the
different importance of these objects, in every step of the work, is
vastly in his favour. It is here that the speculative philosopher's
labour and pleasure end. But he who speculates in order to act, goes
on, and carries his scheme into execution. His labour continues, it
varies, it increases; but so does his pleasure too. The execution
indeed is often traversed, by unforeseen and untoward circumstances, by the perverseness or treachery of friends, and by the
power or malice of enemies: but the first and the last of these animate, and the docility and fidelity of some men make amends for
the perverseness and treachery of others. Whilst a great event is in
suspense, the action warms, and the very suspense, made up of
hope and fear, maintains no unpleasing agitation in the mind. If the
event is decided successfully, such a man enjoys pleasure proportionable to the good he has done; a pleasure like to that which
is attributed to the Supreme Being, on a survey of his works.[18] If
the event is decided otherwise, and usurping courts, or overbearing

---

[16] René Descartes (1596–1650), French philosopher and mathematician, attempted
to restore certainty to the natural sciences and religious belief by the application
of mathematics, the eradication of metaphysics, and the practice of hyperbolical
doubt.

[17] Thomas Burnet (1635–1715), author of *The Sacred Theory of the Earth* (1681), in
its time a highly controversial attempt to provide a mechanistic, Cartesian account
of the Creation.

[18] '. . . and God saw that it was good': Genesis 1: 10, 12, 18, 21, 25, 31.

parties prevail; such a man has still the testimony of his conscience, and a sense of the honour he has acquired, to soothe his mind, and support his courage. For although the course of state-affairs be to those who meddle in them like a lottery, yet it is a lottery wherein no good man can be a loser: he may be reviled, it is true, instead of being applauded, and may suffer violence of many kinds. I will not say, like Seneca, that the noblest spectacle which God can behold, is a virtuous man suffering, and struggling with afflictions:[19] but this I will say, that the second Cato driven out of the forum, and dragged to prison, enjoyed more inward pleasure, and maintained more outward dignity, than they who insulted him, and who triumphed in the ruin of their country. But the very example of Cato may be urged perhaps against what I have insisted upon: it may be asked, what good he did to Rome, by dedicating his whole life to her service, what honour to himself by dying at Utica?[20] It may be said, that governments have their periods like all things human; that they may be brought back to their primitive principles during a certain time, but that when these principles are worn out, in the minds of men, it is a vain enterprise to endeavour to renew them: that this is the case of all governments, when the corruption of the people comes to a great pitch, and is grown universal: that when a house which is old, and quite decayed, though often repaired, not only cracks, but totters even from the foundations, every man in his senses runs out of it, and takes shelter where he can, and that none but madmen continue obstinate to repair what is irreparable, till they are crushed in the ruin. Just so, that we must content ourselves to live under the government we like the least, when that form which we like the most is destroyed, or worn out; according to the counsel of Dolabella in one of his letters to Cicero.[21] But, my Lord, if Cato could not save, he prolonged the life of liberty: the liberties of Rome would have been lost when Catiline attacked them,

---

[19] Seneca, *De Providentia*, II. 7 ('miraris tu, si deus ille bonorum amantissimus, qui illos quam optius atque excellentissimos vult, fortunam illis cum qua exerceantur adsignat?').

[20] The Stoic Marcus Porcius Cato (95–46 BCE), who had urged fierce reprisals against Catiline, committed suicide at Utica in Africa in 46 BCE upon being defeated by Caesar during the civil war; Caesar had beaten the forces of republican Rome after a long and bloody battle at Munda the previous year.

[21] Dolabella to Cicero, *Epistulae ad Familiares*, IX. 9. 3 ('reliquum est, ubi nunc est republica, ibi sumus potius, quam, dum illam veteram sequamur, simus in nulla').

abetted probably by Caesar and Crassus, and the worst citizens of Rome; and when Cicero defended them, abetted by Cato and the best.[22] That Cato erred in his conduct, by giving way too much to the natural roughness of his temper, and by allowing too little for that of the Romans, among whom luxury had long prevailed, and corruption was openly practised, is most true. He was incapable of employing those seeming compliances that are reconcilable to the greatest steadiness, and treated unskilfully a crazy constitution. The safety of the commonwealth depended, in that critical conjuncture, on a coalition of parties, the senatorian and the equestrian: Tully had formed it, Cato broke it. But if this good, for I think he was not an able, man erred in the particular respects I have ventured to mention, he deserved most certainly the glory he acquired by the general tenor of his conduct, and by dedicating the whole labour of his life to the service of his country. He would have deserved more if he had persisted in maintaining the same cause to the end, and would have died I think with a better grace at Munda than at Utica. If this be so, if Cato may be censured, severely indeed, but justly, for abandoning the cause of liberty, which he would not however survive; what shall we say of those, who embrace it faintly, pursue it irresolutely, grow tired of it when they have much to hope, and give it up when they have nothing to fear?

My Lord, I have insisted the more on this duty which men owe to their country, because I came out of England, and continue still, strongly affected with what I saw when I was there.[23] Our government has approached, nearer than ever before, to the true principles of it, since the Revolution of one thousand six hundred and eighty eight: and the accession of the present family to the throne, has given the fairest opportunities, as well as the justest reasons, for completing the scheme of liberty, and improving it to perfection. But it seems to me, that, in our separate world,[24] as the means of asserting and supporting liberty are increased, all concern for it is

---

[22] The conspiracy led by the overambitious aristocrat Catiline (*c.* 108–62 BCE) to subvert the Roman constitution was discovered and harshly prosecuted by Cicero during his consulship in 63 BCE; Marcus Licinius Crassus (*c.* 115–53 BCE) was a member of the first triumvirate with Pompey and Caesar in 60 BCE: Cicero believed him to have been implicated in the Catilinarian conspiracy.
[23] Bolingbroke had returned to France in May 1735.
[24] Virgil, *Eclogues*, I. 36: 'et penitus toto divisos orbe Britannos' ('. . . and the Britons totally cut off from the world').

diminished. I beheld, when I was among you, more abject servility, in the manners and behaviour of particular men, than I ever saw in France, or than has been seen there, I believe, since the days of that Gascon, who, being turned out of the minister's door, leaped in again at his window.[25] As to bodies of men, I dare challenge your Lordship, and I am sorry for it, to produce any instances of resistance to the unjust demands, or wanton will of a court, that British Parliaments have given, comparable to such as I am able to cite to the honour of the parlement of Paris, and the whole body of the law in that country, within the same compass of time. This abject servility may appear justly the more wonderful in Britain, because the government of Britain has, in some sort, the appearance of an oligarchy: and monarchy is rather hid behind it than shown, rather weakened than strengthened, rather imposed upon than obeyed. The wonder therefore is to observe, how imagination and custom (a giddy fool and a formal pedant) have rendered these cabals, or oligarchies, more respected than majesty itself. That this should happen in countries where princes, who have absolute power, may be tyrants themselves, or substitute subordinate tyrants, is not wonderful. It has happened often: but that it should happen in Britain, may be justly an object of wonder. In these countries, the people had lost the armour of their constitution: they were naked and defenceless. Ours is more complete than ever. But though we have preserved the armour, we have lost the spirit of our constitution: and therefore we bear, from little engrossers of delegated power, what our fathers would not have suffered from true proprietors of the royal authority. Parliaments are not only, what they always were, essential parts of our constitution, but essential parts of our administration too. They do not claim the executive power. No. But the executive power cannot be exercised without their annual concurrence. How few months, instead of years, have princes and ministers now, to pass without inspection and control? How easy therefore is it become to check every growing evil in the bud, to change every bad administration, to keep such farmers of governments in awe, to maintain and revenge, if need be, the constitution? It is become so easy by the present form of our government, that corruption alone could not destroy us. We must want spirit, as well as virtue, to

---

[25] Source unidentified.

perish. Even able knaves would preserve liberty in such circumstances as ours, and highwaymen would scorn to receive the wages
and do the drudgery of pickpockets. But all is little, and low, and
mean among us! Far from having the virtues, we have not even the
vices of great men. He who had pride instead of vanity, and
ambition but equal to his desire of wealth, could never bear, I do
not say to be the understrapper to any farmer of royal authority,
but to see patiently one of them (at best his fellow, perhaps his
inferior in every respect) lord it over him, and the rest of mankind,
dissipating wealth, and trampling on the liberties of his country,
with impunity. This could not happen, if there was the least spirit
among us. But there is none. What passes among us for ambition,
is an odd mixture of avarice and vanity: the moderation we have
seen practised is pusillanimity, and the philosophy that some men
affect is sloth. Hence it comes that corruption has spread, and prevails.

I expect little from the principal actors that tread the stage at
present. They are divided, not so much as it has seemed, and as
they would have it believed, about measures: the true division is
about their different ends. Whilst the minister was not hard pushed,
nor the prospect of succeeding to him near, they appeared to have
but one end, the reformation of the government. The destruction
of the minister was pursued only as a preliminary, but of essential
and indispensable necessity to that end. But when his destruction
seemed to approach, the object of his succession interposed to the
sight of many, and the reformation of the government was no longer
their point of view. They divided the skin, at least in their thoughts,
before they had taken the beast,[26] and the common fear of hunting
him down for others made them all faint in the chase. It was this,
and this alone, that has saved him, or has put off his evil day.
Corruption, so much, and so justly complained of, could not have
done it alone.

When I say that I expect little from the principal actors that tread
the stage at present, I am far from applying to all of them what I
take to be true of the far greatest part. There are men among them
who certainly intend the good of their country, and whom I love
and honour for that reason. But these men have been clogged, or

[26] A gallicism: 'vendre la peau de l'ours avant de l'avoir tué'.

misled, or overborne by others; and, seduced by natural temper to inactivity, have taken any excuse, or yielded to any pretence that savoured it. That they should rouse therefore in themselves, or in any one else, the spirit they have suffered, nay helped to die away, I do not expect. I turn my eyes from the generation that is going off, to the generation that is coming on the stage.[27] I expect good from them, and from none of them more than from you, my Lord. Remember that the opposition in which you have engaged, at your first entrance into business, is not an opposition only to a bad administration of public affairs, but to an administration that supports itself by means, establishes principles, introduces customs, repugnant to the constitution of our governments, and destructive of all liberty; that you do not only combat present evils, but attempts to entail these evils upon you and your posterity; that if you cease the combat, you give up the cause: and that he, who does not renew on every occasion his claim, may forfeit his right.

Our disputes were formerly, to say the truth, much more about persons than things; or at most about particular points of political conduct, in which we should have soon agreed, if persons, and personal interests had been less concerned, and the blind prejudice of party less prevalent. Whether the Big-endians or the Little-endians got the better,[28] I believe no man of sense and knowledge thought the constitution concerned; notwithstanding all the clamour raised at one time about the danger of the Church, and at another about the danger of the Protestant succession. But the case is at this time vastly altered. The means of invading liberty more effectually by the constitution of the revenue, than it ever had been invaded by prerogative, were not then grown up into strength. They are so now; and a bold and an insolent use is made of them. To reform the state therefore is, and ought to be, the object of your opposition, as well as to reform the administration. Why do I say as well? It is so, and it ought to be so, much more. Wrest the power of the government, if you can, out of hands that have employed it weakly

---

[27] The 'Boy Patriots', a new generation of oppositional politicians, all aged thirty or under, had entered the Commons after the 1734 election, including George Lyttelton, William Pitt, Richard Grenville, William Murray and Viscount Cornbury; Lyttelton, Pitt and Grenville ('Cobham's Cubs') were all relations of Richard Temple, Viscount Cobham.

[28] These two Lilliputian parties battle over which end to break an egg in Swift, *Gulliver's Travels* (1726), ch. 4.

and wickedly, ever since it was thrown into them, by a silly bargain made in one reign, and a corrupt bargain made in another. But do not imagine this to be your sole, or your principal business. You owe to your country, to your honour, to your security, to the present, and to future ages, that no endeavours of yours be wanting to repair the breach that is made, and is increasing daily in the constitution, and to shut up with all the bars and bolts of law, the principal entries through which these torrents of corruption have been let in upon us. I say the principal entries; because, however it may appear in pure speculation, I think it would not be found in practice possible, no nor eligible neither, to shut them up all. As entries of corruption none of them deserve to be excepted: but there is a just distinction to be made, because there is a real difference. Some of these entries are opened by the abuse of powers, necessary to maintain subordination, and to carry on even good government, and therefore necessary to be preserved in the crown, notwithstanding the abuse that is sometimes made of them; for no human institution can arrive at perfection, and the most that human wisdom can do, is to procure the same or greater good, at the expense of less evil. There will be always some evil either immediate, or remote, either in cause or consequence. But there are other entries of corruption, and these are by much the greatest, for suffering of which to continue open no reason can be assigned or has been pretended to be assigned, but that which is to every honest and wise man a reason for shutting them up; the increase of the means of corruption, which are oftener employed for the service of the oligarchy, than for the service of the monarchy. Shut up these, and you will have nothing to fear from the others. By these, a more real and a more dangerous power has been gained to ministers, than was lost to the crown by the restraints on prerogative.

There have been periods when our government continued free, with strong appearances of becoming absolute. Let it be your glory, my Lord, and that of the new generation springing up with you, that this government do not become absolute at any future period, with the appearances of being free. However you may be employed, in all your councils, in all your actions, keep this regard to the constitution always in sight. The scene that opens before you is great, and the part that you will have to act difficult. It is difficult indeed to bring men, from strong habits of corruption, to prefer honour to profit, and liberty to luxury, as it is hard to teach princes the great art of governing all by all, or to prevail on them to practise it. But if it be a difficult, it is a glorious attempt; an attempt worthy to exert the greatest talents, and to fill the most extended life. Pursue it with courage, my Lord, nor despair of success.

> – deus haec fortasse benigna
> Reducet in sedem vice.[29]

A Parliament, nay one house of Parliament, is able at any time, and at once, to destroy any corrupt plan of power. Time produces every day new conjunctures: be prepared to improve them. We read in the Old Testament of a city that might have escaped divine vengeance, if five righteous men had been found in it.[30] Let not our city perish for want of so small a number: and if the generation that is going off could not furnish it, let the generation that is coming on furnish a greater.

We may reasonably hope that it will, from the first essays which your Lordship, and some others of our young senators, have made in public life. You have raised the hopes of your country by the proofs you have given of superior parts. Confirm these hopes by proofs of uncommon industry and application, and perseverance. Superior parts, nay even superior virtue, without these qualities, will be insufficient to support your character and your cause. How many men have appeared in my time who have made these essays with success, and have made no progress afterwards? Some have dropped, from their first flights, down into the vulgar crowd, have been distinguished, nay heard of, no more! Others with better parts, perhaps with more presumption, but certainly with greater ridicule, have persisted in making these essays towards business all their lives, and have never been able to advance farther, in their political course, than a premeditated harangue on some choice subject. I never saw one of these important persons sit down after his oration, with repeated hear-hims ringing in his ears, and inward rapture glowing in his eyes, that he did not recall to my memory the story of a conceited member of some parlement in France, who was over-

---

[29] 'Perhaps God with kindly change will mend our present ills': Horace, *Epodes*, XIII. 7–8.
[30] Sodom: in Genesis 18: 20–32, Abraham finally bargains the Lord down to ten righteous men.

heard, after his tedious harangue, muttering most devoutly to himself, *Non nobis, Domine, non nobis, sed nomini tuo da gloriam!*[31]

Eloquence, that leads mankind by the ears, gives a nobler superiority than power that every dunce may use, or fraud that every
knave may employ, to lead them by the nose.* But eloquence must
flow like a stream that is fed by an abundant spring, and not spout
forth a little frothy water on some gaudy day, and remain dry the
rest of the year. The famous orators of Greece and Rome were the
statesmen and ministers of those commonwealths. The nature of
their governments and the humour of those ages made elaborate
orations necessary. They harangued oftener than they debated: and
the *ars dicendi*,[32] required more study and more exercise of mind,
and of body too, among them, than are necessary among us. But as
much pains as they took in learning how to conduct the stream of
eloquence, they took more to enlarge the fountain from which it
flowed. Hear Demosthenes,[33] hear Cicero thunder against Philip,
Catiline and Anthony. I choose the example of the first rather than
that of Pericles[34] whom he imitated, or of Phocion[35] whom he
opposed, or of any other considerable personage in Greece; and the
example of Cicero rather than that of Crassus, or of Hortensius,[36]
or of any other of the great men of Rome; because the eloquence of
these two has been so celebrated that we are accustomed to look
upon them almost as mere orators. They were orators indeed, and
no man who has a soul can read their orations, after the revolution
of so many ages, after the extinction of the governments, and of the

---

* Eloquence . . . by the nose.] Eloquence has charms to lead mankind, and gives a
nobler superiority than power, that every dunce may use, or fraud, that every
knave may employ. *1754*

---

[31] 'Not unto us, O Lord, not unto us; but unto thy name give glory': Psalm 115: 1.
[32] 'Art of eloquence'.
[33] Demosthenes (384–322 BCE), the most celebrated of Greek orators, delivered three
Philippics to rouse the Athenians against Philip of Macedon in *c.* 351, 344 and
341 BCE.
[34] Pericles (*c.* 495–429 BCE), statesman, orator and general who led the Athenians in
the Peloponnesian War.
[35] Phocion (*c.* 402–318 BCE), Athenian statesman who opposed Demosthenes' measures against Philip, and resisted later attempts to enter war against the Macedonians.
[36] Quintus Hortensius Hortalus (114–50 BCE), the greatest Roman orator until
eclipsed by Cicero.

people for whom they were composed, without feeling at this hour the passions they were designed to move, and the spirit they were designed to raise. But if we look into the history of these two men, and consider the parts they acted, we shall see them in another light, and admire them in an higher sphere of action. Demosthenes had been neglected, in his education, by the same tutors who cheated him of his inheritance. Cicero was bred with greater advantage: and Plutarch, I think, says that when he first appeared the people used to call him, by way of derision, the Greek, and the scholar.[37] But whatever advantage of this kind the latter might have over the former, and to which of them soever you ascribe the superior genius, the progress which both of them made in every part of political knowledge, by their industry and application, was marvellous. Cicero might be a better philosopher, but Demosthenes was no less a statesman: and both of them performed actions and acquired fame, above the reach of eloquence alone. Demosthenes used to compare eloquence to a weapon,[38] aptly enough; for eloquence, like every other weapon, is of little use to the owner, unless he have the force and the skill to use it. This force and this skill Demosthenes had in an eminent degree. Observe them in one instance among many. It was of mighty importance to Philip to prevent the accession of Thebes to the grand alliance that Demosthenes, at the head of the Athenian commonwealth, formed against the growing power of the Macedonians. Philip had emissaries and his ambassadors on the spot to oppose to those of Athens, and we may be assured that he neglected none of those arts upon this occasion that he employed so successfully on others. The struggle was great, but Demosthenes prevailed, and the Thebans engaged in the war against Philip.[39] Was it by his eloquence alone that he prevailed in a divided state, over all the subtlety of intrigue, all the dexterity of negotiation, all the seduction, all the corruption, and all the terror that the ablest and most powerful prince could employ? Was Demosthenes wholly taken up with composing orations, and haranguing the people, in this remarkable crisis? He harangued them no doubt at Thebes, as well as at Athens, and in

[37] Plutarch, *Life of Cicero*, V. 2.
[38] Demosthenes was the son of a sword-maker; it was a commonplace among rhetoricians that verbal ornaments (*ornatus*) were armaments.
[39] Plutarch, *Life of Demosthenes*, XVII–XVIII.

the rest of Greece, where all the great resolutions of making alliances, waging war, or concluding peace, were determined in democratical assemblies. But yet haranguing was no doubt the least part of his business, and eloquence was neither the sole, nor the principal talent, as the style of writers would induce us to believe, on which his success depended. He must have been master of other arts, subserviently to which his eloquence was employed, and must have had a thorough knowledge of his own state, and of the other states of Greece, of their dispositions, and of their interests relatively to one another, and relatively to their neighbours, to the Persians particularly, with whom he held a correspondence, not much to his honour:* I say, he must have possessed an immense fund of knowledge, to make his eloquence in every case successful, and even pertinent or seasonable in some, as well as to direct it and to furnish it with matter whenever he thought proper to employ this weapon.

Let us consider Tully on the greatest theatre of the known world, and in the most difficult circumstances. We are better acquainted with him than we are with Demosthenes; for we see him nearer, as it were, and in more different lights. How perfect a knowledge had he acquired of the Roman constitution of government, ecclesiastical and civil; of the original and progress, of the general reasons and particular occasions of the laws and customs of his country; of the great rules of equity, and the low practice of courts; of the duty of every magistracy and office in the state, from the dictator down to the lictor; and of all the steps by which Rome had risen from her infancy, to liberty, to power and grandeur and dominion, as well as of all those by which she began to decline, a little before his age, to that servitude which he died for opposing, but lived to see established, and in which not her liberty alone, but her power and grandeur and dominion were lost? How well was he acquainted with the Roman colonies and provinces, with the allies and enemies of the empire, with the rights and privileges of the former, the dispositions and conditions of the latter, with the interests of them all relatively to Rome, and with the interests of Rome relatively to them? How present to his mind were the anecdotes of former times concerning the Roman and other states, and how curious was he to observe the

* not much to his honour] not much to his honor in appearance, whatever he might intend by it *1754*

minutest circumstances that passed in his own? His works will answer sufficiently the questions I ask, and establish in the mind of every man who reads them the idea I would give of his capacity and knowledge, as well as that which is so universally taken of his eloquence. To a man fraught with all this stock of knowledge, and industrious to improve it daily, nothing could happen that was entirely new, nothing for which he was quite unprepared, scarce any effect whereof he had not considered the cause, scarce any cause wherein his sagacity could not discern the latent effect. His eloquence in private causes gave him first credit at Rome, but it was this knowledge, this experience, and the continued habits of business, that supported his reputation, enabled him to do so much service to his country, and gave force and authority to his eloquence. To little purpose would he have attached Catiline with all the vehemence that indignation and even fear added to eloquence, if he had trusted to this weapon alone. This weapon alone would have secured neither him nor the senate from the poniard of that assassin. He would have had no occasion to boast, that he had driven this infamous citizen out of the walls of Rome, *abiit, excessit, evasit, erupit*,[40] if he had not made it before-hand impossible for him to continue any longer in them. As little occasion would he have had to assume the honour of defeating without any tumult, or any disorder, the designs of those who conspired to murder the Roman people, to destroy the Roman empire, and to extinguish the Roman name; if he had not united by skill and management, in the common cause of their country, orders of men the most averse to each other; if he had not watched all the machinations of the conspirators in silence, and prepared a strength sufficient to resist them at Rome, and in the provinces, before he opened this scene of villainy to the senate and the people: in a word, if he had not made much more use of political prudence, that is, of the knowledge of mankind, and of the arts of government, which study and experience give, than of all the powers of his eloquence.

Such was Demosthenes, such was Cicero, such were all the great men whose memories are preserved in history, and such must every man be, or endeavour to be, if he has either sense or sentiment, who presumes to meddle in affairs of government, of a free government I mean, and hopes to maintain a distinguished character in popular

---

[40] 'He has gone, departed, escaped, broken forth': Cicero, *In Catilinam*, II. I. I.

assemblies, whatever part he takes, whether that of supporting, or that of opposing. I put the two cases purposely, my Lord, because I have observed, and your Lordship will have frequent occasions of observing, many persons who seem to think that opposition to an administration requires fewer preparatives, and less constant application than the conduct of it. Now, my Lord, I take this to be a gross error, and I am sure it has been a fatal one. It is one of those errors, and there are many such, which men impute to judgment, and which proceed from the defect of judgment, as this does from lightness, irresolution, laziness, and a false notion of opposition; unless the persons, who seem to think, do not really think in this manner, but serving the public purely for interest, and not for fame, nor for duty, decline taking the same pains when they oppose without personal and immediate reward, as they are willing to take when they are paid for serving. Look about you, and you will see men eager to speak, and keen to act, when particular occasions press them, or particular motives excite them, but quite unprepared for either: and hence all that superficiality in speaking, for want of information, hence all that confusion or inactivity, for want of concert, and all that disappointment for want of preliminary measures. They who affect to head an opposition, or to make any considerable figure in it, must be equal at least to those whom they oppose; I do not say in parts only, but in application and industry, and the fruits of both, information, knowledge, and a certain constant preparedness for all the events that may arise. Every administration is a system of conduct: opposition, therefore, should be a system of conduct likewise; an opposite, but not a dependent system. I shall explain myself better by an example. When two armies take the field, the generals on both sides have their different plans for the campaign, either of defence or of offence: and as the former does not suspend his measures till he is attacked, but takes them beforehand on every probable contingency, so the latter does not suspend his, till the opportunity of attacking presents itself, but is alert and constantly ready to seize it whenever it happens; and in the mean time is busy to improve all the advantages of skill, of force, or of any other kind that he has, or that he can acquire, independently of the plan and of the motions of his enemy.

In a word, my Lord, this is my notion, and I submit it to you. According to the present form of our constitution, every member of either house of Parliament is a member of a national standing council, born, or appointed by the people, to promote good, and to oppose bad government; and, if not vested with the power of a minister of state, yet vested with the superior power of controlling those who are appointed such by the crown. It follows from hence, that they who engage in opposition are under as great obligations, to prepare themselves to control, as they who serve the crown are under, to prepare themselves to carry on the administration: and that a party formed for this purpose, do not act like good citizens nor honest men, unless they propose true, as well as oppose false measures of government. Sure I am they do not act like wise men unless they act systematically, and unless they contrast, on every occasion, that scheme of policy which the public interest requires to be followed, with that which is suited to no interest but the private interest of the prince or his ministers. Cunning men (several such there are among you) will dislike this consequence, and object, that such a conduct would support, under the appearance of opposing, a weak and even a wicked administration; and that to proceed in this manner would be to give good counsel to a bad minister, and to extricate him out of distresses that ought to be improved to his ruin. But cunning pays no regard to virtue, and is but the low mimic of wisdom. It were easy to demonstrate what I have asserted concerning the duty of an opposing party: and I presume there is no need of labouring to prove, that a party who opposed, systematically, a wise to a silly, an honest to an iniquitous, scheme of government, would acquire greater reputation and strength, and arrive more surely at their end, than a party who opposed occasionally, as it were, without any common system, without any general concert, with little uniformity, little preparation, little perseverance, and as little knowledge or political capacity. But it is time to leave this invidious subject, and to hasten to the conclusion of my letter before it grows into a book.

I am, my Lord, &c.

The Idea of a Patriot King

Introduction*

Dec. 1, 1738.*

Revising some letters I wrote to my Lord —,[1] I found in one of them a great deal said concerning the duties which men owe to their country, those men particularly who live under a free constitution of government; with a strong application of these general doctrines to the present state of Great Britain, and to the characters of the present actors on this stage.[2]

I saw no reason to alter, none even to soften, any thing that is* there advanced. On the contrary, it came into my mind to carry these considerations further, and to delineate, for I pretend not to make a perfect draught, the duties of a king to his country; of those kings particularly who are appointed by the people, for I know of none who are anointed by God to rule in limited monarchies. After which I proposed to apply the general doctrines in this case, as strongly and as directly as in the other, to the present state of Great Britain.*

I am not one of those oriental slaves, who deem* it unlawful presumption to look their kings in the face; neither am I swayed

---

* Introduction] The Author's PREFACE
* Dec. 1, 1738] *1749*   * that is] *1749*
* Britain] Britain; tho' not the *Characters* of those who rule, and are to rule, over us.
* deem] think

[1] Henry Hyde, Viscount Cornbury, addressee of *Letters to a Young Nobleman on the Study and Use of History* (1738) and 'On the Spirit of Patriotism'.
[2] 'On the Spirit of Patriotism' ('I expect little from the principal actors that tread upon the stage at present': above, p. 207).

by my Lord Bacon's authority, to think this custom good and reasonable in its meaning, though it savours of barbarism in its institution: *Ritu quidem barbarus, sed significatione bonus.*[3] Much otherwise. It* seems to me, that no secrets are so important to be known, no hearts deserve to be pried into with more curiosity and attention, than those of princes. But many things have concurred, besides age and temper, to set me at a great distance from the present court. Far from prying into the hearts, I scarce know the faces of our royal family.[4] I shall therefore decline all application to their characters, and all mention of any influence which their characters may have on their own fortune, or on that of this nation.*

The principles I have reasoned upon in my letter to my Lord —, and those I shall reason upon here, are the same. They are laid in the same system of human nature. They are drawn from that source from whence all the duties of public and private morality must be derived, or they will be often falsely, and always precariously, established. Up to this source there are few men who take the pains to go: and, open as it lies, there are not many who can find their way to it. By* such as you, I shall be understood and approved: and, far from fearing the censure, or the ridicule, I should reproach myself with the applause, of men* who measure their interest by their passions,* and their duty by the examples of a corrupt age; that is, by the examples* they afford to one another. Such, I think,* are the greatest part of the present generation; not of the vulgar alone, but of those who stand foremost, and are raised highest in our nation. Such* we may justly apprehend too that the next will

---

* Much otherwise. It] Quite on the contrary; it
* family. I shall . . . this nation] family, and ought therefore, on all accounts, to decline all such particular Application.
* Up to this source . . . it. By] ¶ By you, Sir, and
* of men] of other men
* passions] Passion
* examples of a corrupt age; that is, by the examples] Example of a corrupt Age, that is, by the Example
* I think] *1749*   * not of the vulgar . . . Such] and such

[3] Francis Bacon, *De Dignitate et Augmentis Scientiarum*, I. 1 in *Francisci Baconis . . . Opera Omnia* (4 vols., London, 1730), I, *37* (compare Herodotus, *Histories*, I. 99).
[4] Since the accession of George I in 1714, Bolingbroke had been in exile in France in 1715–25 and 1735–38.

be; since they who are to compose it will* set out into the world under a direction that must incline them strongly to the same course of self-interest, profligacy, and corruption.

The iniquity of all the* principal men in any community, of kings and ministers especially, does not consist alone in the crimes they commit, and in the immediate consequences of these* crimes: and, therefore, their guilt is not to be measured by these alone. Such men sin against posterity, as well as against their own age; and when the consequences of their crimes are over, the consequences of their example remain. I think, and every wise and honest man in generations yet unborn will think, if the history of this administration descends to blacken our annals, that the greatest iniquity of the minister,[5] on whom the whole iniquity ought to be charged, since he has been so long in possession of the whole power, is the constant endeavour he has employed* to corrupt the morals of men. I say thus generally, the morals; because he, who abandons or betrays his country, will abandon or betray his friend; and because he, who is prevailed on to act in Parliament* without any regard to truth or justice, will easily prevail on himself to act in the same manner every where else. A wiser and honester* administration may relieve our trade* from that oppression, and the public from that load of debt, under which it must be supposed that he has industriously kept it; because we are able to prove, by fair calculations, that he might have provided effectually for the payment of it, since he came to the head of the Treasury. A wiser and honester administration may draw us back to our former credit and influence abroad, from that state of contempt into which we are sunk among all our neighbours.* But will the minds of men, which this minister has

* that the next . . . compose it will] the next will be, since they
* the] *1749*   * these] those
* I think . . . he has employed] The greatest of all Iniquities which a Prince or Minister can commit, is
* Parliament] Publick
* wiser and honester] wise and honest
* our trade] the Trade of a Nation
* debt, under which . . . our neighbours] Debts, under which a weak or wicked Administration has undoubtedly laid, or industriously kept it; and may draw such a Nation back to its former Credit and influence abroad, from that State of Contempt in which it had been held since by its Neighbours.

[5] Sir Robert Walpole.

narrowed to personal regards alone, will their views, which he has*
confined to the present moment, as if nations were mortal like the
men who compose them, and Britain was to perish with her*
degenerate children; will these, I say, be so easily or so soon
enlarged? Will their sentiments, which are debased from the love of
liberty, from zeal* for the honour and prosperity of their country,
and from a desire of honest fame, to an absolute unconcernedness
for all these, to an abject submission, and a rapacious eagerness after
wealth, that may* sate their avarice, and exceed the profusion of
their luxury; will* these, I say again, be so easily or so soon elevated?
In a word, will the British spirit, that spirit which has preserved
liberty hitherto in one corner of the world at least, be so easily or
so soon reinfused into the British nation? I think not. We have been
long coming to this point of depravation: and the progress* from
confirmed habits of evil is much more slow than the progress to
them. Virtue is not placed on a rugged mountain of difficult and
dangerous access, as they who would excuse the indolence of their
temper, or the perverseness of their will, desire to have it believed;
but she is seated, however, on an eminence. We may go up to her
with ease, but we must go up gradually, according to the natural
progression of reason, who is to lead the way, and to guide our
steps. On the other hand, if we fall from thence, we are sure to be
hurried down the hill with a blind impetuosity, according to the
natural violence of those appetites and passions that caused our fall
at first, and urge it on the faster, the further they are removed from
the control that* before restrained them.

To perform, therefore,* so great a work, as to reinfuse the spirit
of liberty, to reform the morals, and to raise the sentiments of a
people, much time is required; and a work which requires so much
time, may, too probably, be never completed; considering how
unsteadily and unsystematically even the best of* men are apt often

* will the minds ... he has] would the Minds of Men, when once narrowed to
  personal regards alone, would their *Views* when
* and Britain was to perish with her] and destin'd to perish with their
* Will their ... from zeal] Could their *Sentiments*, when debased from the Love of
  Liberty, from a Zeal   * that may] to   * will] could
* will the British ... the progress] could the *Spirit of Liberty*, that *Spirit* which has
  yet preserv'd the Rights of Mankind, in some Corners of the World at least, be
  so easily or so soon *re-infused*? I think not. The Progress
* that] which   * therefore] *1749*   * of] *1749*

to proceed, and how this* reformation is to be carried forward, in opposition to public fashion, and private inclination, to the authority of the* men in power, and to the secret bent of many of those* who are out of power. Let us not flatter ourselves: I did so too long.* It is more to be wished than to be hoped, that the contagion should spread no further than that leprous race, who carry on their skins, exposed to public sight, the scabs and blotches of their distemper. The minister preaches corruption aloud and constantly, like an impudent missionary of vice: and some there are who not only insinuate, but teach the same occasionally. I say, some; because I am as far from thinking, that all those who join with him, as that any of those who oppose him, wait only to be more authorized, that they may propagate it with greater success, and apply it to their own use, in their turn.*

It seems to me, upon the whole matter, that to save or* redeem a nation, under such circumstances, from perdition, nothing less is necessary than some great, some extraordinary conjuncture of ill fortune, or of good, which may purge, yet so as by fire.* Distress from abroad, bankruptcy at home, and other circumstances of like nature and tendency, may beget universal confusion. Out of confusion order may arise: but it may be the order of a wicked tyranny, instead of the order of a just monarchy. Either may happen: and such an alternative, at the disposition of fortune, is sufficient to make a Stoic tremble! We may be saved, indeed, by means of a very different kind; but these means will not offer themselves, this way of salvation will not be opened to us, without the concurrence, and the influence, of a Patriot King, the most uncommon of all phenomena in the physical or moral world.[6]

* this] that   * the] most
* many of those] most
* Let us not . . . too long.] *1749*
* The minister . . . in their turn.] These indeed may preach Corruption aloud, like impudent Missionaries of Vice: but there may be those who whisper and insinuate the same Doctrine; and who wait perhaps only to be more authorised, that they may propagate it with greater success, and apply it to their own Use.
* upon the whole . . . save or] that to
* good . . . purge] good. They may be *purged,*

[6] Compare Machiavelli, *Discorsi*, III. 1, on the necessity of a return to first principles and the desirability of 'some good man' who will arise to redeem the commonwealth.

Nothing can so surely and so effectually restore the virtue and public spirit essential to the preservation of liberty and national prosperity, as the reign of such a prince.

We are willing to indulge this pleasing expectation, and there is nothing we desire more ardently than to be able to hold of a British prince, without flattery, the same language that was held of a Roman emperor, with a great deal,[7]

Nil oriturum alias, nil ortum tale fatentes.[8]

But let us not neglect, on our part, such means as are in our power, to keep the cause of truth, of reason, of virtue, and of liberty, alive. If the blessing be withheld from us, let us deserve, at least, that it should be granted to us. If heaven, in mercy, bestows it on us, let us prepare to receive it, to improve it, and to co-operate with it.

I speak as if I could take my share in these glorious efforts. Neither shall I recall my words. Stripped of the rights of a British subject, of all except the meanest of them, that of inheriting, I remember that I am a Briton still.[9] I apply to myself what I have read in Seneca: *officia, si civis amiserit, hominis exerceat.*[10] I have renounced the world, not in show, but in reality, and more by my way of thinking, than by my way of living, as retired as that may seem. But I have not renounced my country, nor my friends: and by my friends I mean all those, and those alone, who are such to their country, by whatever name they have been, or may be still distinguished; and though in that number there should be men, of whose past ingratitude, injustice, or malice, I might complain, on my own account, with the greatest reason. These I will never renounce. In their prosperity, they shall never hear of me: in their distress, always. In that retreat, wherein the remainder of my days

---

[7] There is evidently an omission here in *1749*, which should perhaps read: 'with a great deal [of truth]'.

[8] 'Nothing like [him] will arise, nor has yet arisen': Horace, *Epistles*, II. 1. 17 (addressed to Augustus).

[9] Bolingbroke had been impeached by Parliament in 1715. Though pardoned in 1723, he was not released from the Act of Attainder until 1725, and even then was not allowed to resume his seat in the Lords.

[10] 'If he has lost the duties of a citizen, let him exercise those of a man': Seneca, *De Tranquilitate Animi*, IV. 4 ('officia civis amisit? hominis exerceat').

shall be spent,[11] I may be of some use to them; since, even from thence, I may advise, exhort, and warn them. *Nec enim is solus reipublicae prodest, qui candidatos extrahit, et tuetur reos, et de pace, belloque censet; sed qui juventutem exhortatur, qui, in tanta bonorum praeceptorum inopia, virtute instruit animos; qui ad pecuniam luxuriamque cursu ruentes, prensat ac retrahit, et, si nihil aliud, certe moratur; in privato publicum negotium agit.*[12]*

The Idea of a Patriot King

*My intention is not to introduce what I have to say concerning the duties of kings, by any nice inquiry into the original of their institution. What is to be known of it will appear plainly enough, to such as are able and can spare time to trace it, in the broken traditions which are come down to us of a few nations. But those who are not able to trace it there, may trace something better, and more worthy to be known, in their own thoughts: I mean what this institution ought to have been, whenever it began, according to the rule of reason, founded in the common rights, and interests, of mankind. On this head it is quite necessary to make some reflections, that will, like angular stones laid on a rock, support the little fabric, the model however of a great building, that I propose to raise.

* We may be saved ... negotium agit.'] ¶ There is no Elegible Remedy that can so surely and so effectually restore the Virtue and Publick Spirit essential to the Preservation of Liberty, and well nigh lost even in Europe, as the Reign of a good and wise Prince. And let me say, that it is in *Britain* alone, and in no other part of Europe, that we can expect that most uncommon of all Phenomena in the Physical or Moral world, I mean a PATRIOT KING, to arise. *Nil oriturum alias, nil ortum tale fatentes.* ¶ It is this Picture I presume to draw; and I will venture to say it is no chimerical one. But that it may not be so, I shall draw it on *that Ground*, on which only it can stand, and on which only it can last; the *Reason of Things*, immediately abstracted from the *Nature* of them.

* CHAP, I. What are the Duties of Kings, from the Nature of their Institution. II. The Source of the Opinions concerning the Divine Right and Absolute Power of Kings.

[11] Bolingbroke had returned to England for good in 1744, and had settled at Battersea.

[12] 'For the man who does good service to the state is not merely he who brings forward candidates, defends the accused, and votes for peace and war, but he who encourages young men, furnishes their minds with virtue when good teachers are lacking, who grasps and pulls back those who are running after riches and luxury and, if nothing else, at least delays them – such a man performs public service, even in private life': Seneca, *De Tranquilitate Animi*, III. 3.

So plain a matter could never have been rendered intricate and voluminous, had it not been for lawless ambition, extravagant vanity, and the detestable spirit of tyranny, abetted by the private interests of artful men, by* adulation and superstition, two vices to which that staring timid creature man* is excessively prone; if authority had not imposed on such as did not pretend to reason; and if such as did attempt to reason had not* been caught in the common snares of sophism, and bewildered in the labyrinths of disputation. In this case, therefore, as in all those of great concernment, the shortest and the surest method of arriving at real knowledge is to unlearn the lessons we have been taught, to remount to first principles, and take nobody's word about them; for it is about them that almost all the juggling and legerdemain, employed by men whose trade it is to deceive, are set to work.

Now he, who does so in this case, will discover soon, that the notions concerning the divine institution and right of kings, as well as the absolute power belonging to their office, have no foundation in fact or reason, but have risen from an old alliance between ecclesiastical and civil policy. The characters of king and priest have been sometimes blended together: and when they have been divided, as kings have found the great effects wrought in government by the empire which priests obtain over the consciences of mankind, so priests have been taught by experience, that the best method to preserve their own rank, dignity, wealth, and power, all raised upon* a supposed divine right, is to communicate the same pretension to kings, and, by a fallacy common to both, impose their usurpations on a silly world. This they have done: and, in the state, as in the Church, these pretensions to a divine right have been generally carried highest by those, who have had the least pretension to the divine favour.

It is worth while to observe, on what principle some* men were advanced to a great pre-eminence over others, in the early ages of

---

* men, by] Men in lower ranks, and by their
* staring .. . . man] timid and staring part of Mankind
* prone, if . . . reason had not] prone. Neither could such Opinions have continued, had not Authority imposed on such as did not pretend to Reason, and had not such as did attempt to Reason
* II. [*footnote* II. The Source of the Opinions concerning the *Divine Right* and *Absolute Power* of Kings.]
* king and priest] Kings and Priests   * upon] on   * some] *1749*

those nations that are a little known to us:* I speak not of such as raised themselves by conquest, but of such as were raised by common consent. Now you will find, in all these proceedings, an entire uniformity of principle. The authors of such inventions, as were of general use to the well being of mankind, were not only reverenced and obeyed during their lives, but worshipped after their deaths: they became principal gods, *Dii majorum gentium.* The founders of commonwealths, the lawgivers, and the heroes of particular states, became gods of a second class, *Dii minorum gentium.*[13] All pre-eminence was given in heaven, as well as on earth, in proportion to the benefits that men received. Majesty was the first, and divinity the second, reward. Both were earned by services done to mankind, whom it was easy to lead, in those days of simplicity and superstition, from admiration and gratitude, to adoration and expectation.

When advantage had been taken, by some particular men, of these dispositions in the generality, and religion and government were* become two trades or mysteries, new means of attaining to this pre-eminence were soon devised, and new and even contrary motives worked the same effect. Merit had given rank; but rank was soon kept, and, which is more preposterous, obtained, too, without merit. Men were then made kings for reasons as little relative to good government, as the neighing of the horse of the son of Hystaspes.[14]

But the most prevalent, and the general motive was proximity of blood to the last, not to the best, king. Nobility in China mounts upwards: and he, who has it conferred upon him, ennobles his ancestors, not his posterity.[15] A wise institution! and especially among a people in whose minds a great veneration for their forefathers has been always carefully maintained. But in China, as well

---

* those nations . . . to us] the Nations that are a little known to us, if not of the World.   * were] *1749*

[13] Cicero, *Tusculan Disputations*, I. 13. 29.
[14] Darius I, who became king of Persia upon winning a bet that his horse would neigh first on a chosen morning: Herodotus, *Histories*, III. 84–6.
[15] See Jean Baptiste du Halde, *The General History of China*, trans. Richard Brookes (4 vols., London, 1736), II, 204. This translation and its folio reprint, *A Description of the Empire of China and Chinese-Tartary* (2 vols., London, 1738), were dedicated to Frederick, Prince of Wales.

as in most other countries, royalty has descended, and kingdoms have been reckoned the patrimonies of particular families.

I have read in one of the historians of the latter Roman empire, historians, by the way, that I will not advise others to misspend their* time in reading, that Sapores, the famous king of Persia against whom Julian made the expedition wherein he lost his life, was crowned in his mother's womb.[16] His father left her with child: the magi declared that the child would be a male; whereupon the royal ensigns were brought forth, they were placed on her majesty's belly, and the princes and the satraps prostrate recognized the embryo-monarch.* But to take a more known example, out of multitudes that present themselves, Domitian, the worst, and Trajan, the best of princes, were promoted to the empire by the same title. Domitian was the son of Flavius, and the brother, though possibly the poisoner too, of Titus Vespasian: Trajan was the adopted son of Nerva.[17] Hereditary right served the purpose of one, as well as of* the other: and if Trajan was translated to a place among the gods, this was no greater a distinction than some of the worst of his predecessors and his successors obtained,* for reasons generally as good as that which Seneca puts into the mouth of Diespiter in the *Apocolocyntosis* of Claudius: *cum sit* e republica esse aliquem, qui cum Romulo possit ferventia rapa vorare.*[18] To say the truth, it would have been a wiser measure to have made these royal persons gods at once; as gods they would have done neither good nor hurt; but as emperors, in their way to divinity, they acted like devils.

If my readers* are ready by this time to think me antimonarchical, and in particular an enemy to the succession of kings by hereditary right, I hope to be soon restored to their* good opinion. I esteem monarchy above any other form of government, and hereditary monarchy above elective. I reverence kings, their office, their

* others to misspend their] you to mispend your
* satraps . . . embryo-monarch.] Satrapes acknowledg'd the Monarch in Embryo.
* of] *1749*   * cum sit] *1749*
* my readers] you   * their] your

[16] Shapur II, King of Persia (309/10–379 CE): Agathias Myrinaeus, *Histories*, IV. 25. 2–4.
[17] Domitian, the last of the Twelve Caesars, was emperor 81–96 (CE); Trajan was emperor 98–117 (CE), after the brief reign of Nerva.
[18] 'And it is for the public good that there should be someone who can devour boiled turnips with Romulus': Seneca, *Apocolocyntosis*, X.

rights, their persons: and it will never be owing to the principles I am going to establish, because the character and government of a Patriot King can be established on no other, if their office and their right are not always held divine, and their persons always sacred.

Now, we* are subject, by the constitution of human nature, and therefore by the will of the author of this and every other nature, to two laws. One given immediately to all men by God, the same to all, and obligatory alike on all. The other given to man by man, and therefore not the same to all, nor obligatory alike on all: founded indeed on the same principles, but varied by different applications of them to times, to characters, and to a number, which may be reckoned infinite, of other circumstances. By the first, I mean* the universal law of reason; and by the second, the particular law, or constitution of laws, by which every distinct community has chosen to be governed.

The obligation of submission to both, is discoverable by so clear and so simple an use of our intellectual faculties, that it may be said properly enough to be revealed to us by God: and though both these laws cannot be said properly to be given by him, yet our obligation to submit to the civil law is a principal paragraph in the natural law, which he has most manifestly given us. In truth we can no more doubt of the obligations of both these laws, than of the existence of the law-giver. As supreme lord over all his works, his general providence regards immediately the great commonwealth of mankind; but then, as supreme lord likewise, his authority gives a sanction to the particular bodies of law which are made under it. The law of nature is the law of all his subjects: the constitutions of particular governments are like the by-laws of cities, or the appropriated customs of provinces. It follows, therefore, that he who breaks the laws* of his country resists the ordinance of God, that is, the law of his nature. God has instituted neither monarchy, nor aristocracy, nor democracy, nor mixed government: but though God has instituted no particular form of government among men, yet by the general laws of his kingdom he

---

* Now, we] CHAP. II. I. What are the Duties of Subjects, from the Constitution of human Nature and Law of Society. II. The true Right of Kings and Obedience of Subjects. III. Which is best, Hereditary Monarchy, or Elective? IV. A Limited Monarchy the best form of Government, and Hereditary the best Monarchy. ¶ We
* I mean] you see that I mean
* laws] *Law*

exacts our obedience to the laws of those communities, to which each of us is attached by birth, or to which we may be attached by a *subsequent and lawful engagement.

*From such plain, unrefined, and therefore, I suppose, true reasoning, the just authority of kings and the due obedience of subjects, may be deduced with the utmost certainty. And surely it is far better for kings themselves to have their authority thus founded on principles incontestable, and on fair deductions from them, than on the chimeras of madmen, or, what has been more common, the sophisms of knaves. A human right, that cannot be controverted, is preferable, surely, to a pretended divine right, which every man must believe implicitly, as few will do, or not believe at all.

But the principles we have laid down do not stop here. A divine right in kings is to be deduced evidently from them: a divine right to govern well, and conformably to the constitution at the head of which they are placed. A divine right to govern ill, is an absurdity: to assert it, is blasphemy.[19] A people may choose, or hereditary succession may raise, a bad prince to the throne; but a good king alone can derive his right to govern from God. The reason is plain: good government alone can be in the divine intention. God has made us to desire happiness; he has made our happiness dependent on society; and the happiness of society dependent on good or bad government. His intention, therefore, was, that government should be good.

This is essential to his wisdom; for wisdom consists, surely, in proportioning means to ends: therefore it cannot be said without absurd impiety, that he confers a right to oppose his intention.

The office of kings is, then, of right divine, and their persons are to be reputed sacred. As men, they have no such right, no such sacredness belonging to them: as kings, they have both, unless they forfeit them. Reverence for government obliges to reverence governors, who, for the sake of it, are raised above the level of other men: but reverence for governors, independently of government, any further than reverence would be due to their virtues if they were private men, is preposterous, and repugnant to common sense. The

* a] *1749*
* II. [*footnote* II. The true Right of Kings, and Obedience of Subjects.]

[19] Compare Alexander Pope, *The Dunciad* (1742), IV, 187–8, 'May you, may Cam and Isis preach it long! / "The RIGHT DIVINE of Kings to govern wrong" '.

spring from which this legal reverence, for so I may call it, arises, is national, not personal. As well might we say that a ship is built, and loaded, and manned, for the sake of any particular pilot, instead of acknowledging that the pilot is made for the sake of the ship, her lading, and her crew, who are always the owners in the political vessel; as to say that kingdoms were instituted for kings, not kings for kingdoms.[20] In short, and to carry our allusion higher, majesty is not an inherent, but a reflected light.

All this is as true of elective, as it is of hereditary monarchs, though the scribblers for tyranny, under the name of monarchy, would have us believe that there is something more august, and more sacred in one than the other. They are sacred alike, and this attribute is to be ascribed or not ascribed, to them, as they answer, or do not answer, the ends of their institution. But there is another comparison to be made, in which a great and most important dissimilitude will be found between hereditary and elective monarchy. Nothing can be more absurd, in pure speculation, than an hereditary right in any mortal to govern other men: and yet, in practice, nothing can be more absurd than to have a king to choose at every vacancy of a throne. We draw at a lottery indeed in one case, where there are many chances to lose, and few to gain. But have we much more advantage of this kind in the other? I think not. Upon these, and upon most occasions, the multitude would do at least as well to trust to chance as choice, and to their fortune as to their judgment. But in another respect, the advantage is entirely on the side of hereditary succession; for, in elective monarchies, these elections, whether well or ill made, are often attended with such national calamities, that even the best reigns cannot make amends for them: whereas, in hereditary monarchy, whether a good or a bad prince succeeds, these calamities are avoided. There is one source of evil the less open: and one source of evil the less in human affairs, where there are so many, is sufficient to decide. We may lament the imperfections of our human state, which is such, that in cases of

* III. [*footnote* III. Which is best, Hereditary Monarchy, or Elective?]
* one] the one

[20] Compare Seneca, *De Clementia*, I. 19. 8 ('. . . non rem publicam suam esse, sed se rei publicae'), later a slogan for Protestant theorists of limited monarchy: Elisabeth Labrousse, ' "Les Rois faits pour les peuples . . ." (à propos de Jurieu)', *Recherches sur le XVIIᵉ siècle* 4 (1980): 183–6.

the utmost importance to the order and good government of society, and by consequence to the happiness of our kind, we are reduced, by the very constitution of our nature, to have no part to take that our reason can approve absolutely. But though we lament it, we must submit to it. We must tell ourselves once for all, that perfect schemes are not adapted to our imperfect state; that* Stoical morals and Platonic politics are nothing better than amusements for those who have had little experience in the affairs of the world, and who have much leisure, *verba otiosorum senum ad imperitos juvenes*,[21] which was* the censure, and a just one too, that Dionysius passed on some of the doctrines of the father of the Academy. In truth, all that* human prudence can do, is to furnish expedients, and to compound, as it were, with general vice and folly; employing reason to act even against her own principles, and teaching us, if I may say so *insanire cum ratione*,[22] which appears on many occasions not to be the paradox it has been thought.

To conclude this head therefore: as I think a limited monarchy the best of governments, so I think an hereditary monarchy the best of monarchies. I said a limited monarchy; for an unlimited monarchy, wherein arbitrary will, which is in truth no rule, is however the sole rule, or stands instead of all rule of government, is so great an absurdity, both in reason informed or uninformed by experience, that it seems a government fitter for savages than for civilized people.

But I think it proper to explain a little more what I mean, when I say a limited monarchy, that I may leave nothing untouched which ought to be taken into consideration by* us, when we attempt to fix our ideas of a Patriot King.*

*Among many reasons which determine me to prefer monarchy to every form of government, this is a principal one. When monarchy

* that] and that   * which was] *1749*
* that] which
* IV. [*footnote* IV. A *limited Monarchy* the best form of Government, and *Hereditary* the best *Monarchy*.]   *wherein] when   *by] either by
* King.] *King*; or by Him, if over God raises one up who intends to be such.
* Chap. III. I. The peculiar Advantage of a limited Monarchy over all other Forms of Government. II. The Absurdity of supposing Arbitrary Power essential to

[21] 'The words of vain old men to inexperienced youngsters': Diogenes Laertius, *Life of Plato*, III. 18, cit. Bacon, *Novum Organum*, I. 71, in *Opera Omnia*, I. *287*.
[22] 'Reasonably to be mad': compare Horace, *Satires*, II. 3. 271 and Terence, *Enuchus*, I. 63.

is the essential form, it may be more easily and more usefully tempered with aristocracy, or democracy, or both, than either of them, when they are the essential forms, can be tempered with monarchy. It seems to me, that the introduction of a real permanent monarchical power, or any thing more than the pageantry of it, into either of these, must destroy them and extinguish them, as a greater light extinguishes a less. Whereas it may easily be shown, and the true form of our government will demonstrate, without seeking any other example, that very considerable aristocratical and democratical powers may be grafted on a monarchical stock, without diminishing the lustre, or restraining the power and authority of the prince, enough to alter in any degree the essential form.

*A great difference is made in nature, and therefore the distinction should be always preserved in our notions, between two things that we are apt to confound in speculation, as they have been confounded in practice, legislative and monarchical power. There must be an absolute, unlimited, and uncontrollable power lodged somewhere in every government;[23] but to constitute monarchy, or the government of a single person, it is not necessary that this power should be lodged in the monarch alone. It is no more necessary that he should exclusively and independently establish the rule of his government, than it is that he should govern without any rule at all: and this surely will be thought reasonable by no man.

I would not say God governs by a rule that we know, or may know, as well as he, and upon our knowledge of which he appeals to men for the justice of his proceedings towards them; which a famous divine has impiously advanced, in a pretended demonstration of his being and attributes.[24] God forbid! But this I may say, that God does always that which is fittest to be done, and that this fitness, whereof neither that presumptuous dogmatist was, nor

Monarchy. III. The Nature of such Limitations as are consistent with Monarchy. IV. Objections against limitations answer'd.

* II. [*footnote* II. The Absurdity of supposing Arbitrary Power essential to Monarchy.]

[23] A contemporary commonplace: compare Jonathan Swift, *Discourse of the Contests and Dissentions between the Nobles and Commons in Athens and Rome* (London, 1701), 3: ' 'Tis agreed that in all Government there is an absolute unlimited Power, which naturally and originally seems to be placed in the whole Body, wherever the Executive Part of it lies.'

[24] Samuel Clarke, *A Demonstration of the Being and Attributes of God* (London, 1705).

any created being is, a competent judge, results from the various natures, and more various relations of things: so that, as creator of all systems by which these natures and relations are constituted, he prescribed to himself the rule, which he follows as governor of every system of being. In short, with reverence be it spoken, God is a monarch, yet not an arbitrary but a limited monarch, limited by the rule which infinite wisdom prescribed* to infinite power. I know well enough the impropriety of these expressions; but, when our ideas are inadequate, our expressions must needs be improper. Such conceptions, however, as we are able to form of these attributes, and of the exercise of them in the government of the universe, may serve to show what I have produced them to show. If governing without any rule, and by arbitrary will, be not essential to our idea of the monarchy of the Supreme Being, it is plainly ridiculous to suppose them necessarily included in the idea of a human monarchy: and though God, in his eternal ideas, for we are able to conceive no other manner of knowing, has prescribed to himself that rule by which he governs the universe he created, it will be just as ridiculous to affirm, that the idea of human monarchy cannot be preserved, if kings are obliged to govern according to a rule established by the wisdom of a state, that was a state before they were kings, and by the consent of a people that they did not most certainly create; especially when the whole executive power is exclusively in their hands, and the legislative power cannot be exercised without their concurrence.

*There are limitations indeed that would destroy the essential form of monarchy; or, in other words, a monarchical constitution may be changed, under pretence of limiting the monarch. This happened among us in the last century, when the vilest usurpation, and the most infamous tyranny, were established over our nation, by some of the worst and some of the meanest men in it. I will not say that the essential form of monarchy should be preserved though the preservation of it were to cause the loss of liberty. *Salus reipublicae suprema lex esto*[25] is a fundamental law; and, sure I am, the safety of

* prescribed] prescribes
* III. [*footnote* III. The Nature of such Limitations as are consistent with Monarchy.]

[25] 'The safety of the commonwealth should be the highest law': Cicero, *De Legibus*, III. 3.

a commonwealth is ill provided for, if the liberty be given up. But this I presume to say, and can demonstrate, that all the limitations necessary to preserve liberty, as long as the spirit of it subsists, and longer than that no limitations of monarchy, nor any other form of government, can* preserve it, are compatible with monarchy. I think on these subjects, neither as the Tories, nor as the Whigs have thought; at least, I endeavour to avoid the excesses of both. I neither dress up kings like so many burlesque Jupiters, weighing the fortunes of mankind in the scales of fate, and darting thunder-bolts at the heads of rebellious giants; nor do I strip them naked, as it were, and leave them at most a few tattered rags to clothe their majesty, but such as can serve really as little for use as for ornament. My aim is to fix this principle: that limitations on a crown ought to be carried as far as it is necessary to secure the liberties of a people; and that all such limitations may subsist, without weakening or endangering monarchy.

*I shall be told, perhaps, for I have heard it said by many, that this point is imaginary; and that limitations, sufficient to procure good government and to secure liberty under a bad prince, cannot be made, unless they are such as will deprive the subjects of many benefits in the reign of a good prince, clog his administration, maintain an unjust jealousy between him and his people, and occasion a defect of power, necessary to preserve the public tranquillity, and to promote the national prosperity. If this was true, here would be a much more melancholy instance of the imperfection of our nature, and of the inefficacy of our reason to supply this imperfection, than the former. In the former, reason prompted by experience avoids a certain evil effectually, and is able to provide, in some measure, against the contingent evils that may arise from the expedient itself. But in the latter, if what is there advanced was true, these provisions against contingent evils would, in some cases, be the occasions of much certain evil, and of positive good in none; under a good prince they would render the administration defective, and under a bad one there would be no government at all. But the truth is widely different from this representation. The limitations necessary to preserve liberty under monarchy will restrain effectually a bad prince, without being ever felt as shackles by a good one. Our constitution

---

* can] *1749*   * IV. [*footnote* IV. Objections against Limitations answered.]

is brought, or almost brought,* to such a point, a point of perfection
I think it, that no king, who is not, in the true meaning of the word,
a patriot, can govern Britain with ease, security, honour, dignity, or
indeed with sufficient power and strength. But yet a king, who* is
a patriot may govern with all the former; and, besides them, with
power as extended as the most absolute monarch can boast, and a
power, too,* far more agreeable in the enjoyment as well as more
effectual in the operation.

*To attain these great and noble ends, the patriotism must be
real, and not in show alone. It is something to desire to appear a
patriot:* and the desire of having fame is a step towards deserving
it, because it is a motive the more to deserve it. If it be true, as
Tacitus says, *contemptu famae contemni virtutem,* that a contempt of
a good name, or an indifference about it, begets or accompanies
always a contempt of virtue;[26] the contrary will be true: and they
are certainly both true. But this motive alone is not sufficient. To
constitute a patriot, whether king or subject, there must be something more substantial than a desire of fame, in the composition;
and if there be not, this desire of fame will never rise above that
sentiment which may be compared to the coquetry of women: a
fondness of transient applause, which is courted by vanity, given by
flattery, and spends itself in show, like the qualities which acquire
it. Patriotism must be founded in great principles, and supported
by great virtues. The chief of these principles I have endeavoured
to trace; and I will not scruple to assert, that a man can be a good
king upon no other. He may, without them and by complexion, be
unambitious, generous, good-natured; but, without them, the exercise even of these virtues will be often ill directed: and, with principles of another sort, he will be drawn easily, notwithstanding these
virtues, from all the purposes of his institution.

*I mention these opposite principles the rather, because, instead
of wondering that so many kings, unfit and unworthy to be trusted

---

* or almost brought,] *1749*   * who] that   * too,] *1749*
* To attain] CHAP. IV. I. That such Limitations will be no Restraints to a Prince
who is truly a Patriot. II. How it happens that so few Princes are Patriots. III. A
Digression. What ought to be the Conduct of those about a Prince, and what is
the Duty of all who approach him. ¶ But to attain
* a patriot] such
* II. [*footnote* II. How it happens that so few Princes are Patriots.]

[26] Tacitus, *Annals*, IV. 38.

with the government of mankind, appear in the world, I have been tempted to wonder that there are any tolerable; when I have considered the flattery that environs them most commonly from the cradle, and the tendency of all those false notions that are instilled into them by precept, and by example, by the habits of courts, and by the interested selfish views of courtiers. They are bred to esteem themselves of a distinct and superior species among men, as men are among animals.

Louis the Fourteenth was a strong instance of the effect of this education, which trains up kings to be tyrants, without knowing that they are so. That oppression under which he kept his people, during the whole course of a long reign, might proceed, in some degree, from the natural haughtiness of his temper; but it proceeded, in a greater degree, from the principles and habits of his education. By this* he had been brought to look on his kingdom as a patrimony that descended to him from his ancestors, and that* was to be considered in no other light: so that when a very considerable man had discoursed to him at large of the miserable condition, to which his people was reduced, and had frequently used this word, 'l'état', though the King approved the substance of all he had said, yet he was shocked at the frequent repetition of this word, and complained of it as of a kind of indecency to himself.[27] This will not appear so strange to our second as it may very justly to our first reflections; for what wonder is it, that princes are easily betrayed into an error that takes its rise in the general imperfection of our nature, in our pride, our vanity, and our presumption? The bastard children, but the children still, of self-love; a spurious brood, but often a favourite brood, that governs the whole family. As men are apt to make themselves the measure of all being, so they make themselves the final cause of all creation. Thus the reputed orthodox philosophers in all ages have taught, that the world was made for man, the earth for him to inhabit, and all the luminous bodies, in the immense expanse around us, for him to gaze at. Kings do no more, no, not so much, when they imagine themselves the final

---

* this education . . . By this] this *Education*; by this　　* that] *1749*

[27] Louis XIV had famously (if apocryphally) protested 'L'état c'est moi' before the Parlement of Paris, 13 April 1655.

cause for which societies were formed, and governments* instituted.

This capital error, in which almost every prince is confirmed by his education, has so great extent and so general influence, that a right to do every iniquitous thing in government may be derived from it. But, as if this was not enough, the characters of princes are spoiled many more ways by their education. I shall not descend into a detail of such particulars, nor presume so much as to hint what regulations might be made about the education of princes, nor what part our Parliaments might take occasionally in this momentous affair, lest I should appear too refining, or too presumptuous, in my speculations.[28] But I may assert in general, that the indifference of mankind upon this head, especially in a government constituted like ours, is monstrous.

I may also take notice of another cause of the mistakes of princes, I mean the general conduct of those who are brought near to their persons. Such men, let me say, have a particular duty arising from this very situation; a duty common to them all, because it arises not from their stations, which are different, but from their situation, which is the same. To enumerate* the various applications of this duty would be too minute and tedious; but this may suffice, that all such men should bear constantly in mind, that the master they serve is to be the king of their country: that their attachment to him, therefore, is not to be like that of other servants to other masters, for his sake alone, or for his sake and their own, but for the sake of their country likewise.

Craterus loves the King, but Hephaestion loves Alexander, was a saying of the last that has been often quoted, but not censured as it ought to be. Alexander gave the preference to the attachment of Hephaestion; but this preference was due undoubtedly to that of Craterus.[29] Attachment to a private person must comprehend a great

---

* governments] Government
* III. [*footnote* III. A Digression. What ought to be the Conduct of those about a Prince, and what is the Duty of all who approach him.]
* princes . . . brought] Princes, the general Conduct of those who are brought by their stations   * enumerate] descend into

[28] An allusion to the bitter disputes in the eighteenth century over the political complexion of the tutors appointed to oversee the education of the successive Princes of Wales.
[29] Plutarch, *Life of Alexander*, XLVII, cit. Bacon, *De Augmentis Scientiarum*, I. I, in *Opera Omnia*, I, 52. Hephaestion was a Macedonian noted for his close friendship with Alexander, Craterus was one of Alexander's generals.

concern for his character and his interests: but attachment to one who is, or may be a* king, much more; because the character of the latter is more important to himself and others; and because his interests are vastly more complicated with those of his country, and in some sort with those of mankind. Alexander himself seemed, upon one occasion, to make the distinction that should be always made between our attachment to a prince, and* to any private person. It was when Parmenio advised him to accept the terms of peace which Darius offered: they were great, he thought them so; but he thought, no matter for my purpose whether justly or not, that it would be unbecoming him to accept them; therefore he rejected them, but acknowledged, that 'he would have done as he was advised to do, if he had been Parmenio.'[30]

As to persons who are not about a prince in the situation here spoken of, they* can do little more than proportion their applause, and the demonstrations of their confidence and affection, to the benefits they actually receive from the prince on the throne, or to the just expectations that a successor gives them. It is of the latter I propose to speak here particularly.* If he gives them those of a good reign, we may assure ourselves that they will carry, and in this case they ought to carry that applause, and those demonstrations of their confidence and affection, as high as such a prince himself can desire. Thus the prince and the people, take, in effect, a sort of engagement with one another: the prince to govern well, and the people to honour and obey him. If he gives them expectations of a bad reign, they have this obligation to him at least, that he puts them early on their guard; and an obligation, and an advantage it will be, if they prepare for his accession as for a great and inevitable evil; and if they guard on every occasion against the ill use they foresee that he will make of money and power. Above all, they should not suffer themselves to be caught in the common snare, which is laid under specious pretences of 'gaining such a prince,

---

* one who is, or may be a] a present or future   * and] or
* about a prince . . . they] immediately about a Prince, they indeed
* benefits they actually . . . here particularly.] just Expectations that the Prince may give them.

[30] Plutarch, *Life of Alexander*, XXIX, cit. Bacon, *De Augmentis Scientiarum*, I. 1, in *Opera Omnia*, I, 53. Parmenio was one of Alexander's best generals; Darius offered Alexander all the country west of the Euphrates, his daughter Statira, and ten thousand gold talents in return for peace.

and of keeping him by public compliances out of bad hands'.[31] That argument has been pressed more than once, has prevailed, and has been fruitful of most pernicious consequences. None indeed can be more absurd. It is not unlike the reasoning of those savages who worship the devil, not because they love him or honour him, or expect any good from him, but that he may do them no hurt. Nay, it is more absurd; for the savages suppose that the devil has, independently of them, the power to hurt them: whereas the others put more power into the hands of a prince, because he has already some power to hurt them; and* trust to the justice and gratitude of one, who wants sense, virtue, or both, rather than increase and fortify the barriers against his folly and his vices.

But the truth is, that men, who reason and act in this manner, either mean, or else are led by such as mean, nothing more than to make a private court at the public expense; who choose to be the instruments of a bad king rather than to be out of power; and who are often so wicked, that they would prefer such a service to that of the best of kings. In fine, these reasons, and every other reason for providing against a bad reign in prospect, acquire a new force, when one weak or wicked prince is, in the order of succession, to follow another of the same character. Such provisions indeed are hardest to be obtained when they are the most necessary; that is, when the spirit of liberty begins to flag in a free people, and when they become disposed, by habits that have grown insensibly upon them, to a base submission. But they are necessary too, even when they are easiest to be obtained; that is, when the spirit of liberty is in full strength, and a disposition, to oppose all instances of maladministration, and to resist all attempts on liberty, is universal. In both cases, the endeavours of every man who loves his country will be employed with incessant care and constancy to obtain them, that good government and liberty may be the better preserved and secured; but in the latter case for this further reason also, that the preservation and security of these may be provided for, not only better but more consistently with public tranquillity, by constitutional methods, and a legal course of opposition to the excesses of regal or ministerial power. What I touch upon here might be

* put . . . them; and], because a Prince has already some Power to hurt them, put more into his hands; and so

[31] Source unidentified.

made extremely plain; and I think the observation would appear to be of no small importance: but I should be carried too far from my subject, and my subject will afford me matter of more agreeable speculation.

It is true that a prince, who gives just reasons* to expect that his reign will be that of a Patriot King, may not always meet, and from all persons, such returns as such expectations deserve: but they must not hinder either the prince from continuing to give them, or the people from continuing to acknowledge them.* United, none can hurt them: and if no artifice interrupts, no power can defeat the effects of their perseverance. It will blast many a wicked project, keep virtue in countenance, and vice, to some degree at least, in awe. Nay, if it should fail to have these effects, if we should even suppose a good prince to suffer with the people, and in some measure for them, yet many advantages would accrue to him: for instance,* the cause of the people he is to govern, and his own cause would be made the same by their common enemies. He would feel grievances himself as a subject, before he had* the power of

---

* It is true ... just reasons] CHAP. V. I. What the Situation will be of a Prince, who during a bad Reign gives Hopes of a good One. His Advantages both before, and after his Accession. II. The Opinion of *Machiavel* on this Point. ¶ The Prince then, who gives the Subjects just Reason.

* may not always ... acknowledge them.] and who does this in the Reign of one who has no Pretence of the Title, must expect himself to become (in how near a Relation soever he may stand to the other) obnoxious both to him and to his Ministers. This cannot fail to be the Case; for to be in Favour with a Court thus constituted, and with the People at once, is an absolute impossibility. All the Expectations that such a Prince raises of a good Reign, all the Testimonies he receives of Gratitude and Affection in return from the People, will create naturally Dislike in the Mind of a King who never had Virtue enough to raise such Expectations, nor to deserve such Testimonies; and this Dislike will be soon work'd up into Jealousy, Envy, Resentment, and Rage, by the Suggestions of his Ministers, and the Ferment of his own Passions. But this certain Effect of their Conduct must not hinder either Prince or People from a steady Pursuit of it.

* Nay, if it ... for instance,] The remote Prospect of a good Government will be of immediate Advantage many ways to the People under a bad one. It may be so even to him who governs; and such Conjunctures may happen, wherein nothing less than that Credit with the People which he dislikes, and those publick and private Virtues which he chuses to persecute rather than to imitate, can keep him on the Throne. ¶ This Advantage an unpopular King may owe to his popular Successor; but however this may turn, the Advantages that will accrue to a good Prince who suffers with the People, and in some measure for them, under a bad King, are certain and invaluable. I might enumerate many such for instance, as these, That

* would be ... would feel] are made the same even by their common Enemies: That he feels

imposing them as a king. He would be formed in that* school out of which the greatest and the best of monarchs have come, the school of affliction: and all the vices, which had* prevailed before his reign, would serve as* so many foils to the glories of it. But I hasten to speak of the greatest of all these advantages, and of that which a Patriot King will esteem to be such; whose ways of thinking and acting to so glorious a purpose as the re-establishment of a free constitution, when it has been shook by the iniquity of former administrations,* I shall endeavour to explain.

What I have here said* will pass among some for the reveries of a distempered brain, at best for the vain speculations of an idle man who has lost sight of the world, or who had never sagacity enough to discern in government the practicable from the impracticable. Will it not be said, that this is advising a king to* rouse a spirit which may turn against himself; to reject the sole expedient of governing a limited monarchy with success; to* labour to confine, instead of labouring to extend, his power: to patch up an old constitution,* which his people are disposed to lay aside, instead of forming* a new one more agreeable to them, and more advantageous to him; to refuse, in short,* to be an absolute monarch, when every circumstance invites him to it? All these particulars, in every one of which the question is begged, will be thus represented, and will be then ridiculed as paradoxes fit to be ranked among the 'mirabilia et inopinata'[32] of the Stoics, and such as no man in his senses can maintain in earnest. These judgments and these reasonings may be expected in an age as futile and* as corrupt as ours: in an age wherein so many betray the cause of liberty, and act not only with-

* king. He would be formed in that] King: That he is formed in the
* had] *1749*
* as] but as
* former administrations] a former administration
* What I have here said] I know that what I shall here say
* Will it . . . king to] That a king should
* to reject . . . constitution] that he should reject the sole Expedient of governing limited Monarchies with Success, (the Attachment of Men to him by personal Dependency) that he should labour to confine instead of extending his
* power: to patch up an old] Power; and to patch up an old tatter'd Constitution
* instead of forming] rather than to form
* to refuse, in short] in short, that he should refuse
* These judgments . . . futile and] Such Judgments and such Reasoning may be expected in an Age

[32] 'Wondrous and unwonted [sayings]': paraphrasing Cicero, *Paradoxa Stoicorum*, IV ('admirabilia contraque opinionem omnium').

out regard, but in direct opposition, to the most important interests of their country; not only occasionally, by surprise, by weakness, by strong temptation, or sly seduction, but constantly, steadily, by deliberate choice, and in pursuance of principles they avow and propagate: in an age when so many others shrink from the service of their country, or promote it coolly and uncertainly, in subordination to their own interest and humour, or to those of a party: in an age, when to assert the truth is called spreading of delusion, and to assert the cause of liberty and good government, is termed sowing of sedition.* But I have declared already my unconcernedness at the censure or ridicule of such men as these; for whose supposed abilities I have much well-grounded contempt, and against whose real immorality I have as just indignation.

Let us come, therefore, to the bar of reason and experience, where we shall find these paradoxes admitted as plain and almost self-evident propositions, and these reveries and vain speculations as important truths, confirmed by experience in all ages and all countries.

Machiavel is an author who should have great authority with the persons likely to oppose me. He proposes to princes* the amplification of their power, the extent of their dominion, and the subjection of their people, as the sole objects of their policy. He* devises and recommends all means that tend to these purposes, without the consideration of any duty owing to God or man, or* any regard to the morality or immorality of actions. Yet even he declares the affectation of virtue to be useful to princes:[33] he is so far on my side in the present question. The only difference between us is, I would have the virtue real: he requires no more than the appearance of it.

In the tenth chapter of the first book of *Discourses*, he appears convinced, such is the force of truth, but how consistently with himself let others determine,* that the supreme glory of a prince

* in an age when . . . sowing of sedition] *1749*
* me. He proposes to princes] me; since he declares the Affectation of Virtue to be useful to Princes, but the real Practice of it hurtful, since he proposes to them
* policy. He] Policy; and since he   * God or man, or] Government, or of
* Yet even he . . . others determine] Yet such is the force of Truth, that even *Machiavel* is on my side in the present Question; how consistently with himself, let those who are concerned to defend him consider. I shall content myself to draw on the Ground he has laid for me, in the 10th Chapter of his first book of Discourses particularly. ¶ In that place he appears so convinced,

[33] Machiavelli, *The Prince*, ch. XVIII.

accrues to him who establishes good government and a free constitution; and that* a prince, ambitious of fame, must wish to come
into possession of a disordered and corrupted state, not to finish the
wicked work that others have begun, and to complete the ruin, but
to stop the progress of the first, and to prevent the last. He thinks
this not only the true way to fame, but to security and quiet; as the
contrary leads, for here is no third way, and a prince must make
his option between these two, not only to infamy, but to danger and
to perpetual disquietude. He represents those who might establish
a commonwealth or a legal monarchy, and who choose to improve
the opportunity of establishing tyranny, that is, monarchy without
any rule of law, as men who are deceived by false notions of good,
and false appearances of glory, and who are in effect blind to their
true interest in every respect: 'nè si avveggono per questo partito
quanta fama, quanta gloria, quanto onore, sicurtà, quiete, con sodis-
fazione d'animo ei fuggono, e in quanta infamia, vituperio, biasimo,
pericolo et inquietudine incorrono'.[34] He touches another advantage
which patriot princes reap, and in that he contradicts flatly the main
point on which his half-taught scholars insist. He denies that such
princes diminish their power by circumscribing it: and affirms, with
truth on his side, that Timoleon, and others of the same character
whom he had cited, possessed as great authority in their country,
with every other advantage besides,* as Dionysius or Phalaris had
acquired, with the loss of all those advantages.[35]

Thus far Machiavel reasons justly; but he takes in only a part of
his subject, and confines himself to those motives that should determine a wise prince to maintain liberty, because it is his interest to
do so. He rises no higher than the consideration of mere* interest,
of fame, of security, of quiet, and of power, all personal to the
prince: and by such motives alone even his favourite Borgia might
have been determined to affect the virtues of a patriot prince;

---

* that] that he thinks
* besides] to boot   * mere] that

---

[34] 'They do not realise how much fame, glory, honour, security, peace of mind and
satisfaction of spirit they are giving up and how much disgrace, calumny, blame,
danger and unease they are going to incur by choosing this course': Machiavelli,
Discorsi, I. 10.
[35] *Discorsi*, I. 10. Timoleon was king of Corinth, Dionysius, of Syracuse; Phalaris
was tyrant of Agrigentum.

more than which this great doctor in political knowledge would not have required of him.[36] But he is far from going up to that motive which should above all determine a good prince to hold this conduct, because it is his duty to do so; a duty that he owes to God by one law, and to his people by another. Now it is with this that I shall begin what I intend to offer concerning the system of principles and conduct by which a Patriot King will govern himself and his people. I shall not only begin higher, but descend into more detail, and keep still in my eye the application of the whole to the constitution of Great Britain, even to the present state of our nation, and temper of our people.

*I think enough has been already said, to establish the first and true principles of monarchical and indeed of every other kind of government: and I will say with confidence, that no principles but these, and such as these, can be advanced, which deserve to be treated seriously; though Mr Locke condescended to examine those of Filmer, more out of regard to the prejudices of the time, than to the importance of the work.[37] Upon such foundations we must conclude, that since men were directed by nature to form societies, because they cannot by their nature subsist without them, nor in a state of individuality; and since they were directed in like manner to establish governments, because societies cannot be maintained without them, nor subsist in a state of anarchy, the ultimate end of all governments is the good of the people, for whose sake they were made, and without whose consent they could not have been made. In forming societies, and submitting to government, men give up part of that liberty to which they are all born, and all alike. But why? Is government incompatible with a full enjoyment of liberty? By no means. But because popular liberty without government will degenerate into licence, as government without sufficient liberty will degenerate into tyranny, they are mutually necessary to each other,

---

* patriot prince; more] Patriot: more　　* a duty . . . by another.] *1749*.
* CHAP. VI. I. What will be the Views, pursuant to the former Principles, of a Patriot King. II. That those Principles and Views will be the same, whether he be Hereditary or Elective.

[36] Cesare Borgia (1475–1507) is particularly praised in *The Prince*, ch. VII.
[37] Locke's first *Treatise of Government* is a systematic refutation of Sir Robert Filmer's *Patriarcha* (1620s), first printed in 1680 as an anti-Exclusion tract.

good government to support legal liberty, and legal liberty to preserve good government.

I speak not here of people, if any such there are, who have been savage or stupid enough to submit to tyranny by original contract; nor of those nations on whom tyranny has stolen as it were imperceptibly, or been imposed by violence, and settled by prescription. I shall exercise no political casuistry about the rights of such kings, and the obligations of such people. Men are to take their lots, perhaps, in governments as in climates, to fence against the inconveniences of both, and to bear what they cannot alter. But I speak of people who have been wise and happy enough to establish, and to preserve, free constitutions of government, as the people of this island have done. To these, therefore, I say, that their kings are under the most sacred obligations that human law can create, and divine law authorize, to defend and maintain, in the first place, and preferably to every other consideration, the freedom of such constitutions.

The good of the people is the ultimate and true end of government. Governors are, therefore, appointed for this end, and the civil constitution which appoints them, and invests them with their power, is determined to do so by that law of nature and reason, which has* determined the end of government, and which admits this form of government as the* proper means of arriving at it. Now, the greatest good of a people is their liberty: and, in the case here referred to, the people has judged it so, and provided for it accordingly. Liberty is to the collective body, what health is to every individual body. Without health no pleasure can be tasted by man: without liberty no happiness can be enjoyed by society. The obligation, therefore, to defend and maintain the freedom of such constitutions will appear most sacred to a Patriot King.

Kings who have weak understandings, bad hearts, and strong prejudices, and all these, as it often happens, inflamed by their passions, and rendered incurable by their self-conceit and presumption; such kings are apt to imagine, and they conduct themselves so as to make many of their subjects imagine, that the king and the people in free governments are rival powers, who stand in competition with one another, who have different interests, and must of course have different views: that the rights and privileges of the people are so many

---

* has] had   * the] a

spoils taken from the right and prerogative of the crown; and that the rules and laws, made for the exercise and security of the former, are so many diminutions of their dignity, and restraints on their power.

A Patriot King will see all this in a far different and much truer light. The constitution will be considered by him as one law, consisting of two tables, containing the rule of his government, and the measure of his subjects' obedience; or as one system, composed of different parts and powers, but all duly proportioned to one another, and conspiring by their harmony to the perfection of the whole. He will make one, and but one, distinction between his rights, and those of his people: he will look on his to be a trust, and theirs a property. He will discern, that he can have a right to no more than is trusted to him by the constitution: and that his people, who had an original right to the whole by the law of nature, can have the sole indefeasible right to any part; and really have such a right to that part which they have reserved to themselves. In fine, the constitution will be reverenced by him as the law of God and of man; the force of which binds the king as much as the meanest subject, and the reason of which binds him much more.

Thus he will think, and on these principles he will act, whether he come to the throne by immediate or remote election. I say remote; for in hereditary monarchies, where men are not elected, families are: and, therefore, some authors would have it believed, that when a family has been once admitted, and an hereditary right to the crown recognized in it, that right cannot be forfeited, nor that throne become vacant, as long as any heir of the family remains. How much more agreeably to truth and to common sense would these authors have written, if they had maintained, that every prince who comes to a crown in the course of succession, were he the last of five hundred, comes to it under the same conditions under which the first took it, whether expressed or implied; as well as under those, if any such there be, which have been since made by legal authority: and that royal blood can give no right, nor length of succession any prescription, against the constitution of a

---

* II. [*footnote* II. That his Principles and Views will be the same, whether he be Hereditary or Elective.]
* under which] *1749*

government?[38] The* first and the last hold by the same tenure.

I mention this the rather, because I have an imperfect remembrance, that some scribbler was employed, or employed himself, to* assert the hereditary right of the present royal family.[39] A task so unnecessary to any good purpose, that, I believe, a suspicion arose of its having been designed for a bad one. A Patriot King will never countenance such impertinent fallacies, nor deign to lean on broken reeds. He knows that his right is founded on the laws of God and man, that none can shake it but himself, and that his own virtue is sufficient to maintain it against all opposition.

I have dwelt the longer on the first and general principles of monarchical government, and have recurred the oftener to them, because it seems to me that they are the seeds of patriotism, which must be sown as soon as possible in the mind of a prince, lest their growth should be checked by luxuriant weeds, which are apt to abound in such soils, and under which no crop of kingly virtues can ever flourish.* A prince, who does not know the true principles, cannot propose to himself the true ends of government; and he who does not propose them will never direct his conduct steadily to them. There is not a deeper, nor a finer observation in all my Lord Bacon's works, than one which I shall apply and paraphrase on this occasion. The most compendious, the most noble, and the most effectual remedy, which can be opposed to the uncertain and irregular motions of the human mind, agitated by various passions, allured by various temptations, inclining sometimes towards a state of moral perfection, and oftener, even in the best, towards a state of moral depravation, is this. We must choose betimes such virtuous objects as are proportioned to the means we have of pursuing them, and as belong particularly to the stations we are in, and to the duties of those stations. We must determine and fix our minds in such manner upon them, that the pursuit of them may become the business, and the attainment of them the end, of our whole lives. Thus

---

* government? The] Government which   * himself, to] himself, under a late
great Patronage   * lest their growth . . . ever flourish] *1749*

[38] A counterblast to those Jacobites and Non-Jurors who refused to recognize the right of the Hanoverians to sit on the British throne (affirmed by the Act of Settlement in 1701) so long as any member of the Stuart family remained alive.

[39] [George Harbin,] *The Hereditary Right of the Crown of England Asserted* (London, 1713), attacked in *Dissertation upon Parties*, 'Letter VIII'.

we shall imitate the great operations of nature, and not the feeble, slow, and imperfect operations of art. We must not proceed, in forming the moral character, as a statuary proceeds in forming a statue, who works sometimes on the face, sometimes on one part, and sometimes on another: but we must proceed, and it is in our power to proceed, as nature does in forming a flower, an animal, or any other of her productions: *rudimenta partium omnium simul parit et producit.* 'She throws out altogether, and at once, the whole system of every being, and the rudiments of all the parts.'[40] The vegetable or the animal grows in bulk and increases in strength; but is the same from the first. Just so our Patriot King must be a patriot from the first. He must be such in resolution, before he grows such in practice. He must fix at once the general principles and ends of all his actions, and determine that his whole conduct shall be regulated by them, and directed to them. When he has done this, he will have turned, by one great effort, the bent of his mind so strongly towards the perfection of a kingly character, that he will exercise with ease, and as it were by a natural determination, all the virtues of it; which will be suggested to him on every occasion by the principles wherewith his mind is imbued, and by those ends that are the constant objects of his attention.

Let us then see in what manner and with what effect he will do this, upon the greatest occasion he can have of exercising these virtues, the maintenance of liberty, and the re-establishment of a free constitution.

The freedom of a constitution rests on two points. The orders of it are one: so Machiavel calls them, and I know not how to call them more significantly.[41] He means not only the forms and customs, but the different classes and assemblies of men, with different powers and privileges attributed to them, which are established in the state. The spirit and character of the people are the other. On the mutual conformity and harmony of these the preservation of liberty

---

* CHAP. VII. I. What will be the Conduct of a *Patriot King*, in order to restore a *Free Constitution*. II. How by the contrary Conduct, a *bad* or *weak Prince* is capable of destroying one. III. But that a *good King* is really sufficient to this Task. IV. The Ability of a Patriot King to restore a *Free Constitution*.
* then see] then proceed to see

[40] Bacon, *De Augmentis Scientiarum*, VII. 3, in *Opera Omnia*, I, *211*.
[41] Machiavelli, *Discorsi*, I. 18.

depends. To take away, or essentially to alter the former, cannot be brought to pass, whilst the latter remains in original purity and vigour: nor can liberty be destroyed by this method, unless the attempt be made with a military force sufficient to conquer the nation, which would not submit in this case till it was conquered, nor with much security to the conqueror even then. But these orders of the state may be essentially altered, and serve more effectually to the destruction of liberty, than the taking of them away would serve, if the spirit and character of the people are lost.

Now this method of destroying liberty is the most dangerous on many accounts, particularly on this; that even the reign of the weakest prince, and the policy of the weakest ministry,* may effect the destruction, when circumstances are favourable to this method. If* a people is growing corrupt, there is no need of capacity to contrive, nor of insinuation to gain, nor of plausibility to seduce, nor of eloquence to persuade, nor of authority to impose, nor of courage to attempt. The most incapable, awkward, ungracious, shocking, profligate, and timorous wretches, invested with power, and masters of the purse, will be sufficient for the work, when the people are accomplices in it. Luxury is rapacious; let them feed it: the more it is fed, the more profuse it will grow. Want is the consequence of profusion, venality of want, and dependence of venality. By this progression, the first men of a nation will become the pensioners of the last;* and he who has talents, the most implicit tool to him who has none. The distemper will soon descend, not indeed to make a deposit below, and to remain there, but to pervade the whole body.

It may seem a singular, but it is perhaps a true proposition, that such a king and such a ministry are more likely to begin, and to pursue with success, this method of destroying a free constitution of government, than a king and a ministry that were held in great esteem would be. This very esteem might put many on their guard against the latter; but the former may draw from contempt the advantage of not being feared: and an advantage this is in the beginning of corruption. Men are willing to excuse, not only to others but to themselves, the first steps they take in vice, and especially in vice that affects the public, and whereof the public has a right to

* II. [*footnote* II. How by the contrary Conduct, a bad or weak Prince is capable of destroying one.]   * the] a   * and the policy of the weakest ministry] *1749*
* If] When   * last] least

complain. Those, therefore, who might withstand corruption in one case, from a persuasion that the consequence was too certain to leave them any excuse, may yield to it when they can flatter themselves, and endeavour to flatter others, that liberty cannot be destroyed, nor the constitution be demolished, by such hands as hold the sceptre, and guide the reins of the administration. But alas! the flattery is gross, and the excuse without colour. These men may ruin their country, but they cannot impose on any, unless it be on themselves. Nor will even this imposition on themselves be long necessary. Their consciences will be soon seared, by habit and by example: and they, who wanted an excuse to begin, will want none to continue and to complete, the tragedy of their country. Old men will outlive the shame of losing liberty, and young men will arise who know not that it ever existed. A spirit of slavery will oppose and oppress the spirit of liberty, and seem at least to be the genius of the nation. Such too it will become in time, when corruption has once grown to this height, unless the progress of it can be interrupted.

How inestimable a blessing therefore must the succession of a Patriot King be esteemed in such circumstances as these, which would be a blessing, and a great one too, in any other? He, and he alone, can save a country whose ruin is so far advanced. The utmost that private men can do, who remain untainted by the general contagion, is to keep the spirit of liberty alive in a few breasts; to protest against what they cannot hinder, and to claim on every occasion what they cannot by their own strength recover.

Machiavel has treated, in the discourses before cited, this question, 'whether, when the people are grown corrupt, a free government can be maintained, if they enjoy it; or established, if they enjoy it not?'[42] And upon the whole matter he concludes for the difficulty, or rather the impossibility, of succeeding in either case. It will be worth while to observe his way of reasoning. He asserts very truly, and proves by the example of the Roman commonwealth, that those orders which are proper to maintain liberty, whilst a

---

* III. [*footnote* III. But that a *good King* is really sufficient to this Task.]
* He, and he alone] He alone

[42] Machiavelli, *Discorsi*, I. 18, paraphrased in this paragraph.

people remain uncorrupt, become improper and hurtful to liberty, when a people is grown corrupt. To remedy this abuse, new laws alone will not be sufficient. These orders, therefore, must be changed, according to him, and the constitution must be adapted to the depraved manners of the people. He shows, that such a change in the orders, and constituent parts of the government, is impracticable, whether the attempt be made by gentle and slow, or by violent and precipitate measures: and from thence* he concludes, that a free commonwealth can neither be maintained by a corrupt people, nor be established among them. But he adds, that 'if this can possibly be done, it must be done by drawing the constitution to the monarchical form of government', 'acciochè quegli uomini i quali dalle leggi non possono essere corretti, fussero da una podestà, in qualche modo frenati'. 'That a corrupt people, whom law cannot correct, may be restrained and corrected by a kingly power.' Here is the hinge on which the whole turns.

Another advantage that a free monarchy has over all other forms of free government, besides the advantage of being more easily and more usefully tempered with aristocratical and democratical powers, which is mentioned above, is this. Those governments are made up of different parts, and are apt to be disjointed by the shocks to which they are exposed: but a free monarchical government is more compact, because there is a part the more that keeps, like the keystone of a vault, the whole building together. They cannot be mended in a state of corruption, they must be in effect constituted anew, and in that attempt they may be dissolved forever: but this is not the case of a free monarchy. To preserve liberty by new laws and new schemes of government, whilst the corruption of a people continues and grows, is absolutely impossible:* but to restore and to preserve it under old laws, and an old constitution, by reinfusing into the minds of men the spirit of this constitution, is not only possible, but is, in a particular manner, easy to a king. A corrupt commonwealth remains without remedy, though all the orders and forms of it subsist: a free monarchical government cannot remain absolutely so, as long as the orders and forms of the constitution subsist. These, alone, are indeed nothing more than the dead letter of freedom, or masks of liberty. In the first character they serve to

* thence] them
* impossible] impossible every where

no good purpose whatsoever: in the second they serve to a bad one; because tyranny, or government by will, becomes more severe, and more secure, under their disguise, than it would if it was barefaced and avowed. But a king can, easily to himself and without violence to his people, renew the spirit of liberty in their minds, quicken this dead letter, and pull off this mask.

*As soon as corruption ceases to be an expedient of government, and it will cease to be such as soon as a Patriot King is raised to the throne, the panacea is applied; the spirit of the constitution revives of course: and, as fast as it revives, the orders and forms of the constitution are restored to their primitive integrity, and become what they were intended to be, real barriers against arbitrary power, not blinds nor masks under which tyranny may lie concealed. Depravation of manners exposed the constitution to ruin: reformation will secure it. Men decline easily from virtue; for there is a devil too in the political system, a constant tempter at hand. A Patriot King will want neither power nor inclination to cast out this devil, to make the temptation cease, and to deliver his subjects, if not from the guilt, yet from the consequence, of their fall. Under him they will not only cease to do evil, but learn to do well; for, by rendering public virtue and real capacity the sole means of acquiring any degree of power or profit in the state, he will set the passions of their hearts on the side of liberty and good government. A Patriot King is the most powerful of all reformers; for he is himself a sort of standing miracle, so rarely seen and so little understood, that the sure effects of his appearance will be admiration and love in every honest breast, confusion and terror to every guilty conscience, but submission and resignation in all. A new people will seem to arise with a new king. Innumerable metamorphoses, like those which poets feign, will happen in very deed: and, while men are conscious that they are the same individuals, the difference of their sentiments will almost persuade them that they are changed into different beings.

But, that we may not expect more from such a king than even he can perform, it is necessary to premise another general observation,* after which I shall descend into some that will be more particular.

* IV. [*footnote* IV. The Ability of a Patriot King to restore a Free Constitution.]
* CHAP. VIII. I. A previous Observation. II. The Measures a Patriot King will take, 1. To purge his Court of the Bad, 2. To chuse the Good and Able.
* we] you   * another . . . observation] one general observation more

Absolute stability is not to be expected in any thing human; for that which exists immutably exists alone necessarily, and this attribute of the Supreme* Being, can neither belong to man, nor to the works of man. The best instituted governments, like the best constituted animal bodies, carry in them the seeds of their destruction: and, though they grow and improve for a time, they will soon tend visibly to their dissolution. Every hour they live is an hour the less that they have to live. All that can be done, therefore, to prolong the duration of a good government, is to draw it back, on every favourable occasion, to the first good principles on which it was founded.[43] When these occasions happen often, and are well improved, such governments are prosperous and durable. When they happen seldom, or are ill improved, these political bodies live in pain, or in languor, and die soon.

A Patriot King affords* one of the occasions I mention in a free monarchical state, and the very best that can happen. It should be improved, like snatches of fair weather at sea, to repair the damages sustained in the last storm, and to prepare to resist the next. For such a king cannot secure to his people a succession of princes like himself. He will do all he can towards it, by his example and by his instruction. But after all, the royal mantle will not convey the spirit of patriotism into another king, as the mantle of Elijah did the gift of prophecy into another prophet.[44] The utmost he can do, and that which deserves the utmost gratitude from his subjects, is to restore good government, to revive the spirit of it, and to maintain and confirm both, during the whole course of his reign. The rest his people must do for themselves. If they do not, they will have none but themselves to blame: if they do, they will have the principal obligation to him. In all events, they will have been free men one reign the longer by his means, and perhaps more; since he will leave them much better prepared and disposed to defend their liberties, than he found them.

*This general observation being made, let us now descend, in some detail, to the particular steps and measures that such a king

* Supreme] sole Supream
* affords] is
* II. [*footnote* II. The Measures a Patriot King will take.]

[43] Machiavelli, *Discorsi*, III. 1.
[44] II Kings 2: 8–14.

must pursue, to merit a much nobler title than all those which many princes of the west, as well as the east, are so proud to accumulate.

*First, then, he must begin to govern as soon as he begins to reign. For the very first steps he makes in government will give the first impression, and as it were the presage of his reign; and may be of great importance in many other respects besides that of opinion and reputation. His first care will be, no doubt, to purge his court, and to call into the administration such men as he can assure himself will serve on the same principles on which he intends to govern.

As to the first point; if the precedent reign has been bad, we know how he will find the court composed. The men in power will be some of those adventurers, busy and bold, who thrust and crowd themselves early into the intrigue of party and the management of affairs of state, often without true ability, always without true ambition, or even the appearances of virtue: who mean nothing more than what is called making a fortune, the acquisition of wealth to satisfy avarice, and of titles and ribands to satisfy vanity. Such as these are sure to be employed by a weak, or a wicked king: they impose on the first, and are chosen by the last. Nor is it marvellous that they are so, since every other want is supplied in them by the want of good principles and a good conscience; and since these defects become ministerial perfections, in a reign when measures are pursued and designs carried on that every honest man will disapprove. All the prostitutes who set themselves to sale, all the locusts who devour the land, with crowds of spies, parasites, and sycophants, will surround the throne under the patronage of such ministers; and whole swarms of little, noisome, nameless insects will hum and buzz* in every corner of the court. Such ministers will be cast off, and such abettors of a ministry will be chased away together, and at once, by a Patriot King.

Some of them perhaps, will be abandoned by him; not* to party fury, but to national justice; not to sate private resentments, and* to serve particular interests, but to make satisfaction for wrongs done to their country, and to stand as examples of terror to future administrations. Clemency makes, no doubt, an amiable part of the character I attempt to draw; but clemency, to be a virtue, must have

---

* 1. [*footnote* 1. First, to purge his Court of the Bad.]   * little . . . buzz]
noisome, nameless Insects will buzz   * not] but not   * and] or

its bounds, like other virtues: and surely these bounds are extended enough by a maxim I have read somewhere, that frailties and even vices may be passed over, but not enormous crimes: *multa donanda ingeniis puto, sed donanda vitia, non portenta.*[45]

Among the bad company, with which such a court will abound, may be reckoned a sort of men too low to be much regarded, and too high to be quite neglected; the lumber of every administration, the furniture of every court. These gilt carved things are seldom answerable for more than the men on a chess-board, who are moved about at will, and on whom the conduct of the game is not to be charged. Some of these every prince must have about him. The pageantry of a court requires that he should: and this pageantry, like many other despicable things, ought not to be laid aside. But as much sameness as there may appear in the characters of this sort of men, there is one distinction that will* be made, whenever a good prince succeeds to the throne after an iniquitous administration: the distinction I mean is, between those who have affected to dip themselves deeply in precedent iniquities, and those who have had the virtue to keep aloof from them, or the good luck not to be called to any share in them. And thus much for the first point, that of purging his court.

As to the second, that of calling to his administration such men as he can assure himself will serve on the same principles on which he intends to govern, there is no need to enlarge much upon it. A good prince will no more choose ill men, than a wise prince will choose fools. Deception in one case is indeed more easy than in the other; because a knave may be an artful hypocrite, whereas a silly fellow can never impose himself for a man of sense. And least of all, in a country like ours, can either of these deceptions happen, if any degree of the* discernment of spirits be employed to choose. The reason is, because every man here, who stands forward enough in rank and reputation to be called to the councils of his king, must have given proofs beforehand* of his patriotism, as well as of

* that will] to
* 2. [*footnote* 2. To make choise of the Good and Able.]   * And] But
* the] *1749*
* have given proofs beforehand] beforehand have given Proofs

[45] 'I think much may be forgiven for men of talent, but only their faults can be overlooked not their abominable acts': Seneca the Elder, *Controverses*, x. Pref. 10.

his capacity, if he has either, sufficient to determine his general character.

There is, however, one distinction to be made as to the capacity of ministers, on which I will insist a little: because I think it very important at all times, particularly so at this time; and because it escapes observation most commonly. The distinction I mean is that between a cunning man and a wise man: and this distinction* is built on a manifest difference in nature, how imperceptible soever it may become to weak eyes, or to eyes that look at their object through the false medium of custom and habit. My Lord Bacon says, that cunning is left-handed or crooked wisdom.[46] I would rather say, that it is a part, but the lowest part, of wisdom; employed alone by some, because they have not the other parts to employ; and by some,* because it is as much as they want, within those bounds of action which they prescribe to themselves, and sufficient to* the ends that they propose. The difference seems to consist in degree, and application, rather than in kind. Wisdom is neither left-handed, nor crooked: but the heads of some men contain little, and the hearts of others employ it wrong. To use my Lord Bacon's own comparison, the cunning man knows how to pack the cards, the wise man how to play the game better:[47] but it would be of no use to the first to pack the cards, if his knowledge stopped here, and he had no skill in the game; nor to the second to play the game better, if he did not know how to pack the cards, that he might unpack them by new shuffling. Inferior wisdom or cunning may get the better of folly: but superior wisdom will get the better of cunning. Wisdom and cunning have often the same objects; but a wise man will have more and greater in his view. The least will not fill his soul, nor ever become the principal there; but will be pursued in subserviency, in subordination at least, to the other. Wisdom and cunning may employ sometimes the same means too: but the wise

---

* CHAP. IX. I. How to judge of the Ability of Ministers. II. Distinction between Wisdom and Cunning.
* escapes . . . commonly] most commonly escapes observation
* this distinction] it is one that   * some] others   * to] for

---

[46] Bacon, *Essays*, 'Of Cunning': 'We take cunning for a sinister, or crooked wisdom' in *Opera Omnia*, III, 332; compare *Dissertation upon Parties*, 3.
[47] 'There be that can pack the cards, and yet cannot play well . . .', Bacon, *Opera Omnia*, III, 332.

man stoops to these means, and the other cannot rise above them. *Simulation and dissimulation, for instance, are the chief arts of cunning: the first will be esteemed always by a wise man unworthy of him, and will be therefore avoided by him, in every possible case; for, to resume my Lord Bacon's comparison, simulation is put on that we may look into the cards of another, whereas dissimulation intends nothing more than to hide our own. Simulation is a stiletto, not only an offensive, but an unlawful weapon: and the use of it may be rarely,* very rarely, excused, but never justified. Dissimulation is a shield, as secrecy is armour:* and it is no more possible to preserve secrecy in the administration of public affairs without some degree of dissimulation, than it is to succeed in it without secrecy. Those two arts of cunning are like the alloy mingled with pure ore. A little is necessary, and will not debase the coin below its proper standard; but if more than that little be employed, the coin loses its currency, and the coiner his credit.

We may observe much the same difference between wisdom and cunning, both as to the objects they propose and to the means they employ, as we observe between the visual powers of different men. One sees distinctly the objects that are near to him, their immediate relations, and their direct tendencies;* and a sight like this serves well enough the purpose of those who concern themselves no further. The cunning minister is one of those: he neither sees, nor is concerned to see, any further than his personal interests, and the support of his administration, require. If such a man overcomes any actual difficulty, avoids any immediate distress, or, without doing either of these effectually, gains a little time, by all the low artifice which cunning is ready to suggest and baseness of mind to employ, he triumphs, and is flattered by his mercenary train, on the great event; which amounts often to no more than this, that he got into distress by one series of faults, and out of it by another. The wise minister sees, and is concerned to see further, because government has a further concern: he sees the objects that are distant as well as those that are near, and all their remote relations, and even their indirect tendencies. He thinks of fame as well as of applause, and

* *footnote* [* Chief Arts of Cunning.]
* rarely,] *1749*
* armour] an Armour
* tendencies] tendency

prefers that, which to be enjoyed must be given, to that which may be bought. He considers his administration as a single day in the great year of government; but as a day that is affected by those which went before, and that must affect those which are to follow. He combines, therefore, and compares all these objects, relations, and tendencies; and the judgment he makes, on an entire not a partial survey of them, is the rule of his conduct. That scheme of the reason of state, which lies open before a wise minister, contains all the great principles of government, and all the great interests of his country: so that, as he prepares some events, he prepares against others, whether they be likely to happen during his administration, or in some future time.

Many reflections might be added to these, and many examples be brought to illustrate them. Some I could draw from the men I have seen at the head of business, and make very strong contrasts of men of great wisdom with those of mere cunning. But* I conclude this head, that I may proceed to another of no less importance.

*To espouse no party, but to govern like the common father of his people, is so essential to the character of a Patriot King, that he who does otherwise forfeits the title.[48] It is the peculiar privilege and glory of this character, that princes who maintain it, and they alone, are so far from the necessity, that they are not exposed to the temptation, of governing by a party; which must always end in the government of a faction: the faction of the prince, if he has ability; the faction of his ministers, if he has not; and, either one way or other, in the oppression of the people. For faction is to party what the superlative is to the positive: party is a political evil, and faction is the worst of all parties. The true image of a free people, governed by a Patriot King, is that of

* mere cunning. But] meer cunning. I could quote among the former my Lord *Somers*, notwithstanding his low Education and his narrow Principles; and among the latter the Marquis of *Wharton*. The Days may come perhaps, (and I trust they will) when you will be able to make such Contrasts as these from your own Experience; for cunning Men there will always be on the publick Stage, and some time or other, perhaps, there may be wise Men. But
* CHAP. X. I. That a Patriot King ought to espouse no Party. II. The Evil of governing by one, either in a State united or divided.

[48] Compare [John Toland], *The Art of Governing by Partys* (London, 1701), 41: '. . . a King can never lessen himself more than by heading of a Party; for thereby he becomes only the King of a Faction, and ceases to be the common Father of his People'.

a patriarchal family, where the head and all the members are united by one common interest, and animated by one common spirit: and where, if any are perverse enough to have another, they will be soon borne down by the superiority of those who have the same; and,* far from making a division, they* will but confirm the union of the little state. That to approach as near as possible to these ideas of perfect government, and social happiness under it, is desirable in every state, no man will be absurd enough to deny. The sole question is, therefore, how near to them it is possible to attain? For, if this attempt be not absolutely impracticable, all the views of a Patriot King will be directed to make it succeed. Instead of abetting the divisions of his people, he will endeavour to unite them, and to be himself the centre of their union: instead of putting himself at the head of one party in order to govern his people, he will put himself at the head of his people in order to govern, or more properly to subdue, all parties. Now,* to arrive at this desirable union, and to maintain it, will be* found more difficult in some cases than in others, but absolutely impossible in none, to a wise and good prince.

If his people are united in their submission to him, and in their attachment to the established government, he must not only espouse but create a party, in order to govern by one: and what should tempt him to pursue so wild a measure? A prince, who aims at more power than the constitution gives him, may be so tempted; because he may hope to obtain in the disorders of the state what cannot be obtained in quiet times; and because contending parties will give what a nation will not. Parties, even before they degenerate into absolute factions, are still numbers of men associated together for certain purposes, and certain interests, which are not, or which are not allowed to be, those of the community by others.* A more private or personal interest comes but too soon, and too often, to be superadded, and to grow predominant in them: and when it does so, whatever occasions or principles began to form them, the same logic prevails in them that* prevails in every church. The interest of the state is supposed to be that of the party, as the interest of religion is supposed to be that of the Church: and, with this

---

* and,] which   * they] *1749*   * Now, *1749*   * be] indeed be
* II. [*footnote* II. The Evil of governing by Party, in a State *united.*]
* absolute] *1749*   * to be, those of the community by others] by others to be those of the Community   * that] as

pretence or prepossession, the interest of the state becomes, like
that of religion, a remote consideration, is never pursued for its own
sake, and is often sacrificed to the other. A king, therefore, who has
ill designs to carry on, must endeavour to divide an united people;
and by blending or seeming to blend his interests with that of a
party, he may succeed perhaps, and his party and he may share the
spoils of a ruined nation: but* such a party is then become a faction,
such a king is a tyrant, and such a government is a conspiracy. A
Patriot King must renounce his character, to have such designs; or
act against his own designs, to pursue such methods. Both are too
absurd to be supposed. It remains, therefore, that as all the good
ends of government are most attainable in a united state, and as the
divisions of a people can serve to bad purposes alone, the king we
suppose here will deem the union of his subjects his greatest advantage, and will think himself happy to find that established, which
he would have employed the whole labour of his life to bring about.
This seems so plain, that I am ready to make excuses for having
insisted at all upon it.

*Let us turn ourselves to another supposition, to that of a divided
state. This will fall in oftener with the ordinary course of things in
free governments, and especially after iniquitous and weak administrations. Such a state may be better or worse, and the great and good
purposes of a Patriot King more or less attainable in it, according to
the different nature of those divisions; and, therefore, we will consider this state in different lights.

A people may be united in submission to the prince, and to the
establishment, and yet be divided about general principles, or particular measures of government. In the first case, they will do by their
constitution what has frequently been done by the Scripture, strain it
to their own notions* and prejudices; and, if they cannot strain it, alter
it as much as is necessary to render it conformable to them. In the
second, they will support or oppose particular acts of administrations,
and defend or attack the persons employed in them; and both these
ways a conflict of parties may arise, but no great difficulty to a prince
who determines to pursue the union of his subjects, and the prosperity of his kingdoms independently of all parties.

---

* but] *1749*   * II. [*footnote* II. The Evil of governing by Party, in a *State*
  divided.]   * notions] actions

When parties are divided by different notions and principles concerning some particular ecclesiastical, or civil institutions, the constitution, which should be their rule, must be that of the prince. He may and he ought to show his dislike or his favour, as he judges the constitution may be hurt or improved, by one side or the other. The hurt he is never to suffer, not for his own sake; and, therefore, surely not for the sake of any whimsical, factious, or ambitious set of men. The improvement he must always desire; but as every new modification in a scheme of government and of national policy is of * great importance, and requires more and deeper consideration than the warmth, and hurry, and rashness of party conduct admit, the duty of a prince seems to require that he should render by his influence the proceedings more orderly and more deliberate, even when he approves the end to which they are directed. All this may be done by him without fomenting division: and, far from forming or espousing a party, he will defeat party in defence of the constitution, on some occasions; and lead men, from acting with a party spirit, to act with a national spirit, on others.

When the division is about particular measures of government, and the conduct of the administration is alone concerned, a Patriot King will stand in want of party as little as in any other case. Under his reign, the opportunities of forming an opposition of this sort will be rare, and the pretences generally weak. Nay, the motives to it will lose much of their force, when a government is strong in reputation, and men are kept in good humour by feeling the rod of a party on no occasion, though they feel the weight of the sceptre on some. Such opportunities, however, may happen; and there may be reason, as well as pretences, sometimes for opposition even in such a reign: at least we will suppose so, that we may include in this argument every contingent case. Grievances then are complained of, mistakes and abuses in government are pointed out, and ministers are prosecuted by their enemies. Shall the prince on the throne form a party by intrigue, and by secret and corrupt influence, to oppose the prosecution? When the prince and the ministers are *participes criminis,*[49] when every thing is to be defended, lest something should come out, that may unravel the silly wicked scheme,

* is of] is a matter of

[49] 'Partners in crime'.

and disclose to public sight the whole turpitude of the administration, there is no* help; this must be done, and such a party must
be formed, because such a party alone will submit to a drudgery of
this kind. But a prince, who is not in these circumstances, will not
have recourse to these means. He has others more open, more noble,
and more effectual in his power: he knows that the views of his
government are right, and that the tenor of his administration is
good; but he knows that neither he nor his ministers are infallible,
nor impeccable. There may be abuses in his government, mistakes
in his administration, and guilt in his ministers, which he has not
observed: and he will be far from imputing the complaints, that
give him occasion to observe them, to a spirit of party; much less
will he treat those who carry on such prosecutions in a legal manner,
as incendiaries, and as enemies to his government. On the contrary,
he will distinguish the voice of his people from the clamour of a
faction, and will hearken to it. He will redress grievances, correct
errors, and reform or punish ministers. This he will do as a good
prince: and as a wise one, he will do it in such a manner that his
dignity shall be maintained, and that his authority shall increase,
with his reputation, by it.

Should the efforts of a mere faction be bent to calumniate his
government, and to distress the administration on groundless pretences, and for insufficient reasons; he will not neglect, but he will
not apprehend neither, the short-lived and contemptible scheme.
He will indeed have no reason to do so; for let the fautors*[50] of
maladministration, whenever an opposition is made to it, affect to
insinuate as much as they please, that their masters are in no other
circumstances than those to which the very best ministers stand
exposed, objects of general envy and of particular malice, it will
remain eternally true, that groundless* opposition, in a well regulated monarchy, can never be strong and durable. To be convinced
of the truth of this proposition, one needs only to reflect how many
well grounded attacks have been defeated, and how few have
succeeded, against the most wicked and the weakest administrations. Every king of Britain* has means enough in his power, to

* is no] is then indeed no   * fautors] factors   * groundless] any groundless
* Every king of Britain] Every King, every King of *Britain*, at least,

[50] Favourers, abettors.

defeat and to calm opposition. But a Patriot King, above all others, may safely rest his cause on the innocency of his administration, on the constitutional strength of the crown, and on the concurrence of his people, to whom he dares appeal, and by whom he will be supported.

To conclude all I will say on the divisions of this kind, let me add, that the case of a groundless opposition can hardly happen in a bad reign, because in such a reign just occasions of opposition must of course be frequently given, as we have allowed that they may be given sometimes, though very rarely, in a good reign; but that, whether it be well or ill grounded, whether it be that of the nation, or that of a faction, the conduct of the* prince with respect to it will be the same; and one way or other this conduct must have a very fatal event. Such a prince will not mend the administration, as long as he can resist the justest and most popular opposition: and, therefore, this opposition will last and grow, as long as a free constitution is in force, and the spirit of liberty is preserved; for so long even a change of his ministers, without a change of his measures, will not be sufficient. The former without the latter is a mere banter, and would be deemed and taken for such, by every man who did not oppose on a factious principle; that I mean of getting into power at any rate, and using it as ill, perhaps worse than* the men he helped to turn out of it. Now if such men as these abound, and they will abound in the decline of a free government, a bad prince, whether he changes or does not change his ministers, may hope to govern by the spirit and art of a faction, against the spirit and strength of the nation. His character may be too low, and that of his minister too odious, to form originally even a faction that shall be able to defend them. But they may apply to their purposes, a party that was formed on far different occasions, and bring numbers to fight for a cause in which many of them would not have listed. The names, and with the names the animosity of parties, may be kept up, when the causes that formed them subsist no longer.

When a party is thus revived or continued in the spirit of a faction, the corrupt and infatuated members of it will act without any regard to right or wrong: and they who have asserted liberty in one reign, or opposed invasions of one kind, will give it up in another reign, and

---

* the] a bad   * perhaps worse than] as

abet invasions of another kind; though they still distinguish themselves by the same appellation, still spread the same banner, and still deafen their adversaries and one another with the same cry. If the national cause prevails against all the wicked arts of corruption and division, that an obstinate prince and flagitious ministry can employ; yet will the struggle be long, and the difficulties, the distresses, and the danger great, both to the king and to the people. The best he can hope for, in such a case, will be to escape with a diminution of his reputation, authority, and power. He may be exposed to something worse; and his obstinacy may force things to such extremities, as they who oppose him will lament, and as the preservation of liberty and good government can alone justify. If the wicked arts I speak of prevail, faction will be propagated through the whole nation, an ill or well grounded opposition will be the question no longer, and the contest among parties will be, who shall govern, not how they shall be governed. In short, universal confusion will follow, and a complete victory, on any side, will enslave all sides.

I have not overcharged the draught. Such consequences must follow such a conduct; and therefore let me ask, how much more safe, more easy, more pleasant, more honourable is it, for a prince to correct, if he has not prevented, maladministration? That he may be able to rest his cause, as I said before, on the strength of the crown and the concurrence of his people, whenever any faction presumes to rise in opposition to him.

This a Patriot King will do. He may favour one party and discourage another, upon occasions wherein the state of his kingdom makes such a temporary measure necessary:* but he will espouse none, much less will he proscribe any.[51] He will list no party, much less will he do the meanest and most imprudent thing a king can do, list himself in any. It will be his aim to pursue true principles of government independently of all and, by a steady

---

* CHAP. XI. I. How to conduct himself with regard to Parties, I. Even in the greatest Extremities, and 2. After a contrary Conduct in former Reigns. II. A Digression, applying this to the Case of the *Jacobites*.
* This a Patriot King will do. He may] But shall a Patriot King never
* necessary:] necessary? Yes, he may for a time favour.

[51] As the Tories had been excluded from holding local and national office after the Hanoverian succession in 1715, when George I firmly tied his dynasty to the one-party oligarchy of the Whigs.

adherence to this measure, his reign will become an undeniable and glorious proof, that a wise and good prince may unite his subjects, and be himself the centre of their union, notwithstanding any of these divisions that have been hitherto mentioned.

Let us now view the divided state of a nation in another light. In this, the divisions will appear more odious, more dangerous; less dependent on the influence, and less subject to the authority of the crown. Such will be the state, whenever a people is divided about submission to their prince, and a party is formed, of spirit and strength sufficient to oppose, even in arms, the established government. But in this case, desperate as it may seem, a Patriot King will not despair of reconciling, and re-uniting his subjects to himself, and to one another. He may be obliged, perhaps, as Henry the Fourth of France was, to conquer his own; but then, like that great prince, if he is the conqueror, he will be the father too, of his people.[52] He must pursue in arms those who presume to take arms against him; but he will pursue them like rebellious children whom he seeks to reclaim, and not like irreconcilable enemies whom he endeavours to exterminate. Another prince may blow up the flame of civil war by unprovoked severity, render those zealous against him who were at worst indifferent, and determine the disaffection of others to open rebellion. When he has prevailed against the faction he helped to form, as he could not have prevailed if the bent of the nation had been against him, he may be willing to ascribe his success to a party, that he may have that pretence to govern by a party: and, far from reconciling the minds that have been alienated from him, and reuniting his subjects in a willing unforced submission to him, he may be content to maintain himself on that* throne, where the laws of God and man have placed him, by the melancholy expedient that usurpers and tyrants, who have no other in their power, employ; the expedient of force. But a Patriot King will act with another spirit, and entertain nobler and wiser views,

---

* 1. [*footnote* 1. Even in the greatest Extremities.]
* and, far] Far   * that] the

52 Henri IV, the first Bourbon King of France (1589–1610), had defended his claim to the French throne by arms at the battle of Jarnac (1569); by his second conversion to Catholicism in 1593 he reunited a country torn apart by the Wars of Religion, and paved the way for the Edict of Nantes, which granted liberty of conscience to Protestants.

from first to last, and through the whole course of such a conjuncture. Nothing less than the hearts of his people will content such a prince; nor will he think his throne established, till it is established there. That he may have time and opportunity to gain them, therefore, he will prevent the flame from breaking out, if by art and management he can do it. If he cannot, he will endeavour to keep it from spreading: and, if the frenzy of rebellion disappoints them in both these attempts, he will remember peace, like the heroic king I just now quoted, in the midst of war. Like him he will forego advantages of pushing the latter, rather than lose an opportunity of promoting the former; like him, in the heat of battle he will spare, and in the triumph of victory condescend; like him, he will beat down the violence of this flame, by his valour, and extinguish even the embers of it, by his lenity.

*It may happen, that a prince, capable of holding such a conduct as this, may not have the opportunity. He may succeed to the throne after a contrary conduct has been held: and when, among other divisions which maladministration and the tyranny of faction have increased and confirmed, there is one against the established government still in being, though not still in arms. The use is obvious, which a faction in power might make of such a circumstance under a weak prince, by ranking in that division all those who opposed the administration; or at least by holding out equal danger to him from two quarters, from their enemies who meant him no harm, and from his enemies who could do him none. But so gross an artifice will not impose on a prince of another character: he will soon discern the distinctions it becomes him to make. He will see, in this instance, how faction breeds, nourishes, and perpetuates faction: he will observe how far that of the court contributed to form the other, and contributes still to keep it in countenance and credit among those who consider more what such men are against, than what they are for. He will observe, how much that of the disaffected gives pretence to the other who keeps a monopoly of power and wealth; one of which oppresses, and the other beggars, the rest of the nation. His penetration will soon discover, that these factions break in but little on the body of his people, and that it depends on him alone to take from them even the strength they have; because

---

* 2. [*footnote* 2. After a contrary Conduct in former Reigns.]

that of the former is acquired entirely by his authority and purse, and that of the latter principally by the abuse which the former makes of both. Upon the whole, the measures he has to pursue towards the great object of a Patriot King, the union of his people, will appear to him extremely easy. How should they be otherwise? One of the factions must be dissolved the moment that the favour of the prince is withdrawn: and the other is disarmed, as soon as it is marked out. It will have no shelter, and it must therefore be so marked out, under a good and wise administration; for, whether the members of it avow their principles by refusing those tests of fidelity which the law requires, or perjure themselves by taking them, they will be known alike. One difference, and but one, will be made between them in the general sense of mankind, a difference arising from the greater degree of infamy that will belong justly to the latter. The first may pass for fools; the latter must pass, without excuse, for knaves.

The terms I use sound harshly, but the censure is just: and it will appear to be so in the highest degree, and upon the highest reason, if we stop to make a reflection or two, that deserve very well to be made, on the conduct of our Jacobites; for I desire no stronger instance on which to establish the censure, and to justify the terms I have used. Now all these, whether they swear or whether they do not, are liable to one particular objection, that did not lie against those who were, in former days, enemies to the king on the throne. In the days of York and Lancaster, for instance, a man might be against the prince on the throne, without being against the constitution of his country. The constitution conveyed the crown by hereditary right in the same family: and he who was a Yorkist, and he who was a Lancastrian, might, and I doubt not did, pretend in every contest to have this right on his side. The same constitution was acknowledged by both: and, therefore, so much indulgence was shown by law to both, at least in the time of Henry the Seventh, that submission to a king *de facto* could not be imputed as a crime to either.[53] Thus again, to descend lower in history, when the exclusion of the Duke of York was pressed in the reign of Charles the Second, the right of that prince to the crown was not disputed.

* II. [*footnote* II. A Digression applying this to the Case of the Jacobites.]
* Now all these,] All these Men.

[53] The 'De facto' Act of 1495; see *Dissertation upon Parties*, 'Letter VIII', p. 73.

His divine right indeed, such a divine right as his grandfather and father had asserted before him, was not much regarded; but his right by the constitution, his legal right, was sufficiently owned by those who insisted on a law as necessary to bar it. But every Jacobite, at this time, goes beyond all these examples, and is a rebel to the constitution under which he is born, as well as to the prince on the throne. The law of his country has settled the right of succession in a new family.[54] He resists this law, and asserts, on his own private authority, not only a right in contradiction to it, but a right extinguished by it. This absurdity is so great, that it cannot be defended, except by advancing a greater: and therefore it is urged, that no power on earth could alter the constitution in this respect, nor extinguish a right to the crown inherent in the Stuart* family, and derived from a superior, that is, from a divine, authority. This kind of plea for refusing submission to the laws of the land, if it was admitted, would serve any purpose as well as that for which it is brought. Our fanatics urged it formerly, and I do not see why a conscientious fifth monarchy-man had not as much right to urge it formerly, as a Jacobite has now. But if conscience, that is private opinion, may excuse the fifth monarchy-man and the Jacobite, who act conformably to it, from all imputations except those of madness and folly; how shall the latter be excused when he forswears the principles he retains, acknowledges the right he renounces, takes oaths with an intent to violate them, and calls God to witness to a premeditated lie? Some casuistry has been employed to excuse these men to themselves and to others. But such casuistry, and in truth every other, destroys, by distinctions and exceptions, all morality, and effaces the essential difference between right and wrong, good and evil. This the schoolmen in general have done on many occasions, the sons of Loyola in particular:[55] and I wish with all my heart that nothing of the same kind could be objected to any other divines. Some political reasoning has been employed, as well as the casuistry here spoken of, and to the same purpose. It has been said, that the conduct of those who are enemies to the establishment, to which they submit and swear, is justified by the principles of the Revolution. But nothing can be more false and frivolous. By the

---

* Stuart] *Stuart*'s

[54] By the Act of Settlement (1701), 12 and 13 William III, c. 2.
[55] St Ignatius Loyola (1491–1556) founded the Jesuit order in 1534.

principles of the Revolution, a subject may resist, no doubt, the prince who endeavours to ruin and enslave his people, and* may push this resistance to the dethronement and exclusion of him and his race: but will it follow, that, because we may justly take arms against a prince whose right to govern we once acknowledged, and who by subsequent acts has forfeited that right, we may swear to a right we do not acknowledge, and resist a prince whose conduct has not forfeited the right we swore to, nor given any just dispensation from our oaths?

But I shall lengthen this digression no further: it is on a subject I have treated in public writings,[56] the refutation of which never came to my hands, and, I think, never will.* I return to the subject of my present discourse. And I say, that such* factions as these can never create any obstruction to a prince who pursues the union of his subjects, nor disturb the peace of his government. The men who compose them must be desperate, and impotent; the most despicable of all characters, when they go together.* Every honest and sensible man will distinguish himself out of their number: and they will remain, as they deserve to be, hewers of wood, and drawers of water,[57] to the rest of their fellow subjects.

They will remain such, if they are abandoned to themselves, and to that habitual infatuation which they have not sense and spirit enough to break. But if a prince, out of goodness or policy, should think it worth his while to take them from under this influence, and to break these habits; even this division, the most absurd* of all others, will not be found incurable. A man who has not seen the inside of parties, nor had opportunities to examine nearly their secret motives, can hardly conceive how little a share principle of any sort, though principle of some sort or other be always pretended, has in the determination of their conduct. Reason has small effect on numbers. A turn of imagination, often as violent and as sudden as a gust of wind, determines their conduct: and passion is taken, by others, and by themselves too, when it grows into habit

* and] *1749*   * it is on a subject . . . never will] *1749*
* And I say, that such] *1749*   * when they go together] *1749*
* absurd] abus'd

[56] *Dissertation upon Parties*, 'Letter VIII'.
[57] Joshua 9: 21, 23.

especially, for principle. What gave strength and spirit to a Jacobite party after the late King's accession?[58] The true answer is,* a sudden turn of the imaginations of a whole party to resentment and rage, that were turned a little before to quiet submission, and patient expectation. Principle had as little share in making the turn, as reason had in conducting it. Men who had sense, and temper too, before that moment, thought of nothing, after it, but setting up a Tory king against a Whig king: and when some of them* were asked, if they were sure a popish king would make a good Tory king, or whether they were determined to sacrifice their religion and liberty to him the answer was, no; that* they would take arms against him if he made attempts on either; that this might be the case, perhaps, in six months after his restoration, but that, in the meantime, they would endeavour his restoration. This is no exaggerated fact: and I leave all men* to judge, to what such sentiments and conduct must be ascribed, to principle or passion, to reason or madness? What gives obstinacy without strength, and sullenness without spirit, to the Jacobite* Tories at this time? Another turn of imagination, or rather the same showing itself in another form; a factious habit, and a factious notion, converted into a notion of policy and honour. They are taught to believe, that by clinging together they are a considerable weight, which may be thrown in to turn the scale in any great event; and that in the meantime, to be a steady suffering party is an honour they may flatter themselves with very justly. Thus, they continue steady to engagements which most of them wish in their hearts they had never taken; and suffer for principles, in support of which not one of them would venture further, than talking the treason that claret inspires.[59]

*It results, therefore, from all that has been said, and from the reflections which these hints may suggest, that in whatever light we

---

* The true answer is] I have said it already   * some of them] *1749*
* that] *1749*   * all men] you   * Jacobite] *1749*
* CHAP. XII. I. Objections rais'd to the Practicability of governing without a *Party*, answer'd. II. The Original and Causes of *Faction*. III. The Example of Queen *Elizabeth*, as to Party.

[58] The accession of George I in 1714 which was soon followed by the Jacobite rising of 1715.
[59] The proverbial drink of Jacobites was claret (from France), that of Whigs, port (imported from Portugal under the terms of the Second Methuen Treaty of 1703).

view the divided state of a people, there is none in which these divisions will appear incurable, nor an union of the members of a great community with one another, and with their head, unattainable. It may happen in this case as it does in many others, that things uncommon may pass for improbable or impossible: and, as nothing can be more uncommon than a Patriot King, there will be no room to wonder if the natural and certain effects of his conduct should appear improbable or impossible to many. But there is still something more in this case. Though the union we speak of be so much for the interest of every king and every people, that their glory and their prosperity must increase, or diminish, in proportion as they approach nearer to it, or are further removed from it; yet is there another interest, by which princes and people both are often imposed upon so far, as to mistake it for their own. The interest I mean, is that of private ambition. It would be easy to show in many instances, and particularly in this, of uniting instead of dividing, and of governing by a national concurrence instead of governing by the management of parties and factions in the state, how widely different, nay how repugnant, the interests* of private ambition and those of real patriotism are. Men, therefore, who are warmed by the first, and have no sense of the last, will declare for division as they do for corruption, in opposition to union and to integrity of government. They will not indeed declare directly, that the two former are in the abstract preferable; but they will affirm, with great airs of sufficiency, that both are incurable; and conclude from hence, that in practice it is necessary to comply with both. This subterfuge once open, there is no false and immoral measure in political management which may not be avowed and recommended. But the very men, who hope to escape by opening it, shut it up again, and secure their own condemnation, when they labour to confirm divisions, and to propagate corruption, and thereby to create the very necessity that they plead in their excuse. Necessity of this kind there is in reality none; for it seems full as absurd to say, that popular divisions must be cultivated, because popular union cannot be procured, as it would be to say that poison must be poured into a wound, because it cannot be healed. The practice of morality, in private life, will never arrive at ideal perfection: must we give up

* interests] Interest

ourselves, therefore, to all manner of immorality? And must those who are charged with our instruction endeavour to make us the most profligate of men, because they cannot make us saints?

Experience of the depravity of human nature made men desirous to unite in society and under government, that they might defend themselves the better against injuries; but the same depravity soon inspired to some the design of employing societies to invade and spoil societies; and to disturb the peace of the great commonwealth of mankind, with more force and effect in such collective bodies, than they could do individually. Just so it happens in the domestic economy of particular states: and their peace is disturbed by the same passions. Some of their members content themselves with the common benefits of society, and employ all their industry to promote the public good: but some propose to themselves a separate interest, and, that they may pursue it the more effectually, they associate with others. Thus factions are in them, what nations are in the world; they invade and rob one another: and, while each pursues a separate interest, the common interest is sacrificed by them all: that of mankind in one case, that of some particular community in the other. This has been, and must always be, in some measure, the course of human affairs, especially in free countries, where the passions of men are less restrained by authority: and I am not wild enough to suppose that a Patriot King can change human nature. But I am reasonable enough to suppose, that, without altering human nature, he may give a check to this course of human affairs, in his own kingdom at least; that he may defeat the designs, and break the spirit of faction, instead of partaking in one, and assuming the other; and that, if he cannot render the union of his subjects universal, he may render it so general as to answer all the ends of good government, private security, public tranquillity, wealth, power, and fame.

If these ends were ever answered, they were so, surely, in this country, in the days of our Elizabeth. She found her kingdom full of factions, and factions of another consequence and danger than these of our days, whom she would have dispersed with a puff of her breath. She could not re-unite them, it is true: the papist

* II. [*footnote* II. The Original and Causes of Faction.]   * and] *1749*
* III. [*footnote* III. Example of Queen *Elizabeth*, as to Party.]
* another] greater

continued a papist, the puritan a puritan; one furious, the other sullen. But she united the great body of the people in her and their common interest, she inflamed them with one national spirit, and, thus armed, she maintained tranquillity at home, and carried succour to her friends and terror to her enemies abroad. There were cabals at her court, and intrigues among her ministers. It is said too, that she did not dislike that there should be such. But these were kept within her court. They could not creep abroad, to sow division among her people, and her greatest favourite the Earl of Essex paid the price of attempting it with his head.[60] Let our great doctors in politics, who preach so learnedly on the trite text *divide et impera*,[61] compare the conduct of Elizabeth in this respect with that of her successor, who endeavoured to govern his kingdom by the notions of a faction that he raised, and to manage his parliament by undertakers:[62] and they must be very obstinate indeed,* if they refuse to acknowledge, that a wise and good prince can unite a divided people, though a weak and wicked prince cannot; and that the consequences of national union are glory and happiness to the prince and to the people, whilst those of disunion bring shame and misery on both, and entail them too on posterity.

*I have dwelt long on the last head, not only because it is of great importance in itself, and at all times, but because it is rendered more so than ever at this time, by the unexampled avowal of contrary principles. Hitherto it has been thought the highest pitch of profligacy to own, instead of concealing, crimes, and to take pride in them, instead of being ashamed of them. But in our age men have soared to a pitch still higher. The first is common, it is the practice of numbers, and by their numbers they keep one another in countenance. But the choice spirits of these days, the men of

---

* undertakers: and they must be very obstinate indeed] undertakers: They must be very obstinate,
* CHAP. XIII. I. That, notwithstanding all Objections, a *King* may be an *honest Man*, and Great, by Patriotism. II. That his Interest and his Country's will be the same. III. What is the particular and true Interest of *Great Britain*.

[60] Robert Devereux, 2nd Earl of Essex (1566–1601), was executed for treason in the wake of his abortive revolt in 1601.   [61] 'Divide and rule'.
[62] The term 'undertaker', to denote a politician who 'undertook' to manage Parliament on behalf of the King, was first used in February 1614 by John Donne: Clayton Roberts, *Schemes and Undertakings: A Study of English Politics in the Seventeenth Century* (Columbus, Ohio, 1985), x.

mode in politics, are far from stopping where criminals of all kinds
have stopped, when they have gone even to this point; for generally
the most hardened of the inhabitants of Newgate[63] do not go so far.
The men I speak of contend, that it is not enough to be vicious by
practice and habit, but that it is necessary to be so by principle.
They make themselves missionaries of faction as well as of corruption: they recommend both, they deride all such as imagine it possible, or fit to retain truth, integrity, and a disinterested regard to
the public in public life, and pronounce every man a fool who is
not ready to act like a knave. I hope that enough has been said,
though much more might have been said, to expose the wickedness
of these men, and the absurdity of their schemes; and to show that
a Patriot* King may walk more easily and successfully in other
paths of government, *per tutum planumque iter religionis, justitiae,
honestatis, virtutumque moralium.*[64] Let me proceed, therefore, to
mention two other heads of the conduct that such a king will hold,
and it shall be my endeavour not to fall into the same prolixity.

A king who esteems it his duty to support, or to restore, if that
be needful, the free constitution of a limited monarchy; who forms
and maintains a wise and good administration; who subdues faction,
and promotes the union of his people: and who makes their greatest
good the constant object of his government, may be said, no doubt,
to be in the true interest of his kingdom. All the particular cases,
that can arise, are included in these general characteristics of a wise
and good reign. And yet it seems proper to mention, under a distinct head, some particular instances that have not been touched,
wherein this wisdom and goodness will exert themselves.

Now, though the true interest of several states may be the same
in many respects, yet is there always some difference to be perceived, by a discerning eye, both in these interests, and in the
manner of pursuing them; a difference that arises from the situation
of countries, from the character of people,* from the nature of
government, and even from that of climate and soil; from circumstances that are, like these, permanent, and from others that may

---

* Patriot] *1749*   * people] the people

[63] One of the most famous of London's prisons.
[64] '. . . the safe, level path of religion, justice, honour, and moral virtues': Bacon, *De
Augmentis Scientiarum*, I. 1, in *Opera Omnia*, I, *32*.

be deemed more accidental. To illustrate all this by examples, would be easy, but long. I shall content myself therefore to mention, in some instances only*, the difference that arises from the causes referred to, between the true interest of our country, and that of some or all our* neighbours on the continent: and leave to extend and apply in own thoughts the comparison I shall hint at, rather than enlarge upon.

The situation of Great Britain, the character of her people, and the nature of her government, fit her for trade and commerce. Her climate and her soil make them necessary to her well being. By trade and commerce we grow a rich and powerful nation, and by their decay we are growing poor and impotent. As trade and commerce enrich, so they fortify, our country. The sea is our barrier, ships are our fortresses, and the mariners, that trade and commerce alone can furnish, are the garrisons to defend them. France lies under great disadvantages in trade and commerce, by the nature of her government. Her advantages, in situation, are as great at least as ours. Those that arise, from the temper and character of her people, are a little different perhaps, and yet upon the whole equivalent. Those of her climate and her soil are superior to ours, and indeed to those of any European nation. The United Provinces have the same advantages that we have in the nature of their government, more perhaps in the temper and character of their people, less to be sure in their situation, climate, and soil. But, without descending into a longer* detail of the advantages and disadvantages attending each of these nations in trade and commerce, it is sufficient for my present purpose to observe, that Great Britain stands in a certain middle between the other two, with regard to wealth and power arising from these springs. A less, and a less constant, application* to the improvement of these may serve the ends of France; a greater is necessary in this country; and a greater still in Holland. The French may improve their natural wealth and power by the improvement of trade and commerce. We can have no wealth, nor*

---

* some instances only] *1749*   * our] of our
* II. [*footnote* II. The particular and true Interest of *Great Britain* from its Situation, Character, and Form of Government.]
* are growing] grow
* longer] lower
* A less, and a less constant, application] A less Application, and a less constant one
* nor] no

power by consequence, as Europe is now constituted, without the improvement of them, nor in any degree but proportionably to this improvement. The Dutch cannot subsist without them. They bring wealth to other nations, and are necessary to the well being of them; but they supply the Dutch with food and raiment, and are necessary even to their being.

The result of what has been said is in general, that the wealth and power of all nations depending so much* on their trade and commerce, and every nation being,* like the three I have mentioned, in such different circumstances of advantage or disadvantage in the pursuit of this common interest; a good government, and therefore* the government of a Patriot King, will be directed constantly to make the most of every advantage that nature has given, or art can procure, towards the improvement of trade and commerce. And this is one of the principal criterions by which we are to judge, whether governors are in the true interest of the people or not.

It results, in particular, that Great Britain might improve her wealth and power in a proportion superior to that of any nation who can be deemed her rival, if the advantages she has were as wisely cultivated, as they will be in the reign of a Patriot King. To be convinced more thoroughly of this truth, a very short process of reasoning will suffice. Let any man who has knowledge enough for it, first compare the natural state of Great Britain, and of the United Provinces, and then their artificial state together; that is, let him consider minutely the advantages we have by the situation, extent, and nature of our island, over the inhabitants of a few salt marshes gained on the sea, and hardly defended from it: and after that, let him consider how nearly these provinces have raised themselves to an equality of wealth and power with the kingdom of Great Britain. From whence arises this difference of improvement? It arises plainly from hence: the Dutch have been, from the foundation of their commonwealth, a nation of patriots and merchants. The spirit of that people has not been diverted from these two objects, the defence of their liberty, and the improvement of their trade and commerce: which have been carried on by them with uninterrupted

* depending so much] depend much
* being,] is
* and therefore] therefore, and consequently

and unslackened application, industry, order, and economy. In Great Britain the case has not been the same, in either respect; but here we confine ourselves to speak of the last alone.

Trade and commerce, such as they were in those days, had been sometimes, and in some instances, before the reign of Queen Elizabeth, encouraged and improved: but the great encouragements were given, the great extensions and improvements were made, by that glorious princess. To her we owe that spirit of domestic and foreign trade which is not quite extinguished. It was she who gave that rapid motion to our whole mercantile system which is not entirely ceased. They both flagged under her successor; were not revived under his son; were checked, diverted, clogged, and interrupted, during our civil wars; and began to exert new vigour after the Restoration, in a long course of peace; but met with new difficulties, too, from the confirmed rivalry of the Dutch, and the growing rivalry of the French. To one of these the pusillanimous* character of James the First gave many scandalous occasions: and the other was favoured by the conduct of Charles the Second, who never was in the true interest of the people he governed. From the Revolution to the death of Queen Anne, however trade and commerce might be aided and encouraged in other respects, they were necessarily subjected to depredations abroad, and overloaded by taxes at home, during the course of two great wars.[65] From the accession of the late king to this hour, in the midst of a full peace, the debts of the nation continue much the same, the taxes have been increased, and for eighteen years of this time we have tamely* suffered continual depredations from the most contemptible maritime power in Europe, that of Spain.[66]

A Patriot King will neither neglect nor sacrifice his country's interest. No other interest, neither a foreign nor a domestic, neither a public nor a private, will influence his conduct in government. He

* pusillanimous] posthumous
* tamely] *1749*

[65] The Nine Years War (1688–97) and the War of the Spanish Succession (1702–13).
[66] The *Patriot King* was drafted in the aftermath of the Convention of Pardo (1738), which reconciled Britain and Spain in the aftermath of numerous commercial grievances, including the seizure of British *guardacostas* in the Caribbean. These insults were greatly resented by the merchant community, and popular protest ultimately helped to drive Walpole's administration into the War of Jenkins's Ear in 1739.

will not multiply taxes wantonly nor keep up those unnecessarily which necessity has laid, that he may keep up legions of tax-gatherers. He will not continue national debts, by all sorts of political and other profusion; nor, more wickedly still, by a settled purpose of oppressing and impoverishing the people; that he may with greater ease corrupt some, and govern the whole, according to the dictates of his passions and arbitrary will. To give ease and encouragement to manufactory at home, to assist and protect trade abroad, to improve and keep in heart the national colonies, like so many farms of the mother country, will be principal and constant parts of the attention of such a prince. The wealth of the nation he will most justly esteem to be his wealth, the power his power, the security and the honour, his security and honour; and, by the very means by which he promotes the two first, he will wisely preserve the two last; for by these means, and by these alone, can the great advantage of the situation of this kingdom be taken and improved.

Great Britain is an island: and, whilst nations on the continent are at immense charge in maintaining their barriers, and perpetually on their guard, and frequently embroiled, to extend or strengthen them, Great Britain may, if her governors please, accumulate wealth in maintaining hers; make herself secure from invasions, and be ready to invade others when her own immediate interest, or the general interest of Europe require it. Of all which Queen Elizabeth's reign is a memorable example, and undeniable proof. I said the general interest of Europe; because it seems to me that this, alone, should call our councils off from an almost entire application to their domestic and proper business. Other nations must watch over every motion of their neighbours; penetrate, if they can, every design; foresee every minute event; and take part by some engagement or other in almost every conjuncture that arises. But as we cannot be easily nor suddenly attacked, and as we ought not to aim at any acquisition of territory on the continent, it may be our interest to watch the secret workings of the several councils abroad; to advise, and warn; to abet, and oppose; but it never can be our true interest easily and officiously to enter into action, much less into engagements that imply action and expense. Other nations, like

---

* tamely] *1749*
* into action . . . and expense.] into Engagements, much less into Action.

the *velites* or light-armed troops, stand foremost in the field, and skirmish perpetually. When a great war begins, we ought to look on the powers of the continent, to whom we incline, like the two first lines, the *principes* and *hastati* of a Roman army: and on ourselves, like the *triarii*,[67] that are not to charge with these legions on every occasion, but to be ready for the conflict whenever the fortune of the day, be it sooner or later*, calls us to it, and the sum of things, or the general interest, makes it necessary.

This is that post of advantage and honour, which our singular situation among the powers of Europe determines us, or should determine us, to take, in all disputes that happen on the continent. If we neglect it, and dissipate our strength on occasions that touch us remotely or indirectly, we are governed by men who do not know the true interest of this island, or who have some other interest more at heart. If we adhere to it, so at least as to deviate little and seldom from it, as we shall do whenever we are wisely and honestly governed, then will this nation make her proper figure: and a great one it will be. By a continual attention to improve her natural, that is her maritime strength, by collecting all her forces within herself, and reserving them to be laid out on great occasions, such as regard her immediate interests and her honour, or such as are truly important to the general system of power in Europe; she may be the arbitrator of differences, the guardian of liberty, and the preserver of that balance, which has been so much talked of, and is so little understood.

'Are we never to be soldiers?' you will say. Yes, constantly, in such proportion as is necessary for the defence of good government. To establish such* a military force as none but bad governors can want, is to establish tyrannical power in the King or in the ministers; and may be wanted by the latter, when the former would be secure without his army, if he broke his minister. Occasionally too we must be soldiers, and for offence as well as defence; but in proportion to the nature of the conjuncture, considered always relatively to the difference here insisted upon between our situation, our interest, and the nature of our strength, compared with those of the other

---

* be it sooner or later] *1749*   * such] *1749*

[67] The *principes* were the front line of the Roman battle array, with the *hastati* behind them, and the *triarii* bringing up the rear; compare Livy, *Histories*, VIII. 8–9, and Machiavelli, *Discorsi*, II. 16.

powers of Europe; and not in proportion to the desires, or even to the wants, of the nations with whom we are confederated. Like other amphibious animals, we must come occasionally on shore, but the water is more properly our element, and in it, like them, as we find our greatest security, so we exert our greatest force.

What I touch upon here, very shortly, deserves to be considered, and reconsidered, by every man who has, or may have, any share in the government of Great Britain. For we have not only departed too much from our true national interest in this respect; but we have done so with the general applause even of well-meaning men, who did not discern that we wasted ourselves by an improper application of our strength in conjunctures when we might have served the common cause far more usefully, nay with entire effect, by a proper application of our natural strength. There was something more than this. Armies grew so much into fashion, in time of war, among men who meant well to their country, that they who mean ill to it have kept, and keep them still up in the profoundest peace: and* the number of our soldiers, in this island alone, is* almost double to that of our seamen.[68] That they are kept up against foreign enemies, cannot be said with any colour. If they are kept for show, they are ridiculous. If* they are kept for any other purpose whatever, they are too dangerous to be suffered. A Patriot King, seconded* by ministers attached to the true interest of their country, would soon reform this abuse,* and save a great part of this* expense; or apply it, in a manner preferable even to the saving it, to the maintenance of a body of marine* foot, and to the charge of a register of thirty or forty thousand seamen. But no thoughts like these, no great designs for the honour and interest of the kingdom, will be entertained, till* men who have this honour and interest at heart arise to power.

* and] till   * is] become
* be said . . . ridiculous; if] always be said with Colour. If they are kept for Shew, and are look'd on as the Play-things of Kings, they are ridiculous. If
* seconded] supported
* would soon reform this abuse] can soon reform any Abuse of this kind
* this] the   * of marine] of three or four Thousand Marine
* But no thoughts . . . entertained, till] And I will venture to say, that Thoughts like these, and Designs like these for the Honour and Interest of the Kingdom, will be entertained, whenever

[68] In fact, during the War of Austrian Succession (1739–48), the average annual personnel of the army was 62,375, of the navy, 50,313.

I come now to the last head under which I shall consider the character and conduct of a Patriot King; and let it not be thought to be of the least importance, though it may seem, at the first mention,* to concern appearances rather than realities, and to be nothing more than a circumstance contained in or implied by the great parts of the character and conduct of such a king. It is of his personal behaviour, of his manner of living with other men, and, in a word, of his private as well as public life that I mean* to speak. It is of that* decency and grace, that *bienséance* of the French, that *decorum* of the Latins, that πρεπον, of the Greeks, which can never be reflected on any character that is not laid* in virtue:[69] but for want of which,* a character that is so laid* will lose, at all times, part of the lustre belonging to it, and may be sometimes not a little misunderstood and undervalued. Beauty is not separable from health, nor this lustre, said the Stoics, from virtue; but as a man may be healthful without being handsome, so he may be virtuous without being amiable.

There are certain finishing strokes, a last hand as we commonly say, to be given to all the works of art. When that is not given, we may see the excellency of a general design, and the beauty of some particular parts. A judge of the art may see further; he may allow for what is wanting, and discern the full merit of a complete work in one that is imperfect. But vulgar eyes will not be so struck. The work will appear to them defective, because* unfinished: so that

---

* I come now to my last head . . . superior strength and power in life (p. 292).] *1749* [= revised text of 'Letter III. Of the Private Life of a Prince'; see 'Note on Texts', p. xliv.]
* I come now . . . be thought] You observe, that among the several Heads under which I have consider'd the Character and Conduct of a Patriot King, I omitted to take notice of One, which you rightly judge not
* at the first mention,] at first
* private as well as public life that I mean] *Private Life*, that you desire me to speak.
* It is of that] ¶ Let me begin then by saying, That all the
* that *bienséance* . . . not laid] (the *Bienseance* of the French, and *Decorum* of the Latins) which becomes this high Character, can never be reflected on this or on any Character, that is not founded
* which] this   * laid] *1749*   * because] and (as it is)

[69] Cicero, *De Officiis*, I. 93. Compare Lord Chesterfield's letter to his son, 24 July 1739: 'I hope by these examples, you understand the meaning of the word *Decency*; which in French is *Bienséance*; in Latin *Decorum*; and in Greek Πρεπον' Chesterfield, *Letters*, ed. David Roberts (Oxford, 1992), 13.

without knowing precisely what they dislike, they may admire, but they will not be pleased. Thus in moral characters, though every part be virtuous and great, or though the few and small defects in it be concealed under the blaze of those shining qualities that compensate for them; yet is not this enough even in private life: it is less so in public life, and still less so in that of a prince.

There is a certain *species liberalis*,[70] more easily understood than explained, and felt than defined, that must be acquired and rendered habitual to him. A certain propriety of words and actions, that results* from their conformity to nature and character, must always accompany him, and create an air and manner that run uniformly through the whole tenor of his conduct and behaviour: which air and manner are* so far from any kind or degree or affectation, that they cannot be attained except by him who is void of all affectation. We may illustrate this to ourselves, and make it more sensible, by reflecting on the conduct of good dramatic or epic writers. They draw the characters, which they bring on the scene, from nature, they sustain them through the whole piece, and make their actors neither say nor do any thing that is not exactly proper to the character each of them represents. *Oderint dum metuant*[71] came properly out of the mouth of a tyrant; but Euripides would never have put that execrable sentence into the mouth of Minos or Aeacus.[72]

A man of sense and virtue both will not fall into any great impropriety of character, or indecency of conduct: but he may slide or be surprised into small ones, from a thousand reasons, and in a thousand manners, which I shall not stay to enumerate. Against these, therefore, even* men, who are incapable of falling into the others, must be still on their guard, and no men so much as princes. When their minds are filled and their hearts warmed with true notions of government, when they know their duty, and love their people, they will not fail in the great parts they are to act, in the council, in the field, and in all the arduous affairs that belong to their kingly office:

---

* results] result   * behaviour: which air and manner are] Behaviour. This air and manner must be   * even] *1749*

[70] 'Gentlemanly appearance': Cicero, *De Officiis*, I. 96; I. 141.
[71] 'Let them hate, so long as they are afraid': Lucius Attius, *Atreus*, cit. Cicero, *De Officiis*, I. 97.
[72] Minos was the legendary king of Crete; like Aeacus, the grandfather of Achilles, he became a judge in the underworld.

at least they will not begin to fail, by failing in them. But as they are men susceptible of the same impressions, liable to the same errors, and exposed to the same passions, so they are likewise exposed to more and stronger temptations than others. Besides, the elevation in which they are placed, as it gives them great advantages, gives them great disadvantages too, that often countervail the former. Thus, for instance, a little merit in a prince is seen and felt by numbers: it is multiplied, as it were, and in proportion to this effect his reputation is raised by it. But then, a little failing is seen and felt by numbers too: it is multiplied in the same manner, and his reputation sinks in the same proportion.

I spoke above of defects that may be concealed under the blaze of great and shining qualities. This may be the case; it* has been that of some princes. There goes a tradition that Henry the Fourth of France asked a Spanish ambassador, what mistresses the king of Spain had? The ambassador replied, like a formal pedant, that his master was a prince who feared God, and had no mistress* but the queen. Henry the Fourth felt the reflection, and asked him in return, with some contempt, 'Whether his master had not virtues enough to cover one vice?'[73] The faults or defects, that may be thus covered or compensated, are, I think, those of the man, rather than those of the king; such as arise from constitution, and the natural rather than the moral character; such as may be deemed accidental starts of passion, or accidental remissness in some unguarded hours; surprises, if I may say so, of the man on the king. When these happen seldom, and pass soon, they may be hid like spots in the sun: but they are spots still. He who has the means of seeing them, will see them: and he who has not, may feel the effects of them without knowing precisely the cause. When they continue (for here is the danger, because, if they continue, they will increase) they are spots no longer: they spread a general shade, and obscure the light in which they were drowned before. The virtues of the king are lost in the vices of the man.

---

* it] as it
* mistress] mistresses

---

[73] This anecdote is attributed to the French historian Pierre Matthieu in Louis Laurent Prault, *L'Esprit de Henri IV* (Paris, 1770), Eng. trans., *Interesting Anecdotes of Henry IV of France* (2 vols., London, n.d.), I, 222.

Alexander had violent passions, and those for wine and women were predominant, after his ambition. They were spots in his character before they prevailed by the force of habit: as soon as they began to do so, the king and the hero appeared less, the rake and bully more. Persepolis was burnt at the instigation of Thais, and Clytus was killed in a drunken brawl.[74] He repented indeed of these two horrible actions, and was again the king and hero upon many occasions; but he had not been enough on his guard, when the strongest incitements to vanity and to sensual pleasures offered themselves at every moment to him: and, when he stood in all his easy hours surrounded by women and eunuchs, by the panders, parasites, and buffoons of a voluptuous court, they, who could not approach the king, approached the man, and by seducing the man, they betrayed the king. His faults became habits. The Macedonians, who did not or would not see the one, saw the other; and he fell a sacrifice to their resentments, to their fears, and to those factions that will arise under an odious government, as well as under one that grows into contempt.

Other characters might be brought to contrast with this; the first Scipio Africanus, for example, or the eldest Cato:[75] and there will be no objection to a comparison of such citizens of Rome, as these were, with kings of the first magnitude. Now the reputation of the first Scipio was not so clear and uncontroverted in private as in public life; nor was he allowed by all, to be a man of such severe virtue, as he affected, and as that age required. Naevius was thought to mean him in some verses Gellius has preserved: and Valerius Antias made no scruple to assert, that, far from restoring the fair Spaniard to her family, he debauched and kept her.[76] Notwithstanding this, what authority did he not maintain? In what esteem and veneration did he not live and die? With what panegyrics has not

---

[74] Plutarch, *Life of Alexander*, XXVII; L–LI. Thais was Alexander's mistress; Clytus, Alexander's best friend.

[75] Publius Cornelius Scipio Africanus Major (237–183 BCE), the conqueror of Hannibal in the Second Punic War, was renowned for his patriotism and continence; Marcus Porcius Cato ('the Elder') (234–149 BCE) was also legendary for his virtue.

[76] Aulus Gellius, *Noctes Atticae*, VII. 8. 5–6; compare Livy, *Histories*, XXVI. 50, where Scipio famously returned a female prisoner to her parents and her betrothed, a Celtiberian chieftain. Bolingbroke also records this episode in the *Letters on the Study and Use of History*, 'Letter III'.

the whole torrent of writers rolled down his reputation even to these days? This could not have happened, if the vice imputed to him had shown itself in any scandalous appearances, to eclipse the lustre of the general, the consul, or the citizen. The same reflection might be extended to Cato, who loved wine as well as Scipio* loved women. Men did not judge in the days of the elder Cato perhaps, as Seneca was ready to do in those of the younger,* that drunkenness could be no crime if Cato drank: but Cato's passion, as well as that of Scipio, was subdued and kept under by his public character. His virtue warmed instead of cooling, by this indulgence to his genius or natural temper: and one may gather, from what Tully puts into his mouth, in the treatise concerning old age, that even his love of wine was rendered subservient, instead of doing hurt, to the measures he pursued in his public character.[77]

Give me leave to insist a little on the two first Caesars, and on Mark Antony. I quote none of them as good men, but I may quote them all as great men, and therefore properly in this place; since a Patriot King must avoid the defects that diminish a great character, as well as those that corrupt a good one. Old Curio called Julius Caesar the husband of every wife, and the wife of every husband, referring to his known adulteries, and to the compliances that he was suspected of in his youth for Nicomedes. Even his own soldiers, in the licence of a triumph, sung lampoons on him for his profusion as well as lewdness.[78] The youth of Augustus was defamed as much as that of Julius Caesar, and both as much as that of Antony. When Rome was ransacked by the panders of Augustus, and matrons and virgins were stripped and searched, like slaves in a market, to choose the fittest to satisfy his lust, did Antony do more? When Julius set no bounds to his debauches in Egypt, except those that* satiety imposed, *postquam epulis bacchoque modum lassata voluptas imposuit*,[79] when he trifled away his time with Cleopatra in the very crisis of the civil war, and till his troops refused to follow him any further in his effeminate progress up the Nile – did Antony do

---

* Scipio] the other   * the days . . . the younger] those days, as *Seneca* was
  ready to do in his   * that] *1749*

[77] Cicero, *De Senectute*, XII–XIV.
[78] Suetonius, *Life of Julius Caesar*, LII. 3; XLIX. 1–2, 4.
[79] '. . . after his exhausted lust set the limit to his feasting and drinking': Lucan, *Pharsalia*, X. 172–3.

more? No; all three had vices which would have been so little borne in any former age of Rome, that no man could have raised himself, under the weight of them, to popularity and to power. But we must not wonder that the people, who bore the tyrants, bore the libertines; nor that indulgence was shown to the vices of the great, in a city where universal corruption and profligacy of manners were established: and yet even in this city, and among these degenerate Romans, certain it is, that different appearances, with the same vices, helped to maintain the Caesars, and ruined Antony. I might produce many anecdotes to show how the two former saved appearances whilst their vices were the most flagrant, and made so much amends for the appearances they had not saved, by those of a contrary kind, that a great part at least of all which was said to defame them might pass, and did pass, for the calumny of party.

But Antony threw off all decorum from the first, and continued to do so to the last. Not only vice, but indecency became habitual to him. He ceased to be a general, a consul, a triumvir, a citizen of Rome. He became an Egyptian king, sunk into luxurious effeminacy, and proved he was unfit to govern men, by suffering himself to be governed by a woman. His vices hurt him, but his habits ruined him. If a political modesty at least had made him disguise the first, they would have hurt him less, and he might have escaped the last: but he was so little sensible of this, that in a fragment of one of his letters to Augustus, which Suetonius has preserved, he endeavours to justify himself by pleading this very habit. 'What matter is it whom* we lie with?' says he: 'this letter may find you perhaps with Tertulla, or Terentilla', or others that he names. 'I lie with Cleopatra, and have I not done so these nine* years?'[80]

These great examples, which I have produced, not to encourage vice, but to show more strongly the advantages of decency in private behaviour,* may appear in some sort figures bigger than the life. Few virtues and few vices grow up, in these parts of the world and these latter ages, to the size of those I have mentioned; and none have such scenes wherein to exert themselves. But the truths I am

---

* whom] who   * nine] two
* not to encourage . . . private behaviour] *1749*

[80] Suetonius, *Life of Augustus*, LXIX. 2. Tertulla (or Tertia) was the sister of Brutus, Terentilla the wife of Maecenas.

desirous to inculcate will be as justly delivered in this manner, and perhaps more strongly felt. Failings or vices that flow from the same source of human nature, that run the same course through the conduct of princes, and have the same effects on their characters, and consequently on their government and their fortune, have all the proportion necessary to my application of them. It matters little whether a prince, who abandons that common decorum which results from nature and which reason prescribes, abandons the particular decorums of this country or that, of this age or that, which result from mode, and which custom exacts. It matters little, for instance, whether a prince gives himself up to the more gross luxury of the west, or to the more refined luxury of the east; whether he become the slave of a domestic harlot, or of a foreign queen; in short, whether he forget himself in the arms of one whore or of twenty; and whether he imitate Antony, or a king of Achin, who is reported to have passed his whole time in a seraglio, eating, drinking, chewing betel, playing with women, and talking of cock-fighting.[81]

To sum up the whole and* draw to a conclusion: this decency, this grace, this propriety of manners to character, is so essential to princes in particular, that whenever it is neglected their virtues lose a great degree of lustre, and their defects acquire much aggravation. Nay more; by neglecting this decency and this grace, and for want of a sufficient regard to appearances, even their virtues may betray them into failings, their failings into vices, and their vices into habits unworthy of princes and unworthy of men.

The constitutions of governments, and the different tempers and characters of people, may be thought justly to deserve some consideration, in determining the behaviour of princes in private life as well as in public; and to put a difference, for instance, between the decorum of a king of France, and that of a king of Great Britain.

Louis the Fourteenth was king in an absolute monarchy, and reigned over a people whose genius makes it as fit* perhaps to impose

---

    * sum up the whole and] *1749*   * as fit] fitter

[81] Achin is a region in the north of Sumatra; on the luxurious habits of its ruler, see 'The Voyage of Captaine John Davis, to the Easterne Indies . . .' in Samuel Purchas, *Hakluytus Posthumus or Purchas His Pilgrimes* (5 vols., London, 1625), I, ii, 122.

on them by admiration and awe, as* to gain and hold them by affection. Accordingly he kept great state; was haughty, was reserved; and all he said or did appeared to be forethought and planned. His regard to appearances was such, that when his mistress was the wife of another man, and he had children by her every year, he endeavoured to cover her constant residence at court by a place she filled about the queen: and he dined and supped and cohabited with the latter in every apparent respect as if he had had no mistress at all.[82] Thus he raised a great reputation; he was revered by his subjects, and admired by his neighbours: and this was due principally to the art with which he managed appearances, so as to set off his virtues, to disguise his failings and his vices, and by his example and authority to keep a veil drawn over the futility and debauch of his court.

His successor, not to the throne, but to the sovereign power, was a mere rake, with some wit, and no morals;[83] nay, with so little regard to them, that he made them a subject of ridicule in discourse, and appeared in his whole conduct more profligate, if that could be, than he was in principle. The difference between these characters soon appeared in abominable effects; such as, cruelty apart, might recall the memory of Nero, or, in the other sex, that of Messalina, and such as I leave the chroniclers of scandal to relate.

Our Elizabeth was queen in a limited monarchy, and reigned over a people at all times more easily led than driven; and at that time capable of being attached to their prince and their country, by a more generous principle than any of those which prevail in our days, by affection. There was a strong prerogative then in being, and the crown was in possession of greater legal power. Popularity was, however, then, as it is now, and as it must be always in mixed government, the sole true foundation of that sufficient authority and influence, which other constitutions give the prince gratis, and independently of the people, but which a king of this nation must acquire. The wise queen saw it, and she saw too, how much popularity depends on those appearances, that depend on the decorum, the decency, the grace, and the propriety of behaviour of which we

---

* as] than

[82] Françoise Athénaïs de Rochehouart, Marquise de Montespan (1641–1707), mistress of Louis XIV 1668–80, and mother of six of his children.
[83] Philippe, Duc d'Orléans (1674–1723), Regent of France 1715–23.

are speaking. A warm concern for the interest and honour of the nation, a tenderness for her people, and a confidence in their affections, were appearances that ran through her whole public conduct, and gave life and colour to it. She did great things, and she knew how to set them off according to their full value, by her manner of doing them. In her private behaviour she showed great affability, she descended even to familiarity; but her familiarity was such as could not be imputed to her weakness, and was, therefore, most justly ascribed to her goodness. Though a woman, she hid all that was womanish about her: and if a few equivocal marks of coquetry appeared on some occasions, they passed like flashes of lightning, vanished as soon as they were discerned, and imprinted no blot on her character. She had private friendships, she had favourites: but she never suffered her friends to forget she was their queen; and when her favourites did, she made them feel that she was so.

Her successor had* no virtues to set off, but he had failings and vices to conceal. He could not conceal the latter; and, void of the former, he could not compensate for them. His failings and his vices therefore standing in full view, he passed for a weak prince and an ill man; and fell into all the contempt wherein his memory remains to this day. The methods he took, to preserve himself from it, served but to confirm him in it. No man can keep the decorum of manners in life, who is not free from every kind of affectation, as it has been said already: but he who affects what he has no pretensions to, or what is improper to his character and rank in the world, is guilty of most consummate folly; he becomes doubly ungracious, doubly indecent, and quite ridiculous. James the First, not having one quality to conciliate the esteem or affection of his people to him, endeavoured to impose in their understandings; and to create a respect for himself, by preaching the most extravagant notions about kings in general, as if they were middle beings between God and other men; and by comparing the extent and unsearchable mysteries of their power and prerogative to those of the divine providence. His language and his behaviour were commonly suited to such foolish pretensions; and thus, by assuming a claim to such respect and submission as were not due to him, he lost a great part of what was due to him. In short, he begun at the wrong end; for

* successor had] Successor, *James* the First, had

though the shining qualities of the king may cover some failings and some vices that do not grow up to strong habits in the man, yet must the character of a great and good king be founded in that of a great and good man. A king who lives out of the sight of his subjects, or is never seen by them except on his throne, can scarce be despised as a man, though he may be hated as a king. But the king who lives more in their sight, and more under their observation, may be despised before he is hated, and even without being hated. This happened to King James: a thousand circumstances brought it to pass, and none more than the indecent weaknesses he had for his minions. He did not endeavour to cure this contempt and raise his character, only by affecting what he had no pretensions to, as in the former case; but he endeavoured likewise most vainly to do it by affecting what was improper to his character and rank. He did not endeavour indeed to disguise his natural pusillanimity and timidity under the mask of a bully, whilst* he was imposed upon and insulted by all his neighbours, and above all by the Spaniards; but he retailed the scraps of Buchanan,[84] affected to talk much, figured in church controversies, and put on all the pedantic appearances of a scholar, whilst he neglected all those of a great and good man, as well as king.

Let not princes flatter themselves. They will be examined closely, in private as well as in public life: and those, who cannot pierce further, will judge of them by the appearances they give in both. To obtain true popularity, that which is founded in esteem and affection, they must, therefore, maintain their characters in both; and to that end neglect appearances in neither, but observe the decorum necessary to preserve the esteem, whilst they win the affections of mankind. Kings, they must never forget that they are men; men, they must never forget that they are kings. The sentiments, which one of these reflections of course inspires, will give a humane and affable air to their whole behaviour, and make them taste in that high elevation all the joys of social life. The sentiments, that the other reflection suggests, will be found very compatible

* bully, whilst] Bully, nor wear a long Sword, look fierce, and talk big, whilst

[84] George Buchanan (1506–82), Scottish humanist and republican resistance theorist, had been tutor to the young King James in Scotland. James rarely cites him but to attack him.

with the former: and they may never forget that they are kings, though they do not always carry the crown on their heads, nor the sceptre in their hands. Vanity and folly must entrench themselves in a constant affectation of state, to preserve regal dignity: a wise prince will know how to preserve it when he lays his majesty aside. He will dare to appear a private man, and in that character he will draw to himself a respect less ostentatious, but more real and more pleasing* to him, than any which is paid to the monarch. By never saying what is unfit for him to say, he will never hear what is unfit for him to hear. By never doing what is unfit for him to do, he will never see what is unfit for him to see. Decency and propriety of manners are so far from lessening the pleasures of life, that they refine them, and give them a higher taste: they are so far from restraining the free and easy commerce of social life, that they banish the bane of it, licentiousness of behaviour. Ceremony is the barrier against this abuse of liberty in public; politeness and decency are so in private: and the prince, who practises and exacts them, will amuse himself much better, and oblige those, who have the honour to be in his intimacy and to share his pleasures with him, much more, than he could possibly do by the most absolute and unguarded familiarity.

That which is here recommended to princes, that constant guard on their own behaviour even in private life, and that constant decorum which their example ought to exact from others, will not be found so difficult in practice as may be imagined; if they use a proper discernment in the choice of the persons whom they admit to the nearest degrees of intimacy with them. A prince should choose his companions with as great care as his ministers. If he trusts the business of his state to these, he trusts his character to those; and his character will depend on theirs much more than is commonly thought. General* experience will lead men to judge that a similitude of character determined the choice; even when* chance, indulgence to assiduity, good nature, or want of reflection, had their share in the introduction of men unworthy of such favour. But, in such cases,* certain it is that they, who judged wrong at first concerning him, will judge right at last. He is not a trifler, for instance. Be it so: but if he takes trifling, futile creatures, men of mean characters, or of no character, into his intimacy, he shows a dispo-

---

* pleasing] agreeable
* to those; . . . thought. General] to those. Not only general
* the choice; even when] it; but if   * But, in such cases,] *1749*

sition to become such; and will become such, unless he breaks these habits early, and before puerile amusements are grown up to be the business of his life.* I mean, that the minds of princes, like the minds of other men, will be brought down insensibly to the tone of the company they keep.*

A worse consequence, even than this, may follow a want of discernment in princes how to choose their companions, and how to conduct themselves in private life. Silly kings have resigned themselves to their ministers, have suffered these to stand between them and their people, and have formed no judgments, nor taken any measures on their own knowledge, but all implicitly on the representations made to them by their* ministers. Kings of superior capacity have resigned themselves in the same manner to their favourites, male and female, have suffered these to stand between them and their most able and faithful counsellors: their judgments have been influenced, and their measures directed by insinuations of women, or of men as little fitted as women, by nature and education, to be hearkened to, in the great affairs of government. History is full of such examples; all melancholy, many tragical! Sufficient, one would imagine, to deter princes, if attended to,* from permitting the companions of their idle hours, or the instruments of their pleasures, to exceed the bounds of those provinces. Should a minister of state pretend to vie with any of these, about the forms of a drawing-room, the regulation of a ruelle,[85] the decoration of a ball, or the dress of a fine lady, he would be thought ridiculous, and he would be truly so. But then are not any of these impertinent, when they presume* to meddle in things at least as much above them, as those that have been mentioned are below the others? And are not princes, who suffer them to do so, unaccountably weak?

What shall I say further on this head? Nothing more is necessary. Let me wind it up, therefore, by asserting this great truth, that results from what has been already said. As he can never fill the

---

* He is not . . . his life] *1749*
* keep.] keep. They are not *Triflers* for Instance. Be it so: But if they take Men of mean Characters, or of no Characters, into their Intimacy, they show a Disposition to *become* such; unless they break those Habits *early*, and before puerile Amusements are grown up to be the business of their Lives.
* their] those
* Sufficient, one . . . attended to] Sufficient, if attended to (one would imagine) to deter Princes.　　* presume] pretend

[85] A morning reception in a lady's bedchamber.

character of a Patriot King, though his personal great and good qualities be in every other respect equal to it, who lies open to the flattery of courtiers, to the seduction of women, and to the partialities and affections which are easily contracted by too great indulgence in private life; so the prince, who is desirous to establish this character, must observe such a decorum, and keep such a guard on himself, as may prevent even the suspicion of being liable to such influences. For as the reality would ruin, the very suspicion will lessen him in the opinion of mankind: and the opinion of mankind, which is fame after death, is superior strength and power in life.

And now, if* the principles and measures of conduct, laid down in this discourse, as necessary to constitute that greatest and most glorious* of human beings, a Patriot King, be* sufficient to this purpose; let us* consider, too, how easy it is, or ought to be, to establish them in the minds of princes. They are founded on true propositions, all of which are obvious, nay, many of them self-evident.* They are confirmed by universal experience. In a word, no understanding can resist them, and none but the weakest can fail, or be misled, in the application of them. To a prince, whose heart is corrupt, it is in vain to speak: and, for such a prince, I would not be thought to write. But if the heart of a prince be not corrupt, these truths will find an easy ingression, through the understanding, to it. Let us consider* again, what the sure, the necessary effects of such principles and measures of conduct must be, to the prince, and to the people. On this subject let the* imagination range through the whole glorious scene of a patriot reign: the beauty of the idea will inspire* those transports, which Plato imagined the vision of virtue would inspire, if virtue could be seen.[86] What* in truth can be so lovely, what so venerable, as to

* And now, if] And now Sir, if you think
* glorious] noble
* be] *1749*
* let us] *1749*
* self-evident.] self-evident, and some of them are Objects even of intuitive Knowledge.
* Let us consider] Consider   * the] your   * inspire] give
* seen. What] seen. There will be nothing in it unreasonable, nothing chimerical. What

[86] Plato, *Phaedrus*, 250D, cit. Cicero, *De Finibus* II. 16. 52; compare *Dissertation upon Parties*, p. 122.

contemplate a king on whom the eyes of a whole people are fixed, filled with admiration, and glowing with affection? A king, in the temper of whose government, like that of Nerva, things so seldom allied as empire and liberty are intimately mixed,[87] co-exist together inseparably, and constitute one real essence? What spectacle can be presented to the view of the mind so rare, so nearly divine, as a king possessed of absolute* power, neither usurped by fraud, nor maintained by force, but the genuine effect of esteem, of confidence, and affection;* the free gift of liberty, who finds her greatest security in this power, and would desire no other if the prince on the throne could be, what his people wish him to be, immortal? Of such a prince, and of such a prince alone, it may be said with strict propriety and truth,*

> Volentes
> Per populos dat jura, viamque affectat Olympo.[88]

Civil fury will have no place in this draft: or, if the monster is seen, he must be seen as Virgil describes him,

> Centum vinctus ahenis
> Post tergum nodis, fremit horridus ore cruento.[89]

He must be seen subdued, bound, chained, and deprived entirely

---

* absolute] an absolute   * of confidence, and affection] and of confidence
* immortal? Of such ... and truth,] Immortal. A Prince, who infusing the Spirit of Liberty into his People, makes them deserve to be free; and who restoring and strengthening the Free Constitution of their Government, rewards them for deserving it: As it is said of the Divinity, that he first infuses Grace to make men virtuous, and then rewards them for being so. One who rescues them from those private Vices, which making them bad Men, introduce those publick Vices which make them bad Citizens; and exalts them to that happiest State of Social Creatures, where Law and Reason, not Will and Passion, are the Rule of Government.

---

[87] '... divus Nerva res olim insociabiles miscuisset, imperium et libertatem': Bacon, *Of the Advancement of Learning* in *Opera Omnia*, II, 439, adapting Tacitus, *Agricola*, III. 2 ('Nerva Caesar res olim dissociabiles miscuerit, principatum et libertatem'). Compare Clarendon, who thought the reign of Charles I a time when '*imperium et libertas* were as well reconciled as possible': Clarendon, *The History of the Rebellion*, ed. W. Dunn Macray (6 vols., Oxford, 1888), I, 96.

[88] '[The conqueror] gives laws to willing nations, and pursues the path to Olympus': Virgil, *Georgics*, IV. 561–2 (of Augustus), cit. Bacon, *De Augmentis Scientiarum*, I. 1, in *Opera Omnia*, I, 56.

[89] '... bound with a hundred brazen knots behind his back, he roars horribly with blood-stained mouth': Virgil, *Aeneid*, I. 295–6.

of power to do hurt. In his place, concord will appear, brooding peace and prosperity on the happy land; joy sitting* in every face, content in every heart; a people unoppressed, undisturbed, unalarmed; busy to improve their private property* and the public stock; fleets covering the ocean,* bringing home wealth by the returns of industry, carrying assistance or terror abroad by the direction of wisdom, and asserting triumphantly* the right and the honour of Great Britain, as far as waters roll and as winds can waft them.*

Those who live to see such happy days, and to act in so glorious a scene, will* perhaps call to mind, with some tenderness of sentiment, when he is no more, a man, who contributed his mite to carry on so good a work, and* who desired life for nothing so much, as to see a king of Great Britain the most popular man in his country, and a Patriot King at the head* of an united people.

* Civil fury . . . joy sitting] Peace and Prosperity will appear thro' his Country; Joy
* property] Properties
* fleets covering the ocean] while their Fleets shall cover the Ocean
* triumphantly] triumphantly thro' the World
* as far as waters roll and as winds can waft them] *1749*
* Those who live . . . scene, will] You Sir, may probably see those happy Days, and live to act in that glorious Scene. If you do, you will
* sentiment, when . . . work, and] Sentiment, a deceased Friend,
* at the head] *1749*

Biographical notes

Bacon, Francis (1561–1626), Baron Verulam, Viscount St Albans. English statesman and philosopher, successively solicitor general, attorney general, privy councillor, Lord Keeper and Lord Chancellor under James I, he was fined, imprisoned and banished from public life on charges (later overturned) of taking bribes. Bolingbroke admired Bacon as much for the mastery of his English prose in the *Essays* as for his pioneering intellectual methods in *The Advancement of Learning* (1605) and *Novum Organon* (1620).

Boulainvilliers, Henri de (1658–1722), French historian and political writer, leading ideologue of the *thèse nobiliaire*, author of the posthumously published historical works, the *Etat de la France*, *Mémoires Historiques* and *Lettres sur les Anciens Parlements de France*, which Bolingbroke attacked in the *Dissertation upon Parties*. His historical and intellectual importance – like Bolingbroke's – was overlooked as long as he was dismissed as simply an aristocratic reactionary.

Burnet, Gilbert (1643–1715), Scottish Whig bishop, historian and controversialist, author of the posthumously published *History of My Own Time* (1723–34) on which Bolingbroke relied for his detailed knowledge of the reigns of Charles II and James II. Burnet was a zealous supporter of toleration and a confidant of William III who was rewarded with the bishopric of Salisbury in return for his pro-Williamite propagandizing during the Glorious Revolution.

Cicero, Marcus Tullius (106–43 BCE), a 'new man' who rose to prominence by means of his eloquence and, as consul in 63 BCE, by

295

his harsh prosecution of the Catilinarian conspiracy; in the declining
years of the Roman Republic, he retired from public life to concen-
trate on rhetoric, political philosophy and ethics, thereby providing
later philosopher-politicians (Bolingbroke among them) with a
model for their retirement and material for their speculations.

Clarendon, Edward Hyde, 1st Earl of (1609–74), English statesman and historian, sat as MP for Wootton Bassett (as Bolingbroke
would do sixty years later) in the Short Parliament. A leading constitutional royalist during the civil wars, Clarendon became chief
counsellor to Charles II in exile and, as Lord Chancellor after 1660,
was the engineer of the Restoration settlement in Church and state.
Impeached in 1667, he spent his remaining years in France, partly in
writing his *History of the Great Rebellion*, which provided a literary
model for Bolingbroke's historiography, just as his political life
foreshadowed Bolingbroke's own triumphs and disasters.

Cornbury, Henry Hyde, Viscount (1710–53), Clarendon's great-
grandson, Tory MP for Oxford University 1732–50, and (before
1735) Jacobite conspirator; a leading figure among the young aristo-
crats who formed a charismatic but ineffectual opposition circle of
'Boy Patriots', he was the dedicatee of the letter 'On the Spirit of
Patriotism' and the *Letters on the Study and Use of History* (1736).

Frederick Louis, Prince of Wales (1707–51), eldest son of
George II and Queen Caroline, despised by his father, despaired of
by his mother, and embraced by the opposition after he quarrelled
with the King in 1737. By his literary and political patronage, Frederick provided a focus of opposition to his father's chief minister,
Walpole, though (as even his closest advisers realized) he was in
great need of the princely counsel that *The Idea of a Patriot King*
hopefully supplied.

Lyttelton, George, Lord (1709–73), equerry and later secretary to
Frederick, Prince of Wales, opposition MP, and leading light among
the 'Boy Patriots' of the late 1730s; a principled opponent of Walpole and prolific political author of both Bolingbrokean humanist
history (*Observations on the Life of Cicero* (1733)) and Montesquieu-
ian political satire (*Letters from a Persian in England* (1735)), Lyttelton was the addressee of *The Idea of a Patriot King*, though by the

time of its publication in 1749 his former opposition to Walpole had become an embarrassment and he asked that all reference to him in the work be removed.

Pope, Alexander (1688–1744), poet and close friend of Bolingbroke, to whom he dedicated the *Essay on Man* (1733–34), a Tory associate of Swift, and later leading light in the Scriblerian club, he held aloof from the practice of opposition politics despite his associations with opposition politicians and poets, and a lingering touch of Jacobitism; Bolingbroke entrusted works to his care, and acted as his literary executor, though he blackened Pope's memory for printing an extensive edition of *The Idea of a Patriot King* against his wishes.

Seneca, Lucius Annaeus (the Younger) (4 BCE–65 CE), philosopher, statesman and dramatist. Once tutor to Nero, he withdrew from the court under political pressure, before committing suicide upon being suspected of plotting to assassinate the emperor. Like Cicero, he provided an important model for the retired statesman, and particularly influenced the epistolary style of philosophizing which Bolingbroke developed while exiled in France.

Walpole, Sir Robert (1676–1745), like Bolingbroke, first entered Parliament in 1701 and held the office of secretary of war (1708). He rose to become Chancellor of the Exchequer after the Whig landslide in the elections of 1714, and weathered the South Sea Bubble crisis to become Chancellor again in 1721. Shrewd management of the House of Commons and the confidence of his monarchs helped him to retain his grip on power until he was unseated as chief minister in 1742, whereafter he went to the Lords as Earl of Orford.

Index of persons

*Subjects marked with an asterisk are treated in the 'Biographical notes'

Walpole, Horatio 3
*Walpole, Sir Robert viii, xi, xiv, xv,
    xxiii, 4, 8, 197, 199, 207, 219, 221
Welwood, James *cit.* 47
Wildman, John *cit.* 102
William I (the Conqueror) 115
William III vii, viii, 36, 46, 50, 66, 67,

70, 71, 72, 74, 80, 97, 102, 171,
    175
William IV xxiii
Wright, John xli
Wyndham, Sir William xvii

York, Duke of *see* James II

Index of subjects

abdication x, 5, 66
absolutism xiv, 21, 94, 115, 119, 209,
    286–7
Achin 286
Act for the Confirmation of Judicial
    Proceedings (1660) 78
Act of Recognition (1604) 13, 78, 79, 80
Act of Settlement (1701) xv, 9, 267
Act of Settlement (Ireland, 1662) 40
Act of Uniformity (1662) 20
advisers 254
alliances 278
ambition 270
aristocracy xix, 98, 125, 127, 135, 139,
    140, 141–2, 146, 152–3, 156, 160,
    164–5, 225, 231; natural xx, 89,
    193–5; see also Lords, House of
army 26, 279, standing xii, xvi, 10, 51,
    63, 92, 102, 117, 279
Athens 212

balance of power: constitutional, 135,
    136; European 10, 277, 278; see also
    property, balance of
Bank of England xi
benevolence, public 6
Bible cit. Deuteronomy 159; Exodus 158;
    Ezra 84; Genesis 203, 210; Joshua
    181, 199, 268; II Kings 252;
    Numbers 159; I Samuel 112; II
    Thessalonians 180
'blue-water' policy x, 277
'Boy Patriots' xix, 208
Breda, Declaration of (1660) 18

Britons, ancient 113

Cabal 24, 25, 40
Capetians 147–8
Cappadocia 111
Carolingians 146
Castile xviii, 132–4, 137–9
casuistry 267
Catholicism, Roman 14; see also popery
'cavaliers' 15, 22, 45
China 225
Church of England ix, x, 6, 7, 16, 17, 19,
    22, 40, 41, 64, 66, 76, 208
civil list 25, 102, 174, 178, 182
Civil War 14, 15, 22
Claim of Right (1689) 101
claret 269
climate 273–4
colonies xxii, 277
commerce xxii, 10, 163, 219, 274–6, 277,
    294
Commons, House of 98, 99, 124, 125,
    140, 160, 163
conquest 34, 68; Norman xviii, 153–4
Constantine, donation of 123
constitution xvi, 77–8, 84–5, 86, 88, 89,
    91, 93, 95, 103, 118, 119, 121, 122,
    155, 166, 169, 184, 187, 188, 206,
    240, 245, 247, 266; ancient xv, 22,
    82, 94, 110, 113–15, 153, 154;
    definition of 88; mixed viii, xii, xvii,
    xviii, 96, 120–1, 124, 125–6, 127,
    163; simple 126–7; Castilian 132–4,
    137–9; French 143–51, 152, 156–7;

302

legislative power 143, 153, 163, 165, 166, 232

liberty 5, 9, 14, 15, 28, 32, 35, 49, 50, 52, 53, 55, 65, 77, 84, 85–6, 91, 93–4, 95, 97, 99, 101, 103, 104, 107, 108, 111, 112, 128–9, 133, 137, 138, 139, 153, 155, 157, 158, 167, 168, 184, 186, 190, 195, 199, 204, 205–6, 207, 208, 213, 222, 232–3, 241, 242, 244, 247–8, 249, 278, 293; British 113–21, 163, 169, 222, 171, 176, 220; legal 112–13, 196, 243–4, 250; natural 90; principles of 23, 201; public 10, 53, 56, 98, 170, 176, 202, 243; social 90; spirit of 8, 54, 56, 82–3, 91, 220, 238, 249, 251, 262

limitations xxi–xxii, 59, 96, 232, 233

London Courant cit. xvii

London Journal cit. 121

Lords, House of 40, 58, 67, 125, 141, 160, 164–5

luxury 53, 55, 182–3, 184, 248

Magna Carta 23, 81, 95

manners 56; *see also* decorum

marines 279

measures 262

militia 26, 58

ministers 255–7, 261, 262, 291

mirror for princes xxi, xxii, xxiii, xli

monarchy xxi; elective 29, 245; hereditary 225–6, 229, 230; limited 9, 83, 135, 136, 137, 206, 217, 240, 242, 250, 273; Israelite 112; *see also* constitution; divine right of kings; right, hereditary; kingship; Patriot King

nature, human 218

navy 278–9, 294

necessity xv, 49, 81, 86, 270; *see also* reason of state

Neo-Stoicism xix, xxiv; *see also* Stoicism

Nijmegen, Treaty of (1678) 33

Non-Jurors 74

non-resistance; *see* obedience, passive

obedience 83, 228; passive, x, 5, 22, 51, 66, 69

opinion 31, 117

opposition vii, viii, xi, xiii–xiv, xvi, xvii, xix, 76, 208, 215, 238, 260, 261–2

Oxford, University of 66

Papacy 79

Parliament 4, 109, 124, 126, 206, 215–16; annual viii, 102, 106; corruption of xviii, 94, 98, 99, 140–1, 157, 160–1, 166, 170; triennial 105; Cavalier (1661–78) 25–9, 31, 35, 40, 41; Exclusion (1679–81) 36, 49, 59; Convention (1689) ix, 15, 80, 81; *see also* Commons, House of; Lords, House of

party ix, xiv, 5, 6, 37, 38, 71–2, 99–100, 186, 187, 257, 259, 263; *see also* Country party; Court party; faction; Tory Party; Whigs

patriarchalism xiii, xxii, 257–8

Patriot King xxi–xxiii, 162; accession 249, 251, 253; administration 254–5, 291; character 280–92; conciliator 260, 264–6, 271, 273; commercial policy 275, 276–7; court 253–4; duties 217; influence 292–4; legitimacy 227, 246; non-partisan executive 257–64; patriarch 257–8; principles 234, 243–5, 247; rarity 221, 251, 270, 293; reformer 251–4, 261

patriotism xix, xx, xxii, xxiii, xxiv, 200, 201–3, 233–4, 254

politeness 290

popery ix, 19, 21, 24, 26, 49, 61, 64

Popish Plot (1678) vii, 32, 34, 35, 38, 40, 42, 58

popularity 287, 289

prerogative 16, 20, 33, 44, 53, 54, 78, 119, 170, 183–4, 185, 186; *see also* dispensing power, reason of state

Presbyterianism, Presbyterians 17, 18, 40, 43

principles, first 224, 252

property 5, 98, 129–30, 156, 164, 172; balance of 155, 162, 163, 167; *see also* balance of power

proscription vii, 22, 261

protection 126–7

quo warranto 52

reason 195–6, 223

reason of state 109, 179, 232, 257; *see also* necessity; prerogative

Remarks on the History of England (Bolingbroke) xii, 13, 157

Cambridge Texts in the History of Political Thought

Titles published in the series thus far

Aristotle *The Politics* and *The Constitution of Athens* (edited by Stephen Everson)

Arnold *Culture and Anarchy and other writings* (edited by Stefan Collini)

Astell *Political Writings* (edited by Patricia Springborg)

Austin *The Province of Jurisprudence Determined* (edited by Wilfrid E. Rumble)

Bakunin *Statism and Anarchy* (edited by Marshall Shatz)

Baxter *A Holy Commonwealth* (edited by William Lamont)

Beccaria *On Crimes and Punishments and other writings* (edited by Richard Bellamy)

Bentham *A Fragment on Government* (introduction by Ross Harrison)

Bernstein *The Preconditions of Socialism* (edited by Henry Tudor)

Bodin *On Sovereignty* (edited by Julian H. Franklin)

Bolingbroke *Political Writings* (edited by David Armitage)

Bossuet *Politics Drawn from the Very Words of Holy Scripture* (edited by Patrick Riley)

The British Idealists (edited by David Boucher)

Burke *Pre-Revolutionary Writings* (edited by Ian Harris)

Christine de Pizan *The Book of the Body Politic* (edited by Kate Langdon Forhan)

Cicero *On Duties* (edited by M. T. Griffin and E. M. Atkins)

Constant *Political Writings* (edited by Biancamaria Fontana)

Dante *Monarchy* (edited by Prue Shaw)

Diderot *Political Writings* (edited by John Hope Mason and Robert Wokler)

The Dutch Revolt (edited by Martin van Gelderen)

Early Greek Political Thought from Homer to the Sophists (edited by Michael Gagarin and Paul Woodruff)

The Early Political Writings of the German Romantics (edited by Frederick C. Beiser)

Erasmus *The Education of a Christian Prince* (edited by Lisa Jardine)

Ferguson *An Essay on the History of Civil Society* (edited by Fania Oz-Salzberger)

Filmer *Patriarcha and other writings* (edited by Johann P. Sommerville)

Sir John Fortescue *On the Laws and Governance of England* (edited by Shelley Lockwood)